History of the Joint Chiefs of Staff

The Joint Chiefs of Staff and The Prelude to the War in Vietnam 1954–1959

The Joint Chiefs of Staff, 22 January 1954. *Left to right:* General Nathan F. Twining, Chief of Staff, USAF; Admiral Arthur W. Radford, USN, Chairman, Joint Chiefs of Staff; General Matthew B. Ridgway, Chief of Staff, USA; General Lemuel C. Shepherd, Jr., Commandant, USMC; and Admiral Robert B. Carney, Chief of Naval Operations, USN.

The Joint Chiefs of Staff in March 1956. *Left to right*: Admiral Arleigh A. Burke, Chief of Naval Operations, USN; General Nathan F. Twining, Chief of Staff, USAF; Admiral Arthur W. Radford, USN, Chairman, Joint Chiefs of Staff; General Maxwell D. Taylor, Chief of Staff, USA; General Randolph McC. Pate, Commandant, USMC.

The Joint Chiefs of Staff in September 1957. *Left to right:* General Thomas D. White, Chief of Staff, USAF; General Maxwell D. Taylor, Chief of Staff, USA; General Nathan F. Twining, USAF, Chairman, Joint Chiefs of Staff; Admiral Arleigh A. Burke, Chief of Naval Operations, USN; and General Randolph McC. Pate, Commandant, USMC.

History of the Joint Chiefs of Staff

The Joint Chiefs of Staff and The Prelude to the War in Vietnam

1954–1959

Willard J. Webb

Office of Joint History
Office of the Chairman of the Joint Chiefs of Staff
Washington, DC ♦ 2007

Library of Congress Cataloging-in-Publication Data

Webb, Willard J.
  The Joint Chiefs of Staff and the prelude to the War in Vietnam, 1954-1959 / Willard J. Webb.
    p. cm. – (History of the Joint Chiefs of Staff)
  Based of the classified manuscript.
    Includes bibliographical references and index.
    1. Vietnam–History–1945-1975. 2. United States–Foreign relations–Vietnam. 3. Vietnam–Foreign relations–United States. 4. United States–Foreign relations–1945–1989. 5. United States. Joint Chiefs of Staff–History. I. Title.

DS556.9.W43 2008
959.704'31--dc22

2007050224

For sale by the Superintendent of Documents, U.S. Government Printing Office
Internet: bookstore.gpo.gov   Phone: toll free (866) 512-1800; DC area (202) 512-1800
Fax: (202) 512-2104 Mail: Stop IDCC, Washington, DC 20402-0001

ISBN 978-1-78039-282-0

Foreword

Established during World War II to advise the President regarding the strategic direction of the armed forces of the United States, the Joint Chiefs of Staff (JCS) continued in existence after the war and, as military advisers and planners, have played a significant role in the development of national policy. Knowledge of JCS relations with the President, the National Security Council, and the Secretary of Defense in the years since World War II is essential to an understanding of their current work. An account of their activity in peacetime and during times of crisis provides, moreover, an important series of chapters in the military history of the United States. For these reasons, the Joint Chiefs of Staff directed that an official history be written for the record. Its value for instructional purposes, for the orientation of officers newly assigned to the JCS organization and as a source of information for staff studies, will be readily recognized.

Written to complement *The Joint Chiefs of Staff and National Policy* series, *The Joint Chiefs of Staff and The Prelude to the War in Vietnam, 1954–1959*, focuses upon the activities of the Joint Chiefs that were concerned with events in Vietnam during these years. The nature of the activities of the Joint Chiefs of Staff and the sensitivity of the sources used caused the volume to be written originally as a classified document. Classification designations are those that appeared in the classified publication.

This volume describes those JCS activities related to developments in Vietnam during the period 1954–1959. At times, the role of the Joint Chiefs in events in Vietnam may appear to be submerged in the description of foreign relations, politics, economics, and other areas having little to do with military matters. However, developments in these areas provide essential background for understanding the military activity of the 1960s.

Originally a collaborative effort of the entire Historical Section, JCS, the classified publication on which this volume is based was written by Mr. Willard J. Webb. The current version has been updated by Dr. Jack Shulimson. Dr. Graham A. Cosmas reviewed Dr. Shulimson's work, and Dr. David A. Armstrong edited the resulting manuscript. Ms. Susan Carroll prepared the Index and Ms. Penny Norman prepared the manuscript for publication.

The volume was reviewed for declassification by the appropriate US Government departments and agencies and cleared for release. The volume is an official publication of the Joint Chiefs of Staff but, inasmuch as the text has not been considered by the Joint Chiefs of Staff, it must be construed as descriptive only and does not constitute the official position of the Joint Chiefs of Staff on any subject.

Washington, DC

DAVID A. ARMSTRONG
Director for Joint History

Preface

The Historical Division, Joint Chiefs of Staff, the predecessor of the present Joint History Office, produced the manuscript "The Joint Chiefs of Staff and the War in Vietnam, 1954–1959," in 1972 as a Top Secret document. Based largely upon then classified State Department and Defense department records, the History consists of eight chronological chapters and an Appendix describing the formation and functioning of the Southeast Asia Treaty Organization (SEATO). The chronological chapters cover the growing relationship of the United States after the Geneva Treaty of 1954 with the new Republic of Vietnam (South Vietnam) under President Ngo Dinh Diem; Diem's defeat of the various independent sects and his dominance over the South Vietnamese military; the awkward relationship between the US mission and the remaining French units in Vietnam; the continuing hostility between the two Vietnams; and the beginning of the "Viet Cong" insurrection in the later years of the study.

After the manuscript was declassified with only a few deletions, Dr. David A. Armstrong, the Director for Joint History, asked me to review and revise the declassified version for publication. After a preliminary review, I suggested that the text needed little revision except for some updating and occasional smoothing of transitions. Consequently, changes in the body of the text were largely confined to small inserts with most of the new information and updates presented in the footnotes which have also been revised to indicate where formerly classified materials appear in collections such as the *Pentagon Papers* and the State Department series, *Foreign Relations of the United States*. I wish to thank Dr. Armstrong and Dr. Graham A. Cosmas of the Joint History Office for their support.

Jack Shulimson

Contents

1. **The Geneva Conference and Its Aftermath—1954** 1
   The Geneva Background 1
   The Situation in Vietnam 3
   Reassessment of US Policy 8
   NSC 5429 8
   The Views of the Joint Chiefs of Staff 10
   NSC 5429/1 and NSC 5429/2 11
   The Manila Conference 13
   Restudy of US Policy toward the Far East (NSC 5429/3) 13

2. **Three Troubled Months—August-October 1954** 19
   Political Turmoil 19
   The Washington Conference 22
   South Vietnam: Continuing Political Deadlock 24
   French Policy 28
   The Question of Independence 31
   The Situation in North Vietnam 32

3. **The Collins Mission** 35
   The Seven-Point Program 36
   The Problem of Creating an Effective VNA 37
   Economic Problems 47
   Strengthening and Broadening the Diem Government 49
   A Provisional National Assembly 51
   The Question of Diem's Replacement 52
   Review of US Policy 55

4. **The Crisis of April and May 1955** 59
   The Sect Problem 59
   The "United Front of Nationalist Forces" 62
   Fighting in Cholon, 29–30 March 64
   The Recommendations of Generals Collins and Ely 66
   The Binh Xuyen Insurrection 71
   Trilateral Talks in Paris 74

5. **The Outlook Brightens in South Vietnam** 79
   Diem's Refusal to Consult 79
   Franco-Vietnamese Relations 83
   The Campaign against the Sects. 85
   Organizing for Pacification. 86
   Diem's Political Program 87
   The Training Relations Instruction Mission (TRIM) 90
   Revision of Vietnamese Force Levels 91
   MAAG's Personnel Problems. 92
   The Security Threat. 94

6. **Developments in North Vietnam**. 97
   Evacuation of Refugees 97
   Evacuation of MDAP Equipment 100
   French Industry Leaves Tonkin 101
   Reconstruction and Expansion of the Agricultural Economy 102
   Reconstruction and Expansion of the Industrial Economy. 105
   Agriculture and Industry: The Three Year Plan and After. 106
   The DRV Government 107
   The Opposition 109
   DRV Foreign Policy, 1954–1960 110

7. **The Republic of Vietnam: 1956, A Year of Progress** 115
   Elections and a New Constitution. 116
   The Succession Controversy. 117
   US Aid to RVN. 119
   The Security Threat. 122
   RVN Forces 122
   Regular Forces 123
   Temporary Equipment Recovery Mission. 126
   VNAF and VNN 127
   Increase in MAAG Personnel 127
   Paramilitary Forces: The Civil Guard 128
   Paramilitary Forces: The Self Defense Corps 130
   Development of a New Policy Statement. 131

8. **South Vietnam, 1957-1959**. 137
   Economic Developments and Agrarian Reforms 140
   The GVN Defense Establishment 143
   The RVNAF 143
   The ARVN 144

The VNAF 148
　　The VNN 148
　　Assessment of RVNAF 149
　　Diem's Attempt at Political Unity 151
　　The Insurgency in Vietnam, 1957-1959 155

Appendix: The Evolution of the Southeast Asia
　　Treaty Organization 163
　　A Military Concept for Southeast Asia 170
　　The International Working Group 173
　　The Bangkok Conference: 23–25 February 1955 174
　　The Bandung Conference: 18–24 April 1955 176
　　Setting Up Machinery 177
　　SEATO's Accomplishments and Failures 183

Abbreviations and Acronyns 187

Principal Civilian and Military Officers 189

Notes 101

Index 221

History of the Joint Chiefs of Staff

The Joint Chiefs of Staff and The Prelude to the War in Vietnam 1954–1959

1

The Geneva Conference and Its Aftermath—1954

In the summer of 1954, the conclusion of the Geneva Conference marked the final failure of the French attempt to regain the control over Indochina that they had lost during World War II. To a lesser extent, this defeat was shared by the United States.

Following the war, the United States had denied any assistance to the French in restoring their colonial rule; however, in 1949 the victory of the Chinese Communists led the United States to reassess its policy toward Indochina. The decision to assist noncommunist governments in Asia in resisting subversion was strengthened, and its implementation lent urgency, by the attack on South Korea in June 1950.

By the spring of 1954, events in Indochina had crystallized US concern for Southeast Asia, consumed almost $3 billion of US assistance, and diminished US prestige. As the French faltered, the United States considered military intervention, but British refusal to lend their support, which President Eisenhower saw as a necessary condition, closed that option. The alternative chosen, in the hope of saving the remainder of Southeast Asia, was the development of a regional security pact. Since preliminary negotiations on a regional pact moved slowly, the United States went to the Geneva Conference in mid-1954 isolated by the tenuous military French position and the reluctance of the British to support immediate military action.

The Geneva Background

In early 1954 the United States, the United Kingdom, France, and the Soviet Union agreed to meet at Geneva to seek a peaceful settlement of the Korean conflict. The government of Communist China was invited to attend and agreed to do so. The United

States reluctantly gave in to French demands that the participants also discuss "the problem of restoring peace to Indochina." Accordingly, representatives of the five powers assembled in Geneva on 26 April 1954, and after two weeks of futile discussions on Korea, turned to Indochina. In addition to the "Big Four" and Communist China, the three Associated States—Cambodia, Laos, and Vietnam—and the Democratic Republic of Vietnam (DRV) also participated in the sessions on Indochina.

The Geneva deliberations on Indochina proved long and difficult, but finally, in mid-July, the Conference produced three separate agreements—one each concerning Cambodia, Laos, and Vietnam—and a Final Declaration of the Conference.[1]

The agreements, signed on 20 July 1954, provided for the cessation of all hostilities in the three Indochinese states. They prohibited the establishment of new military bases throughout the territory of the three states and called for the liberation and repatriation of all prisoners of war and civilian internees. In addition, the agreements contained, in varying degrees, restrictions on foreign armed forces in the territories of the three states.

The agreement on Vietnam was the most complex of the three. It provided for a provisional military demarcation line (PMDL), generally following the 17th parallel and dividing Vietnam approximately in half, and a five-kilometer demilitarized zone (DMZ) on either side of the PMDL to serve as a buffer area. After the cease-fire, the combatant forces were to regroup on either side of the PMDL, with the Viet Minh (the People's Army of Vietnam), to the north of the line and the French Union forces to the south. In addition, the agreement on Vietnam forbade the introduction of any troop reinforcements or additional military personnel, and reinforcements "in the form of all types of arms, munitions and other war material." The agreement allowed, however, rotation and replacement of forces already in country and the replacement, piece for piece and of the same type, of materials, arms, and munitions destroyed, damaged, worn out, or used after the cessation of hostilities.

The agreement on Vietnam also provided for the creation of a Joint Commission, composed of equal representation from the two sides, to facilitate execution of the agreement. Further, the agreement established an International Commission to supervise and control its implementation. Composed of representatives from India (presiding), Canada, and Poland, the commission would use fixed and mobile inspection teams to verify that the terms of the agreement were being carried out and would inform the conference members of violations.

The Final Declaration on Indochina, issued on 21 July 1954 by all the conference participants except the United States and the State of Vietnam, noted the provisions of the Geneva Agreements and expressed satisfaction at the ending of hostilities. With regard to Vietnam, the Final Declaration stated that the "essential purpose" of the agreement was to end hostilities and that "the military demarcation line should not in any way be interpreted as constituting a political or territorial boundary." Expressing the conviction that the execution of its provisions and those of the agreement on Vietnam would create "the necessary basis for the achievement in the near future of a political settlement in Vietnam," the Final Declaration called for general elections in Vietnam during July 1956, under the supervision of an International Commission composed again of India, Canada, and Poland.

The declaration concluded with a pledge by the signers of the Geneva Agreements to respect "the sovereignty, the independence, the unity, and the territorial integrity" of Cambodia, Laos, and Vietnam; to refrain from any interference in internal affairs of the three states; and to consult together on any question referred to them by the International Commission in order to study such measures as might be necessary to assure that the agreements were respected.

The delegation of the State of Vietnam would not agree to the division of Vietnam and refused to sign the Final Declaration of the Conference. Objecting to both the manner and conditions of the agreement on Vietnam, the Government of Vietnam reserved to itself "complete freedom of action to guarantee the sacred right of the Vietnamese people to territorial unity, national independence, and freedom."[2]

The United States took the position that primary responsibility for the settlement in Indochina rested with the nations that had participated in the fighting. Since it had not been a belligerent in the war, the United States did not sign the Geneva Agreements or the Final Declaration, and it did not consider itself bound by the decisions of the Geneva Conference. On 21 July 1954, the United States issued a unilateral declaration promising to refrain from the threat or use of force to disturb the Geneva Agreements and stating that it would view any renewal of aggression in violation of the agreements "with grave concern," as a serious threat to international peace and security. The US declaration affirmed the policy of seeking to achieve the unity of divided nations through free elections supervised by the United Nations. The United States noted the protest by the State of Vietnam to the agreement and reiterated the US policy "that peoples are entitled to determine their own future." It stated that it would not join in an arrangement which would violate this principle.[3]

The Situation in Vietnam

The political situation in Vietnam changed significantly during the course of the Geneva Conference. The French Government of Premier Joseph Laniel had promised on 3 July 1953 to grant independence to the three Associated States of Indochina. In pursuit of this pledge, France and the Vietnamese Government of Premier Buu Loc had initiated negotiations in Paris in early 1954. Differences over the definition of independence stalemated the negotiations at first, but in an effort to present a united Franco-Vietnamese front at Geneva, France gave in to Vietnamese demands. Consequently, on 28 April, two days after the first session of the Geneva Conference, Premier Laniel and Vietnamese Vice Premier Nguyen Trung Vinh issued a joint declaration agreeing to the signature of two treaties, one granting Vietnam independence and the other establishing "a Franco-Vietnamese association within the French Union."[4]

Five weeks later on 4 June, France and Vietnam formally initialed the two treaties in Paris. In the independence treaty, France recognized Vietnam "as a fully independent and sovereign State invested with the Jurisdiction recognized by international law." In addition, the treaty, abrogated all "earlier and contrary acts and dispositions," and France transferred to Vietnam "all jurisdictions and public services still held by her on Vietnamese territory." In the association treaty, France and Vietnam pledged to maintain "in friendship and confidence" the ties which united them and to associate "freely within the French Union...."[5]

Although the initialing of the two treaties ended 70 years of French "presence," the event sparked no outburst of joy in Vietnam. In fact, it is doubtful that the Vietnamese people recognized the treaties for what they were. Between 1949 and 1954 there had been seventeen French declarations granting various degrees of independence, and the Vietnamese greeted this latest act with some skepticism.

Meanwhile, as the conferees were meeting in Geneva, Premier Buu Loc resigned on 15 June 1954, and Chief of State Bao Dai called upon Ngo Dinh Diem to form a new government. Diem, who came from a prominent mandarin family, had held no public office in Vietnam for twenty years, but he was ardently anticommunist and a dedicated nationalist with a reputation for scrupulous honesty and moral uprightness. A militant Catholic, Ngo Dinh Diem was aloof, courageous, stubborn, and diligent.[6]

Diem, who was in France, returned to Vietnam and set about forming a government. On his arrival in Vietnam, he declared that he was "destined to open the way to national salvation and to bring about a revolution in all fields," adding that he would seek to "eliminate the last vestiges of foreign domination."[7]

Diem formally constituted his government on 7 July 1954, which as "Double Seven" (seventh day, seventh month) would be celebrated as a national holiday in coming years. The new government was nationalistic, youthful, and small with nine ministries (Agriculture, Economics and Finance, Education, Foreign Affairs, Health, Interior, Labor and Youth, National Defense, and Public Works) and eight state secretariats. Diem retained the two important ministries of National Defense and Interior within his portfolio. Several other members of the new government were related to Diem or his family: Tran Van Chuong, the Minister of Economics and Finance, was the father-in-law of Diem's brother Ngo Dinh Nhu; Tran Van Do, Chuong's brother was named Foreign Minister; Tran Van Bac, a Diem relation, was appointed Minister of Education; and Diem's brother, Ngo Dinh Luyen, was designated as a roving ambassador for the government. Reliance on his family was characteristic of Diem.[8]

As Diem assumed office he faced a number of serious and pressing problems; the most immediate was the impending Geneva settlement. Diem and his new government adamantly refused to sanction, even temporarily, the partition of Vietnam

The Geneva Conference and Its Aftermath—1954

into communist and noncommunist states. But the major powers pushed on to a final agreement dividing Vietnam at the 17th parallel; the State of Vietnam lost more than half of its territory and population.

Facing many obstacles, the Diem government began its tenure with little popular appeal. Diem had lived abroad for the previous four years and had no following in Vietnam. The conduct of Bao Dai, who had abdicated as Emperor in 1945 and been restored by the French in 1949 as Chief of State, tarnished the image of the new government. Since his restoration, Bao Dai had been less and less inclined to participate in the affairs of government. He avoided Saigon altogether and lived in luxury at the Vietnamese mountain resort of Dalat or on the French Riviera, accumulating a vast personal fortune and surrounded by corrupt friends.

In addition to lacking popular support, the Diem government did not have the institutions, the administrative machinery, or the experience, especially at the local level, needed by an independent state. The State of Vietnam had no constitution or elected assembly; it had only decrees and ordinances and a Provisional National Council. Bao Dai had established this council by ordinance in July 1953; its members were appointed and its powers strictly advisory. There had been elections for municipal and provincial councils in 1953, but these elections were limited to areas and villages under government control and restricted to those who had registered in the 1951 census. As a result, the residents of one village in three had been permitted to vote and only about one million Vietnamese among a population of approximately twenty-seven million had participated in the elections. Thus, in 1954 only a small fraction of the people of the State of Vietnam had participated, in any way, in the processes of self-government.

At independence, the State of Vietnam did not control large areas of its territory. Even though the Geneva settlement provided for the withdrawal of all Viet Minh forces from Vietnam south of the 17th parallel, large areas remained under Viet Minh influence. In many areas of the South Vietnamese countryside, village administration was openly controlled by Viet Minh elements. In village after village where the government sent its officials, they found that the business of government and the administration of justice were carried out behind the scenes by the Viet Minh. Although the Viet Minh were evacuating large numbers of their uniformed troops to the north, they kept a clandestine administrative and propaganda network in the south. It was impossible to tell how many of the evacuating forces were young people sent north for Viet Minh training and indoctrination or to estimate how many soldiers remained behind as civilians to pursue guerrilla activities. Even in Saigon and the other cities of the south, where government control had always been the strongest, the Viet Minh had many sympathizers among the poorer classes, the intellectuals and professionals. Viet Minh sponsored parades and rallies were frequent.

The United States government was well aware of the Viet Minh threat in the State of Vietnam. A National Intelligence Estimate (NIE) of early August, on the post-Geneva outlook in Indochina, predicted that the communists would continue their efforts to secure control of all of Indochina, resorting to psychological and "paramilitary" means rather than armed invasion, and avoiding violation of the armistice. The NIE stated that the Viet Minh would seek to retain "sizable military and political assets" in South Vietnam, noting that many of both regular and irregular Viet Minh soldiers currently in the south were natives of the area and would probably remain there. The Geneva Agreements' restrictions on the importation of arms and military equipment, foreign military personnel, and new military bases and alliances would increase the already severe problem of establishing and maintaining security in South Vietnam. The Viet Minh were almost certain to attempt to discredit a new South Vietnamese administration, to embitter Franco-South Vietnamese relations further, and to appeal to the strong feeling for national unification in Vietnam. If scheduled national elections were held in 1956, and if the Viet Minh did not prejudice its political prospects, the Viet Minh would almost certainly win.[9]

Not only did Ngo Dinh Diem and his new government face the danger of the externally controlled Viet Minh; they were also opposed by certain noncommunist groups in South Vietnam. Two politico-religious sects, the Cao Dai and the Hoa-Hao, and the Binh Xuyen, a group of former river pirates who had extensive vice and gambling monopolies and who controlled the Saigon-Cholon police, were major political forces in South Vietnam at this time. All three groups maintained their own private armed forces, totaling about 40,000 men. They controlled large areas of the South Vietnamese countryside and collected tolls and taxes from the local population in these areas. A strong central government would challenge their positions; the three groups viewed Diem with suspicion, if not hostility.

Confronted with both the Viet Minh and the private armies of the sects and the Binh Xuyen, Diem also lacked the confidence of the French. Because of his strong anti-French sentiments, departing French officials had no great affection for Diem. Initially, they did not oppose him outright, but neither did they support him. They concentrated instead on salvaging some remnant of their position and influence in Vietnam. Under French pressure, Bao Dai and his clique showed themselves increasingly disenchanted with Diem; his honesty and diligence threatened their perquisites.

France was quite frank in telling the United States that it did not consider Diem qualified to head the new government in Vietnam. The French praised Diem's "high moral character" and felt that he should be a member of any future Vietnamese government if he could make peace with the sects. But they held that Diem did not fully represent the population in the south, that he would be unable to carry out necessary agricultural reforms promptly, and that he would not depose Bao Dai and create a republic when it became appropriate.[10]

To cope with the forces arrayed against him, Diem needed a strong national army which he did not have. Fearing that a Vietnamese national army would turn against them, the French had delayed its formation until 1951, the year that Vo Nguyen Giap formed the first regular Viet Minh division. In 1954 the

Vietnamese National Army (VNA) was still in its formative stages and, although it was numerically equal to the forces of the DRV, one observer termed it was "organizationally only a miscellaneous conglomeration of ill-sorted battalions."[11] The military victory of the Viet Minh at Dien Bien Phu, and its diplomatic confirmation at Geneva, had seriously undermined the morale of the VNA. Not only was the VNA disorganized, poorly trained, and demoralized, but many of the high ranking officers, including Chief of Staff General Nguyen Van Hinh, opposed Diem.

Diem also had major economic, financial, and social problems to solve. The Geneva partition had divided the agricultural south from the industrial north, leaving South Vietnam with a scarcity of skilled labor. The war had destroyed approximately 60 percent of South Vietnam's roads, many bridges, and one-third of the railroad track. Further, there were serious administrative and technical problems involved in transferring control of foreign trade, banking, and currency from French to Vietnamese hands. South Vietnam did have economic assets in its rice and rubber producing capacity, but it was a tremendous task to build and orient a self-sufficient economy.

In the months following the Geneva settlement, thousands of North Vietnamese refugees fled south. Crowded into tent cities without even the basic necessities of life, and with growing antagonism between them and the native southerners, care and integration of the refugees presented yet another challenge to the resources of the government.

Closely related to the problem of refugee settlement was the matter of land reform. Land reform had been considered as early as 1949, but even though Premier Nguyen Van Tam had decreed a program in 1953, nothing had been done. In a country where a large part of the population consisted of landless peasants tilling large estates and plantations, and where small tenant farmers were burdened with high rents and usurious interest rates, land reform was essential, if the government was to compete with the propaganda of the Viet Minh.

Beset by political insecurity and chaos, and confronted with immense economic and social problems, the State of Vietnam required outside assistance to survive. After seven years of war in Vietnam, and having severed its formal ties with the three former Associated States, France no longer could provide such assistance. Recognizing the importance of Vietnam, the United States realized that the West could ill afford the loss of all of Vietnam to the communists. Not only was the existence of a noncommunist South Vietnam threatened, the United States government believed, but so too was that of a free Indochina and, ultimately, all of Southeast Asia. Earlier in 1954, President Eisenhower had enunciated his belief in the "falling domino" principle, likening Indochina's position among Southeast Asian states to the first in a row of dominos set on end: if the first were toppled, the rest would follow.[12]

Reassessment of US Policy

The results of the Geneva Conference, and the perilous situation in South Vietnam, prompted the United States to undertake a wide-ranging reassessment of its Far East policy in the summer of 1954. Recognizing that France would no longer be responsible for Indochina, the United States had to decide to what extent it would commit itself to prevent further communist encroachment there. Moreover, the relationship of Indochina to the surrounding area made it mandatory that the United States review its policy toward all the nations and regions of the Far East, particularly Communist China. In the short space of five years, Communist China had driven the Nationalist Government of China from the mainland, fought impressively in Korea, and contributed significantly to the victory of the Viet Minh in Indochina. It had also forged a strong alliance with the Union of Soviet Socialist Republics (USSR), gained great prestige and respect among the Asian and African nations, and now menaced its small and generally weak neighbors.

NSC 5429

The American government's formal reassessment of its policy began immediately after the Geneva Conference with a draft statement of policy toward the Far East circulated to the National Security Council on 4 August 1954 as NSC 5429. The draft had been prepared by the NSC Planning Board which represented the various executive departments and agencies charged with the development of national security policy. Beginning with an outline of the consequences of the Geneva Conference for the United States, the draft included four sections: (1) courses of action to increase the security of the Pacific offshore island chain; (2) general political and economic measures for the Far East; (3) courses of action for Southeast Asia; (4) policy toward Communist China. The latter two sections gave US policymakers the most trouble. The Defense, JCS, and Office of Defense Mobilization (ODM) representatives on the Planning Board believed that US policy toward China should be determined first, with policy toward "the peripheral areas" then established in light of that determination. They proposed that the section on Communist China be made the first section of the policy statement.

The section on Southeast Asia called for a new initiative to protect the US position and restore US prestige. According to the draft statement, the situation in that area had to be stabilized to prevent further losses to communism through either "creeping expansion" and "subversion" or overt aggression. As a major objective, the United States should negotiate a Southeast Asia security treaty with the United Kingdom, Australia, New Zealand, France, the Philippines, Thailand, and other free South and Southeast Asian countries willing to participate. The United States would continue to provide limited military assistance and training missions to friendly Southeast Asian states to bolster the will to fight, stabilize legal governments, and control subversion.

In a paragraph titled "Action in the Event of Local Subversion," NSC 5429 presented two alternatives. The first, recognizing that "the above-mentioned economic and military measures" might be inadequate to cope with communist expansion and subversion in Indochina, called for the issuance "at the earliest practicable moment" of a declaration to the Chinese Communists that further communist expansion on the mainland of Southeast Asia would not be tolerated. Such a declaration should warn that continued communist expansion would "in all probability" lead to the application of military power "not necessarily restricted to conventional weapons against the source of the aggression (i.e. Communist China)." The second alternative proposed that, in addition to the negotiation of a Southeast Asia security treaty, the United States prepare, either unilaterally or under the terms of that treaty, and if requested by a legitimate local government, to assist that government with military force, if required and feasible, to defeat local communist subversion or rebellion not constituting external armed attack.

For Indochina, NSC 5429 recommended the following political and covert actions: (1) making every effort, not openly inconsistent with the US position on the Geneva Agreements, to defeat communist subversion and influence, to maintain and support friendly noncommunist governments in Cambodia, Laos, and South Vietnam, and to prevent communist victory through all-Vietnam elections; (2) urging France to recognize promptly and deal with Cambodia, Laos, South Vietnam as independent sovereign nations; (3) strengthening US representation in, and dealing directly with, the governments of Cambodia, Laos, and South Vietnam; (4) working through the French only insofar as necessary, assisting Cambodia, Laos, and South Vietnam to maintain military forces necessary for internal security and economic conditions conducive to the maintenance of strong noncommunist regimes; (5) aiding emigration and resettlement of peoples unwilling to remain under communist rule in North Vietnam; (6) exploiting available means to make Viet Minh control of North Vietnam more difficult; (7) exploiting available means to prevent North Vietnam from becoming permanently incorporated in the Soviet bloc, using consular relations and non-strategic trade as feasible and desirable, or, alternatively, treating North Vietnam as already permanently incorporated into the communist bloc with the application of economic controls similar to those applied to Communist China; and (8) conducting covert operations on a large scale to support the foregoing.

Reaching agreement on the section of the draft dealing with policy and courses of action for US relations with Communist China proved the most difficult. In this section, the Planning Board offered four alternative policies with appropriate implementing courses of action. The four alternatives, enumerated as Alternatives A through D, were: (1) putting US relations with Communist China on the same footing as those with the Soviet Union; (2) reducing, by means short of war, the relative power of Communist China in Asia; (3) reducing the power of Communist China in Asia even at the risk of, but without deliberately provoking, war, and (4) initiating "an increasingly positive policy toward Communist China designed to confront the regime with a clear likelihood of US military action against China proper," unless Communist China took public action to change its belligerent support of communist expansion.[13]

The Views of the Joint Chiefs of Staff

Since the draft policy statement was to be considered at a NSC meeting on 12 August 1954, the Joint Chiefs immediately reviewed the draft. In a memorandum of 11 August 1954, they told the Secretary of Defense that NSC 5429 did not represent a comprehensive policy statement for the Far East. It did not delineate US objectives for the whole area or courses of action that would logically flow from the establishment of such objectives. They affirmed their proposal of the previous April that the United States formulate a comprehensive policy treating the Far East as a strategic entity. The Chiefs recommended that NSC 5429 be returned to the NSC Planning Board with guidance for derivation and exposition of US objectives in the Far East and the development of broad courses of action to achieve these objectives.

Although the JCS agreed on the general inadequacy of NSC 5429, they differed on specific provisions of the policy statement. The Chief of Naval Operations, the Chief of Staff of the Air Force, and the Commandant of the Marine Corps, concurred in the view of the Defense, JCS, and ODM representatives on the Planning Board that US policy toward Communist China should be determined first, with policy for "the peripheral areas" following that determination. They recommended that, in the final version of NSC 5429, the section on Communist China be first and then made detailed comments on individual portions of the draft policy statement. With regard to US actions in Indochina, the JCS majority preferred a revision of the course of action for exploitation of available means to make Viet Minh control of North Vietnam more difficult. They would substitute continued exploitation of "opportunities to further US long-range objectives toward uniting Vietnam under a democratic form of government." If this change were accepted, they believed, it would eliminate the need for either of the alternative actions of preventing North Vietnam from becoming permanently attached to the Soviet bloc or treating North Vietnam as already permanently incorporated in the communist bloc.

With respect to the four alternative policies toward Communist China, they considered the first two inadequate and the fourth extreme. Consequently, they preferred the third alternative—reduction of the power of Communist China in Asia even at the risk of, but without deliberately provoking war—with certain revisions in the courses of action to implement this alternative. This policy, with their proposed revisions, would provide a positive approach to the problem of reducing the threat of further Communist Chinese expansion in Asia, furnishing a basis for action against indirect aggression that was lacking in the first two alternatives, while avoiding the "more extreme measures, with their greatly enhanced risks," contained in the fourth alternative.

The Army Chief of Staff had more basic reservations regarding NSC 5429. He stated that the proposed policy was not a comprehensive review of Far Eastern policy, adding that the problem confronting the United States in the Far East could not be stated except in relation to, and as an element in, a US foreign policy of "global scope." Although not suggesting what such a global policy should be, it seemed axiomatic to him that "one principal OBJECTIVE" should be to split Communist China from the Soviet bloc. As a result, the Army Chief found none of the four alternative policies toward Communist China acceptable. He stated that there were elements in each alternative that, if combined, might offer a better alternative, emphasizing that the United States need not either appease Communist China or destroy it. Returning to the "objective" of driving a wedge between Communist China and the USSR, he said that, if this objective were accepted, the "statesman-like approach would seem to be to bring Peking to a realization that its long-range benefits would derive from friendliness with America, not with the USSR." These benefits would, of course, be forthcoming "in time" and only if Communist China "would mend its ways."[14]

NSC 5429/1 and NSC 5429/2

The National Security Council considered NSC 5429 on 12 August 1954; it did not accept the JCS recommendation to return the draft to the Planning Board. The NSC accepted the sections dealing with the Pacific offshore island chain and general political and economic measures (Sections I and II) without change. In its consideration of the Southeast Asia section (Section III), the NSC could not agree on either alternative action to meet local subversion. Nor did the council accept the recommendation of the Chief of Naval Operations, the Chief of Staff of the Air Force, and the Commandant of the Marine Corps, with regard to the action to make Viet Minh control of North Vietnam more difficult. Instead, the NSC approved the provision as stated in NSC 5429 and chose also the alternative of exploiting available means to prevent North Vietnam from becoming permanently incorporated in the Soviet bloc.

Reviewing the four alternative policies toward Communist China, the NSC was unable to decide on one of them. As a result, the council adopted the first three sections of NSC 5429 with the exception of paragraph 8 in Section III treating local subversion. The council agreed to reconsider this paragraph, together with the section on Communist China, on 18 August. The President approved Sections I, II, and III, with the exception of paragraph 8, and directed their use as a general guide to US policy in the Far East. This revised NSC 5429 was published as NSC 5429/1, dated 12 August 1954.[15]

When the National Security Council met on 18 August 1954, it had before it the four alternative policies toward Communist China presented in NSC 5429, ranging from putting US relations with that nation on the same footing as those with the Soviet Union to military action against the Chinese mainland. The council adopted alternative C, providing for the reduction of the power of Communist China in Asia even at the risk of war, but without deliberately provoking it. The language of the policy as finally adopted followed closely that suggested by the majority of the Joint Chiefs of Staff, with the addition of a course of action calling for the creation of "internal division" in the Chinese regime as well as impairment of Sino-Soviet relations by all feasible overt and covert means—as proposed by the Army Chief of Staff in the split JCS views.

At the 18 August meeting, the National Security Council also reconsidered the question of how to deal with communist subversion in Southeast Asia. The council selected neither alternative proposed in NSC 5429—(1) a unilateral US declaration to Communist China threatening the use of force in the event of continuing communist expansion in Southeast Asia or the United States; or (2) preparedness to act, either unilaterally or under the projected Southeast Asia security treaty, to assist local governments facing local communist subversion. Rather, the council adopted a new paragraph calling on the President to consider asking Congress for authority to use US forces in Southeast Asia. Specifically, the new paragraph stated:

> If requested by a legitimate local government which required assistance to defeat local Communist subversion or rebellion not constituting armed attack, the U.S. should view such a situation so gravely that, in addition to giving all possible covert and overt support within Executive Branch authority, the President should at once consider requesting Congressional authority to take appropriate action, which might if necessary and feasible include the use of U.S. military forces either locally or against the external sources of such subversion or rebellion (including Communist China if determined to be the source).

With all the disagreements resolved, the National Security Council adopted the entire statement of US policy for the Far East on 18 August 1954 with the understanding that the section on Communist China would be used as the basis for further consideration in light of a review by the Secretary of State scheduled to be completed in about one month. The President approved this statement of policy on 20 August with the same understanding. The approved policy, NSC 5429/2, was issued on the same day, with the section on Communist China first.[16]

The Manila Conference

With an approved policy toward the Far East and Southeast Asia, the US Government moved to create a regional security arrangement. Preliminary negotiations for such an arrangement had been in progress since April 1954. Representatives of the United Kingdom, France, Australia, New Zealand, and the United States joined by Pakistan, Thailand, and the Philippines met in Manila in early September 1954 to draft such a treaty and, on 8 September, signed the Southeast Asia Collective Defense Treaty (SEACDT). The signatories recognized that an attack on any one of them would endanger the peace and safety of all and pledged that each would "act to meet the common danger in accordance with its constitutional processes." In the event of a threat other than armed attack to their territory, sovereignty, or political independence, the signers agreed to consult on appropriate measures for common defense. The area covered by the treaty provisions included Southeast Asia, the entire territories of the Asian members and the general area of the Southwest Pacific, including the area north of 21° 30' north latitude. A separate protocol extended the security provisions of the treaty to "the States of Cambodia and Laos and the free territory under the Jurisdiction of the State of Vietnam." The United States, however, signed the treaty with the understanding that the provisions covering aggression and armed attack applied only to communist aggression, but consented to consult in the event of "other aggression or armed attack." The SEACDT established a council to consider implementation of the treaty. The treaty also incorporated economic provisions, each party promising to cooperate in promotion of the economic well being and social progress. Signed by the eight states on the same day, the Pacific Charter proclaimed their determination to resist any attempt "to subvert their freedom or to destroy their sovereignty or territorial integrity."[17]

Restudy of US Policy toward the Far East (NSC 5429/3)

The requirements of the August 1954 NSC decision, together with the continuing critical situation as well as the Secretary of State's report following the Manila Conference, caused the Planning Board in the fall of 1954 to undertake a review of US policy in the Far East. Subsequently, the Planning Board circulated a new draft statement of US policy toward the Far East (NSC 5429/3) to the NSC members of 19 November 1954.

The new draft statement was organized into three sections—general considerations, objectives, and courses of action. Under general considerations the Planning Board set forth the primary problem of the United States in the Far East as meeting the serious threat resulting from the spread of communist power on the continent of Asia—over mainland China, North Korea, and the northern part of Vietnam. Not only had the Chinese Communist regime apparently succeeded in consolidating its power on the mainland but it had also developed working relations with the Soviet Union. The task of the United States in coping with the communist threat was complicated by a number of factors. The noncommunist countries in Asia were vulnerable militarily, politically, economically, and psychologically to further communist inroads and all had intense nationalistic feelings with residual resentments against European colonialism. In addition, a sense of "weakness and inadequacy in the face of the worldwide power struggle" inhibited many Far Eastern and Southeast Asian countries from cooperating with the United States. The divergent Far Eastern policies followed by US European allies, particularly with regard to Communist China, limited US political and economic pressures against Asian communist regimes.

The draft included four principal objectives and reflected the JCS view that any full statement of US policy for the area should include the goals that the United States was seeking to achieve in the Far East as a whole. The objectives to be pursued with clear and strong resolve, and "if necessary at the risk of but not provocative of war" included: preservation of the territorial and political integrity of the noncommunist countries in the area against further communist expansion or subversion; progressive improvement of the relative political, economic, and military position of the noncommunist countries; reduction of Chinese Communist power and prestige; and disruption of the Sino-Soviet alliance through actions designed to intensify existing and potential areas of conflict or divergence of interest between the USSR and Communist China. The draft statement also contained a fifth objective, proposed by the Defense, JCS, Commerce, ODM, Foreign Operations Administration (FOA), and Central Intelligence Agency (CIA) representatives on the Planning Board, but opposed by the Department of State representative. It provided for creation in noncommunist Asia, and ultimately within Communist China, of political and social forces that would spread the "greater values of the free world" and expose "the falsity of the communist ideological offensive."

To achieve these objectives, the Planning Board proposed courses of action, falling into two categories—those designed to "preserve the territorial and political integrity of, the area" and those required to "enhance the individual and collective strength of the non-Communist nations." The first category included: maintenance of the security of the Pacific offshore island chain; conclusion of a mutual defense treaty with the Republic of China covering Formosa and the Pescadores; use of force, as appropriate, in the event of armed attack on the Republic of Korea or in an area covered by the Manila Pact; and preparedness to seek Congressional authority for necessary action, including use of force, to meet armed attack or imminent threat of attack against any other country in the area not covered by a security treaty to which the United States was a party. Further actions in this category were: prompt punitive action in the event of unprovoked communist armed attack against US personnel, aircraft, or vessels; encouragement of a Western

Pacific collective defense arrangement; assistance, where necessary and feasible, to noncommunist governments in the Far East to counter communist subversion and economic domination; and maintenance of US forces in the Far East as clear evidence of US intentions in the area. With regard to internal communist subversion or rebellion, the first category of actions included the same provision that had been included in NSC 5429/2 only after a lengthy consideration—calling for the United States to give all possible covert and overt support within the Executive Branch authority and for the President to be prepared to request Congressional authority for appropriate action, including military force, if appropriate.

The second category of actions, those required to enhance the individual and collective strength of the noncommunist states, called for: increased efforts to develop the basic stability and strength of the noncommunist countries to resist communist expansion; continued recognition of the Government of the Republic of China, with direct military and economic assistance to that government; encouragement of the organization of an economic grouping of free Asian states, accompanied by all feasible measures to increase opportunities for trade among these countries and with the free world; provision of economic and technical assistance, encouraging use of US advisers where appropriate; attempts to increase the understanding of, and orientation of the Asian peoples toward, the free world as well as to expose the menace of Chinese imperialism and world communism; and encouragement of the application of private capital to the development of free Asia.

With respect to Indochina, the new draft policy statement continued the policy adopted in NSC 5429/2, with the addition of a new paragraph. Reflecting US concern over a growing problem, the new paragraph called for the United States to expose communist violations of the armistice in Indochina.

Included in NSC 5429/3 was a proposal for study of the feasibility of the negotiation of a Far Eastern settlement that might encompass such elements as recognition and seating in the United Nations of the two Chinas; opening trade with Communist China; unifying Korea; obtaining the abandonment of subversive communist pressures in South Vietnam; admission of Japan to the United Nations; and obtaining an undertaking by Communist China to refrain from support of subversive groups in any part of Asia. Realizing that such a proposal would require detailed study and planning, the Planning Board stated that, in the meantime, the United States must weaken or retard the growth and power of Communist China, and also called for continued refusal to recognize Communist China and other Asian communist regimes, utilization of all feasible overt and covert means to create discontent and internal division within the communist dominated area, and maintenance of a trade embargo against Communist China. On the matter of the trade embargo, however, the members of the Planning Board could not agree. Although all supported continuation of the embargo, the Defense, JCS, Commerce, and ODM representatives favored use of "the total bargaining position of the United States to gain acceptance of the embargo, or near embargo, by all other noncommunist countries." The State, Treasury, Budget, and CIA representatives, on the other hand, would continue to exert US influence on other free world countries for maintenance of the current level of trade controls against Communist China but without using US influence in such a manner as to be "seriously divisive."[18]

In preparation for a 1 December NSC consideration of NSC 5429/3, the Joint Chiefs provided the Secretary of Defense their comments on the draft policy statement on 26 November, noting that they had had only three days to prepare their views. They informed the Secretary that US policy for the Far East was dependent, in large degree, upon the "Basic National Security Policy of the United States." Since the Basic National Security Policy was currently under review by the National Security Council, the Joint Chiefs cautioned that their views on the Far East draft policy statement must be considered tentative.

The new draft, the JCS said, would constitute a comprehensive policy for the area as a whole and would provide guidance for the formulation of Subsidiary policies. With respect to the principal objectives, they endorsed all five goals. They believed, however, that the objective calling for the reduction of the power and prestige of Communist China lacked clarity and suggested the following expansion of that objective:

> The reduction of Chinese Communist power and prestige with the objective of securing by reorientation a government on the mainland of China whose objectives do not conflict with the vital interests of the United States.

They supported the disputed fifth objective (for the creation in noncommunist Asia of the political and social forces to spread the values of the free world and expose the falsity of the communist ideological offensive), stating that such an objective was "wholly consistent" with the basic goals of the United States in the Far East and should be retained in the policy statement. The Joint Chiefs of Staff found the draft policy with respect to Indochina, including the new paragraph dealing with armistice violations, "acceptable from the military point of view."

The Joint Chiefs of Staff strongly opposed the proposal for study of the feasibility of negotiation of a Far Eastern settlement by swapping concessions with Communist China. They based their stand not so much on the value of the concessions to be bartered as on their belief that Communist China would not live up to any agreement not suiting its purposes. They stated that such a settlement would grant the Chinese Communists far-reaching concessions, while relying upon "the as yet undemonstrated faith of that regime." They pointed out that experience in Korea and currently in Indochina with respect to the armistice provided ample evidence that the communists would "distort, evade, or violate any agreements when it suits their purposes to do so." In addition, the Joint Chiefs of Staff believed it "highly unrealistic" to expect the Chinese Communists to abandon their subversive efforts in South Vietnam and elsewhere in Asia, regardless of any commitments to the contrary.

Concerning the question of the trade embargo on Communist China, the Joint Chiefs of Staff supported the more restrictive approach. They conceded that some of the proposed courses of action in that approach might not be feasible in view of existing free world trade agreements, but they considered that the broad objective of US security policy would not be achieved if the United States was forced to defer to the counsel of the most cautious among its allies or "if it was unwilling to undertake certain risks inherent in the adoption of dynamic and positive security measures."[19]

On 1 December 1954, the National Security Council considered NSC 5429/3 and expanded the objective toward Communist China, essentially as suggested by the Joint Chiefs of Staff. In addition, the council retained the disputed fifth objective and, after some deliberation, deleted the proposal for study of the feasibility of achieving a Far Eastern settlement by bartering concessions with Communist China. In addition under the courses of action to preserve territorial and political integrity of the Far East, the council enlarged the one providing for punitive action in the event of unprovoked Communist attack on US personnel, aircraft, or vessels, including provision for pursuit of the attacking communist force into hostile airspace or waters, if feasible, and for retaliatory action as appropriate and approved by the President. The Department of State, however, considered that such pursuit should be undertaken only on specific order of the senior commander in the area. On the question of the trade embargo, the council was unable to agree, and the draft policy statement on the Far East, as revised at the 1 December meeting, was subsequently circulated on 10 December as NSC 5429/4, with the issues of hostile pursuit and the trade embargo still unresolved.[20]

The Secretary of Defense requested the JCS views on NSC 5429/4, and the Joint Chiefs of Staff furnished them on 17 December 1954. They accepted the expansion of the course of action dealing with punitive action and hostile pursuit in the case of unprovoked attack. With regard to the Department of State qualification concerning who should authorize such pursuit, they considered that, under certain circumstances, "the United States commander on the spot" should have authority to initiate hot pursuit but that such authority should be incorporated in the directives to the armed forces rather than in a broad policy statement.

On a trade embargo for Communist China, the Joint Chiefs of Staff once again strongly supported the more restrictive approach. They considered that the policy for the control of trade with Communist China should be developed within the context of the overall US economic defense policy, adding that "maximum restrictions" on trade with the Chinese Communists would be desirable.[21]

The National Security Council on 21 December 1954 again considered US policy toward the Far East but was unable to resolve the matters of hostile pursuit and the trade embargo on Communist China. Consequently, on the following day, the President approved the statement of policy in NSC 5429/4 with the exception of the portions dealing with these two matters, and the approved policy was circulated as NSC 5429/5, superseding NSC 5429/2.[22]

On 5 January 1955, the National Security Council reviewed the unresolved issues of the US policy toward the Far East. The Secretary of State presented the council a new draft section dealing with unprovoked attack and hostile pursuit prepared in coordination with the Assistant Secretary of Defense International Security Affairs (ISA). This draft provided that the United States Government should issue a directive to its armed forces that, in the event of unprovoked communist attack against US personnel, aircraft, or vessels outside communist territory, US forces in the area would take "immediate and aggressive protective measures" against the attacking force including, if necessary and feasible, "hot pursuit... into hostile airspace or waters." In addition, the proposal retained provision for such additional punitive actions as might be specifically approved by the President; the Council adopted it without change.

With respect to the trade embargo, on 5 January the National Security Council adopted a section calling for maintenance of the current level of US trade controls with Communist China and for administration of these controls in such a manner "as to endeavor not to lessen the active cooperation in the multilateral control program of other Free World countries." Under this provision, the United States would urge other free world countries to maintain the current level of trade controls on Communist China, promoting the willingness of such nations to do so by appropriate handling of routine exceptions. Additionally, whenever the Secretary of State determined that maintenance of the current multilaterally agreed level of export controls could be "seriously divisive" among US allies, or lead nations needing trade with Communist China toward an accommodation with the Soviet bloc, he would report the matter to the National Security Council for prompt consideration. The council also agreed to study, "on an urgent basis," all aspects of US economic defense policy applicable to trade with the communist bloc, including Communist China.[23] The President approved both NSC actions, and NSC 5429/5 was revised accordingly.[24]

Thus, at the beginning of 1955, after five months of effort, the United States had an approved policy that, it was hoped, would cope with the serious challenge to vital US security interests in the Far East in general, and in South Vietnam in particular. During the development of this policy, Communist China was seen ever more clearly as the principal threat to US interests in the area. In the preparation of the policy, the problem of dealing with Communist China tended to dominate the consideration of US policymakers. The basic decision was to halt the spread of communism in the Far East and, if possible, to roll it back.

In a sense, the policy toward Indochina was developed as a corollary to the broad and basic policy. But Indochina, especially South Vietnam, was perceived as a seriously endangered area that would require substantial help if it was to resist further communist inroads. During the months that the policy was under consideration, the situation in South Vietnam had deteriorated so rapidly that the United States was forced to act without benefit of an approved policy.

2

Three Troubled Months—August–October 1954

The summer and autumn of 1954, an important period in Indochinese history, was a time of turmoil, political instability, and strife. Although Laos and Cambodia achieved a measure of stability, South Vietnam became embroiled in civil conflict. Plans for political, economic, and military reform were lost in the anarchy surrounding the South Vietnamese Government of Premier Ngo Dinh Diem. French and US authorities had not been able to agree upon what measures ought to be adopted. The Vietnamese National Army was still prevented by politics from extending the authority of the Saigon government to the countryside. Hordes of refugees poured in from North Vietnam, clogging inadequate reception facilities. The Viet Minh were gaining strength in the south. By mid-November, when President Eisenhower sent General J. Lawton Collins, USA, to Indochina in a renewed effort to save Vietnam, the crisis was in its third month, and there appeared to be little chance of keeping South Vietnam in the noncommunist camp.

Political Turmoil

After the Geneva Conference, the Vietnamese political scene was a tangle of conflicting power groups struggling for dominance in postwar Vietnam. Except for US support, the Diem government stood alone. The Cao Dai and Hoa Hao politico-religious sects and the Binh Xuyen criminal organization sought Diem's downfall because of his refusal to face "political reality," that is, the traditional prerogative of governmental officials in Vietnam to enrich themselves at public expense. The Chief of Staff of the VNA, General Nguyen Van Hinh, led a group of ambitious young officers who, championing the restoration of public order, began laying plans for a coup d'etat. Other prominent but unaffiliated politicians such as Nguyen Van Tam, Nguyen Van Xuan, and Tran Van Huu intrigued with both the army and the sects in an attempt to regain positions of power. It was no secret that Chief of State Bao Dai, who was living on the French Riviera, was strongly opposed to the Diem government. Bao Dai's living in France was largely financed by the sects and the Binh Xuyen, and he no doubt realized that he stood a good chance of being deposed as Chief of State if Diem called a constituent assembly.

Diem's immediate problem, however, was to cope with his local opponents, for they represented widespread political strength. Possessing no organized following of his own, Diem was compelled to negotiate with them. The sects and the Binh Xuyen in August offered to participate in Diem's government, but on terms that would have reduced the Prime Minister to a figurehead. Diem's counterproposals on the other hand, would have given the sects no real measure of power. In the deadlock that followed, the sects began to collaborate with General Hinh to devise a plan for supplanting Diem by a military dictatorship. Both General Paul Ely, French Commissioner-General, and US Ambassador Donald H. Heath brought pressure to bear on Diem, the sects, and Hinh to moderate their demands and patch together a coalition government that could begin the work of pacification, resettlement, and constitutional reform.[1]

These efforts by General Ely and Ambassador Heath were offset by France's lack of enthusiasm for Prime Minister Diem. The French were unsettled by Diem's militant Francophobia. Like the Hinh coterie, they pointed to Diem's seeming inability to restore order as evidence of his unsuitability. General Ely, although personally convinced that Diem had to be replaced, apparently worked sincerely, if reluctantly, with Ambassador Heath to prevent Diem's downfall. Some of General Ely's subordinates, however secretly encouraged both Hinh and the sects to overturn the Diem regime. Ambassador Heath reported that, although he did not doubt the "impartiality and integrity [of] General Ely," it was clear that other French officers were giving "quiet encouragement if not unofficial support" to General Hinh. Moreover, the administrators at the "operating level in Paris," as well as "most French officials" in Saigon, wished either to unseat Diem as quickly as possible or to load his government with pro-French individuals.[2]

The French persistently sought to convince the US Government that Diem should be given a figurehead role, with actual authority vested in a stronger person. Tam, Xuan, Huu, Prince Buu Loc and Prince Buu Hoi were all mentioned. But none of the French candidates was acceptable to the United States, because of past identification with either France or the Viet Minh. The name most persistently put forward was that of Nguyen Van Tam, father of General Hinh and former Interior Minister, whose repressive police techniques had kept order in Saigon and thus endeared him to the French. The campaign in behalf of Tam reached a climax in mid-September when Diem complained that Deputy Commissioner-General Jean Daridan had demanded that Tam be taken into the government and implied that, otherwise, Diem would be out "in [a] matter of days." Ambassador Heath reported the allegation to Washington, and the Department of State registered an official protest with Premier Mendes-France personally. The Premier denied knowledge of pressure in favor of Tam but agreed to instruct Saigon to "go easy." French advocacy of Tam, however, did not abate in succeeding months.[3]

By early September, the political atmosphere in Saigon had become so highly charged that a break in the deadlock clearly had to come soon. It came on 10 September. One of Diem's agents had infiltrated a General Staff meeting where plans for a coup d'etat were being drafted. His report confirmed Diem's suspicions, and the Prime Minister arrested two of the ringleaders, Colonel Lan and Captain Giai. Couching his protest as a thinly veiled threat, Hinh demanded that the two officers be reinstated. This so incensed Diem that he summarily removed Hinh from command of the army and ordered him out of the country. Diem had moved boldly but without carefully laying plans for subsequent action. He appointed General Nguyen Van Vy to fill the post vacated by Hinh, but Vy temporized and finally refused. Diem then placed Vy on inactive status and instructed Colonel Ho Thong Minh to assume command. When Minh refused, Diem could find no other available officer whom he considered sufficiently loyal to the government to hold the important position. As a last resort, Le Ngoc Chan, the civilian Secretary of State for Defense, took over Hinh's duties in addition to his own. Hinh, with direct orders to go abroad on a "study mission," procrastinated and at length barricaded himself in his home. Fully equipped infantry and a number of armored vehicles were brought in "to protect him from the President." Diem withdrew into Norodom Palace and strengthened the palace guard. Again the situation was deadlocked.[4]

Diem's mishandling of Hinh's ouster gave the General an opportunity to present the conflict as an attack by the government on the integrity of the army. Hinh was soon explaining that, although he would be happy to take a vacation in France, he could not leave without turning his command over to a qualified officer whom the army trusted. Besides, he asserted, the situation was no longer in his control. He had become a "moral prisoner" of the army. Judging his hand strong enough, he appealed to Bao Dai to intervene by discharging Diem and constituting a government that could restore order. General Ely, Ambassador Heath, and Lieutenant General John W. O'Daniel, Chief, Military Assistance Advisory Group (MAAG) Indochina, used all of their persuasive powers to prevent Hinh from acting rashly.[5] They sought to influence the Premier to moderate his position enough to adopt a compromise that would save face for Hinh.[6]

Fortunately for Diem, the Hinh crisis had been accompanied by increasing disposition of the sects to participate in the government. They had been unable to agree among themselves on a formula for dividing control of a new administration, and Ambassador Heath had left little doubt that precipitate action might jeopardize the flow of US aid.[7] As a result, the sects had moderated their demands and begun negotiating with Diem. Agreement in principle was reached early in September, although at the last minute the Binh Xuyen withdrew rather than share authority with the two sects. By 21 September, the Cao Dai and Hoa Hao were on the verge of entering the government. But at this critical Juncture, a Cao Dai functionary reported to Ambassador Heath that General Raoul Salan, Deputy Commander in Chief, French Union Forces, had called in the sects and declared that General Le Van Vien, Binh Xuyen leader, had received a mandate from Bao Dai to form a government led by the Binh Xuyen, and that France and the United States had accepted this solution. From Diem came intelligence that General Salan had threatened the sects with termination of their subsidies if they joined the government, and that Deputy Commissioner General Daridan was reported to be exerting "heavy pressure" on the sects not to participate.[8] A Hoa Hao officer "wistfully" remarked to Ambassador Heath that General Ely had counseled them to cooperate with the Prime Minister, and General Salan had advised them to the contrary. As a result they were "dizzy."

Ambassador Heath assured the sects that the United States had not changed its attitude toward Diem. On 24 September Diem announced the inclusion in his Cabinet of Cao Dai and Hoa Hao representatives, and rumors of an impending military coup spread through Saigon as VNA troops clashed with Diem's palace guard.[9]

The Washington Conference

Against this background French and US negotiators met in Washington on 27 September to find a solution to the political tangle in Saigon and to work out military and fiscal problems. General Ely and Ambassador Heath flew to Washington to participate. No sooner had they departed from Saigon than Bao Dai intervened in the crisis by ordering Diem to take Generals Hinh, Xuan, and Vien into his government. Diem stalled and negotiated while his future was determined in Washington.[10]

The cross-purposes at which France and the United States had been working in Vietnam pointed clearly to the need for developing a unified approach to Vietnamese political problems. On their part, the French were anxious to obtain a US commitment for financial support of the French Expeditionary Corps (FEC), as well as an indication of US plans for future aid programs to the three Associated States.[11] The United States sought, as its principal objective in the Washington talks, to reach agreement with France on a political program for Vietnam. In the view of Secretary of State John Foster Dulles, if no such agreement were reached there would be "no point in our discussing further aid."[12]

During the conference, M. Guy La Chambre, Minister for Relations with the Associated States, and Under Secretary of State Walter Bedell Smith discussed at length the relative merits of the various personalities on the Vietnamese political scene. Minister La Chambre favored a plan whereby Prince Buu Loc, a member of Bao Dai's entourage, would be designated the representative of Bao Dai and sent to Saigon to form a new government. Secretary Smith insisted, however, that Diem had to be fully supported by the United States and France. The United States, he explained, felt that Bao Dai, although he should be constitutionally deposed at a more propitious time in the future, now ought to be persuaded to intervene in behalf of Diem. To attain this end, the United States suggested that Ambassador Heath and General Ely fly to Cannes and impress upon the Chief of State that the United States and France had determined to back Diem. Minister La Chambre finally agreed to the US plan.[13]

The French were obviously reluctant to insist strongly that Diem be replaced because of their dependence upon the US for financial support of the FEC. The United States had stopped paying FEC expenses incurred after the cease-fire, and the French were very anxious to have the flow of dollars resumed. France had declared in August that it could not reasonably be expected to continue to provide manpower for the defense of Southeast Asia unless US financial assistance were continued.[14] Most US authorities believed that the presence of the FEC in Indochina was necessary until indigenous forces could be developed, and that France would probably withdraw the FEC if the United States refused to contribute to its upkeep. The United States had determined, however, to make no definite promises until French intentions could be assessed and until the matter was considered further.[15]

At the Washington Conference, M. La Chambre stated that the FEC would be reduced from its current force of 175,000 to 100,000 by the end of 1955. Under this plan, the financial requirement during 1955 would total approximately 500 million, of which France could afford only 170 million. The United States, the French thought, should furnish about 330 million to make up the difference. In reply, Foreign Operations Administrator Harold Stassen pointed out that Congress had appropriated FEC support funds before the armistice and for the express purpose of winning the Indochinese war. This objective was no longer attainable. No answer, he added, could be given until about 1 December, for Congress had to be consulted before new commitments were made.[16]

Of more immediate concern to the United States was the problem of obtaining French agreement to the principle of direct aid to the Indochinese countries. Not only would the objectives of the United States be best served if the Indochinese people could distinguish between French and US activities, but the provision of US aid through French channels was inconsistent with the independent status of the three countries. For these reasons the principle of direct aid had been adopted by the National Security Council (NSC) and written into the Mutual Security Act by Congress.[17]

The French, when informed by Secretary Dulles in August that the United States intended to alter its aid procedures, had objected strongly. Direct aid, they asserted, would violate the Geneva Agreements and would needlessly provoke the Chinese Communists. Furthermore, the French believed that permitting the Indochinese any greater control over expenditure of aid funds would promote waste, graft, and corruption, and intensify the political struggle. As US Ambassador to France, C. Douglas Dillon, summed up this viewpoint, the French

... are convinced that if the Vietnamese are given, without restriction, an erector set with all the parts for a ten story building they will end up with a one story cabin and the remaining parts will either be sold or end up in the pockets of the builders. On the other hand if the parts are handed out with care and supervision, a well-built five story building will emerge after many trials and tribulations. Furthermore, the French believe that their past sacrifices on behalf of Vietnam and their obligation as a member of [the] French Union dictate that they should be the construction supervisor.[18]

At the Washington Conference, Minister La Chambre advanced a plan whereby aid would be administered jointly by Franco-American committees. These organizations, one each for Laos, Cambodia, and Vietnam, would be headed by General Ely and would not include representatives of the Associated States. Each committee would serve, said M. La Chambre, as a "US-French brain trust." Under Secretary of State Smith was inclined to accept the La Chambre plan, but his colleagues, principally Assistant Secretary of State Walter Robertson and Counselor Douglas MacArthur II, pointed out that this procedure contradicted the US policy of dealing with the Associated States on a basis of equality. A compromise wording, for insertion in a Minute of Understanding, was proposed by Under Secretary Smith and accepted by M. La Chambre. It stated: "Such [aid] programs will be planned and closely coordinated to assure maximum effectiveness through appropriate machinery established in agreement with interested governments." This wording, said Secretary Smith, could mean some form of tripartite organization, and he hoped it would be interpreted as such.[19]

This substitution of vague language for definite agreement failed to put France on notice that the United States was opposed to French participation in the distribution of US assistance. Minister La Chambre returned to Paris convinced that the United States had consented to a form of tripartite control. Mr. Robertson, however, later advised Secretary Dulles that no real understanding had been achieved on how aid funds were to be distributed.[20]

South Vietnam: Continuing Political Deadlock

Prime Minister Diem, confronted on the eve of the Washington Conference with Bao Dai's directive to take Xuan, Hinh, and Vien into his government, negotiated with the three generals in an effort to play for time. In accordance with the agreement reached in Washington that France and the United States would continue to support Diem, Ambassador Heath and General Ely flew to Cannes for a talk with Bao Dai. As a result of their representations, the Chief of State withdrew his ultimatum to Diem, and instructed Xuan, Hinh, and Vien to cooperate with the Premier. Although the crisis was temporarily eased, Diem was still in a precarious position. A mistake could trigger a revolt of the National Army and the Binh Xuyen Surete in Saigon. The military forces of the sects, which were now supporting Diem, would be of little help, for they were dispersed throughout the provinces. Each day brought fresh rumors that the army was planning to strike on the following day.[21]

In this heated atmosphere, Diem became more inflexible. Despite the repeated advice of Ambassador Heath and General Ely to move with extreme caution, Diem insisted that Hinh leave the country immediately. But Hinh had now joined with Vien and Xuan in a seemingly unshakable coalition that pressed exorbitant demands upon the Prime Minister. Hinh refused to surrender command of the army; Xuan was still determined to become Vice President and Defense Minister and Vien contended that the Binh Xuyen should control the Ministry of the Interior. Diem's acceptance of these demands would have reduced his role to that of a figurehead. Diem attempted to sow dissension among the three generals, but failed. Each time he offered a compromise the triumvirate raised its demands. The situation became increasingly tense, with all evidence pointing to an army coup on 13 October. Ambassador Heath and General Ely summoned Hinh and warned him that resorting to violence would cause a suspension of US aid. Thereafter, the threat of an uprising declined slightly, but the problem of the three generals remained to torment Diem.[22]

In the provinces, meanwhile, conditions steadily grew worse as a result of the prolonged paralysis of the government. Minister La Chambre, returning to France from a visit to Indochina, declared that the Viet Minh in Annam were openly exerting their influence, were cool, competent, assured, and acting like conquerors. Local Vietnamese officials were inefficient and powerless. Deputy Commissioner Daridan thought there was no possibility of retaining Annam, and that emphasis should be directed instead to saving Cochin-China. Ambassador Heath journeyed to Annam and confirmed Daridan's pessimistic report.[23]

In Cochin-China, communist strength was less obvious, but the French suspected that large numbers of Viet Minh troops had cached their arms and blended with the population. As the Viet Minh armies withdrew, the armies of the Cao Dai and Hoa Hao rapidly moved in to establish themselves in time to levy duties on the rice crop. Although the sects were cooperating in the Saigon government, open warfare was reported between them for control of the provinces. A "usually reliable Hoa Hao source" informed Ambassador Heath that at least one battle between Hoa Hao and Cao Dai troops had been deliberately engineered by the local French commander. The French, said Ambassador Heath's confidant, were following a "divide and rule" policy and were trying to create discord between the sects in order to weaken their cooperation in the Diem government.[24]

The VNA, involved in politics, poorly trained, and heavily dependent upon French leadership, could not bring order to the rural areas. The US Military Attaché at Saigon reported that the VNA had shown itself incapable of performing even minor police actions without French staff and logistical support. One operation, originally conceived entirely as a Vietnamese project, after much confusion had to be planned and executed by a French colonial infantry regiment, French

Union troops were thus brought into action against Vietnamese nationals, an eventuality France had wished to avoid.[25]

Little could be accomplished in the provinces until the political stalemate in Saigon was broken. Diem's cause received an appreciable stimulus in mid-October with the publication in the United States of the Mansfield Report, which was expected to have great influence on Congress and the Department of State. United States Senator Mike Mansfield had visited Vietnam early in October. Upon his return he had written an analysis of the situation in Indochina. "The political issue in South Vietnam," declared Senator Mansfield,

> is not Diem as an individual but rather the program for which he stands. It is unlikely that any independent non-Communist government can survive in Vietnam, let alone recover the Vietminh-held areas unless it represents genuine nationalism, unless it is prepared to deal effectively with corruption, and unless it demonstrates a concern in advancing the welfare of the Vietnamese people.

Ngo Dinh Diem offered the best chance of filling this prescription, thought the Senator. Should Diem be forced out of office, it was improbable that new leadership dedicated to these principles could be found. Senator Mansfield's conclusion, therefore, was that if the Diem government fell, "the United States should consider an immediate suspension of all aid to Vietnam and the French Union forces there, except that of a humanitarian nature, preliminary to a complete reappraisal of our present policies in Free Vietnam."[26]

The Mansfield Report produced noteworthy reactions in both South Vietnam and France. In South Vietnam, the "unfortunate Mansfield statement," as Xuan termed it, had a moderating effect both upon Diem's opponents and upon French officialdom. On the other hand, Diem and his supporters were "jubilant" and the Prime Minister became more uncompromising. In France, where Diem had long since been given up as a lost cause, Paris officials felt the Mansfield formula violated the decision at the Washington Conference to support an alternate if Diem failed. Factions advocating conciliation of the Viet Minh pointed out that Senator Mansfield's observations merely reinforced their own arguments. The United States, if it followed the Senator's recommendations, would withdraw should Diem fall; Diem, they believed, could not possibly succeed; therefore, France should start "betting on [the] Viet Minh to win [the] race."[27]

The Mansfield Report was followed closely by a crash program designed by the National Security Council to stabilize the Diem regime. When the National Security Council met on 22 October, the Diem-Hinh conflict was in its fortieth day, with no end in sight and the Viet Minh promising to win South Vietnam by default unless prompt and vigorous actions were taken. The NSC decision was followed on the same day by instructions to Ambassador Heath to deliver a letter from President Eisenhower to Prime Minister Diem, reiterating US support and offering to begin discussions immediately on a program of direct economic and military assistance to South Vietnam. Ambassador Heath also was authorized to acquaint French and Vietnamese officials with the US attitude and to work out with General Ely a plan for neutralizing the opposition of Generals Hinh, Xuan, and Vien. A joint State-Defense message, also of 22 October, repeated for both Ambassador Heath and General O'Daniel the US policy to support Diem and directed them to begin a crash program to improve the loyalty and effectiveness of the Vietnamese armed forces. To accomplish this task, all the assets of the US Government in Vietnam would be available. Ambassador Dillon, in Paris, was instructed to present the French with the US program and to suggest that France had not been giving Diem all the support of which it was capable.[28]

This crash program and, in particular, the charge that France had fallen short in its support of Diem had an electric effect upon the French. Minister La Chambre replied that the President's letter to Diem, offering to work out immediate procedures of direct aid, was a clear-cut violation of the Washington Agreement. La Chambre recalled that Under Secretary Smith had distinctly agreed to tripartite distribution of assistance funds. Moreover, the accusation that France had not been working actively to consolidate the Diem regime was not only untrue but a direct reflection upon himself, General Ely, and the honor of the French Government. Although convinced that Diem was leading Vietnam to disaster, Minister La Chambre declared that France was still willing to support him. "We prefer to lose in Vietnam with the US rather than to win without them," said the Minister. "We would rather support Diem knowing he is going to lose and thus keep Franco-US solidarity than to pick someone who could retain Vietnam for the free world if this meant breaking Franco-US solidarity."[29]

Upon learning of this conversation, Secretary Dulles drafted a formal message to Premier Mendes-France. The United States, said the Secretary, considered the crash program "as being in furtherance of the understandings reached at Washington." In addition, although the United States had not "the slightest idea of questioning the good faith of the French Government," the fact remained that "many French officials have not concealed their belief that Diem has failed... and that he should be replaced." The result of this attitude was the "impasse in Saigon." Minister La Chambre received Mr. Dulles' message "with little comment." He did, however, suggest a "way out of the mess." Tam, he thought should be made Minister of the Interior in Diem's government, for "Here is a man who knows how to fight Communists."[30]

The indignation in Paris notwithstanding, Ambassador Heath and General O'Daniel, in Saigon, devised a comprehensive plan, with political, economic, and military courses of action, to put the NSC decisions into effect.[31] The more important political features envisioned statements of mutual reconciliation by Diem and Hinh and Hinh's departure for France on a "study mission." Xuan was to be put aside and Vien taken into the government, although not in control of the Interior Ministry. Diem was to effect a house-cleaning of his administration, and personally circulate among the people. In the economic field, a general statement would be made declaring the government's intention to inaugurate a comprehensive land reform program.[32]

The plan of action was based on three admittedly untested assumptions: that Diem could be persuaded to accept the Ambassador's proposals; that Hinh would carry out his promise, recently made to General O'Daniel, to give the government his loyal support; and that the French would cooperate, in fact as well as in name, at all echelons.[33] None of these assumptions proved immediately valid. Diem remained as stubborn as ever; Hinh continued his intrigues; and there was no noticeable improvement of local French support. The crash program, as a result, made little headway. The political stalemate continued; the Diem government grew weaker; and communist influence spread through the countryside.

French Policy

Aggravating the stalemate in Vietnam was the contradictory French policy toward Indochina. In formulating a policy, the Mendes-France government was apparently torn by factions striving toward conflicting objectives. Some members of the government wished to join with the United States in halting the spread of communism in Indochina and the rest of Southeast Asia. Others thought coexistence with the Viet Minh offered the only chance to protect French commerce, business, industry, and cultural institutions in North Vietnam. Still others were interested only in preserving the paramount position of France, and in blocking the growing influence of the United States, in South Vietnam. The French, however, had two strong incentives for adapting their policy to US ideas. They needed US financial support of the FEC, and they wished to avoid friction in Franco-American relations. France, therefore, subscribed, at the Washington Conference, to a four-point program to be undertaken in concert with the United States. First, France would "support the independence" of the Associated States. Second, within the limitations imposed by Geneva, France would "oppose the extension of [Viet Minh] influence or control" in Indochina. Third, France would undertake, in cooperation with the United States, programs of economic and military assistance to strengthen the Associated States. Finally, France would support Prime Minister Diem in establishing a strong anticommunist regime in South Vietnam.[34] These principles were later reaffirmed in conversations held between President Eisenhower and Premier Mendes-France in November.

France consistently professed its adherence to the policy adopted at the Washington Conference. Nevertheless, US leaders doubted the resoluteness of the Mendes-France government in carrying out this policy. The Americans were concerned about what appeared to be France's accommodating attitude toward the new Viet-Minh regime.

French policy toward the Viet Minh can be explained partly by a widespread belief in France that the Viet Minh would inevitably win all of Vietnam despite French and US efforts, and that the French economic and cultural investment in Tonkin might not be lost if France approached the Viet Minh in a conciliatory fashion. Moreover, as Ambassador Dillon reported in November, Premier Mendes-France had found in Vietnam a "situation ideally designed to test [the] basis of his fundamental political philosophy" of "peaceful coexistence," and his government had become increasingly "disposed to explore and consider a policy looking toward an eventual peaceful North-South rapprochement" on terms favorable to the Viet Minh.[35]

As a result of this thinking, the French insisted upon what some US diplomats thought an overly strict interpretation of the Vietnam Agreement. There was strong sentiment in the Department of State for avoiding at all costs the projected 1956 elections in Vietnam. This purpose could be accomplished without great difficulty since the armistice provisions governing elections were extremely vague. In addition, South Vietnam had not been a party to the Geneva Agreements and was, therefore, not pledged to conduct elections. The French, however, were unalterably opposed to any policy that might be construed, even remotely, as a violation of Geneva. The French would accept the results of general elections, thought Ambassador Dillon, "however academic that exercise may eventually prove to be." Premier Mendes-France had declared publicly that France intended to demand elections and abide by the results, and Minister La Chambre had stated that, if Ho Chi Minh won by a majority of a single vote, France would permit him to have all of Vietnam.[36]

The influence of the proponents of coexistence was apparent, for example, in the dispatch to Hanoi of Jean Sainteny, who had negotiated the March 1946 accords with the DRV.[37] Sainteny was charged with working out agreements with the Viet Minh for protection of French interests in Tonkin. Although his terms of reference contemplated purely consular activities, Sainteny's mission could not help but have political overtones, especially in view of his past activities in behalf of rapprochement with the Viet Minh.[38]

The Sainteny Mission greatly disturbed General Ely. He confided to Ambassador Heath his fear that Sainteny would soon tire of a dull consular role and begin to promote political friendship and cooperation with North Vietnam. General Ely declared that he would have been much happier had Paris sent a "stupid type of consular officer" rather than a man of Sainteny's "active stripe." Seriously concerned over this French policy, he flew to France to learn just what Paris intended to do. There he informed Premier Mendes-France that he was not disposed to retain his assignment if French policy, as reflected by the Sainteny Mission, was to play a "double game" in North and South Vietnam with the intention of eventually backing the side that came out on top. The Premier gave General Ely unqualified assurance that the policy of the French Government was to give maximum support to anticommunist elements in South Vietnam and to do everything possible to contribute to the success of these elements in the 1956 elections. Placated, the General returned to Saigon, but there was no perceptible change in French policy.[39]

Sainteny's efforts to safeguard French economic interests led, in December, to an agreement with Ho Chi Minh permitting French enterprise to carry on without discrimination. On the surface the agreement appeared to be an important concession, but French businessmen in Indochina were not optimistic. They pointed out that, although Ho had guaranteed freedom of operation without discrimination, he had insisted that French enterprises be regulated by Viet Minh legislation. The communists could thus do as they pleased with French business merely by passing appropriate legislation. Ho had granted the right to sell freely in the Tonkinese market and to transfer profits to the franc zone. But the Viet Minh piaster had no value outside the communist orbit, and no purpose would be served by transfer. Most French concerns decided that potential profits were not worth the risks, and they prepared to withdraw from North Vietnam. Sainteny, nonetheless, remained in Hanoi as France's "general delegate" to the Democratic Republic of Vietnam.[40]

Although at the Washington Conference, the French had pledged themselves to support the Diem government, the promise had been given with obvious reluctance. Officials in Saigon, receiving no authoritative leadership from Paris, not only persisted in their antagonism toward Diem but worked more openly to undermine his regime. Paris continued its efforts to convince the United States that Diem ought to be replaced by men such as Tam, Xuan, or Vien. Already recognized by the French as a Francophobe, Diem added to French hostility toward his government by interfering with Sainteny's prospects for a settlement with Ho Chi Minh.[41]

Prince Buu Hoi, a member of Bao Dai's court, had in past years been friendly to the Viet Minh cause, and he quickly became the outstanding contender for Diem's job. By November, Buu Hoi had enlisted an impressive array of supporters, and Ambassador Dillon reported that Premier Mendes-France and Minister La Chambre were inclined to favor the Prince as an eventual alternate to Diem. Alarmed at the proportions the Buu Hoi campaign was assuming, Secretary of State Dulles instructed Ambassador Dillon to inform the French Government that "So far as Buu Hoi is concerned we can state that if he or a person of his political ideologies" were to replace Diem as Prime Minister "a basic re-examination of our present policy with respect to Viet-Nam would be entailed." This declaration was received "without grace" in the French Foreign Office, and French officials continued to champion Buu Hoi.[42]

The conflicting currents of French policy put the United States at a disadvantage in dealing with France vis-à-vis Indochina. France repeatedly insisted that its policy was to oppose the extension of communism in Vietnam, but much evidence suggested that the Mendes-France government was reconciled to an all-communist Vietnam. France also insisted that it was fully supporting Diem, but officials in Saigon consistently gave support to his political enemies, while diplomats in Paris advanced a galaxy of unacceptable candidates for the consideration of the United States.

The Question of Independence

Intricately tied to the French turmoil over Indochina policy was the question of the independence of the Associated States. Prior to the Washington Conference, the United States had made clear its interest in seeing France accord full independence to the three States, as promised at Geneva. France believed, said Ambassador Dillon, that the United States had an "almost psychotic attachment to 'independence' without giving sufficient thought and attention to the practical problems and risks involved." This belief did not, however, deter Ambassador Dillon from pointing out that the United States would be more inclined to consider generous aid programs in Indochina if France attacked the problem of independence immediately and vigorously.[43] Specifically, France should satisfy the nationalistic aspirations of the Vietnamese. Laos and Cambodia presented no particular difficulty. Both had recently been granted independence, and although France had maintained considerable influence in Laotian affairs, the Cambodian Government believed itself to be truly independent, and acted accordingly.

The policy of the Mendes-France government toward South Vietnam was, as Minister La Chambre expressed it, to grant total independence "without retaining anything in the back of [the] bureau drawer." But this policy did not imply relaxation of the average Frenchman's resolute attachment to the concept of the French Union. He believed that full sovereignty and membership in the Union were entirely compatible, and he would sanction no policy that did not include Vietnam in the French Union. The Union offered economic and commercial advantages, the trappings of world power, and the opportunity to advance French culture overseas. No French Government dared defy public opinion by permitting severance of Union ties. Nevertheless, as the United States had pointed out at Geneva, any relationship that failed to recognize the right of South Vietnam to withdraw from the French Union was not true independence.[44]

An entirely new formula for granting independence to South Vietnam was now developed by the Mendes-France government, which planned to discard the treaty of independence initialed by the Laniel government in June 1954. Minister La Chambre, in explaining this surprise move, declared that previous governments had followed a "terrible policy." They had negotiated basic treaties and then had attempted to hold back the attributes of sovereignty by narrow interpretation of technical accords. Moreover, because of the partition of Vietnam, conclusion of a formal treaty might give the impression of creating a permanently divided country. The treaty was therefore to be replaced by a three-phase program. First, all possible technical services would be turned over to the Vietnamese immediately. Second, a four-power meeting would examine matters of common interest. Finally, any remaining French functions in Vietnam would be transferred as soon after the four-power conference as possible.[45]

Pursuant to the first phase of this program, General Ely transferred to Vietnam the direction of the port of Saigon, all local administrative and judicial functions, meteorological services, and civil aviation. France retained, nonetheless, an influential role in South Vietnam's military affairs, and the FEC remained, in the eyes of the local population, a bar to genuine independence. Premier Mendes-France had promised to withdraw the FEC upon request. Accordingly, the Diem government in September asked Paris to evacuate the FEC by May 1956, in order that South Vietnam might face national elections free of this symbol of French colonialism.[46]

Delegates from France and from each of the Associated States met in Paris on 26 August to reorganize the financial and economic relationships of the four countries to accord with the status of independence. The conferees decided to liquidate the Bank of Indochina and institute separate banks of issue and separate currencies. For the time being, however, each State would retain the piaster as the unit of currency, with the same rate of exchange with the franc as earlier. As the United States had urged, the delegates did not link the piaster to the Viet Minh currency. Furthermore, Premier Diem assured the United States that no exchange relationship would be established. The four-power customs union was abolished, leaving France to negotiate bilateral accords with each State for special economic privileges as a member of the French Union.[47]

Although agreement on breaking up the quadripartite organizations came quickly, the conference dragged on for four months. Cambodians and Vietnamese, jealous of their national rights, argued endlessly over navigation of the Mekong River, preferential treatment for Cambodia in the port of Saigon, and division of assets formerly held in common. When the meeting finally adjourned in December, the three States had agreed to found a tripartite control board to supervise navigation on the Mekong, and to negotiate bilateral accords giving Cambodia and Laos special facilities in Saigon and transit rights through Vietnam.[48]

The transfer of services and abolition of the four-power organizations wiped out almost the last vestiges of French colonialism in Indochina. For all practical purposes the Indochinese States were now independent. In the native mind, however, real independence was not possible while French troops remained and while membership in the French Union was compulsory.

The Situation in North Vietnam

While the situation in South Vietnam in the months following the Geneva Conference grew more chaotic, the outlook in North Vietnam was quite the reverse. The Viet Minh moved immediately to assert and consolidate their control. The tricolor was lowered over Hanoi on 9 October 1954, and the French garrison withdrew to Haiphong. Viet Minh troops in Soviet trucks and jeeps entered the city, to be greeted by wildly cheering Vietnamese. In succeeding weeks the Viet Minh followed the pattern of discipline, orderliness, and moderation that characterized the early period of communist rule in China. The administrative system was not materially changed, and most Vietnamese civil servants retained their posts in the municipal government. Corruption in any form was attacked, and prostitution and other vices that had flourished in Hanoi were abolished. Before long, however, the marks of authoritarian rule became evident. Propaganda posters cluttered the city, and the population was mobilized into "discussion groups" that were required to listen to lectures, learn slogans, and sing communist songs. Also the Viet Minh, although they announced the abolition of press censorship, took over the newspapers and printed nothing but communist party-line material.[49]

United States Consul Thomas G. Corcoran and five assistants remained in Hanoi after the French withdrew. The Viet Minh radio charged that this US presence constituted "a violation of the diplomatic sovereignty of the Democratic Republic of Vietnam," a violation "completely contrary to the Geneva agreements." Although no attempt was made to expel Mr. Corcoran, the communists applied increasing administrative and logistical pressure designed to harass US consular officials and disrupt, if not block, all consular activities.[50]

In the metropolitan display-case of Hanoi, the Viet Minh made a great show of respecting the Vietnam Agreement. Outside the city they were less moderate and freely evaded the armistice agreement wherever convenient. The most flagrant violations were evident in the Viet Minh effort to prevent refugees from migrating to the south. Road blocks were erected, refugees physically intimidated, children snatched from their parents, group leaders arrested, and boat-loads of emigrants bombarded with mortars and fired upon with automatic weapons. The Viet Minh insisted upon absurdly strict interpretation of regulations and impossible administrative restrictions. Refugees were forbidden to sell their property. Those who were turned back or failed to find transportation were prohibited from reoccupying their land. These measures deterred untold numbers of Tonkinese from fleeing the communist regime.[51]

The Viet Minh respected the military provisions of the armistice no more than those dealing with refugees. General Vo Nguyen Giap continued to expand and modernize his army. Intelligence sources reported that, during the last six months of 1954, the Viet Minh formed four new infantry divisions and one heavy division, and added an organic artillery battalion to each division. The same sources reported the importation from China, in violation of the Geneva Agreements, of 150 artillery pieces, over 500 mortars, 9,000 automatic weapons, 500 recoilless rifles, 400 military vehicles, and large quantities of ammunition.[52]

Truce violations by the Viet Minh were not confined to Tonkin. In South Vietnam the politico-military cadres left by the departing Viet Minh began preparing, clandestinely, for the 1956 elections. In Cambodia the government suspected that not all Viet Minh soldiers had been withdrawn and knew that the Khmer Resistance Forces had not been disbanded. In Laos, Pathet Lao troops remained in control of the two provinces bordering Tonkin and refused to recognize the rule of the Royal Laotian Government.[53]

The International Control Commissions (ICCs) in Laos, Cambodia, and Vietnam were almost powerless to enforce the armistice regulations. The Indian, Canadian, and Polish members of the teams rarely agreed on any issue. The Canadians sought to discharge their duties in an objective and unbiased fashion, but the Indians took a neutral stance, preferring negotiation rather than voting with either side. Both the Indians and the Canadians, however, felt that all chances of cooperation would be destroyed if they permitted either side to use the findings of the commissions for propaganda purposes. The Poles, on the other hand, were not so scrupulous. To the disillusionment of the Indians, the Poles proved obstructive, biased, and unreasonable; they directed their energies less to the business of the commissions than to gathering propaganda material for the Viet Minh.[54]

Attempts by the commission assigned to Vietnam to investigate violations in Tonkin were consistently thwarted by the Viet Minh. Investigators were harassed with onerous administrative requirements as well as with restrictions on travel. They had to give advance notice before arriving in a given area, thus permitting the Viet Minh ample time to set the stage and terrorize prospective witnesses. By contrast, representatives of the commission operated with complete freedom in South Vietnam. Nevertheless, in at least five incidents investigated during the last few months of 1954, the commission unanimously placed the blame on South Vietnam. An Indian official confided to an Embassy officer that the VNA was "inexperienced and trigger-happy," and that in some cases Vietnamese officers had ordered crowds of their own people dispersed with hand grenades. He also admitted that Viet Minh agents were probably agitating the populace, but evidence could rarely be obtained to confirm the suspicion.[55]

Interference with the ICC was but one manifestation of the ruthless and efficient control that the Viet Minh was rapidly extending over Tonkin. Contrasted with the Saigon government, the Democratic Republic of Vietnam was, as one correspondent expressed it, "indisputably strong, confident, and unified." By the end of 1954, the Viet Minh were well advanced in converting Tonkin into a genuine totalitarian communist state, with every phase of national and private life rigidly controlled by the Hanoi government. Only the Haiphong enclave remained in French hands, and the Viet Minh were poised to obliterate this last remnant of the old order when the evacuation period expired in May 1955.

3

The Collins Mission

By November 1954, South Vietnam had been in the grip of political anarchy for over three months, and French and US officials in Saigon saw little hope of preventing Annam and Cochin-China from going the way of Tonkin. A concerned President Eisenhower concluded that the deteriorating situation in South Vietnam called for extraordinary measures. In an attempt to restore order and hope in the future of the beleaguered nation, the President dispatched General J. Lawton Collins, USA, then serving as the US member on the Military Committee of NATO, on a special mission to Saigon. Collins was designated Special United States Representative in Vietnam with the rank of Ambassador and given broad authority to direct, utilize, and control all agencies and resources of the United States in South Vietnam.

On the eve of General Collins' departure, the President outlined his mission as follows:

> The immediate and urgent requirement... is to assist in stabilizing and strengthening the legal government of Viet-Nam under the premiership of Ngo Dinh Diem. Accordingly, the principal task of your mission is to coordinate and direct a program in support of that government to enable it to: (a) promote internal security and political and economic stability, (b) establish and maintain control throughout the territory, and (c) effectively counteract Viet Minh infiltration and paramilitary activities south of the military demarcation line. As an initial framework for a concrete program of action you should (a) use the joint instructions which the Departments of State and Defense transmitted to the American Embassy in Saigon on October 22 and (b) take into consideration the latter's reply of October 27, 1954.[1]

When the President's action was communicated to General Ely, whose cooperation was essential to the success of the Collins' mission, the response was not encouraging. Although expressing warm friendship and high esteem for General Collins, General Ely declared that such a mission would inevitably create an unfavorable impression in both France and free Vietnam, for it would be interpreted as evidence that the United States was planning to take over Indochina. He even implied that he might have to resign if the United States insisted on the assignment.[2] But General Ely did not resign, and on 11 November 1954, General Collins arrived in Saigon.

The Seven-Point Program

General Collins found himself confronted with a situation of discouraging complexity. For weeks, Diem's government had been virtually paralyzed by the defiance of General Nguyen Van Hinh, who was supported by a large portion of the army, by General Le Van Vien and the Binh Xuyen, by ex-President Nguyen Van Xuan, and sub rosa, by many French officials. The Cao Dai and Hoa Hao sects, having finally been persuaded to join the government, nevertheless, pursued their own selfish goals with scant regard for the national interest. In addition to powerful political opposition, the Diem government was burdened with the immense task of caring for the thousands of refugees pouring in from North Vietnam. Only a fraction of the refugees could be resettled in the rural areas, for many provinces had fallen under control of Viet Minh shadow governments, and others had become feudal domains of the sects or, worse, objects of dispute between them. "From nearly every point of view," General Collins recalled, "'free' Vietnam appeared headed toward absorption by the Viet Minh," either "through a French-managed accommodation with the Communists or through the restoration of a scarcely veiled colonial system." The latter, added the General, "could have been sustained against the Viet Minh only by the weight of arms which, paradoxically the French had made clear they had no intention of using."[3]

Devising a comprehensive and orderly approach to this tangled situation was indeed a formidable undertaking. General Collins, however, proposed to General Ely that they unite their efforts to attain six specific objectives designed to counteract the political, economic, and military chaos of Vietnam. General Ely agreed, and at his request a seventh, dealing with educational matters, was added.

The first objective of this seven-point program was the solution of the problem of the Vietnamese armed forces, especially the army. The VNA's support of General Hinh had been largely responsible for prolonging the political impasse, which in turn was delaying both political and economic reforms. Until it was molded into an efficiently organized, tightly disciplined, well-trained force loyal to the legal government, the VNA could not extend the authority of the central government to the provinces. And until the provinces were brought under the effective administrative control of Saigon, the US objective of a stable, anticommunist Vietnam could not be realized.

The second objective was strengthening and broadening the Diem government. The Premier was running what was virtually a one-man operation, and General Collins believed that the key ministries should be filled at once with capable and energetic men. A complementary goal was to set up some sort of national assembly as soon as possible. Except for municipal and provincial councils, for which the last elections had been held in 1953, South Vietnam had no representative institutions, and the Diem government badly needed a measure of identification with democracy.

The closely allied problems of land reform and refugees occupied prominent positions in the Collins-Ely program. The task was not only to care for the immediate wants of the emigrants from Tonkin but also to devise a long-range program that would win their political support, bring into productivity the uncultivated land, and give South Vietnamese tenant farmers an investment in freedom by granting them ownership of the land they tilled. Measures to modernize the financial and economic structure of Vietnam, to develop local talent in all fields, especially civil service, and to improve education completed the seven-point program.

Generals Collins and Ely formed specialized working groups from their respective staffs to draw up detailed programs in each of the seven categories. These working groups would submit draft plans to the two generals, who would resolve differences and settle upon an agreed Franco-American position. This position would then be used as the basis for recommendations to Premier Diem and for consultations with representatives of the Vietnamese government agencies responsible for putting the program into effect. French and US information agencies were to concentrate on giving Diem full credit for any progress that might be made.[4]

In subsequent weeks, a close and highly satisfactory relationship developed between Generals Collins and Ely. The distaste with which Ely had received the appointment of General Collins was apparently overcome. Although General Ely sincerely cooperated with General Collins in carrying out most features of the seven-fold approach, the attitudes of the government in Paris and the French community in Saigon limited his authority. In the end, therefore, it was General Collins who initiated most of the concrete measures of reform, and who provided the impetus that carried them forward in the face of many obstacles.

The Problem of Creating an Effective VNA

Even before General Collins went to Saigon, the United States had realized that Vietnam desperately needed a strong, well-trained army to cope with its formidable internal security problem. The role of the United States in developing such an army, however, became a subject of disagreement between the Department of State and the Joint Chiefs of Staff.

The dispute was touched off by General O'Daniel, Chief, MAAG Indochina.[5] In the week following the signing of the Geneva Agreements, General O'Daniel had urged that the United States undertake, without French interference, a priority program for training the VNA. Pointing out that the Vietnam Agreement prohibited the enlargement of foreign contingents in Vietnam after 11 August 1954, he recommended that MAAG Indochina be immediately increased in order to carry out a realistic training program. Seeing that final decision would be delayed beyond 11 August, General O'Daniel took advantage of the presence in Saigon of one hundred Air Force mechanics traveling to Manila to expand his roster of authorized personnel.[6]

Ambassador Heath and his superiors in the State Department strongly concurred with General O'Daniel's recommendations, but the Joint Chiefs of Staff did not. They had no wish to be drawn into a situation where the United States would have responsibility for a program that faced a good chance of failure through factors beyond US control. The Joint Chiefs of Staff, therefore, defined four "preconditions" they considered should be met before the United States assumed any training obligations in Vietnam or Cambodia. First, a strong and stable civil government should be in control of the country. "It is hopeless," warned the Joint Chiefs of Staffs, "to expect a US military training mission to achieve success unless the nation concerned is able effectively to perform those governmental functions essential to the successful raising and maintenance of armed forces." Second, each state should formally request US financial support and training assistance. Third, the French should grant full independence to the Associated States and provide for a phased withdrawal of French troops, officers, and advisers. Without this provision, reasoned the Joint Chiefs of Staff, there would be lack of motivation and an unsound basis for the establishment of indigenous armed forces. As a corollary of this stipulation, the United States from the beginning should deal directly with the native governments, "completely independent of French participation or control." Finally, the size and composition of the forces should be based on "local military requirements and the overall US interests." Only when these conditions were fulfilled, they believed, should the United States commit itself to training and financing the native forces.[7]

Secretary of State Dulles pointed out in reply that Cambodia already had met the four conditions. Cambodia had formally requested US assistance, it qualified as politically stable, and it enjoyed complete sovereignty. The command of the Royal Khmer Army had been handed over to the King, and with the exception of a few French advisers attached to Cambodian military forces, French troops had been removed from Cambodian soil. Although Vietnam could not meet the JCS specifications, Secretary Dulles believed that the United States should nevertheless undertake a training program. Strengthening the army, he reasoned, was in fact a prerequisite to political stability. Conceding that the problem was the "familiar hen-and-egg argument," he nonetheless asserted that "one of the most efficient means of enabling the Vietnamese Government to become strong is to assist it in reorganizing the National Army and in training that Army." The FEC had not been withdrawn from Vietnam, but "it would be militarily disastrous to demand the withdrawal of French forces... before the creation of a new National Army." Secretary

Dulles saw no reason why the United States could not train the Vietnamese forces at the same time the French were gradually phasing out their troops.[8]

Meanwhile, however, the National Security Council had decided that political factors outweighed the military considerations on which the Joint Chiefs of Staff had based their opinion. NSC 5429/1, adopted by the Council on 12 August and approved by the President on the same day, stated that, "working through the French only insofar as necessary," the United States would assist in the buildup of indigenous "military forces necessary for internal security." Events were to prove this policy much more easily conceived than executed.[9]

With provision for assumption of training responsibilities by the United States incorporated into Far Eastern policy, Secretary Dulles notified the French in August that the United States intended to assign a training mission to MAAG Saigon. But the Joint Chiefs of Staff still believed that their four conditions should be fulfilled before the United States launched a training program. Reviewing the problem on 22 September they concluded that these conditions had not yet been met. They accordingly recommended that no commitment to train the VNA be made during forthcoming talks with French officials.[10]

The State Department, on the other hand, reasoned that the French, if presented with the JCS conditions, certainly would not agree to exchange French for US influence in Vietnamese military affairs. The United States then would have either to discard the conditions or withdraw its support for Vietnam. The latter alternative was unacceptable because of the extensive investment of US money and prestige in Indochina, and the obligations recently assumed under the Manila Pact. The position of the United States, therefore, was to make no commitments on training the VNA but to concentrate on more immediate problems.[11]

The training issue, in the following weeks, became enmeshed in a dispute between the State Department and Joint Chiefs of Staff over Vietnamese forces levels. The Joint Chiefs of Staff proposed a VNA of 184,000 and a militia of 50,000, with a small air force and navy. Since the forces could be equipped with Mutual Defense Assistance Program (MDAP) material already on hand, there would be no initial expenditure, the annual operating cost would total $475 million.[12]

Secretary of State Dulles objected to this plan. He asserted that NSC 5429/2 envisaged maintenance in Indochina only of those forces necessary for internal security. In the event of a threat to security from external sources, the Manila Pact would become operative. With these facts in mind, concluded the Secretary, the JCS manpower and cost estimates appeared excessive.[13]

The JCS, in turn, replied that US policy, as set forth in NSC 162/2, the Basic National Security Policy, relied on ground defense in the Far East by indigenous troops. If every nation developed only those forces required for internal security, no forces would be available to go to the defense of another country. The mission of the VNA, therefore, should be not only to police Vietnam but also "to deter Viet Minh aggression by a limited defense of the Geneva armistice demarcation line." On this note, the question of size and composition of Vietnamese forces was deferred for a month. But Secretary Dulles' persistence had at the same time brought the Joint Chiefs of Staff to reconsider their opposition to a training program in Vietnam. Although they still believed that, from a military viewpoint, the United States should not participate in the training of Vietnamese forces, they conceded that, from a political viewpoint, the risk might be justified. If so, the Joint Chiefs of Staff concluded, they "would agree to the assignment of a training mission to MAAG Saigon with safeguards against French interference with the US training effort."[14]

This decision by the Joint Chiefs of Staff came at the time when the Operations Coordinating Board was considering what political, economic, and military measures could be taken to resolve the crisis in Vietnam.[15] The State Department drafted a message outlining a crash program to be carried out by all US agencies in Vietnam. Although the OCB envisaged, as one of several measures, a limited and interim training program, Admiral Arthur W. Radford, Chairman of the Joint Chiefs of Staff, believed the message, as drafted, would set in motion the long-range program that General O'Daniel had proposed. The Joint Staff therefore drew up another message to substitute for the State Department's draft, but before this version could be considered by the JCS, the National Security Council, on 22 October, approved both the OCB plan and a draft joint State-Defense message to Saigon. This cable was dispatched the same day and authorized Ambassador Heath and General O'Daniel to "collaborate in setting in motion a crash program designed to bring about an improvement in the loyalty and the effectiveness of the Free Vietnamese forces." The "how" was left to the Ambassador and the Chief, MAAG.[16]

In the absence of final decision on a long-range program, Ambassador Heath and General O'Daniel, with General Ely's concurrence, decided to extend US military influence by placing a MAAG officer in the Defense Ministry, three in VNA headquarters, and one at each regional headquarters. But an effective training program had to await on detailed planning in Washington, formal agreement with France, and reorganization of MAAG Saigon.[17]

Upon General Collins' arrival in Vietnam, and even before he and General Ely had reached final agreement on the seven-fold approach, the two generals took up the problem of the VNA. It was the opinion of General Collins that the army represented the key to success in Vietnam, but in almost every respect the VNA was unprepared to cope with the responsibilities and dangers posed by the political and military situation in Vietnam.

In November 1954, the VNA, consisting of 170,000 regulars, was badly organized and trained and possessed no units above the regimental level. Still primarily an instrument of the French High Command, it remained under French operational control and was entirely dependent upon the French for logistical support. Twenty percent of the infantry and fifty percent of the support and technical units were at least partially staffed by French cadres. The French had failed to develop qualified leaders in the VNA, and native officers, even when given authority and responsibility, were inclined to rely heavily on French advisers. Moreover, the Hinh rebellion had disrupted the planning activities of the General Staff and had fostered insubordination and irresponsibility throughout the army.[18]

General Collins' plan of action for the VNA was designed to remedy these defects. It provided, first, for reaching agreement with France and South Vietnam on force levels, composition, and mission of indigenous forces. This done, General O'Daniel would assume responsibility for organizing and training Vietnamese forces. The Collins plan also called for French agreement to a program aimed at granting full autonomy to the Vietnamese military establishment by the summer of 1955 and a determined effort to straighten-out the tangled political loyalties of the army. After France and South Vietnam had agreed to these principles, and the reorganization and training ventures had been launched, the army would be employed to pacify and rehabilitate the country.[19]

Before any degree of success could be assured, resolution of the Hinh rebellion was essential. This feud had lasted three months, and friction between Diem and Hinh had become so acute that reconciliation was impossible. If the principle of civil supremacy over the military were to be maintained, Hinh had to be removed from Vietnam.

Shortly after General Collins arrived in Saigon, Hinh's defiance was effectively neutralized. Surprisingly, the impulse for Hinh's removal came from Bao Dai. Early in November, US diplomats in France surmised that Bao Dai, hoping to insure the security of his position as Chief of State, had decided to exhibit more respect for US policy in Vietnam. In any event, he sent an emissary to Saigon with orders for Bay Vien and the Binh Xuyen to cooperate with the government, and for General Hinh to report to him in Cannes immediately. After two weeks of indecision, during which he attempted to secure a reprieve from this summons, Hinh made a belligerent farewell speech and on 19 November departed for France. Upon his arrival, he sealed his own fate by publicly expressing defiance of Bao Dai's authority. Bao Dai summarily removed Hinh from his position of Chief of Staff of the VNA and named General Le Van Ty to succeed him. At the same time Bao Dai designated General Nguyen Van By to assume the duties of Inspector General, recently given up by the French General Marcel Alessandri.[20]

Bao Dai's action removed one of the more serious irritants from the Vietnamese political scene. The way was now cleared for reconciliation between government and army. Diem issued a public declaration affirming complete confidence in the loyalty of the army, and thereafter, the army did not pose a serious threat to Vietnamese political stability.

But before it could be considered an effective arm of the government, the important questions of the size, organization, and mission had to be settled. Therefore, General Collins moved quickly to secure endorsement by his superiors in Washington and acceptance by the French and Vietnamese of his concept of the future of Vietnamese armed forces. Such questions were not easily resolved, however, for the Departments of State and Defense remained in fundamental disagreement on the crucial issue of force levels that the United States should support. General Collins was aware of this disagreement and asked, on 11 November, that Washington take no action on indigenous force levels until he had had an opportunity to make his own recommendations on the matter. The Department of Defense agreed to this on 13 November.[21]

General Collins' recommendations, which were received on 16 November, represented a compromise between the positions of the Departments of State and Defense. Although he had been charged with assisting the Vietnamese to develop a force capable only of establishing and maintaining internal security, General Collins considered that some divisional combat elements should be included in the VNA. They were necessary not only to assist the FEC to absorb the shock of invasion if hostilities were renewed but also, if called upon, to reinforce the security troops in pacification activities. Moreover, to cut the army in half without at the same time providing forces organized for combat rather than merely for security duty was certain to have a bad effect upon the morale of both the VNA and the Vietnamese people.

Accordingly, General Collins recommended that the United States support in fiscal year 1956, a small, well-balanced, defense force totaling 83,685 military and 4,400 civilian personnel—almost 100,000 less than the Joint Chiefs of Staff had proposed in September. To establish and maintain internal security, the VNA would include thirteen security regiments and an airborne regimental combat team. It would also include three field divisions to delay any communist invasion until external assistance from the Manila powers arrived. With support troops, this army would number 77,685 officers and men, as well as 4,000 civilians. A small navy and air force would complete the Vietnamese military establishment. General Collins estimated the total support cost, to be borne by the United States, at $201.6 million for fiscal 1956.[22]

The Joint Chiefs of Staff on 17 November approved the recommendations of General Collins and, substituting his figures for those drawn up by the Joint Strategic Plans Committee (JSPC), submitted the figures, and their views on the whole problem, to the Secretary of Defense. In doing so, the Joint Chiefs of Staff warned that these forces alone could not provide adequate insurance against external aggression after French forces were withdrawn. With the Viet Minh increasing the size and effectiveness of its armies, and with no forces actually committed to mutual defense by the Manila powers, an organized military assault by the Viet Minh would encounter no more than "limited initial resistance" from the VNA. The Secretary of Defense concurred in the recommendations and views of the JCS and provided them to the Secretary of State on 26 November.[23]

These observations brought into focus another problem—the size of the French Expeditionary Corps. The French were already withdrawing elements of the Corps, planning to cut it to 100,000 by the end of 1955. At the Washington

Conference in September, they had made clear that retention even of this number depended upon the flow of dollars, estimating that $330 million would be required. The United States had promised an answer by 1 December.

United States policymakers, however, had reservations about continuing to support the FEC. A State-JCS meeting revealed that military and diplomatic leaders alike thought it better that France pull its troops out of Vietnam altogether. Overt aggression was not thought likely. The real threat was civil war, and the French had several times declared that they would not intervene in such a conflict. Since an immediate objective of US policy was to restore order in Vietnam and bolster the Diem government, the FEC hardly seemed worth its cost, but both General Collins and Ambassador Heath disagreed with this view. They believed that the United States should help maintain the Corps, although not to the extent of $330 million. Complete withdrawal of French troops in 1955, they reasoned, would create a vacuum that only the Viet Minh could fill, for the VNA would be unable to cope with communist irregular forces for some time to come. Moreover, without French cooperation any US project in Vietnam was doomed, and a US decision to cut off support funds would gravely jeopardize such cooperation.[24]

General Collins and Ambassador Heath's view prevailed. The United States informed France it would contribute $100 million to maintenance of the FEC during calendar 1955, after which no further support was contemplated. The United States also put France on notice that for 1954 it would "continue to reimburse French 1954 budget year expenditures," but proposed to "declare ineligible for reimbursement all expenditures on material, equipment and supplies which cannot or will not be delivered to Indochina by December 31, 1955."

The provision of US funds for support of the FEC and for the reimbursement of French expenditures for material, equipment, and supplies was made contingent upon consultations with (and presumably approval of) Congress and "subject [to] Ely and Collins and [the] two governments mutually agreeing on what is to be done in Indochina."[25]

The sum of $100 million was well below the $330 million the French had anticipated, and they made clear that the US decision would entail a drastic reduction of French troops serving in Indochina. Paris accordingly stepped up withdrawal of the FEC and predicted that by the end of 1955 only 40,000 French soldiers would remain in South Vietnam. The Foreign Office emphasized that although this action was based entirely on monetary considerations, there was also much sentiment in France for transferring the FEC to North Africa. This sentiment stemmed from the belief that in Vietnam French troops were serving the interests of the free world; since the free world would not pay its upkeep, the FEC should be sent to North Africa where it would better serve the interests of France and the French Union.[26]

The Paris decision to accelerate reduction of the Expeditionary Corps forced General Ely to revise his strategic plans for the defense of South Vietnam and to place more reliance on the Manila Pact as a deterrent. Also, he intimated to General Collins that, because Washington chose not to support French and Vietnamese force levels adequate for defense of the country, the United States had automatically assumed equal responsibility with France for the security of Vietnam. This proposition General Collins categorically rejected.[27]

Although the French wished to commit the United States to greater responsibility for South Vietnam, they consented only with great reluctance to any significant change in the VNA. This became clear during the protracted discussions on Vietnamese military problems. General Collins had drawn up a draft minute of understanding to be used as a basis for negotiations with General Ely. The minute outlined the US concept of size, composition, and mission of Vietnamese force and defined the basic principles on which a training program had to be founded if success were to be achieved.

First and foremost, General Collins wanted assurances that "full autonomy will have been granted by France to the armed forces of the state of Vietnam by not later than 1 July 1955." Full autonomy, to General Collins, meant "actual command of all units of Vietnam armed forces by Vietnamese personnel." In addition,

> full responsibility for assisting the Government of Vietnam in the organization and training of its armed forces will be assumed by the United States on 1 January 1955. Exercise of this responsibility will be entrusted to the Chief of the United States Military Assistance Advisory Group.

The draft minute explained how this would work in practice. General O'Daniel, acting under the broad authority of General Ely in his capacity as the French Commander in Chief in Indo-China, would direct training activities. Reliance would be initially placed on French advisory personnel but with progressive introduction of US instructors, the French officers would be gradually phased out.[28]

General Ely's reaction to the draft minute was mixed. He feared that the Manila Pact was not an effective deterrent to aggression but reluctantly accepted the mission and reduced force base proposed by General Collins. General Ely also agreed to assumption by the United States of training responsibility, going so far as to declare that the agreement on Vietnam would not be an obstacle to augmentation of MAAG beyond the 342 spaces authorized when the cease-fire took effect. At the same time, General Ely expressed his conviction that no French government could accept replacement of Frenchmen by Americans in the training apparatus. In the opinion of General Collins, the opposing US and French views on this question represented the basic difference in the thinking of the two countries on the future role of France in Vietnamese military affairs. Phase-out of French instructors was one of the conditions that the Joint Chiefs had insisted be met before the United States entered the training field. The United States, if it were to have responsibility for development of an effective army, had to be free to use US methods and doctrines. Moreover, as General Collins pointed out to General Ely, it was necessary to convince the Vietnamese that the French really intended to give up their influence in the armed forces of Vietnam.[29]

Premier Mendes-France was much less inclined than General Ely to accept the Collins blueprint. The Premier arrived in Washington during the third week of November and quickly expressed his disagreement with the draft minute. France, he said, was willing to grant autonomy to the VNA, but he doubted that it could be accomplished by 1 July 1955. Also, increasing the size of MAAG for training purposes clearly violated the Vietnam Agreement. But the portion of the Collins plan that most aroused the opposition of the Premier was the provision for phase-out of French instructors. In his view it would be difficult for the French people to accept; they would not understand why France must relinquish its influence to the United States while continuing to support a heavy burden in Indochina. In addition, the phase-out of French instructors would be a severe blow to the morale of the French Expeditionary Corps. Although objecting to elimination of French instructors, the Premier at the same time attempted strenuously to establish for the record that primary responsibility for the policy of the free world in the Far East, including Indochina, rested with the United States. Neither Premier Mendes-France nor Secretary Dulles would yield, and in the end the matter was referred to Generals Collins and Ely for compromise and agreement.[30]

Three weeks of negotiation in Saigon produced an agreed minute that both Generals Collins and Ely signed on 13 December. During the discussions preceding agreement, General Collins had flatly asserted that he could not recommend US participation in training unless General O'Daniel possessed real authority, subject to the overall responsibility of General Ely, to direct training activities. As approved by General Collins and General Ely, the agreement differed little from General Collins' draft minute of understanding, though the wording was softened to make the document less offensive to French pride. Perhaps the most significant change was introduced by the French. Instead of providing for phase-out of French instructors alone, the minute was worded to provide for phase-out of both French and US instructors as the efficiency of Vietnamese forces increased. The signed Minute of Understanding was immediately dispatched to Paris and Washington for final approval.[31]

Although the United States quickly approved the Collins-Ely agreement, France embarked upon a campaign of delay. In mid-December, a US-French review of Indochinese affairs was held in Paris. Secretary Dulles and Admiral Radford represented the United States and General Ely was also present. During the course of discussion Premier Mendes-France informed Secretary Dulles that the French Government would have to study the Minute of Understanding closely for possible conflicts with the Vietnam Agreement especially the question of strengthening the US MAAG. Both Secretary Dulles and Admiral Radford assured the Premier that the United States intended only to rotate personnel, not to assign additional strength. Nevertheless, Mendes-France replied, a legal question still remained. Even though the agreement permitted rotation, he feared that substitution of training for administrative personnel, or officers for enlisted men, was a violation. The Viet Minh, he added, had already officially protested to the International Control Commission.[32]

When apprised of these remarks, General Collins cabled the Secretary of State that, if France intended to hedge the agreement with legal restrictions of this type, the United States should not undertake a training venture. He added that Premier Mendes-France had promised to accept any agreement negotiated by General Ely. The Premier's latest action, in General Collins' opinion, raised the serious question of whether Paris intended to support the authority of its top officials in Vietnam.[33]

While the United States applied increasing pressure on France to honor General Ely's signature, the issue was debated within the French Government. At length, the French informed Washington that they had no quarrel with the substance of the Minute of Understanding, but objected to its form. The Vietnamese Government, they said, should not be confronted with a fait accompli, but rather with a series of recommendations agreed to by France and the United States. With this in mind, the French Embassy in Washington submitted a redraft of the Minute to the Department of State on 7 January 1955.[34]

This action added to General Collins' mounting impatience. It clearly indicated, he believed, that the French were stalling. He had never intended to present the Vietnamese with the Minute, and the French proposal actually would do just that. Moreover, in redrafting the Minute, the French had eliminated all reference to autonomy of Vietnamese armed forces and had omitted phrases spelling out General O'Daniel's authority over French training personnel. "I will certainly not agree to it unless specifically instructed by higher authority," General Collins concluded. When General Ely returned from the Paris meeting, General Collins told him that the French seemed to be deliberately dragging their feet. He emphasized that it was imperative that France approve the original Minute of Understanding at once because, using it as the basis for discussion, he had already begun negotiating with Vietnamese Defense Minister Ho Thong Minh. General Ely replied that there had evidently been a serious misunderstanding. The French Government had approved the original agreement, and he was perfectly willing that negotiations with Minh should continue.[35]

Although the US Embassy in Paris reported that the French Government, so far as could be ascertained, had not in fact approved the Minute, General Collins continued his talks with Minh. Here he encountered a further obstacle, for the Minister of Defense strongly objected to the proposed force levels.

Minh's arguments were telling. He contended that the army would be reduced to a size not much larger than the paramilitary forces of the Cao Dai, Hoa Hao, and Binh Xuyen. This would alter the power relationship in South Vietnam and greatly enhance the political bargaining strength of the sects. The problem would be aggravated by enlistment of discharged soldiers in the armies of the sects. Furthermore, rapid reduction of the armed forces from 217,000 to 88,000 would flood the country with unemployed veterans, thus producing severe social, economic, and psychological effects, with consequent political complications. General Collins admitted that this was a real problem but declared that the United States simply could not afford the cost of a large Vietnamese military establishment. He did offer to modify the projected reduction. Instead of aiming for a force of 88,000 by 1 July 1955, the United States would agree to a goal of 100,000 by 31 December 1955, even though it would cost an extra $14.5 million. This Minh reluctantly accepted. An exchange of letters between the Vietnamese Government and General Collins on 19 and 20 January constituted formal agreement between the United States and Vietnam for US financial support of Vietnamese armed forces and responsibility for their organization and training.[36]

Despite the success of these negotiations, the whole question of the VNA was far from resolved. The United States and France were still deadlocked over the Collins-Ely Minute of Understanding. The United States refused to accept the redraft submitted on 7 January and, according to an official of the French Foreign Office, Premier Mendes-France, for political reasons, simply could not accept responsibility for formally approving the minute General Ely had signed in December. The impasse was finally broken by US initiative. In a personal message to Mendes-France, Secretary Dulles, with the concurrence of General Collins, advanced a compromise proposal. The Secretary of State suggested that both the Minute of Understanding and the French redraft be discarded and that France dispatch two letters over General Ely's signature. The first would be sent to Diem guaranteeing complete autonomy to Vietnamese forces by 1 July 1955, the second to General Collins agreeing that both US and French training personnel would be under the immediate direction of General O'Daniel, acting under the overall authority of General Ely.[37]

With certain changes of wording, this solution proved acceptable to France. The French, however, still wished to present the 7 January redraft to the Diem government as joint Franco-American recommendations. The French desired, they said, an agreement that could be used in Parliament or made public if the need arose. The Department of State found this distinctly unpalatable, for the redraft, without the clarifying letters, was unsatisfactory to the United States. But General Collins was anxious to break the deadlock, and the United States finally agreed to use the redraft if the French promised to implement it in conjunction with the two letters contemplated by Secretary Dulles. On 11 February, General Ely carried out the compromise plan, and the next day General O'Daniel assumed responsibility for organizing and training the military forces of Vietnam.[38]

Economic Problems

Although military questions occupied much of the energies of Generals Collins and Ely, they had by no means neglected the other features of the seven-point program. Two closely related items of the program were the utilization of uncultivated land and the absorption of the refugees, most of whom still were housed in temporary rehabilitation camps.

American and French agencies in Vietnam undertook exhaustive studies involving far-reaching changes in the pattern of land tenure and use. The immediate requirement, however, was a short-range, emergency program to meet the more critical aspects of the two problems. Generals Collins and Ely encouraged Diem to adopt an emergency plan of governmental requisition of idle farm land for three years in order to resettle refugees from Tonkin, as well as displaced southerners and discharged soldiers. Diem was also advised to create a special agency within the Ministry of Agriculture, both to administer the short-range program and to plan the long-range program.[39]

Although Diem accepted these recommendations, US economic experts found it an entirely different matter to develop agreed procedures with subordinate Vietnamese officials. The Minister of Agriculture was a member of the Hoa Hao sect, which controlled large amounts of Vietnam's rice-producing lands, and the Hoa Hao feared the effect land reform would have on its vested interests. As a result, the Americans made little progress with officials of the Ministry of Agriculture.[40]

Nevertheless, on 10 February Diem signed decrees putting into effect the emergency program proposed by the French and United States officials. Two weeks earlier, on the Vietnamese New Year, he had announced adoption of a long-range agrarian reform program.[41] It remained to be seen how realistically these measures would be executed when the Hoa Hao found its prerogatives being undermined.

In the financial field, the primary objective of the seven-point program was to gear the Vietnamese monetary structure to direct US aid, scheduled to be in effect in early January. To accomplish this change, it was necessary to institute within the Vietnamese Government fiscal and budgetary procedures designed to qualify South Vietnam for receipt of US aid. The Vietnamese had no objection, but the principle of direct aid was still abhorrent to the French. They saw plainly the inevitable consequence for French commerce. The United States planned to provide the Vietnamese with over $325 million in economic and military aid funds during 1955. Because these dollars would no longer be converted into francs before reaching the Vietnamese, a gradual shift of the trade pattern into the dollar area would develop. The French press was already loudly denouncing the United States for trying to squeeze out French commercial interests.[42]

Moreover, France had not yet entirely reconciled itself to exclusion from US aid councils. At the Washington Conference in September, Under Secretary of State Walter Bedell Smith had agreed to the establishment of "appropriate machinery" to control aid disbursements in Vietnam. The French had chosen, not without reason, to interpret this as acquiescence in their concept of joint or tripartite committees. On 29 October, however, Secretary Dulles had outlined to Premier Mendes-France the US concept of "appropriate machinery," and the definition ruled out all but informal exchanges of information to prevent duplication of effort.[43]

Premier Mendes-France attempted, without success, to secure a modification of the US position, and in Saigon General Ely formally proposed to General Collins that Franco-American committees be established to examine specific programs submitted by the French and US aid missions. But the United States continued to hold to the line drawn by Secretary Dulles. After some complaint about the United States backing down on commitments made by Under Secretary Smith, the French dropped the subject.[44]

By February 1955, some progress had been made toward all the economic objectives of the seven-point program. The same was not true, however, of the most important political objective—shoring up the tottering Diem government by decentralizing administration and introducing capable and honest men into the operating ministries.

Strengthening and Broadening the Diem Government

Premier Diem had been repeatedly charged with running a one-man government and relying too heavily on the generally poor advice of his brothers. In addition, he retained personal control of the two most important ministries, Defense and Interior. It seemed particularly important to French and US officials that at least these two ministries should be filled by able men who could in some measure offset the Premier's deficiencies. But the Cao Dai and Hoa Hao sects, whose representatives held over half the cabinet posts in the government, opposed the installation of any strong personality who might prove a threat to their influence on national policy or their established position in the economic, social, and political life of the country. Although Diem was apparently sincere in his desire to broaden the government, he believed, perhaps with some justification, that he could not afford to antagonize the sects until the army was able to neutralize their military forces.

General Collins centered his efforts on an attempt to have Dr. Phan Huy Quat, an able man with an independent mind, taken into the Diem government. Dr. Quat, however, had two serious liabilities: as a member of the Dai Viet Party from Tonkin, he, like Diem, lacked organized political support in the south; and worse, as Defense Minister in the government of Tran Van Huu in early 1950, Quat had endeavored to abolish the private armies of the sects and aroused their lasting hostility. General Collins believed that, in spite of these drawbacks, Quat would be an important addition to the government, and he urged Diem to appoint Quat to the Defense Ministry, retaining the energetic and capable Ho Thong Minh as Deputy Defense Minister. Diem readily consented and offered the post to Quat.[45]

Strong opposition to Quat quickly developed within the Diem government. The Premier's brothers, Ngo Dinh Luyen and Ngo Dinh Nhu, brought their considerable influence to bear to prevent the appointment. Both men, General Collins believed, were determined to keep the armed forces out of the hands of a strong personality who might prove a serious contender for the premiership. The sect representatives in the Cabinet also expressed their antipathy for Quat. Particularly vociferous were Hoa Hao General Tran Van Soai and Cao Dai General Nguyen Thanh Phuong, the latter strongly supported by the Cao Dai Pope, Pham Cong Tac. Both Soai and Phuong declared they would resign rather than sit in the same cabinet with Quat. Diem feared that if Quat were appointed the Hoa Hao would cut off Saigon's rice supply and the Cao Dai would precipitate an armed rebellion in the city. In addition, Acting Defense Minister Minh, whom Premier Diem as well as Generals Collins and O'Daniel wished to keep in the government, viewed the proposed appointment as a threat to his own ambitions. Minh declared that he would neither serve under Quat nor in any other department except Defense. He was certain that, as Acting Defense Minister, he had the army well in hand and was making progress in healing the wounds left by the Hinh episode.[46]

The pressures from these sources were stronger than Diem could resist, and he withdrew his offer to Quat. Early in January, Diem elevated Minh to the rank of Defense Minister, delegating him full authority, and this solution proved satisfactory.[47] In succeeding weeks, not only did Minh perform ably but Diem refrained from meddling in the affairs of the Ministry.

General Collins had less success in persuading Diem to surrender the Interior Ministry, for no candidate could be found with the necessary qualities of honesty, patriotism, and technical competence. General Ely proposed the old French favorites, Tam and Vien, but Diem pointed out that Tam was the complete antithesis of everything the Diem government stood for. Diem believed that Vien would also be an unfortunate choice since, apart from his unsavory personal reputation, his appointment would be politically dangerous. The Binh Xuyen already controlled the Saigon police, and to extend its police powers to the entire country by giving Vien the Interior Ministry would immeasurably enhance the Binh Xuyen's ability to challenge the supremacy of the government.[48]

Moreover, Diem himself did not wish to relinquish control of the Interior Ministry. Diem believed that he alone had adequate knowledge of both central and southern Vietnam and was convinced that he should have at least one major operating department under his personal control.[49] Therefore, the Ministry of the Interior remained under Diem's personal direction.

General Collins considered the unsuccessful outcome of this effort a major setback. But this failure was offset somewhat, by an encouraging advance in the plan to reinforce the executive arm of the government with a legislative arm. By February, prospects were bright for incorporating a national assembly, albeit a primitive one by US standards, into the Vietnamese governmental structure.

A Provisional National Assembly

General Collins was convinced that a provisional national assembly of some sort ought to be constituted as quickly as possible. An assembly was necessary not only to give the Diem government a measure of democratic backing but to provide a training ground for future political leaders. Accordingly, this item had been given a prominent place on the seven-point agenda drawn up by Generals Collins and Ely. But finding the exact formula to govern the composition and functions of the assembly was not an easy task. It was contemplated that the interim body would serve until security conditions permitted genuine national elections for a constituent assembly. It was important that the provisional assembly be as representative as possible without opening a Pandora's box of irresponsible discussion by politically inexperienced deputies. The assembly also had to have enough power to justify its existence but not enough to cause complications for the struggling government of Premier Diem.

While the staffs of Generals Collins and Ely were drawing up plans for such an assembly, the Vietnamese themselves had not been idle. The Minister of Reform on 25 November had presented the Cabinet with a draft decree outlining a proposed assembly. In succeeding weeks, this draft underwent four revisions as attempts were made to resolve the differences between the Vietnamese concept and that of the US and French staffs.

The first conflict of opinion arose over the representative character of the assembly. Both Generals Collins and Ely believed that, if the assembly were to provide an element of democracy for the Diem government and a forum for the development of political talent, its elective character was more important than extensive powers. But the original Vietnamese concept had provided only that deputies from the north, south, and center of South Vietnam be nominated by Diem and approved by Bao Dai. This provision was subsequently changed to provide that 91 assemblymen be chosen by Diem after consultation with the municipal and provincial councilors, and 130 after consultation with the sects and other special interest groups. The Vietnamese plan still did not give the assembly a very solid popular foundation, but in the end Diem conceded more than had been expected. He agreed to an assembly chosen by municipal and village councilors, who had been elected to their offices in 1953. General Collins believed this plan to be as democratic as conditions in South Vietnam permitted at the time.[50]

A second area of disagreement concerned the nature of powers and prerogatives of the assembly. In General Collins' opinion, the powers of the assembly had to be strictly limited and carefully defined. The Vietnamese, he reasoned, were still politically immature and had no democratic traditions. To give the assembly important powers, or vaguely defined powers, would invite even greater political chaos than already existed.[51]

Diem wished to delegate to the assembly greater constituent power than General Collins thought prudent. The Premier intended the assembly to draft, within three months, a provisional charter delineating the establishment of governmental institutions until such time as an elected constituent assembly drew up a permanent constitution. General Collins argued that this would involve defining the position of Bao Dai in the governmental hierarchy, and with a conflict between Diem and the sects apparently in the offing, this was decidedly not the time to antagonize the Chief of State. Although Diem seemed inclined to challenge Bao Dai regardless of consequences, he finally accepted the advice of General Collins. As a result, restrictions denying the assembly all constituent powers were carefully written into the decree.[52]

In contrast to the position he had taken on constituent powers, Diem insisted on narrowly limiting the powers and functions of the assembly. The US officials concerned believed that such circumscription would unavoidably lead to the charge that the assembly was a meaningless institution without influence. The focal point of this issue was the assembly's right of interpellation. The original draft decree had provided for interpellation in all matters of foreign and domestic policy. This was modified in the second draft to prohibit debate or vote following the government's reply to interpellation. Finally, the right to ask questions was substituted for the right of interpellation.[53] Clearly, Diem did not want to create an assembly that might turn on him. Despite General Collins' arguments, Diem would not give in. Although the final revision of the decree did provide for interpellation, it still forbade discussion or vote on the answer of the government. In addition to this limited privilege, the decree permitted the assembly to discuss matters referred to it by the Premier and approve and supervise execution of the budget.[54]

Although the fifth draft still contained many defects, both Generals Collins and Ely felt it the best they were likely to get, and the Cabinet approved this version early in February. The delicate question then arose over who was to sign the decree, Diem or Bao Dai. This was satisfactorily resolved when Bao Dai obligingly authorized Diem, "by delegation of powers," to sign it. The Diem government made the decree public on 16 February, and the Minister of Reform optimistically announced that the assembly might be convened within six weeks. General Collins believed that, all in all, a substantial step forward had been taken.[55] Fortunately for Diem, the step came at a time when the United States was wavering in its resistance to French efforts to abandon him. Along with other evidence of South Vietnam's progress, Diem's approval of plans for a national assembly led the United States to reaffirm its support of the Premier.

The Question of Diem's Replacement

The replacement of Diem was an issue that had clouded US-French relations for some time. The French had acquiesced in retention of Diem as Premier only because of US insistence, but Diem's Francophobia, his galling personality, and his inability to stabilize the situation in South Vietnam were sources of constant irritation to France. Nevertheless, at Washington in mid-November, Premier Mendes-France reaffirmed the Smith-La Chambre agreement of 29 September 1954, in which the United States and France had pledged themselves to support the Diem government. In doing so, however, Mendes-France said that, before long, replacement of Diem would have to be seriously studied. If he failed to put an energetic program into execution within one or two months, the United States and France would have to consider jettisoning him.[56] This was the signal for heavy French pressure aimed at weakening US support for Diem. In a US-French review of policy toward Indochina a month later, and through the Foreign Office in Paris and the Embassy in Washington, the French made clear their conviction that the time had come for a change.

Finding the United States would not accept the elevation of Prince Buu Hoi to Diem's place, the French brought up other proposals. One alternative they favored was to have Bao Dai designate a "Viceroy" with full authority to use the powers of the Chief of State for the purpose of unifying the disparate political forces. The French suggested that Tran Van Huu, Nguyan Van Tam, or perhaps Dr. Quat could perform this mission.[57] A second formula contemplated the immediate return to South Vietnam of Bao Dai himself. The Chief of State would form a government with Huu as Premier, Tam as Interior Minister, and Quat as Defense Minister. France had already received assurances that Huu would accept such an appointment and that Tam would consent to join his government.[58] Huu meanwhile was in Saigon busily plotting to bring about such an eventuality. He was reported to have summoned representatives of various political groups to inquire what posts they would require in the "Huu Government," and was even alleged to have offered twenty million piasters to Hoa Hao dissident General Lam Than Nguyen for his support.[59]

The French were not alone in their adverse judgment of Diem. Ambassador Heath had found his political and administrative capabilities distinctly limited. From the first, General Collins had been skeptical about Diem's capacity to lead Vietnam through its crisis, and on 13 December, he suggested that the Department of State consider three alternative plans that might be put into operation should Diem fail to show improvement. None offered much promise. First, Bao Dai could be urged to name Quat as Premier. This admittedly was a long shot, for Quat's liabilities were many. But with full support of Bao Dai, General Collins believed, Quat might have a chance. Second, Bao Dai himself could return under a "state of emergency." This would have to be accompanied by convincing and dramatic evidence that Bao Dai had reformed, and he would have to establish a government of capable, honest and patriotic men. Finally, if neither of these solutions were thought advisable, the United States might withdraw from Vietnam altogether. Although the third possibility was not at all desirable, General Collins concluded, "in all honesty and in view of what I have observed to date it is possible this may be [the] only solution."[60]

By 17 December, General Collins had become convinced that Diem lacked the leadership to unify the country and translate his fine words into concrete deeds. This conviction was strengthened by the Premier's failure to appoint Quat to the Defense Ministry. General Collins, therefore, recommended that the United States, while continuing to support Diem a short while longer, urgently consider the return of Bao Dai. He suggested that, if this was unacceptable to US policymakers, the United States should re-evaluate its programs in South Vietnam. In addition, he proposed that, if the situation continued without substantial improvement, the United States withhold support to the VNA and increase its support of the FEC while evacuating its MDAP materiel.[61]

The Department of State, however, was reluctant to countenance General Collins' proposals. Ambassador Heath, who was in Washington, told Assistant Secretary of State Walter Robertson that "General Collins' recommendations ignore the basic factor that we would assist a Communist takeover by a withholding of our aid, even if it must necessarily be given to a government which is less than perfect." Ambassador Heath also pointed out to Assistant Secretary Robertson that the Secretary of State had analyzed the situation in South Vietnam as "a time buying operation" in which the United States must attempt to stave off the communist takeover while it strengthened Cambodia, Laos, and Thailand.[62]

Moreover, consultations with Senator Mike Mansfield had revealed that Congressional opinion would not accept such action. In a recent conversation with Assistant Secretary Robertson, Senator Mansfield had concluded that although the prospects for helping Diem strengthen South Vietnam were 'dim' at best, the United States should, nevertheless, "continue to exert its efforts and use its resources"—even at great cost—to hold Vietnam since any other course would have a disastrous effect on Cambodia, Laos, and the rest of Southeast Asia. He believed that the United States should continue to support Diem (regardless of his weaknesses as an administrator and his inability to delegate responsibility), should put pressure on Bao Dai to stop his long distance "wire pulling," and should prevent the Chief of State's return to Vietnam if possible.[63]

On 19 December, Secretary Dulles discussed the problem with Premier Mendes-France and General Ely in Paris. Although admitting that Diem had been a disappointment, Dulles declared that the United States and France had to exhaust all pressure on him before considering alternatives. Nonetheless, the Secretary of State agreed that Generals Collins and Ely should study alternative plans and also the time of Diem's replacement.[64] The French chose to interpret Secretary Dulles' position as a US commitment to consider a change, with which Bao Dai would be associated, by 15 January 1955. The United States stoutly denied having committed itself to a deadline or to any formula definitely involving Bao Dai. The French stoutly insisted that this was the tenor of the conversations and that Collins and Ely had a mandate to study alternatives and report to their respective governments.[65]

Upon his return to Washington, Secretary Dulles reviewed for General Collins in Saigon and Ambassador Dillon in Paris what he considered to be the basic factors of the Vietnam problem and spelled out the guidelines for future US action. "Although there are many complex and difficult factors confronting Free Viet-Nam," Dulles stated, "there is no reason to admit defeat. During the past five months since Geneva, the situation has not disintegrated. The people are fundamentally anti-Communist.... In some ways developments may be better than we predicted." With respect to the future, Secretary Dulles stated that the United States must create such a situation that the Viet Minh could take over only by internal violence, adding that investment in Vietnam was justified even if only to buy time. Bao Dai's return would not solve the problem, Secretary Dulles told General Collins and, consequently, the United States had no choice but to continue its aid to Vietnam and support Diem. He also stated that revitalization of the VNA would give hope for an improved security condition and that the United States should exploit the land reform issue.[66]

Even as the discussion of these differences continued, the United States was in the midst of a reappraisal of its position in South Vietnam. General Collins' fear that the United States might soon be faced with the choice of supporting Bao Dai's return or withdrawing from South Vietnam altogether had prompted another US Government review of its Indochina policy.

Review of US Policy

Study of US policy toward Vietnam began in the Department of Defense early in January 1955. Secretary of Defense Charles E. Wilson, surveying the latest developments in Vietnam, on 5 January advised the Joint Chiefs of Staff that a delicate and unstable situation existed in South Vietnam, and that the Department of Defense should be prepared for any eventuality. Accordingly, he asked the Joint Chiefs to submit their views on courses of action open to the United States.[67]

The JCS considered this question on 21 January but declared that they were not in a position to recommend the course of action the United States ought to pursue in South Vietnam. Although national policy prescribed making every effort to save South Vietnam, the degree to which the United States was prepared to support that policy in men, money, materials, and additional war risks had not become apparent to the Joint Chiefs. They stated that before they could recommend courses of action in Vietnam, a firm decision on these matters at the national level was mandatory.

The JCS saw four possible courses of action open to the United States. First, the United States, with the cooperation of France and Vietnam, could continue aid as currently being developed. Second, the United States could institute, through an advisory system, a unilateral program of direct guidance to the Vietnamese Government, making assistance dependent upon Vietnamese adherence to US direction. If neither of these courses of action proved adequate to insure the viability of South Vietnam, self-sustaining US forces might be deployed to Indochina, either unilaterally or as part of a Manila Pact force. Finally, the United States could withdraw all support from South Vietnam and concentrate on saving the remainder of Southeast Asia.

Although the Joint Chiefs of Staff declined to recommend a favored course, they made clear the implications for the United States if the rest of Vietnam fell to the communists. Laos and Cambodia would probably be lost through subversion soon afterward. A friendly government could perhaps be maintained in Thailand but only through a greatly expanded US aid program. Clearly the fall of South Vietnam would heighten the chance that US armed forces would be required to support US policy in Southeast Asia.[68]

A week after the JCS discussion of South Vietnam, General Collins, who was on a visit to Washington, gave the National Security Council essentially the same appraisal in even more positive terms. The General no longer thought that the United States should consider complete withdrawal from Vietnam. "In view of the importance of Vietnam to all of Southeast Asia," he advised the Council:

> I am convinced that the United States should expend the funds, materiel, and effort required to strengthen the country and help it retain its independence. I cannot guarantee that Vietnam will remain free, even with our aid. But I know that without our aid Vietnam will surely be lost to Communism. If the chances of success are difficult to calculate the results of a withdrawal would hasten the rate of Communist advances in the Far East as a whole and could result in the loss of Southeast Asia to Communism. In my opinion the chance of success is not only worth the gamble; we cannot afford to let free Vietnam go by default.[69]

General Collins was no longer as convinced in January as he had been in December that Diem should be superseded. The Premier had demonstrated in recent weeks that he was capable of making some progress. Through Defense Minister Minh, Diem had done much to patch up his feud with the army, and the way was almost clear for inauguration of a US training program for the VNA. Diem had begun an energetic campaign against graft and corruption in political circles, and his closing of the Binh Xuyen's palatial gambling establishment, the Grand Monde, had been received with approbation at home and abroad. He had made encouraging advances on land reform programs, and the plans for a national assembly were approaching completion. Even more spectacular had been Diem's visits to the provinces, where, surprisingly, he had been enthusiastically received as the champion of Vietnamese independence.[70]

These successes, though modest, still offered hope that Diem might be able to unify South Vietnam. Despite lingering doubts concerning Diem's ability to build popular confidence in his government, General Collins advised the National Security Council that, everything considered, "Diem's integrity, strong nationalism, tenacity, and spiritual qualities render him the best available Prime Minister to lead Vietnam in its struggle against Communism."[71]

As a result of General Collins' recommendations, the National Security Council endorsed a strong US policy in Vietnam. The United States would continue to support the Diem government and continue to press France to carry out the commitments made by La Chambre during the Washington Conference. The council approved in principle the programs of military and economic aid drawn up to implement the recommendations of General Collins. Finally, the council decided that, at the forthcoming Bangkok Conference, scheduled by the SEATO members for the last week of February to work out a formal treaty organization, the United States would seek reaffirmation by the Manila powers of their determination to react under the treaty if hostilities were resumed in Indochina. Patently, the United States intended to remain in South Vietnam.[72]

As General Collins flew back to Indochina, the US Chargé d'Affairs in Saigon, Randolph Kidder, reported a noticeable relaxation of tension on the Vietnamese political scene. There was a "quickening of almost reluctant optimism," he said, which had been commented upon by numerous foreign observers. Diem's recent successes, together with the efforts of General Collins and the constancy of US support, thought Mr. Kidder, was responsible for the atmosphere of greater hope.[73]

Despite the optimism in Saigon, there was still much reason for concern. Diem, encouraged by his newly discovered popularity in the provinces, had developed an exaggerated self confidence and seemed anxious to take on all opponents at once. The drive to wipe out corruption was uniting the Premier's foes and inspiring in them even greater determination to eliminate him from the scene. All at the same time, Diem had investigations under way against former Presidents Tam, Xuan, Huu, and Buu Loc, as well as a number of less prominent public figures. As Mr. Kidder remarked, "hornets' nests seem to have an irresistible fascination for Diem." The war against corruption even had its effect on Bao Dai. Cannes became the headquarters of disgruntled Vietnamese politicians urging the Chief of State to dismiss Diem. Buu Loc, Buu Hoi, General Hinh, and Phan Van Giao, who had left Saigon a jump ahead of Diem's agents, were all in Cannes engaged in this activity. Bao Dai was reported to be resisting these blandishments, but his earlier sources of income were steadily diminishing. Diem's closure of the Grand Monde, from whose profits Bao Dai had reaped sizable returns was an especially unpleasant blow to the Chief of State. Although for the time being he was faithfully adhering to the lines of US policy, Bao Dai's future cooperation was by no means assured.[74]

Of still more significance for the future was the growing hostility between the government and the Cao Dai, Hoa Hao, and Binh Xuyen. French subsidies to the sects had progressively diminished and were cut off entirely early in February. The National Army was unable to absorb all the sect troops and still remain within the force levels prescribed by the United States. All in all, the course of events seemed to be steadily closing in on the three sects, and their leaders were growing more and more restless. In the seemingly inevitable conflict with the sects, however, Diem could take confidence from the fact that, once again, the United States appeared to be solidly behind his government.

4

The Crisis of April and May 1955

By April 1955 the internal conflicts of South Vietnam had become so serious that they had to be resolved before the more important task of establishing a solidly anticommunist state could be continued. The most dangerous of these conflicts had developed between Prime Minister Diem and the sects.

The Sect Problem

As early as January 1955, it had become evident to US diplomats in Saigon that, sooner or later, either the sects or Premier Diem would have to give way. The three sects were strong and well organized. They were determined to retain at all costs their privileged position in Vietnamese life, and so powerful was their grip on the country that they had a good chance of succeeding. From key posts in the government, Cao Dai and Hoa Hao ministers could sabotage the reform programs drawn up by the French and Americans. The private armies of the sects, built up by the French during the war to fight the Viet Minh, were equipped with artillery, mortars, and machine guns. In those provinces administered by the Cao Dai and Hoa Hao, their control of the population was absolute. In Saigon, law enforcement was exclusively the function of the Binh Xuyen.

Diem could not tolerate these conditions indefinitely without sacrificing the principles by which he had attracted international support and with which he hoped to win the allegiance of the Vietnamese people. Although the sects argued that they were the strongest and most devotedly anticommunist groups in South Vietnam, their answer to communism was particularism. As a permanent solution, this was unacceptable not only to Diem but also to the United States. In the final analysis, there was no place for the sects, with their undisguised ambition for power and wealth, in the political, economic, and social order that had to be created if South Vietnam were to win the ideological battle with communism, obtain foreign recognition, and retain US backing.

These were the factors underlying the growing tension between Diem and the sects. But the event that shook the sects from their complacency, and began the chain of circumstances culminating in the April revolt, was the French decision to stop paying subsidies for maintenance of their troops. Because the power of the sects rested on their private armies, this was a severe blow. With their primary source of income drying up, the sects were forced to turn to the Vietnamese Government for the necessary money.

Diem appreciated that the unpaid armies of the sects could be a genuine problem for the nation. He feared that at best the sects would increase their exactions from the population; at worst turn to large-scale banditry at a time when the forces of law and order were unprepared to cope with it. Therefore, the Premier began paying the sects part of the income they had formerly received from the French.[1] This measure was obviously not a long-term solution, however, and the sects were of course fully alert to the danger of their position. They resolved, according to the analysis of General Collins, upon three basic objectives designed to safeguard their interests.

The most important of these objectives was to preserve their private military forces by integrating intact as many sect units as possible into the National Army. The size of the VNA, however, was governed by the level of US aid, and the United States had consented to support no more than about 80,000 men. By January 1955, only about 6,000 of the 30,000 to 40,000 Cao Dai and Hoa Hao troopers had been integrated, and it was clear that few more could be absorbed. In fact, there was every indication that, in executing the program for reducing the army, some of those already integrated would have to be discharged.

The second objective of the sects was to obtain governmental assistance to ease the transition to civil life of the sect troops who had to be demobilized. Generals Collins and Ely believed it desirable to provide severance pay for these troops and resettle them on confiscated lands. General Collins thought that if the French could furnish funds for severance pay, US aid might be used to finance a resettlement project. The two Generals agreed to establish a special working group within the Training Relations Instruction Mission (TRIM), which was composed of US and French personnel charged with training the South Vietnamese armed forces.[2] This group was to study the problem and draw up a plan that would be recommended to Diem.

The final objective actually constituted the crux of the sects' problem. The sects wanted recognition of their areas of influence together with assurances that, once their military strength was reduced, the government would not encroach on these areas. But this Diem had no intention of doing. On the contrary, his actions demonstrated that his plans for the future of Vietnam did not include an influential role for the sects. In fact, the Premier had already initiated a policy and program of applying gradually increasing pressure to the sects.[3]

Diem's anti-sect program alarmed the Hoa Hao in particular. The VNA moved into areas of central and southwestern Vietnam that the Hoa Hao considered its exclusive preserve, and, according to the Hoa Hao, deliberately provoked Hoa Hao troops. The Hoa Hao leader, Ba Cut, responded by initiating open warfare against the government, and in turn, the National Army mounted an all-out counteroffensive. Ba Cut had the sympathy and active support of old General Tran Van Soai, military chief of the Hoa Hao, who was also acting as a minister in the Diem government. Soai felt his power and authority slipping as a result of Diem's policies, especially after the Prime Minister won over two Hoa Hao dissidents, Colonels Ngo and Hue, together with their troops.[4]

The Hoa Hao were especially incensed by Diem's tactic of playing off the Cao Dai against the Hoa Hao. Principally, this took the form of concessions to the Cao Dai in the integration of its troops into the VNA—an act designed to win Cao Dai adherence in the contest with the Hoa Hao. From the viewpoint of the Hoa Hao, the crowning blow came when its arch enemy, Cao Dai dissident Trinh Minh The, rallied to the government on the condition, allegedly, that his troops be employed in a campaign against Ba Cut.[5]

Although the Hoa Hao was on the verge of open warfare with the government and, in the case of Ba Cut, had already begun the war, it was the Binh Xuyen that constituted the most serious menace. Binh Xuyen commandos were concentrated in the capital city, where they posed an immediate threat to the Diem government. Moreover, Bay Vien, the leader of the Binh Xuyen, was a formidable adversary. He was the most ruthless, determined, and intelligent of all the sect chieftains. He believed that the United States was too interested in South Vietnam to withdraw its support even if Diem were overthrown, and he was determined to obtain, by one means or another, a new government that did not include Diem.[6]

Diem, for his part, had only contempt for Vien and his followers. The Premier had not yet applied as great pressure to the Binh Xuyen as to the Hoa Hao, but he had considerably reduced its commercial monopolies. Binh Xuyen control of the National Police and Surete especially rankled Diem, and he planned to regain the police for the government at the first opportunity. The United States, which could not reconcile itself to the idea of a band of former gangsters and pirates running the police apparatus, attempted to help Diem on this issue. The US Embassy in Paris suggested to Bao Dai that he revoke the decrees bestowing police powers on the Binh Xuyen. But Bao Dai replied that this move would not be likely to improve the political situation, and indeed would probably lead to further deterioration. Besides, he doubted that Diem had men capable of taking over responsibility for law enforcement.[7]

Through January and February, the police issue loomed larger and larger in Diem's mind. It was only a question of time until he felt strong enough to challenge the Binh Xuyen, and it was improbable, in view of Bay Vien's attitude that the Binh Xuyen would refuse the challenge when offered.

Even the Cao Dai, which Diem had chosen not to antagonize too openly, had grievances. The Cao Dai Pope, Pham Cong Tac, was bitterly hostile toward Diem and made no effort to conceal his animosity. Tac, however, was losing influence with the military arm of the Cao Dai, and he was unable to force Generals Phuong and The, the principal temporal leaders, to turn on Diem. Phuong and The, probably for reasons of financial gain, kept the Cao Dai more or less behind the Diem government. But they too were having difficulties in maintaining their troops, and they trusted Diem's intentions little more than did the Hoa Hao and Binh Xuyen.[8]

All three sects felt confronted by a common threat to their existence. They had tried uniting against Diem in August 1954 but had failed to find ground for agreement. Once again, in the spring of 1955, they attempted to form an alliance aimed at supplanting the Diem government with one less hostile to their objectives.

The "United Front of Nationalist Forces"

On 4 March the Cao Dai Pope called a press conference in Saigon. Acting as spokesman for the leaders of the Cao Dai, Hoa Hao, and Binh Xuyen, whose representatives were present, Tac announced the formation of the "United Front of Nationalist Forces." The Binh Xuyen political adviser read a declaration stating that the objectives of the new political group were to unify Vietnam, perfect its independence as a democracy, and assure its sovereignty. The declaration was obviously designed largely for US consumption, for it denounced feudalism and corruption, endorsed the Manila Pact, and refrained from directly attacking Premier Diem. Nevertheless, it frankly called for a new government, one based on "equitable, just and progressive foundations." Signing the declaration for the Hoa Hao were Generals Soai, Nguyen, and Ba Cut; for the Binh Xuyen, Bay Vien; and for the Cao Dai, Pham Cong Tac. Significantly absent among the signatures were those of Cao Dai Generals Phuong and Trinh Minh The, and the former Hoa Hao dissidents, Colonels Hue and Ngo. In fact, The and Ngo quickly issued public statements affirming their support of the Diem government.[9]

United States and French observers in Saigon took the declaration of the United Front as evidence that the sect opposition had switched to the political front. The danger of civil war, they thought, had abated. Diem appeared to be the least perturbed of all. He recognized certain immediate and local dangers to his position, but to General Collins, he did not seem greatly concerned by the apparent new unity among the sects.[10]

Diem's optimism soon seemed justified. The arrival of a delegation in Cannes to importune Bao Dai to withdraw Diem's powers as Premier followed closely the receipt by the Chief of State of a personal message from President Eisenhower outlining US objectives in Vietnam and the progress made by General Collins toward achieving these objectives. This message was immensely reassuring to the Chief of

State, who in recent weeks had suffered a growing fear that the United States was preparing to eliminate him from the Vietnamese scene. As a result of this encouragement, Bao Dai denied the request of the sect representatives, and they returned to Saigon empty handed.[11]

The United Front next tried a more direct approach. At a second press conference in Saigon on 21 March, the Front released the text of a declaration and "motion," which had been sent to Diem the previous afternoon. The declaration recited all the familiar charges against Diem, attacking him for favoritism, partisanship, press censorship, a provocative and uncompromising attitude toward his opposition, and ineffectual foreign and domestic policies. The attached "motion" was a thinly veiled ultimatum. It "requested" Diem to "undertake within five days complete reorganization of the present cabinet and its replacement by a new cabinet with the approval of the United Front of Nationalist Forces." The ultimatum was signed by the same sect leaders, with the addition of Generals Phuong and The, as the declaration of 4 March. According to General The, who was present when these documents were drafted, a broad program of governmental action was to have been attached, but the sects had been unable to reach agreement. Again, they were finding it much easier to oppose existing programs than to propose new ones.[12]

The same day, Diem discussed the latest maneuver of the United Front with his Cabinet, less the sect representatives, and all agreed that he could do nothing but refuse the demands of the sects. General Collins concurred and advised Diem to stand firm. The General also informed Diem that, although his failure to broaden the government made it difficult for the United States to continue to support him, US policy toward his government remained unchanged.[13]

Nevertheless, the defection of Phuong and The, whom Diem had been providing with liberal subsidies, was a heavy blow to the Premier. Michel Wintrebert, the French Chargé d'Affaires, found Diem so profoundly depressed on the evening of 21 March that he appeared on the verge of giving up. This alarmed Wintrebert and, as General Ely was in Paris and Deputy Commissioner-General Daridan out of town, he decided to act on his own initiative. Without consulting General Collins, he cabled Paris recommending an immediate demarche to secure Bao Dai's intervention and "perhaps his return to Indochina." The Foreign Office, supported by General Ely, urged the United States to join in such a move.[14]

But Diem recovered from his despondency, and General Collins, upon learning of Wintrebert's recommendation, cabled the Secretary of State that Bao Dai's return could accomplish nothing but cut the ground from under Diem. Daridan, who had returned to Saigon, made the same comment to Paris. Both recommended rejection of the proposal.[15]

The French, however, still believed that the only avenue out of the crisis was to use Bao Dai as mediator between Diem and the sects. This could be accomplished, they said, by either having Bao Dai return to Vietnam or having him summon Diem and the sect leaders to Cannes to negotiate their differences. The US Government believed it far more appropriate that a joint declaration be issued to the sects warning them that the United States and France were opposed to violence. The warning should contain the statement that the FEC would prevent movement of sect troops to reinforce the Binh Xuyen in Saigon. General Collins had been trying for a week to get General Ely to agree to employ French troops for this purpose, for he was convinced that Vien would not challenge the government by arms if he could not count on assistance by Hoa Hao troops. General Ely, supported by Paris, made it clear that the FEC would be used only to protect the lives and property of French and foreign nationals.[16]

The French next proposed that Generals Collins and Ely present the text of a joint demarche to both Diem and the sects urging moderation and compromise. The United States Government pointed out that such a move would put the sects on the same plane with Diem. It was absolutely necessary, the Department of State emphasized, to uphold the authority of the central government. The sects were rebels and should be treated as such. Both General Collins and Deputy Commissioner Daridan advised that the joint approach not be made. They agreed that they had already informed Diem and the sects of every point contained in the text of the proposed demarche.[17]

General Collins, in fact, had called in Phuong and The and lectured them rather sternly on the absurdity of demanding a solution in five days. Certainly, he pointed out, they could not expect the United States to continue supplying funds for troop support if they overthrew the government by violence. Subsequently, General Collins stated that discussion with the two generals was like trying to reason with small children. But his lecture apparently had some effect, for General The soon withdrew from the United Front, declaring that he had only joined it to exercise a moderating influence on the other members.[18]

As the deadline imposed by the United Front expired, the situation became highly explosive. The sect leaders refused to extend the deadline or to meet with Diem. The Premier moved reinforcements into Saigon and converted the grounds of the Presidential Palace into an armed camp. Battalions of Vien's green-bereted commandos concentrated in the southwestern section of the capital, while Hoa Hao troops occupied positions on the highways leading south from Saigon.[19]

Fighting in Cholon, 29–30 March

Diem chose this moment to challenge the Binh Xuyen. Just before dawn of 28 March, a tank-led company of National Army soldiers seized the Central Police headquarters near the arroyo separating Saigon from the Chinese community of Cholon. The Binh Xuyen guards did not resist but withdrew into the adjoining police school to await orders from Bay Vien. Next day, Diem informed Defense Minister Minh that he intended that afternoon to replace the Binh Xuyen police commissioner with his own appointee and to occupy the Surete headquarters in central Saigon. Minh protested that Diem should first consult his Cabinet. The Premier refused and Minh submitted his resignation on the spot. When General Ely learned of Diem's intention, he sent M. Wintrebert and General Pierre Jacquot to reason with him. They were more successful than Minh, and Diem agreed to defer his move against the Surete.[20]

This was a fortunate decision for the Prime Minister, for on the night of 29-30 March, the Binh Xuyen struck. They thus stamped themselves as rebels attacking the legal government.

Shortly after midnight, Binh Xuyen commandos, whom Diem's soldiers had driven from Central Police headquarters on 28 March, counterattacked in an attempt to regain their stronghold. About eighty Binh Xuyen soldiers, supported by mortar fire, stormed the police compound but were repulsed by National Army paratroopers and later driven from the neighborhood. Another Binh Xuyen force attacked National Army headquarters on nearby Boulevard Gallieni; this assault also was beaten off by VNA defenders. At the same time, mortar shells fell in the grounds of the Presidential Palace, wounding a number of Vietnamese soldiers. When government forces moved to retaliate by attacking the Surete headquarters, still in Binh Xuyen hands, the French ordered the National Army to remain on the defensive and, to insure compliance, temporarily cut off gasoline and ammunition supplies. By 0330 fighting had ceased.[21]

The Binh Xuyen attack made Diem more than ever determined to destroy its power. Now that Vien had resorted to violence, Diem saw no alternative except to remove control of the National Police and Surete from the Binh Xuyen Director General, Lai Van Sang, as quickly as possible. The government, he told General Ely, could not escape its responsibilities. The Binh Xuyen had to be disarmed or wiped out, and the VNA had enough strength in Saigon to carry out this mission.[22]

General Ely was emphatically opposed. The army could take the Surete headquarters at any time, he told General Collins; that was not the issue. The important point was that Diem did not have sufficient strength to defeat the sects decisively and rapidly throughout the country; and if Diem used force, a long and bloody civil war would inevitably result. Angered by Diem's attitude, General Ely declared that Diem was suffering from hallucinations and was on the verge of megalomania. Diem had no appreciation of the means at his disposal, yet he was ready to "put the city to sword and flame to establish his authority." General Ely believed it would be criminal for the French to get mixed up in a civil war, and he stated that he would do no more than separate the opposing forces if asked to intervene. On the other hand, he asserted that he intended to maintain order even if it entailed placing Diem under arrest.[23]

General Collins, while urging moderation, sympathized with Diem. He believed the Binh Xuyen had taken action to demonstrate that Diem could not control the country; and, if Diem did not remove Police Director General Sang and fight back, he would have to let the sects maintain their feudal systems. If General Collins had been in Diem's place, he told General Ely, he would have met the Binh Xuyen challenge by shelling Binh Xuyen headquarters and going after Bay Vien personally. The French, however, already had a different interpretation of the events of 29-30 March, one that coincided substantially with that of the United Front. The Binh Xuyen, said the French, might not have been the aggressors after all. There was reason for believing that the National Army had begun hostilities and the Binh Xuyen had only acted in self-defense.[24]

This interpretation by the French was merely the first in a series of actions that, in the US view, seemed illogical. The explanation of this French behavior lay, apparently, in the vicious war of words the French and Vietnamese press had been waging for many weeks. The French had become so sensitive to the intemperate attacks on "colonialism," for which they held Diem responsible, that they were predisposed in favor of Diem's opponents regardless of political complexion.

Diem found himself in an unenviable position. The crisis had quickened the disintegration of his government and revealed flaws in the top military command. Ho Thong Minh had already resigned from the Defense Ministry in protest against Diem's policies. Four Hoa Hao cabinet members now resigned, and, despite elaborate ceremonies on 31 March integrating Cao Dai forces into the National Army, four Cao Dai ministers also resigned. Foreign Minister Do and his followers submitted their resignations, then withdrew them. But they ceased to be consulted by Diem or to have any influence upon him. The Inspector General of the National Army, Nguyen Van Vy, made no secret of his opposition to using the army against the Binh Xuyen, and publicly expressed the French view that the government had attacked the Binh Xuyen first. General Collins reported that Army Chief of Staff Le Van Ty was proving to be in this emergency the "weak reed we feared he might be." Diem now more than ever was operating a one-man government and, except for his brothers, stood virtually alone in his determination to resist the sects.[25]

On 31 March, both the government and the Binh Xuyen accepted French General Jean Gambiez as mediator, and a forty-eight hour truce was arranged. Several de facto extensions lengthened the truce through April, but tension continued to mount in Saigon, heightened by almost daily incidents. Generals Collins and Ely, as well as Washington and Paris, sought to find a solution that would resolve the sect problem.

The Recommendations of Generals Collins and Ely

To the men on the scene, it seemed that Diem simply was incapable of changing his methods sufficiently to form or maintain anything but a rubber-stamp cabinet. He had alienated almost every political group in Vietnam and antagonized the French community. Only the United States and General Ely, much against his personal predilections, stood behind Diem. Generals Collins and Ely soon concluded, however, that a major political change was essential if civil war were to be averted.

It was General Ely who now raised the question of Diem's replacement. He met with General Collins on 7 April, with no French staff present. Diem, he said, could no longer be maintained as Premier except by overcoming enormous difficulties. After a full day of "soul searching," General Ely continued, he was forced to conclude that, in order to preserve Vietnam for the free world, Diem had to be replaced. He was prepared to accept anyone but Diem, and this was his final conclusion.[26]

General Collins was reaching a similar conclusion. In fact, as early as 31 March he had informed the Department of State that it was necessary again to consider alternates to Diem.[27] Following his conversation with General Ely on 7 April, General Collins wrote Secretary of State Dulles as follows:

> Even before receiving your kind letter I had been considering writing you personally as to my estimate of President Diem's chances of successfully remaining as President of Viet Nam. I have just filed a dispatch giving General Ely's final views on this point. You and the President are entitled to my judgment in light of this and other recent events.
>
> As you know, I have been doing everything within my power to assist Diem in accordance with my original directive from the President and subsequent instructions from you and the Department. In various messages, and in my January report, I have indicated my growing doubts as to Diem's capacity for leadership under the difficult and complex conditions existing in Viet Nam.
>
> I must say now that my judgment is that Diem does not have the capacity to achieve the necessary unity of purpose and action from his people which is essential to prevent this country from falling under Communist control. I say this with great regret, but with firm conviction.
>
> During the five months that I have been here I have come to admire Diem greatly in many ways. He has valuable spiritual qualities, is incorruptible, is a devoted nationalist, has great tenacity. However these qualities, linked with his lack of practical political sense, his inability to compromise his inherent incapacity to get along with other able men, and his tendency to be suspicious of the motives of any one who disagrees with him, make him practically incapable of holding this government together. As I have often pointed out, he pays more attention to the advice of his brothers Luyen and Nhu than he does to General Ely or me. He has consistently failed to decentralize responsibility to his ministers, or to consult with them in advance of reaching important decisions. This has resulted in the resignation of the few able men in his cabinet who were not repeat not "yes men."
>
> I agree with the appraisal of General Ely and of men like Dr. Quat, Do and Minh, that Diem will not succeed in getting any new men of ability to join even a reorganized government. Damaging as the above facts are, perhaps even more serious is the President's apparent incapacity for creative thinking and planning. At no time since I have been here has he offered to me a single constructive thought of his volition. All of the progressive programs which we have attributed to him have in fact been developed through the cooperative efforts of General Ely and me, and our staffs. I am still not sure whether Diem really grasps the full significance of these programs, or the great difficulties of implementing them.

Instead of sticking to the clear but difficult road leading to the conversion of these paper plans into accomplished facts, Diem has been ever ready like Don Quixote to dash off on side excursions to tilt with windmills. And while bent on these excursions, whether they be to displace officers of the Army whom he regarded as loyal to General Hinh, to take action against Soai or Ba Cut, or to relieve a police chief, he loses all sense of direction toward the essential goals, and it is almost impossible to bring him back to the high road. We have had many such tiltings.

In summary, despite his several fine qualities, it is my considered judgment that the man lacks the personal qualities of leadership and the executive ability successfully to head a government that must compete with the unity of purpose and efficiency of the Viet Minh under Ho Chi Minh.

In saying this I hasten to add that I do not believe that Diem is indispensable for the accomplishment of our purposes in Viet Nam, that is, to save the country from Communism. Programs which General Ely and I have developed are, I believe, sound and susceptible of accomplishment. But our successors here must have a President and a Cabinet to work with, which to some degree will talk our language and will stick steadfastly to the implementation of these programs.

I believe that Tran Van Do or Dr. Quat could form and successfully head such a government. If our government should accept such a change, I would urge that we stipulate as a prior condition the removal, by President Diem with the complete support of Bao Dai, of the control of the National Police and Surete from the Binh Xuyen. You may feel that if this is done, Diem should be given further time to see whether he can broaden his government and speed up progress. I believe it would be better not to wait. By having saved a certain amount of face for Diem by the transfer of police powers from the Binh Xuyen we should then accede to the appointment of Do or Quat as President of the country.

I fully appreciate [the] gravity of the recommendations I have made above. I need not tell you with what a heavy heart I file this message. However, it is by no means with a feeling of defeat for our objective here. I still feel that under proper native leadership, which can be had, the programs which we have initiated can still be made effective and can save Viet Nam from Communism.[28]

The Secretary of State in reply, indicated that he could not see how replacement of Diem would solve the problem of the sects. Any successor to Diem with qualities that would warrant continued US support would still have the sects to contend with. Moreover, a change in premiers would be damaging to US prestige throughout the Far East. The United States would be charged with paying lip service to the cause of Asian nationalism, then abandoning a nationalist leader when "colonial interests" applied enough pressure. An additional consideration was the pro-Diem sentiment in Congress. The Mutual Security Bill was being debated, and Senator Mansfield made it clear that Congress would be reluctant to appropriate funds for Vietnam if Diem were superseded. Nevertheless, Secretary Dulles was willing to consider a change in US policy if General Collins would fly to Washington for consultations with Department of State officials and congressional leaders.[29]

Even before receipt of General Collins' views, Secretary Dulles had been under strong pressure from Paris to unseat Diem. The United States was informed in

The Crisis of April and May 1955

blunt terms that the US policy of maintaining and strengthening Diem was wholly unrealistic. The time had come for formation of a government responsive to the dominant political forces of Vietnam. The French had in mind the creation of a "Conseil Superieur." This body would be composed of representatives of Diem and his supporters, the sects (Cao Dai Pope, for example), intellectuals (Buu Hoi, the French suggested), politicians (Tam, Huu, and Quat), and the army (General Hinh). The supreme council would formulate policy to be executed by a cabinet of "non-political" technicians headed by Diem. The United States rejected this formula and replied that Franco-US policy should be to let Diem strike back at the Binh Xuyen with force, and to support him both morally and logistically in this move.[30]

Despite this ostensible support of Diem, the United States, following General Collins' proposal to switch premiers, decided to explore possible alternative solutions with France and addressed to the Foreign Office a series of questions designed to elicit a concrete French plan. The United States asked the French who should succeed Diem, when the change would take place, how it would be accomplished, what would be done about removing the police from the Binh Xuyen, and how support of the new government by the sects would be assured. The French reply was that the answers to these questions should be developed jointly by the United States and France. For the French alone to answer the questions would be to depart from the agreed policy of achieving a joint Franco-US approach to Indochinese problems. Unless this policy were continued, said the Foreign Office, France would have to state publicly that the United States was now fully responsible for developments in Vietnam.[31]

The United States stood firm, however, and the French, increasingly apprehensive over the mounting tension in Saigon, at length submitted answers to the US questions. They still declined to propose a successor to Diem, declaring that this must be the result of joint consultations. But they did outline, on 17 April, a plan by which a change might be accomplished. Generals Collins and Ely would prepare a slate of acceptable candidates for the premiership and various cabinet posts. Washington and Paris would reach agreement on this list and submit it to Bao Dai. The Chief of State would then summon representatives of the contending factions to Cannes and, on the basis of French and US recommendations, negotiate a solution, including the transfer of the police from the Binh Xuyen to the government. Support of the new government by the sects would be assured by their membership in a high council, together with a program of honors, indemnification, and integration of sect troops into the National Army.[32]

In Saigon, meanwhile, French officials became more and more adamant in their view that Diem must be replaced, calling his removal the will of the Vietnamese people. But General Collins pointed out that this was merely an opinion since there was no way to determine the Vietnamese will. He further noted that it would be difficult to explain Diem's ouster to the American people, adding that US congressional reaction could not be predicted. Despite this, General Collins himself was finding Diem harder and harder to do business with. On 20 April, after reporting to Washington that Diem was willing to agree, but only on his own narrow terms, to a proposal that he participate in a coalition government, General Collins informed Secretary Dulles, "I see no alternative to the early replacement of Diem."[33]

While the Department of State was studying the French reply of 17 April, General Collins arrived in Washington on 21 April to discuss the replacement of Diem. He affirmed his recommendation on the early abandonment of Diem during conversations at the Department of State. Specifically he stated: it would be a major error in judgment to continue to support Diem, who had demonstrated marked inability to understand the political, economic, and military problems of Vietnam; Diem was currently governing by himself with the advice of his brothers and a few close friends to the exclusion of other capable men; in five months Diem had not had one constructive suggestion, idea, or plan; Dr. Quat and former Foreign Minister Do were the most able men available in South Vietnam; general elections in South Vietnam were not possible and the best form of government would be a constitutional monarchy. He had already told Diem, General Collins reported, that he did not see how anyone could save the Diem government and that Bao Dai would probably remove him.[34]

The day General Collins arrived in Washington, Bao Dai injected a further complication into the already troubled situation. On 21 April, Bao Dai told the US Embassy in Paris that it would be impossible to find a solution to the South Vietnamese problems as long as Diem remained Premier. Consequently, he proposed a plan, similar to the plan the French were so strenuously advocating, calling for him to summon representative Vietnamese to Cannes, designate Phan Huy Quat Premier, and instruct Quat to form a "nonpolitical" cabinet of technicians. A high council also would be organized with membership from all factions of Vietnamese society, including the sects, army, peasants, artisans, and trade unions. If the United States rejected this plan, declared Bao Dai, he could no longer take responsibility for events in South Vietnam. Bao Dai asserted that if the United States did not reply to his proposal by 27 April, he would take action unilaterally.[35]

While officials of the US Embassy in Paris sought to defer Bao Dai's move, Secretary Dulles and General Collins, after conferring with Congressional leaders reached a position on the question of Diem's replacement. The United States was now willing to consider shifting its support from Diem to either Quat or ex-Foreign Minister Do. The US Government, however, would not discuss the subject with the French until they submitted a full and frank statement of their intentions in South Vietnam. This statement should include unequivocal assurance of wholehearted French backing of any new political arrangements in Saigon, as well as resolution of "certain ambiguities" in French policy toward North Vietnam. Until Paris produced such a declaration, the United States would continue to support the Diem government.[36] But even before these views were communicated to the French, the shaky truce in Saigon exploded.

The Crisis of April and May 1955

The Binh Xuyen Insurrection

Since the fighting of 20–30 March, Diem had been determined to remove Lai Van Sang from the post of police commissioner; but French and US officials, as well as most of Diem's Cabinet, had advised caution. The Binh Xuyen would surely fight back and the consequences were unpredictable. Nevertheless, Diem on 25 April issued a decree charging Sang with "very grave official misconduct," and naming Colonel Nguyen Ngoc Le to replace Sang as Director General of National Police and Surete. The decree also announced the transfer of police headquarters to the prefectural police school building on Boulevard Gallieni and directed all personnel to report at that address by 1430 hours on 28 April or be considered as having abandoned their posts. Sang replied to Diem's decree over the United Front radio. He had been appointed by Bao Dai, he said, and only Bao Dai could dismiss him. Use of force in attempting to execute Diem's decree would have disastrous consequences for which Diem alone would bear the blame.[37]

The Binh Xuyen were not bluffing. Shortly before noon on 28 April, fighting broke out between the VNA and the Binh Xuyen around Bay Vien's headquarters in Cholon. A little later, mortar shells again fell on the Presidential Palace. Diem responded promptly by ordering the National Army to attack. The fighting, featuring light and heavy machine guns and mortars as well as 105 mm howitzers, spread through the fringe of the crowded Chinese community and onto Boulevard Gallieni. The VNA acted with vigor, if not always with tactical brilliance, and within nine hours the Binh Xuyen had been driven back into Cholon. With fires raging out of control in Cholon, and hundreds dead and wounded, an uneasy truce fell on Saigon.[38]

Diem had by no means won his battle. On 28 April Bao Dai, true to his warning of 21 April, acted. He dispatched telegrams summoning Diem and General Ty to France for "consultations," and vesting command of the army in General Vy, well known for his Binh Xuyen sympathies. Next day, he telegraphed that he was sending General Hinh, Diem's arch-enemy, to Vietnam with instructions for Vy. The Chief of State was clearly intent on overthrowing Diem and, in fact, he so informed US diplomats in France. The United States, he charged, had refused his counsel and had blindly supported Diem in the hope that he would attack the Binh Xuyen. Diem had done so, and now Bao Dai would use his own judgment. The Prime Minister, however, was not to be intimidated, and for the first time he openly defied Bao Dai. With full cabinet support, Diem announced that he would neither heed Bao Dai's summons nor transfer command of the army to General Vy.[39]

Diem's announcement appeared to have considerable public support. The government press had portrayed Bao Dai and the Binh Xuyen as the instruments of French colonialism, and the hostilities had already taken on the cast of a war against French colonialism by nationalist forces. The French, for their part, did little to dispel the impression that they were not, as Diem charged, backing the Binh Xuyen both morally and logistically. The Vietnamese saw French liaison officers entering and leaving Binh Xuyen lines. They also saw the cordon of French troops that barred the VNA from cleaning out the three Binh Xuyen outposts in the European quarter.[40] As the French and Vietnamese press and radio intensified their propaganda campaigns, animosity increased.

The atmosphere was propitious for the emergence of a political group reflecting the mounting anti-French, anti-Bao Dai sentiment. On 30 April the National Revolutionary Congress of the Vietnamese People was born. Backed by Cao Dai Generals Phuong and The, and Hoa Hao General Nguyen Ngo, this new political group claimed it represented almost all political parties of South Vietnam. It issued a declaration repudiating Bao Dai, declaring the Diem government dissolved, and calling upon Diem to form a new government with the specific mission of holding elections for a national assembly, whose first task would be to draft a constitution.[41]

Although the new party consisted largely of individuals with a history of opportunism and was actually representative only of its founders, Diem found its program alluring. At Diem's invitation on the night of 30 April, about thirty members of the Revolutionary Committee of the Congress went to the Presidential Palace for discussions with the Premier. Encountering General Vy in the corridors, they stripped him of his insignia and were about to kill him when Diem interceded. The committee then forced Vy to read to the press a prepared statement declaring that he was breaking with Bao Dai and going over to Diem.[42]

Next morning, safely out of the Palace, Vy called his own press conference, declared that the legal government had ceased to exist, and announced his own assumption of control pending designation of a new Premier by Bao Dai. Vy then moved troops to key points in Saigon, many within the European sector. The French obligingly lowered the barricades to admit units they thought were now loyal to Vy. But the Chief of Staff, General Ty, countermanded all of Vy's orders, and the troops obeyed Ty. Vy then fled Saigon for Dalat, leaving Diem master of the situation.[43]

Meanwhile behind the scenes, bitter disagreement had been building up between the top French and US officials in Saigon. In this period, since General Collins was enroute to Vietnam from his conferences in Washington, Chargé d'Affaires Randolph Kidder was the principal US representative in Saigon. Mr. Kidder reported that General Ely had become incapable of discussing calmly any matter involving Diem. The Premier, according to General Ely, was an "irresponsible madman." He had broken the truce by firing Sang and bringing reinforcements into Saigon and therefore was to blame for the civil war. The United States was also to blame for not having agreed to a political solution before the fighting broke out. Now, said the General, Diem was hysterical beyond the point of reason. In Mr. Kidder's opinion General Ely himself verged on hysteria, and his emotional involvement had compromised his usefulness to both France and the United States.[44]

According to Mr. Kidder, General Ely was also apprehensive that the fighting, if unchecked, would spread to the European sector. He had attempted to persuade Mr. Kidder and the British Ambassador to join in a demarche to Diem aimed at securing a cease-fire. But both diplomats were determined to avoid interference in the conflict, and they had categorically refused. General Ely's concern for the French community was again manifested on 1 May in what Mr. Kidder described as a "violent tirade." After a meeting with Diem, Mr. Kidder had informed General Ely that in Diem's view the continued presence of Binh Xuyen troops in the French security zone created a potentially explosive situation. The General responded vehemently, declaring that Diem was obviously planning trouble for the night of 1 May and had called in Mr. Kidder for the express purpose of clearing himself in advance. Mr. Kidder, said General Ely, must go to Diem and warn him that any incidents between French and Vietnamese soldiers would be the Premier's sole responsibility. When reminded that Diem himself had deplored the possibility of incidents with the French, and that such a declaration would in effect be labeling Diem a liar, General Ely replied: "He is a liar and you should tell him exactly that." Despite heavy pressure from General Ely, Mr. Kidder flatly refused to intervene, and General Ely declared that, if his advice were not heeded, the responsibility for bloodshed would rest with Mr. Kidder personally.[45]

General Ely's prediction that Diem intended to provoke incidents between the VNA and FEC on the night of 1 May proved unfounded. Diem was planning, however, to launch a final offensive against the remaining Binh Xuyen strong points. At noon on 2 May, National Army troops crossed the Chinese arroyo in boats and attacked the Binh Xuyen forces in Cholon. By the following morning the power of the Binh Xuyen had been broken and the remnants of Vien's army had been driven into the countryside south of Cholon.[46]

As Diem was launching his cleanup operation, General Collins arrived in Saigon. He found Diem strongly inclined to associate himself with the Revolutionary Committee and use it to dispose of Bao Dai. General Collins feared that, more likely, the Premier might himself become a captive of the committee. In any event, elimination of Bao Dai would destroy the legal foundations of the Vietnamese Government and leave the country at the mercy of a self-appointed group of known opportunists. Moreover, a number of functionaries on the committee had past affiliations with the Viet Minh. The French intelligence services were convinced that Viet Minh agents had infiltrated the committee and intended to use it for their own purposes. The United States also had an uneasy feeling that communists were lurking somewhere in the committee's organization. General Collins, therefore, strongly urged Diem to use all his influence to hold the Revolutionary Committee in check, to reconstitute his government, to get on with the reform programs, and to leave the question of Bao Dai to an elected national assembly.[47]

This advice may have made Diem more cautious in his relations with the Revolutionary Committee. In any event, he attempted to give the movement against Bao Dai a more representative character by summoning 700 elected councilors from 39 provinces to consider the legality of Bao Dai's role in South Vietnam. This "Estates General," or Congress of Elected Representatives, chose 50 of its number to draw up a program. On the afternoon of 5 May, these men met at the Presidential Palace. Angry words were soon being exchanged between Diem's supporters from Annam and Tonkin and the Cochin-China delegates who had long been hostile to Diem. At length, 18 of the 22 delegates from Cochin-China walked out of the meeting. The remaining councilors then drafted a resolution demanding that Bao Dai transfer all civil and military powers to Diem, who would exercise them until a national assembly met, within six months, to draw up a constitution.

At the same time, 4,000 activists, claiming to represent 95 political parties, met at a downtown theater to consider the Revolutionary Committee's platform. Much of the committee's driving force had been lost with the death of Trinh Minh The in fighting on 3 May, but extremism and demagoguery were still the order of the day. Three motions were enthusiastically adopted. They called for Bao Dai's overthrow, Diem's dismissal, and formation of a provisional government under Diem to govern as agent of the Revolutionary Committee.[48]

Little of a concrete nature emerged from the confused conflict of diverse political factions and personalities and the fulminations against colonialists and puppet emperors. The committees and congresses in Saigon generated much heat, but the real fate of Diem and Bao Dai was being worked out between the United States and France. Secretary Dulles and Premier Edgar Faure, who had succeeded Mendes-France in February, in the second week of May sat down at conference tables in Paris to discuss the future of Ngo Dinh Diem. For the fourth time in nine months, the French and US Governments attempted to resolve this question, and this time they were in even more fundamental disagreement than at any previous time.

Trilateral Talks in Paris

The United States, on the eve of the Binh Xuyen insurrection, had finally agreed to discuss Diem's removal with the French. But the dramatic events in Saigon completely changed the situation, and on 1 May Secretary of State Dulles cabled the embassies in both Saigon and Paris that, in view of Diem's apparent military successes, Congressional and public opinion simply would not sanction any relaxation in US support of the Vietnamese Premier.[49] The United States was again solidly behind Diem, but the almost total divergence of views between the French and Americans in Saigon, and between Washington and Paris, threatened to immobilize free world efforts in Indochina. Understandably, therefore, the Vietnamese question occupied a prominent place on the agenda when the Foreign Ministers of the United States, France, and Great Britain met in Paris on 8 May at a conference called to discuss problems of European defense.

With British Foreign Secretary Harold Macmillan sitting in, Prime Minister Faure and Secretary Dulles discussed their positions on South Vietnam. Clearly, US support of Diem had hardened, and Mr. Dulles emphasized that the United States must either continue to support Diem or withdraw from Vietnam altogether. No one else who had so far appeared on the Vietnamese scene could warrant commitment of US resources and prestige—certainly not Bao Dai. The Chief of State, nonetheless, should be retained as a constitutional figurehead, said the Secretary, until the Vietnamese people themselves decided his fate. This would ensure maintenance of the much discussed "thread of legality."

The French position on Diem had also hardened. Diem, said Premier Faure, was not only incapable but mad. He had deliberately taken advantage of General Collins' absence to engineer a coup de force by attacking the Binh Xuyen, and now he was surrounded by Viet Minh elements. To retain Diem would, one way or another, bring on a Viet Minh victory, focus the hostility of everyone on France, and result in a breach in Franco-US relations. Prime Minister Faure concluded:

> Diem is a bad choice, impossible solution, with no chance to succeed and no chance to improve the situation. Without him some solution might be possible, but with him there is none.... What would you say if we were to retire entirely from Indochina and call back the FEC as soon as possible.... I think I might be able to orient myself to it if you say so. It would have the advantage of avoiding all future reproach to France of "colonialism" while at the same time giving response to Diem's request that France should go. Since it contemplates the liquidation of the situation and the repatriation of the FEC, would the United States be disposed to help protect French civilians and the refugees?[50]

Secretary Dulles feared that the French were not bluffing, and that the choice was now between French or US withdrawal from Indochina. He proposed that the discussion be continued later and called upon Washington for counsel. The question was referred to the Joint Chiefs of Staff for comment. To the Joint Chiefs neither alternative appeared acceptable. They believed that withdrawal of the FEC would leave South Vietnam in a precarious position. The VNA was as yet not capable of filling the vacuum that would be created, and the United States was debarred by the Geneva Agreements from supplying the forces that would be necessary to insure protection of French lives and property. Nor should the United States withdraw, for without its moral and material support France could not develop effective and cohesive indigenous forces. In the opinion of the JCS, if either country withdrew, South Vietnam would probably fall to the communists. The Chiefs considered that the question of continuing to support Diem was one for resolution at the governmental level, but expressed their opinion that the Diem government offered the best hope of achieving internal stability.[51]

General Collins was also strongly opposed to any solution involving withdrawal of the FEC. In the first place, the FEC was responsible, under the aegis of the Manila Pact, for defense of Indochina, and it was apparent that neither the United States nor the British Commonwealth was prepared to take over this responsibility. In addition, French military assistance was essential to the development of Vietnamese forces. The FEC still provided almost complete logistical support of the

VNA, and furnished the French instructors working with the MAAG in the training program. Finally, General Collins, while recognizing that the presence of French troops caused much bitterness among the Vietnamese, believed that the FEC was a stabilizing influence in the strife-ridden politics of South Vietnam.[52]

With these comments as background, Secretary Dulles met with Premier Faure again on 11 May. The Secretary of State emphasized that Indochina, despite its importance, should not be permitted to injure relations between the United States and France. The United States still insisted on Diem's retention, he declared, but some common ground ought to be found. He proposed that France agree to support a broadened Diem government until elections could be held for a national assembly. The assembly would then decide the ultimate political structure of South Vietnam. It might or might not include Diem, but it would be the free expression of the will of the Vietnamese people.[53]

Prime Minister Faure, much against his personal views and the pressure of French opinion, accepted the US proposal on the following conditions: enlargement of the Diem government and acceleration of the electoral process; peaceful resolution of the sect problem; cessation of anti-French propaganda; retention of Bao Dai as Chief of State; reciprocal removal from South Vietnam of French and US officials deemed disturbing to Franco-US harmony; and assurances by the United States that French economic, cultural, and financial relations in South Vietnam would be nurtured.

Secretary Dulles agreed to the French conditions, but pointed out that Diem was not a puppet of the United States. United States diplomats could give him advice but not orders. Therefore, the United States could not promise that the conditions involving Vietnamese action would be fulfilled. In concluding, the Secretary made an especially significant point. The Vietnamese problem, he said, did not lend itself to a contractual agreement between France and the United States. Accordingly, both countries should state their policies and proceed with knowledge of what the other was doing. In other words, the attempt at achieving a joint policy would be discarded, and in the future the United States would act more independently of France.[54]

In South Vietnam the crisis had passed. Diem had dealt the Binh Xuyen as well as the United Front a crippling and, although the French refused to believe it, a fatal blow. Bay Vien and his henchmen, declared outlaws by Diem, had taken to the hills. They were presumed to be conspiring with Bao Dai's emissary, General Hinh, who had wisely avoided Saigon upon arriving in South Vietnam. Whether they could rally the beaten Binh Xuyen forces and join with the Hoa Hao to challenge Diem again was an open question in May 1955. Certainly the VNA, fired by recent success, would be better able to meet the challenge than previously. The United States was again giving Diem its unqualified support, and France had again promised to do so even if reluctantly, with conditions. Moreover, Bao Dai was no longer the threat to Diem he had been formerly. He had blundered badly in trying to overthrow Diem, and had lost much support in South Vietnam.

On 10 May, the rebellion broken, Diem had reconstituted his government, naming a group of relatively unknown "technicians" to support him until elections were held. The Cabinet was the immediate target of criticism both at home and abroad. From all indications, it was another rubberstamp government that would assure the continued primacy of the Ngo brothers in the policies of the nation.[55]

A special US intelligence estimate in early May assessed the situation in South Vietnam as follows:

> The success of Premier Diem in operations against the Binh Xuyen, and his stand against Bao Dai, the French and General Vy, has created a new and potentially revolutionary situation in Vietnam. While the situation in Vietnam is extremely fluid, Diem appears to hold the initiative in the phase that is about to begin.

The estimate concluded that:

> In present circumstances, we do not believe that Diem could be persuaded voluntarily to resign. If he were forced from office, many of Diem's followers would probably undertake revolutionary opposition, including maquis resistance to the successor regime.... [Nevertheless,] Although Diem has improved his position, we believe that it will still be extremely difficult, at best, for Diem or any Vietnamese government to build sufficient strength to meet the long-range challenge of the Communists.[56]

As South Vietnam embarked upon a new chapter in its struggle to become a united, free, prosperous, and democratic nation, the Collins Mission drew to a close. The General left Saigon on 14 May, and later in the month Ambassador G. Frederick Reinhardt presented his credentials to Diem. On 2 June, General Ely also terminated his assignment in Indochina thus making good his oft-repeated declaration that he would not stay in Vietnam if Diem remained Premier. General Jacquot assumed the duties of Commissioner-General pending assignment of General Ely's successor.

5

The Outlook Brightens in South Vietnam

Emerging victorious from the battle of Saigon in May 1955, Prime Minister Ngo Dinh Diem found himself in a position of new strength. He had seriously crippled the sects and all but broken Bao Dai's grip on Vietnamese politics. His resolute stand against the sects had gained him respect abroad and popular confidence at home. It had dispelled grave doubts in Washington about his personal fitness and had won him renewed US support as well as renewed, though qualified, French support.

Important as his success had been, however, Diem still faced many pressing problems. The sect armies had scattered into the provinces where, together with Viet Minh elements, they made pacification a more urgent requirement than ever. The constitutional question also remained to be resolved. Bao Dai's "thread of legality" had to be severed, and a constitutional government, deriving strength from popular participation and decision, had to be erected.

Further, problems with France demanded attention. The political, military, economic, and financial relationships between the two countries all required resolution and implementation. Finally, and most pressing, the Vietnam Agreement and the question of nationwide elections remained to be dealt with.

Diem's Refusal to Consult

Diem was far more interested in consolidating his regime, disposing once and for all of Bao Dai and the sects, and settling accounts with the French than in dealing with the requirements of the Vietnam Agreement. The Final Declaration of the Geneva signatories, however, had called for nation-wide elections for the unification of Vietnam to be held in July 1956 and for consultations between the interested parties to begin a year earlier.

The Declaration was obscure on the identities of the interested parties.[1] As the ruling power in Vietnam, France had signed the Agreement and was thus responsible for carrying out its provisions. By July 1955, however, French power in Vietnam had eroded so badly that France was no longer able to fulfill its responsibilities without the cooperation of the Diem government. But Diem had refused to sign the Agreement and had emphatically protested when France signed. He still refused to admit that his country was bound by the Agreement.

French policymakers were under increasing pressure from public opinion to give the DRV no pretext for renewing hostilities while the FEC remained in Indochina. It was, therefore, an urgent matter that some means be found to fulfill the requirement for consultations in July. Since any formula for holding elections would have to be approved by South Vietnam, the realistic solution was to persuade Diem to confer with the Viet Minh.

The French had help from the British. Because of the leading role they had played in bringing about the Geneva settlement, the British wanted South Vietnam to follow a course they could represent as conforming to that settlement. They believed it essential that Diem recognize the principle of consultations and elections even if he did not consult immediately. At all costs, he should be prevented from publicly repudiating the Agreement. Accordingly, British diplomats in Saigon joined the French in urging Diem to consult with the DRV.[2]

Although the United States had not signed the Vietnam Agreement, in the year following the war it had become the power with the greatest interest and influence in South Vietnam. The views of the US Government on elections were eagerly awaited not only by the British and French but also, no doubt, by the communists. Several times during the winter General Collins had called for an expression of US policy on the subject, and early in 1955 the NSC Planning Board began work on a draft statement of "U.S. Policy on All-Vietnam Elections" (NSC 5519).

The Planning Board concluded that neither South Vietnam nor the United States could afford to give the impression of obstructing popular elections. By adopting such a position, the Diem government would enable the communists to pose as the sole champions of Vietnamese unification and would badly complicate its own task of winning popular support at home. As for the United States—which had advocated national elections in Korea, Austria, and Germany—such a position would appear as more than mildly inconsistent. However, while recommending that the United States encourage Diem to consult with the Viet Minh, the Planning Board cautioned that he should be advised and assisted by the United States. Above all, Diem should reach no agreement with the Viet Minh that did not guarantee free elections and provide for effective supervisory machinery.[3]

When asked to comment on NSC 5519, the Joint Chiefs of Staff, after close study, recommended to the Secretary of Defense that he concur in its approval with one important modification. The change sought by the Joint Chiefs concerned Paragraph 10 of the draft policy statement:

> 10. If pursuit of the above policy should result in a renewal of hostilities by the Communists, the U.S., in the light of the circumstances then prevailing, should be prepared to oppose any Communist attack with U.S. armed forces, if necessary and feasible . . . preferably in concert with the Manila Pact allies of the U.S., but if necessary alone.

Taking exception to that portion of the paragraph that envisioned the possibility of employing US forces "alone" to oppose communist attack, the JCS suggested that the language following "oppose any Communist attack" be replaced with "by immediately invoking the Manila Pact and taking vigorous action thereunder to repel the Communist military aggression." The Joint Chiefs wished to avoid committing US forces to battle in Southeast Asia without the armed assistance and support of the SEATO allies.[4]

The Secretary of Defense forwarded the views of the Chiefs to the National Security Council, and these views, along with the draft policy statement in NSC 5519, were considered by the Council on 9 June. The Council chose, however, to shelve the whole question of all-Vietnam elections for the time being. It decided that no statement of policy on elections was required at that time and noted that US policy in the event of a renewal of fighting would be governed by paragraph 5d of NSC 5429/5 pending a review of that paragraph by the Planning Board.[5] This revision, as it turned out, was not accomplished for over a year.[6]

Despite the failure of the National Security Council to adopt NSC 5519, the main features of the policy outlined in the paper had, in fact, already been carried out by the Department of State. On 7 June the new United States Ambassador to South Vietnam, G. Frederick Reinhardt, had told Diem that, although the United States recognized that South Vietnam was not bound by Geneva, it believed that consultations, under carefully defined conditions, should be held with the Viet Minh. The United States Government considered that only North and South Vietnam should be parties to the negotiations and that, in particular, the International Control Commission should be kept out of the picture. The Ambassador emphasized that in the US view the crucial question was that of safeguards. Unless the communists agreed to free elections by secret ballot, further discussion should be avoided for fear of arousing public expectation that elections were to be held even in the absence of safeguards. To insure free elections Diem should insist upon the same conditions that Sir Anthony Eden had drafted, and the west had supported, for German unification. These conditions included individual freedom from intimidation or coercion before, during, and after elections, and creation of a commission with full powers to supervise the elections and to guarantee against coercion prior to the elections and reprisal afterwards.[7]

Although Diem listened to the advice of US, British, and French diplomats, he could not bring himself to sit down at the conference table with the Viet Minh. He had already made public his opinion that so momentous a question ought to be referred to the future national assembly for debate and decision. Moreover, he felt that he could not negotiate with DRV officials without giving the impression that he recognized the Geneva settlement as binding on South Vietnam. Finally, he believed that his bargaining position would not be firm until he had the same united and strong western support enjoyed by Chancellor Adenauer in Germany and President Rhee in the Republic of Korea.[8]

What Diem really wanted was to disassociate South Vietnam entirely from the Geneva Agreements, but he finally agreed to a less extreme solution. After much debate with the British Ambassador in Saigon, the Prime Minister on 16 July made public his position. Although carefully explaining that he did not reject the principle of free elections, he declared that South Vietnam could not "consider any proposal from the Communists" without proof that they had mended their ways and were prepared to submit to the conditions necessary for genuinely free elections.[9]

Diem's statement seemed to be a rejection of both consultations and elections, and it came at a particularly embarrassing time for the West. The Big Four "summit" talks were scheduled to open at Geneva on 18 July, and the Western powers feared that the USSR would try to force consideration of the issue during the conference. Already, Soviet Premier Bulganin and Indian Premier Nehru, during the latter's visit to Moscow on 23 June, had issued a communique agreeing that all signatories of the Geneva Agreements should "do their utmost fully to discharge their obligations." They had pointedly urged "that where elections are to be held as preliminary to a political settlement the efforts of the governments concerned should be directed to the full implementation of the provisions of the agreement."[10] And hardly had the summit conference of 1955 opened when DRV Premier Pham Van Dong, as if to dramatize the issue for the diplomats at Geneva, called on Diem to appoint representatives to meet with the Viet Minh any time after 20 July to discuss procedures for holding elections.[11]

British, French, and US officials went to the summit meeting in full agreement that the West would try to avoid any discussion of Indochina, would resist any Soviet pressure for inviting the Chinese Communists to participate in a five-power conference on Indochina, and would oppose any attempt to reconvene the Geneva Conference of 1954.[12] With the Soviets wearing the guise of affability and moderation, the conference might well have ended without touching the ticklish problem of Indochina, but two days after it began Saigon made world headlines.

The first anniversary of the signing of the Geneva Agreements fell on 20 July 1955. Anticommunist demonstrations, protesting the partition of Vietnam, broke out in Saigon. Rioters sacked two hotels housing the ICC, and police made only token efforts to prevent the mob from destroying the personal effects of members of the Commission. Several Americans were rescued from the mob by officers of the US Embassy. Diem promptly apologized and offered indemnification to the governments whose nationals were involved, but the damage had been done.[13]

Pointing out that continued supervision of the armistice was being jeopardized by conditions of lawlessness, the ICC called on the co-chairmen of the Geneva Conference of 1954 (Eden and Molotov) for new instructions—which, it said, the riots had made necessary. Prime Minister Nehru of India also cabled Eden and Molotov. Stressing South Vietnam's hostile attitude towards the ICC, he supported the Commission's appeal for new instructions.[14]

At Geneva, the questions raised by the ICC and Nehru were kept off the agenda, and Eden and Molotov discussed the matter informally. As the French and Vietnamese had promptly given assurances that the ICC would be protected in the future, the Soviet and British Foreign Ministers decided to advise Nehru that the ICC could now assume that adequate security existed.[15]

The immediate crisis had been met, but the election issue had only been aggravated. The communists served notice that they would make as much of it as possible. In his closing speech at Geneva, Bulganin stated that "the Geneva agreements on Indochina and other problems will not tolerate postponement." Several days later Chou En-lai attacked the Diem regime for permitting mob violence to ICC personnel and declared that "the most urgent need at present is . . . consultations on the question of general elections." Ho Chi Minh followed with a warning that the US imperialists were planning to keep Vietnam partitioned indefinitely. Even the French joined in the communist demand. Premier Faure warned President Eisenhower at Geneva that unless steps were taken to arrange nation-wide elections in Vietnam, the West might face a full-scale crisis in Indochina.[16]

Franco-Vietnamese Relations

Diem's public announcement on 16 July only partially revealed the motives that had led him to reject consultations. In the Premier's mind this question was intimately bound to the continued presence in Vietnam of the French High Command and the French Expeditionary Corps (FEC).

Although the Vietnamese National Army had been operating independently of the French in the war against the sects, a French officer still retained the title of Commander in Chief, as well as paper responsibility for internal security, and the FEC still provided a pervasive military influence. Diem reasoned that this situation made South Vietnam vulnerable to communist propaganda depicting it as a French colony and, as long as this was so, his negotiators could not meet with the Viet Minh as representatives of a sovereign country.[17]

Diem therefore insisted that the French honor their promise, made by Premier Mendes-France at the Geneva Conference of 1954, to turn over the High Command to the VNA and to withdraw the French Army from Vietnam. He sent one of his ministers, Nguyen Huu Chau, to France to negotiate this question and also to secure a revision of Franco-Vietnamese economic, financial, and cultural accords. Chau was to obtain the withdrawal of French ground troops but was to ask the French to leave naval and air forces under Vietnamese command, to provide logistical support for Vietnamese armed forces, and to pose a continuing threat to the Viet Minh.[18]

Although there was little chance that the French would place their military units under Vietnamese command, they were anxious to withdraw the FEC and seemed willing to turn over the High Command to the VNA. Therefore, as Nguyen Huu Chau arrived in Paris, he had good reason for optimism. But at this juncture Diem raised another issue that antagonized the French and interfered with the military talks. He began to press for a change in the diplomatic relationship between France and Vietnam.

The Premier demanded that Vietnamese affairs in France be handled by the Foreign Office instead of by the Ministry of Associated States, and that General Ely's successor, former UN Representative Henri Hoppenot, be accredited to the Vietnamese Government in the same fashion as other foreign diplomats. The French curtly refused the first request but did go so far as to give Hoppenot the title of Ambassador instead of High Commissioner. His duties, however, would include responsibility for Laos and Cambodia as well as Vietnam and in all other respects would be the same as those of the old High Commissioner. The High Commissariat would not become an Embassy even in name. As a French diplomat explained to an American, for reasons of French domestic politics, the transition to new diplomatic forms could not be done so abruptly as to raise delicate constitutional questions affecting the French Union.[19]

Because Diem refused to accept their terms, the French held up the military talks with Minister Chau. In July, however, Diem at length relented and accepted "Ambassador" Hoppenot. But no sooner had the Hoppenot problem been resolved than Diem arrested two French officers suspected of complicity in the bombing of several electric power stations in Saigon and announced that they would be tried in Vietnamese courts for menacing the security of the state. Deeply angered, the French again suspended the military talks until such time as Diem released the officers.[20]

The deadlock continued for several months until, late in 1955, the French moved to ease relations with Vietnam. First, they transferred responsibility for Vietnamese affairs from the Ministry of Associated States to the Quai d'Orsay. Next, they attempted to quiet Diem's suspicions by refusing to accept the assignment of a diplomatic representative of the DRV to Paris and by making clear that the Sainteny Mission was in Hanoi for the sole purpose of protecting French economic and cultural interests in North Vietnam. Finally, following Diem's victory in the popular referendum (see below), they recognized the Republic of Vietnam (RVN) with Diem as its President. For his part, Diem at last released the two French officers to French custody.[21]

These concessions, however, failed to clear the way for harmonious relations, for Diem seemed intent upon convincing even the most hard-headed Frenchman that the French simply were not welcome in Vietnam. In December he suddenly terminated the economic and financial accords that had been so laboriously negotiated in late 1954. He imposed stringent commercial regulations upon French businessmen, forcing them to leave the country in increasing numbers. The outrage the French felt at this trend was not assuaged by the realization that the mounting activity of the United States in Vietnam was fast driving their former colony from the franc into the dollar area. As a final blow to French pride, Diem withdrew South Vietnam's representatives from the French Union Assembly.[22]

The Campaign against the Sects

Part of the confidence that led to Diem's defiance of France stemmed from his victory over the sects in May. This victory had secured his position in Saigon, but in order to prepare the way for his political program, Diem also attempted to eliminate sect opposition from the provinces. He undertook this ambitious task with an untrained army whose loyalty had been only partially tested and with a political following of uncertain strength.

The Binh Xuyen and Hoa Hao remained Diem's strongest adversaries. Remnants of Bay Vien's Binh Xuyen army, about 1,200 in number, had established themselves in the swamps south of Saigon, where they preyed upon river traffic. The Hoa Hao posed a more serious threat. Although some 6,000 Hoa Hao troops either had been integrated into the VNA or had pledged loyalty to Diem, another 10,000 under Tran Van Soai and Ba Cut ranged across South Vietnam from the Cambodian frontier to the South China Sea. The headquarters of both men became rallying points for anti-Diem elements, including Bao Dai's emissary, former Chief of Staff Nguyen Van Hinh. United States military intelligence officials were convinced that French officers were supplying these Hoa Hao units and encouraging them to attack the VNA.[23]

The Cao Dai carried a double standard. The Pope, Pham Cong Tac, was cooperating with the other hostile sect leaders in trying to overthrow Diem, but the Cao Dai military leader, Ngugen Thanh Phuong, supported Diem. Phuong concluded an agreement with Diem, integrating the 15,000-man Cao Dai army into the VNA and eventually succeeded in stripping Tac of his temporal powers. Except for an abortive attempt to take over the Revolutionary Committee, formed during the Saigon crisis in May, the Cao Dai ceased to be a major problem for Diem.[24]

By late spring US intelligence officials believed that they had solid evidence that the French were supporting the sects against Diem. Not only had French officials actively hindered Diem's efforts to finish off the Binh Xuyen, but they were known to be advising and supporting with money and ammunition both the Cao Dai and the

JCS and the Prelude to the War in Vietnam 1954–1959

Hoa Hao. The Deputy Director for Intelligence, Joint Staff, informed the Chairman, Joint Chiefs of Staff, on 1 June that, "It appears that the present French plans include the support of the dissident sects against the Diem government in an effort to cause eventual widespread revolt in South Vietnam, making it necessary for the French Expeditionary Corps to intercede, re-establish internal security, and to sponsor a new government, tied closely to France . . . through Bao Dai."

French help did not save the sects. After the battle for Saigon, Diem immediately threw thirty VNA battalions against the Hoa Hao. Both Soai and Ba Cut, badly outnumbered, suffered one defeat after another. By mid-July the Hoa Hao organization had disintegrated and its leaders had taken refuge temporarily in Cambodia. The flag of South Vietnam was planted on all seven peaks of the Hoa Hao stronghold in the Seven Mountains region of Southwest Vietnam. On 20 September Diem opened the long-awaited campaign against the Binh Xuyen south of Saigon. Twenty-two VNA battalions were concentrated in the area and in a surprisingly short time wiped out organized resistance.

By the end of 1955 the Hoa Hao, Binh Xuyen, and Cao Dai had been eliminated as organized threats to the government. There remained, however, the major operations of methodically destroying, in province and village, the scattered bands of sect guerrillas and the subversive Viet Minh elements. The need for a more extensive organization to accomplish this task had become apparent even before the sects were crushed.[25]

Organizing for Pacification

With the military defeat of the sects, the security problem in South Vietnam assumed a new form. Hitherto, the sects, militant and selfish but thoroughly anticommunist, had constituted one menace to internal stability and orderly government. The Viet Minh, with numerous armed agents in addition to political cadres and front organizations, had constituted another. As the sects lost hope of prevailing over the national forces in combat, however, their leadership fell prey to infiltration by Viet Minh cadres. The influence of the Viet Minh soon became apparent in the tactics of the sects. They began to concentrate less on military forays against the VNA and more on subjugating the villages by intimidation and propaganda. At the same time, intelligence agencies in Saigon reported that the Viet Minh had strengthened its capability for infiltration, sabotage, and terrorism at the village level. Communist subversive pressures were making themselves felt both through the sects and through the Viet Minh's own apparatus.

The VNA had been deployed throughout South Vietnam in a manner that kept the Viet Minh and the sects from becoming too aggressive. But in the late fall of 1955, the General Staff began to regroup many of the scattered battalions and form them into divisions for training purposes. Thus, extensive security forces were clearly needed: first, to check and ultimately destroy the Viet Minh-sect combination; and second, to gain for the government the confidence and allegiance of the people.[26] At the same time a need existed to improve the quality of indigenous officers engaged in pacification operations. One plan for filling this need that found favorable attention in Washington was drawn up by Colonel Edward G. Lansdale, USAF.

Colonel Lansdale reasoned that US doctrines of unconventional warfare could be strengthened by including distinctively Asian tactics that had proved sound in practice. The situation in Vietnam, he believed, closely paralleled that faced by the Philippines during the Huk war of 1950–1951. Because the Filipinos were very proud of the unconventional methods they had employed to eliminate the Huk menace, Colonel Lansdale suggested that the United States devise a program for training Vietnamese officers in the Philippines by Filipino officers who were veterans of the Huk campaign.[27]

Upon learning of Colonel Lansdale's proposal, the Chairman, Joint Chiefs of Staff, Admiral Radford, referred it to the Army Chief of Staff, General Maxwell D. Taylor, for comment. General Taylor agreed with Colonel Lansdale that the benefits of successful Asian anticommunist doctrine would be lost if the United States insisted solely on its own methods. Moreover, he pointed out, "The psychological impact of Asian aid for another Asian country, without apparent US involvement, has the definite advantage of furthering the concept of Asian self-help and unity in the face of Communist subversion."[28]

The Joint Chiefs on 12 September agreed with General Taylor's analysis and solicited CINCPAC's views. In reply, Admiral Felix B. Stump enthusiastically endorsed the Lansdale Plan and, having found Filipino military leaders anxious to help, recommended that a training program in counter-subversion be set up in the Philippines, within the SEATO framework, to train selected Vietnamese officers, who in turn would serve as instructors in Vietnam. On 1 November 1955, the JCS approved Stump's recommendation and, after securing the concurrence of the Secretary of Defense, authorized him to budget for and plan such a program.[29]

Diem's Political Program

Diem, by making significant gains in reducing the menace of lawless and subversive elements, advanced his chances of success on the political front. He began the campaign on this front in the summer of 1955 with important assets that he had lacked before the crisis of April and May. His victory in the battle of Saigon, and the apparent progress of the pacification program, increased the Prime Minister's popular following throughout the country. Also, the United States had now reached the firm conclusion that the Diem government offered the only hope of achieving a stable, democratic, and secure Republic of Vietnam. Consequently, both

Diem and his opponents, foreign and domestic, knew that US support and financial assistance for South Vietnam was virtually assured as long as Diem remained at the helm. Finally, Diem had purged the army leadership of officers friendly to the sects, and the army's loyalty to him personally increased with each victory over the sects.

As Diem's strength and self-confidence grew, those features of his administration that had long worried US diplomats became more evident. Despite his profession of democratic principles, Diem appeared more and more authoritarian and less and less tolerant of opposition—trends for which informed Vietnamese citizens and foreign missions held the United States responsible. The Cabinet of "technicians" was completely dominated by Diem, who in turn was heavily influenced by his brothers. The Prime Minister seemed to have no intention of changing the composition of his regime until after the institutions of constitutional government had been established, and those he now meant, apparently, to build and control himself.

Diem's plans for national political action reflected both his new self-confidence and his growing authoritarianism. These plans called for achieving constitutional government in three stages. As a first step, Diem intended to hold a national referendum in late October. The people would be asked to decide whether or not to depose Bao Dai as Chief of State, and whether or not to designate Diem Chief of State with a mandate to organize a government. If this referendum turned out as expected, a second would follow in November, in which the people would be asked to approve a draft constitution prepared by Diem. Communal and municipal elections would also be held. Then, to complete the sequence, direct elections for a national assembly would take place in December.[30]

Ambassador Reinhardt viewed these ambitious plans with some concern. He pointed out to Diem that the complex mechanics of such a program would be difficult to execute and that its undemocratic features would be apparent both at home and abroad. Elections for a national assembly should be held first, he advised, and then that organization could deal with the questions of Bao Dai and a constitution. But Diem argued that an assembly would take too long to depose Bao Dai and to approve a constitution. In the end it might produce an unacceptable constitution that provided too much parliamentary authority over the government. Vietnam, he emphasized, could not in this phase of its development afford to risk the instability of French-style parliamentary government. Underlying Diem's attitude, in the Ambassador's opinion, was a determination to prevent a national assembly from gaining too much power before he had fully established his own political supremacy.

Diem had made it clear to the Ambassador that he did not need the advice of the United States to carry out his political program. As the Ambassador informed Washington, US influence in this matter was distinctly limited because Diem realized that the United States was committed to backing him and that US support could therefore be taken for granted. Despite the undesirable features in Diem's political program, Ambassador Reinhardt believed it "preferable to further procrastination and haggling."[31]

Diem announced that the first referendum would be held on 25 October. From his chateau on the French Riviera, Bao Dai made a last vain attempt to reassert his former authority. He appealed to the United States, France, and Great Britain to disregard the results of the "undemocratic" referendum. Several days later he hurried to Paris and issued a decree dismissing Diem as Prime Minister of Vietnam.[32] The decree proved as effectual as the appeal. Bao Dai's ability to influence Vietnamese politics had vanished with the power of the discredited sect chieftains, and Diem was no longer dependent upon either for support. Recognizing this fact, the Western powers ignored the fulminations of the Chief of State.

The Vietnamese people trooped to the polls on the appointed day and were given a ballot printed with pictures of a scowling Bao Dai on one side and a smiling Diem on the other. Over 98 percent of the voters tore the ballot in two, dropping Bao Dai's picture on the ground and Diem's picture into the ballot box.[33] The balloting clearly expressed the overwhelming desire of the Vietnamese to rid themselves of Bao Dai. What else it expressed was open to question. The pre-election campaign had been energetic and one-sided, with the activities of opposition groups impeded by governmental restrictions. Diem's undeniable success, reported Ambassador Reinhardt, lay not so much in his victory percentage as in the large turnout of voters and the orderly and democratic fashion in which the balloting had been conducted.[34]

Apparently emboldened by the unexpected success of his experiment with democracy, Diem modified the remainder of his program and in effect did what the United States had been urging. The day after the election he issued a Provisional Constitutional Act establishing Vietnam as a republic, naming himself President, and changing the titles of all Ministers to Secretaries and all Ministries to Departments. He then created a commission to draft a constitution that would be submitted, not to the people as had been planned, but to the future national assembly. A commission was also set up to arrange elections for the assembly.[35]

After publication of the Provisional Constitutional Act, Vietnamese political parties, in anticipation of election day, took on clearer lines. The two largest and most powerful parties, the National Revolutionary Movement (NRM) and the Revolutionary Workers Party (RWP), were solidly behind Diem. The NRM, an outgrowth of the old Revolutionary Committee, was largely controlled by Diem's brother, Ngo Dinh Can. The RWP was led by another of Diem's brothers, Ngo Dinh Nhu. The most important opposition parties, such as the Dai Viet, were only mildly opposed to Diem.[36] Nevertheless, they announced that they would boycott the election because he refused to permit them greater freedom to campaign against him. This position made an overwhelmingly pro-Diem assembly almost a foregone conclusion.[37]

President Diem's autocratic brand of "democracy" was distasteful to officials in the Department of State. They feared that by restricting the freedom of opposition parties he was antagonizing elements that might add strength to the Vietnamese Government in the future. On the other hand, the realities of Vietnamese politics had to be faced. As Ambassador Reinhardt pointed out, there was almost no Vietnamese political leader, either in or out of the government, who was sincerely motivated by democratic principles. In the interest of the United States as well as Diem, a strong and stable government was more important than encouraging democratic trends. In the view of the Department of State, therefore, it was necessary at least temporarily for Diem to dominate both the government and the national assembly of Vietnam.[38]

In this regard, US officials had little to fear. Diem had shown clearly that he meant to dominate both the government and its legislative body. When Diem spoke now he spoke for a government no longer dependent on France, a government no longer verging on collapse. As a measure of Diem's personal success, he had, in the eight months following the sect revolt, strengthened his political position, gained substantial public support, eliminated his main rivals, and proclaimed South Vietnam a Republic with himself as titular, and de facto, head.

The Training Relations Instruction Mission (TRIM)

At Diem's insistence the French began gradually to withdraw their military forces from South Vietnam during 1955. Although the US Government welcomed the French withdrawal, the phase-out of French troops combined with other developments to retard progress of the program Generals Collins and Ely had worked out in December 1954 to strengthen the Vietnamese forces.

According to the Collins-Ely Minute of Understanding, signed on 13 December 1954, the Chief of the MAAG, acting under the French Commander in Chief for Indochina, was to be responsible for training the Republic of Vietnam Armed Forces. Although this agreement, because of diplomatic procrastination in Paris did not go into effect until 12 February 1955, General O'Daniel began immediately to organize the joint Franco-American group that became known as the Training Relations Instruction Mission.

This mission, separate from the MAAG, consisted of all French and US advisory and training personnel in Vietnam, as well as French cadres with Vietnamese units. It was organized in two echelons. The TRIM staff advised and assisted the Vietnamese Ministry of Defense, the General Staff, and the Arms and Services Directorate, while the TRIM Advisory Group advised and assisted subordinate headquarters, schools, training center, agencies, and installations. The various sections of TRIM were commanded either by a US officer with a French associate or by a French officer with a US associate. All were responsible to General O'Daniel, who served as Chief of both TRIM and MAAG.[39]

During 1955 TRIM occupied itself in organizing a military school system, setting up programs for training officers and specialists in the United States and other countries, and reducing the language barrier between the US and French instructors and their Vietnamese pupils. Much time and thought went into planning for reorganizing and training the army on a divisional rather than a battalion basis. In this area, however, TRIM accomplished little beyond the planning stage during 1955.[40]

One reason for this slow progress was the continued employment of the army in operations against the sects. Another was the reduction of French personnel assigned to TRIM. As the French reduced the strength of the FEC, they also cut the strength of the French component of TRIM. Between April and November 1955, for instance, the number of French assigned to TRIM dropped from 268 to 122. The justification offered by the French for this reduction was that the French members of TRIM were being relegated to secondary and passive roles. Yet, in the same period the French jealously guarded the Vietnamese Navy and Air Force from even token US influence, and the training of those services remained almost exclusively under French control.[41]

The rapid reduction of the FEC, together with the continuing need for employing the VNA in the pacification program, not only slowed the pace of training activities but also left South Vietnam unprepared to cope with aggression by the DRV. This lack of forces capable of meeting external aggression led the RVN to press for US support of higher force levels.

Revision of Vietnamese Force Levels

In November 1954 the United States, on General Collins' recommendation, had agreed to support a Vietnamese force of 88,000 men; the 170,000 men of the armed forces were to be reduced to this figure by 1 July 1955. However, in January 1955 the RVN had persuaded the US Government to support a force of 100,000 men by December 1955, but it had soon become apparent that even this goal was unrealistic. The conflict with the sects, the continued buildup of Viet Minh subversive pressures, and the reduction of the FEC emphasized the undesirability of scaling down the army too soon. Moreover, the Vietnamese lacked the necessary administrative machinery to demobilize efficiently within the time allotted. The RVN were also able to make a good case that large-scale demobilization would add heavily to the burden of an economy already strained by its effort to support large numbers of unemployed refugees from the north.[42]

In August 1955, therefore, General O'Daniel proposed a new adjustment in force levels. He recommended that for the balance of 1955 the US Government support a military establishment of 150,000 men, plus 10,000 sect troops; by the end of FY 1956 this 160,000-man force would be reduced to 150,000 men. The 150,000-man force would be organized into four field and six light divisions, thirteen territorial regiments, one airborne Regimental Combat Team (RCT), and support troops. The force bases would include an air force and a navy of limited size.[43]

Ambassador Reinhardt and the Commander in Chief, Pacific (CINCPAC), fully endorsed General O'Daniel's proposal, and the Joint Chiefs advised the Secretary of Defense that the recommended force basis should be accepted. The Department of Defense subsequently approved the O'Daniel Plan, and the MAAG immediately began planning for the reorganization of Vietnamese forces according to US concepts and at the new level.[44]

The revision of force levels, the independence of the RVN, and the withdrawal of the French seemed to call for a reassessment of the mission of the RVNAF. Drafting US policy towards Vietnam in August 1954, the NSC, apparently expecting the FEC to deter or block any Viet Minh invasion, had defined the mission of Vietnamese forces as maintenance of internal security. For almost two years this was to remain the only mission approved by the NSC. In fact, however, the United States had organized and supported Vietnamese forces on the assumption that they might be called upon to perform an additional mission—limited, but effective, initial resistance to external aggression.

The record makes it clear that Vietnamese forces were being developed to perform both missions, for in 1955 the stated objective of the Mutual Defense Assistance Program in South Vietnam was to assist in organizing, equipping, and training Vietnamese forces in order to "insure the maintenance of internal security and provide limited initial resistance to attack by the Viet Minh." Moreover, the JCS recommended as one US military objective in Vietnam the promotion of eventual Vietnamese participation in the Southeast Asia Treaty Organization (SEATO); they believed that the members of the pact should have the capability of resisting armed attack.[45]

When the question of force levels arose in July 1955, Ambassador Reinhardt pointed out the desirability of re-examining the mission as defined by the NSC, and Admiral Stump declared that failure to include the mission of deterring aggression and delaying a Viet Minh attack invited such an attack and reduced the value of US aid to Vietnam. But, despite the need felt by these US officials for revision of the NSC definition of the RVNAF mission, the NSC statement remained unchanged until September 1956.[46]

MAAG's Personnel Problems

The increase in force levels and the cutback in the French training mission put TRIM in a difficult position. Even with French help, advisers and instructors had been too thinly spread through the Vietnamese military establishment. Now the training requirement was greater and the personnel to accomplish it fewer. MAAG had similar problems. General O'Daniel had transferred 220 of his 342 men to TRIM in February 1955, and with the French withdrawing personnel engaged in processing MDAP equipment, MAAG found it difficult to supervise redistribution and use of this material. As early as February, before the French began to withdraw, General O'Daniel had reported that he needed twice his authorized strength to accomplish the mission assigned him.[47]

But the United States had decided that, although not a signatory, it would abide by the provisions of the agreement on Vietnam. Thus, according to Department of State interpretation, Article 16 of the agreement, which limited foreign military personnel in Vietnam to the number present in July 1954, limited the number of MAAG spaces to no more than 342. Both Admiral Stump and General O'Daniel argued forcefully for a change in the Department of State's ruling. CINCPAC believed that the policymakers in Washington were, to an alarming degree, permitting fear of offending the ICC to influence the course of US policy. Their attitude he characterized as one of "leaning over so far backward we are apt to fall on our faces."[48]

On 2 November 1955 Admiral Stump, in a long cable, laid his case before the Chief of Naval Operations. He argued that in restricting foreign military personnel in Vietnam, the Vietnam Agreement specified no nationality and clearly dealt in totals of communist and noncommunist foreign troops. Unless there was an increase in the total number of noncommunist troops in Vietnam, he said, it could not be validly contended that the armistice agreement had been violated. Therefore, replacement of French by US personnel did not violate Article 16 of the agreement and should be promptly authorized. It was bad enough to be pictured in Asia as a paper tiger, he concluded, but "even a paper tiger would lose face if he showed fear of possible Communist words."[49]

Admiral Arleigh Burke took CINCPAC's plea to the Joint Chiefs, adding his own strong endorsement. They agreed, and in a memorandum to the Secretary of Defense stated:

> The Joint Chiefs of Staff concur in the views of CINCPAC. They believe that it would be realistic to interpret the provisions of the Geneva Agreement to permit replacement of French military personnel, withdrawn from the Combined Training Organization (TRIM) without replacement, by U.S. military personnel. Similarly, it should be permissible to replace French military technicians, withdrawn without replacement from execution of the MDAP redistribution activities, by U.S. military technicians. Accordingly, it is recommended that the Secretary of Defense inform the National Security Council of the gravity of the situation in Vietnam, requesting authority to raise the 342 limitation on U.S. military personnel in Vietnam to replace, as required, French personnel withdrawn without replacement from the training and MDAP equipment redistribution program.[50]

Transmitting these views to the Secretary of State on 13 December, the Secretary of Defense added his own emphatic concurrence. Conceding that the political impact of such a move as advocated by the JCS would have to be carefully studied, Secretary Wilson suggested that this time military considerations might well outweigh political considerations. The Chief, MAAG, he continued, had been made responsible for the mission defined by the NSC, but had been denied the means to accomplish it. "If a favorable solution to this problem is not forthcoming in the immediate future," wrote Secretary Wilson, "It is considered that the NSC military objective should be revised downward so as to reflect a mission which might reasonably be accomplished by MAAG, Viet Nam."[51]

The "NSC military objective" in Vietnam was not revised nor was the Chief, MAAG, immediately given the additional personnel he deemed essential; the explanation may, in part at least, lie in the relative calm in Southeast Asia and the more sanguine view taken by US officials of the security threat.

The Security Threat

Although in 1954 the Viet Minh went through the outward motions of compliance with the Vietnam Agreement calling for the withdrawal of their forces, it had been apparent that they, in fact, were not doing so. The year 1955 brought renewed evidence that the Viet Minh were not abiding by the Agreement. Intelligence sources continued to report that the Viet Minh were leaving behind substantial numbers of trained military personnel in civilian guise while withdrawing new recruits to North Vietnam for training and indoctrination. French and VNA units moving into areas evacuated by the Viet Minh frequently discovered arms and ammunition caches, confirming that the Viet Minh had further plans for South Vietnam.

By late 1955, when the last Viet Minh units had left South Vietnam, a number of agents remained behind to direct the subsequent phases of the enemy campaign to unite the Vietnamese under Hanoi's rule. United States officials did not have an accurate estimate of the number of cadres left behind but clearly saw the threat these men represented. "The biggest danger facing South Vietnam (other than outright renewal of hostilities) is that of a Viet Minh decision to exercise its very extensive capability for widespread terrorist-guerrilla activities," the Deputy Director for Intelligence, Joint Staff, informed Admiral Radford on 22 November 1955. The decision to engage in such warfare would be taken by Hanoi only after it found itself unable, because of South Vietnam's increasing strength and stability, to conquer through political means. Admiral Radford noted, however, that it would be "increasingly difficult" for the Viet Minh to "get away with" terrorist activities as they had done in the past.

General O'Daniel did not believe that the Viet Minh had a very "extensive" guerrilla capability. They had, he thought, much less paramilitary strength than they had a year before. He predicted that this strength would continue to dwindle. Accepting this judgment, the Deputy Director for Intelligence informed the Chairman, Joint Chiefs of Staff, on 19 December 1955 that the present Viet Minh guerrilla capability was not sufficient to take over the country and that only through a resumption of hostilities could they win South Vietnam.[52]

The Outlook Brightens in South Vietnam

Thus as 1955 drew to a close the trend of events in South Vietnam appeared favorable to US policy. This trend seemed to bode well for the establishment of a reasonably stable government and a security climate in which the new republic might well become a dependable link in the chain of resistance to communist expansion in Asia.

6

Developments in North Vietnam

When the Geneva settlement formally acknowledged de facto Viet Minh control in the northern half of Vietnam, the Democratic Republic of Vietnam had been exercising authority over large areas in the north for nine years.

This pre-Geneva experience provided a governmental framework that eased the DRV's task of assuming complete governmental control in 1954; the DRV soon found, however, that economic and political problems had been substituted for military ones. Before Geneva, the regime could command the support of the population simply by waging an effective war for independence and, when faced with economic and social problems, could convincingly attribute them in one way or another to colonialism. Thus the Viet Minh, and hence the DRV, although bearing few of the responsibilities and costs of real governmental power, had enjoyed great popularity and public cooperation. The Geneva Agreements ended this state of affairs and visited new demands upon the DRV government.

Evacuation of Refugees

The Vietnam Agreement provided that French and Viet Minh forces be regrouped in their respective zones within 330 days after the armistice became effective. Withdrawal of French forces was to be accomplished in three stages: from the Hanoi perimeter by the end of 80 days; from the Haiduong perimeter by the end of 100 days; and from the Haiphong perimeter by the end of 300 days. Hanoi and Haiduong were evacuated on schedule, leaving Haiphong the last French foothold in the north. The transfer of the Haiphong enclave from French to Viet Minh hands began on 22 April 1955 and was completed on 16 May, two days before the deadline. The transfer was accomplished without incident, and the DRV thus assumed full responsibility, pending a final political settlement and unification of the country, for the administration of all Vietnamese territory north of the 17th parallel.

In addition to the regrouping of military forces, the Vietnam Agreement also provided that civilians on either side of the demarcation line desiring to move to the other side should be permitted and helped to do so. The agreement specified the same period of time for such transfers as for the removal of the military forces—300 days.

Within a few days of the signing of the Geneva Agreements, however, it became apparent that the French and the South Vietnamese would be unable to handle the evacuation of the thousands of refugees electing to migrate from North to South Vietnam. Ambassador Heath reported early in August 1954 that the refugee program was being gravely endangered by Viet Minh terrorism, South Vietnamese incompetence, and "incorrigibly weak" French staff work. The President should be advised, he added, that only bold US leadership could prevent failure.[1] Thus alerted, the United States Government responded with alacrity when the French and South Vietnamese, on 7 August 1954, requested assistance. General O'Daniel, as coordinator of refugee affairs, mobilized all appropriate US, French, and Vietnamese agencies to carry out what had been christened "Operation Exodus." Rear Admiral Lorenzo S. Sabin was designated by CINCPAC to organize Task Force 90, consisting of 41 troop and cargo ships and ten support vessels. Task Force 90 was charged with assisting the French, who were conducting both sea and air lift, to transport refugees from Haiphong to reception centers at Saigon and Cap St. Jacques.[2]

United States officers found the staging areas at Hanoi, Haiduong, and Haiphong in a state of confusion and disorganization. Swarms of refugees jammed tent cities, public buildings, and even the streets. Sanitary conditions were deplorable. Viet Minh agents used all manner of tactics to induce or compel the emigrants to return to their homes. Communist photographers patrolled the beaches, photographing what one American described as the French "herding operation." French officers showed great reluctance to cooperate with the Americans. Admiral Sabin was denied permission to send a communications team ashore unless it was integrated into the French Army, and United States medical officers were unable to secure an audience with representatives of the French medical service to discuss preventive medicine for the refugees. One French officer, with more candor than discretion, advised a US observer that "You people have the job of supplying the money and the ships. Please don't try to tell us how to run our end of the show. We will run it the way we think best."[3]

Conditions at the reception centers about Saigon were somewhat better than in the staging areas. A joint US-French-Vietnamese headquarters was established to coordinate refugee activities, and the development of reception centers was undertaken as a joint enterprise. France and the United States supplied large quantities of tentage, messing, sanitary, and hospital facilities, as well as supervisory personnel. The South Vietnamese, for their part, furnished military units to be used as labor battalions. A number of private relief organizations assisted greatly at all stages of the effort. Expansion of the centers, however, failed to keep pace with the influx of immigrants, owing mainly to South Vietnamese vacillation and incompetence, rotation of personnel, and differences between the VNA and the Saigon government. The planned resettlement of refugees also lagged, thereby contributing to the congestion at the reception centers. Effective and extensive land reform, which would have absorbed most of the immigrants, became an impossibility as the Diem-Hinh conflict delayed the pacification program. Although 30,000 Tonkinese had been established as farmers on uncultivated lands in Bien Hoa by 14 September, the majority of the refugees had to wait months in the reception camps.[4]

The French employed their entire naval force in Indochina to carry out the evacuation of refugees. In addition, thirty C–47s of the French Air Force were used to evacuate refugees. The first US vessel to participate directly began evacuating personnel on 16 August. During August, the peak month for evacuation, 177,000 persons were carried southward to Saigon. The flow began dropping off in September with 155,000 civilian and military personnel being evacuated during that month. The United States Military Attaché in Saigon ascribed this diminution to Viet Minh terror tactics and the inadequacy of the reception and relocation program at Saigon. During November the number of evacuees dropped to 65,000. Nevertheless, by 20 November a total of 473,000 persons had been recorded leaving North Vietnam. This did not include many thousands of Vietnamese who, out of fear of Viet Minh reprisals, had walked southward across the 17th parallel.[5]

The evacuation of refugees continued until 16 May 1955 when the closure of Haiphong officially terminated Operation Exodus. Between August 1954 and May 1955, a total of 620,000 refugees had elected to leave the communist north for an uncertain future in the south. Most of these were Roman Catholics likely to be singled out for persecution if they had remained. Approximately half of the emigrants were moved to the south by the US Navy, and, in all, Task Force 90 transported 304,704 refugees, 68,727 tons of cargo, and 8,114 vehicles.[6]

The total number of refugees would doubtless have been much higher but for the terrorist tactics consistently applied by the Viet Minh to would-be emigrants throughout the entire 300-day period. Intimidation of refugees by the Viet Minh led to widespread sentiment in the free world for extending the truce deadline beyond 18 May 1955. The South Vietnamese delegation to the Bandung Conference discussed the subject with the Viet Minh delegation, and early in May Prime Minister Diem had brought the matter to the attention of Secretary of State Dulles. In the meantime, General Ely had informed the Canadian member of the International Control Commission that France strongly favored an extension of the 300-day period to compensate for the policy of obstruction employed by the Viet Minh. Finally, Sir Anthony Eden, co-Chairman of the Geneva Conference, broached the topic to his opposite number, Soviet Foreign Minister Molotov. The DRV proved receptive, probably because Ho Chi Minh hoped that the principle of freedom of movement might be expanded to include freedom of circulation between zones and lead eventually to cultural and economic exchanges, which the communist press and radio had been advocating for several months. Freedom of movement would greatly enhance opportunities for infiltration and subversion of South Vietnam. Accordingly, the DRV agreed on 20 May to extend the deadline for one month and subsequently allowed the date again to be moved forward, this time to 20 July 1955. Although these concessions were not accompanied by relaxation of Viet Minh oppression, an estimated 150,000 more refugees left North Vietnam after the closure of Haiphong. According to a Department of State estimate, approximately 900,000 refugees eventually made their way to South Vietnam.[7]

Evacuation of MDAP Equipment

The question of MDAP equipment shipped to Tonkin for use by French Union Forces during the war had caused much concern to US officials, including Congressmen, who feared that quantities of it might fall into the hands of the Viet Minh. This concern had been heightened by evidence that the French were not carrying out the evacuation program in a manner calculated to ensure removal of the material by the end of the 300 days. The United States expressed its apprehension to the French during the Smith-La Chambre talks in September 1954. On this and subsequent occasions, the French promised that no US equipment would be left in Haiphong for the Viet Minh, and they were able to make good their promise. By February 1955, all large items of military equipment had been shipped to Saigon.[8]

General O'Daniel reported in March that equipment with an acquisition cost of almost $206 million had been recovered from Tonkin and stockpiled in South Vietnam. The United States planned to distribute most of this to Vietnamese, Cambodian, and Laotian troops, and ship the remainder to other recipients of MDAP aid in the Far East. This could not be done, however, until the French completed an inventory of all the excess equipment. As French accounting, storage, and distribution procedures left much to be desired, the inventory proved to be a time-consuming operation. But the MAAG preferred accuracy to speed, and did not attempt to rush the French.[9]

One category of equipment still remained in Haiphong, and the French appeared to be making no effort to remove it. This was the heavy machinery, financed by the Foreign Operations Administration, in the Hon Gay coal mines. General Ely had repeatedly assured the United States that this equipment would not be left behind when the French evacuated Tonkin. But General Ely was also under instructions to do nothing that might provoke trouble with the Viet Minh, and the French feared that the Viet Minh would not permit the equipment to be evacuated peacefully. So they procrastinated, and the United States was confronted with the unpleasant prospect of US-financed equipment providing fuel and power for communist industry. But General Ely had given his word. While Paris gave US diplomats qualified promises and talked in ambiguous legalities, the General boldly began to evacuate the machinery. The first items were dismantled and shipped to Saigon early in February, and the operation was completed on 28 March.[10]

French Industry Leaves Tonkin

A partial explanation of the dilatory French approach to the evacuation of industrial equipment lay in the fact that they hoped to retain their commercial interests in North Vietnam following the withdrawal of their military forces. The "Sainteny policy" of maintaining the economic, industrial, and cultural presence of France in the north, begun under Mendes-France, had been adopted by the Faure government. Paris had attempted to persuade French companies to remain in the north and operate under the communist regime, but these firms had refused to carry on without certain financial guarantees that the French Government was unwilling to provide. After some consideration of a proposal to persuade Ho Chi Minh to internationalize Haiphong and exempt French industry and shipping from regulation by the DRV, Sainteny induced the French Government to try to plan for mixed French-Viet Minh companies. According to Sainteny's formula, French industry in Haiphong, after the transfer of the enclave in May, would cede its physical properties to the Viet Minh. A new corporate ownership would be formed in which the DRV had controlling interest. The remaining interest would be divided between the French Government and the private French industrialists concerned. Sainteny's mission in Hanoi was authorized to begin negotiations with Ho Chi Minh for establishing a pilot project to test the feasibility of this proposal. The firm selected was Charbonnages du Tonkin, which administered the Hon Gay coal mines containing the US-financed machinery.[11]

The French tried to convince the United States that this proposal was in the interest of the free world. If the French withdrew from the enterprise, the Foreign Office explained, Chinese or other communist technicians would be brought in to operate the French installations. If the French remained, however, Ho's dependence on the communist bloc would be lessened. As an official of the US Embassy in Paris pointed out, the French had not yet given up their belief that the DRV could be kept from becoming a communist satellite.[12]

To US officials, the French approach in general, and the Sainteny plan in particular, seemed to be based more on wishful thinking than on a realistic appraisal of past experience with the communists. Apart from this consideration, the US Government believed that Sainteny's proposal to work with the communist north contradicted French professions of support for the Diem government in Saigon. The United States also concluded that mixed companies could not qualify as "western installations," for which special exceptions were made to the embargo on trade in strategic materials with the communist countries of the Far East. Without US support, French-DRV companies could not hope to secure permission to import strategic materials essential to their operations. Furthermore, Ho Chi Minh, in negotiations with Sainteny and representatives of Charbonnages du Tonkin, had demanded 95 percent interest in the mixed companies, terms that hardly appealed to the Charbonnages directors. To the disappointment of the authorities in Paris, Charbonnages du Tonkin therefore refused to continue operations. Accordingly, the company concluded arrangements for the sale of its installations and equipment to the DRV, thus setting an example soon followed by the other French concerns in the Haiphong area. As a result, the Foreign Office informed the United States that France had decided to abandon the project for maintaining French business in Tonkin. When the DRV took over Haiphong in May, no French industry and very few French technicians remained.[13]

Reconstruction and Expansion of the Agricultural Economy

One of the most densely populated areas in the world, North Vietnam has historically been a food (rice) deficit area. From the outset, the DRV was determined to develop an agricultural self-sufficiency that would free it from dependence on outside sources. Although collectivization was the ultimate objective of the DRV's economic programs, the regime did not adhere blindly to communist dogma. The collectivization of agriculture, initially at least, was pursued cautiously, if firmly.[14]

The DRV had good reason to proceed with care. The war with France had seriously disrupted the already marginal agricultural economy of the north and the Geneva settlement had interrupted the importation of rice from the south. Moreover, the situation grew even worse with the failure of the rice crop. Despite 100,000 tons of rice supplied by Red China, North Vietnam's rice deficit jumped from 200,000 tons in 1954 to 700,000 tons in 1955. The DRV blamed the landowner class for "sabotaging agricultural reforms," and in February 1955 instituted rationing and controls. But many areas of Tonkin continued to suffer acute food shortages, and rice prices doubled in Hanoi.

Although an extensive land reform program was launched, paddy taxes continued to absorb 40 percent of the peasant's output. Heavy sales and inventory taxes were clamped on merchants, and the scope of private trade diminished as the government began to take over all commercial intercourse. Flight of foreign business and technicians forced even greater reliance on imports and enlarged the chronic deficit in the balance of payments of the Tonkin region. Depreciation of currency and forced labor added to the problems of the regime and burdens of the populace.

At the end of the DRV's first year in power, US intelligence officials found it difficult to assess the character and intensity of resistance within North Vietnam. The evidence available indicated that, despite governmental oppression and depressed living standards, discontent was not finding expression in organized opposition to the regime. The people saw that the government was strong, cohesive, and prepared to crush any opposition with complete ruthlessness. Further, for the most part they retained respect for the Viet Minh as the nationalist movement that had expelled the hated French.[15]

One area in which the DRV could make considerable progress without fear of popular resentment was in the matter of rehabilitation of unproductive land. During 1955–1956, while the other phases of the agricultural program stumbled along, efforts at land rehabilitation were vigorously and successfully pursued, with the result that by the end of 1956, 85 percent of the arable land in the north was under cultivation, a 15 percent increase over the previous year.[16]

The other major element of the regime's agricultural program was the distribution of the property of large landowners (church and communal land was included) among the landless agricultural workers. The fact that there was apparently no great economic need in the north for redistribution suggests that the regime's program was carried out for political or propaganda purposes. During the long years of revolution, the Viet Minh had claimed that land reform would be one of the benefits which would result from the expulsion of the French and had gone so far as to carry out some reforms in the area under its control. These "campaign promises" were especially significant in the south where the existence of large individual holdings and absentee ownership made land reform particularly appealing to the southern peasantry. Unlike the situation in the south, the pattern of land ownership in the north had for many years been characterized by large numbers of small owner-operated farms, and relatively little absentee ownership. Only about 17 percent of the total area under cultivation in the north was made up of "large properties," i.e., more than 3.6 hectares. Redistribution would, however, set the stage for the socialization of agriculture, and by destroying the small class of large landowners the regime would, it was hoped, eliminate the primary potential source of resistance to collectivism and induce a sense of loyalty in the recipients of the redistribution.[17]

During its first year in power (1954–1955) the DRV did not press land redistribution, because, apparently, it did not want to tamper with an operating system. Moreover, the go-slow formula of the first year may have in part reflected the regime's desire not to appear extremist in the eyes of the west or of the peasants of South Vietnam. In 1955, however, a National Planning Board, established with the help of Chinese and Soviet personnel, announced the first of two annual "plans" which were to begin the transformation of agriculture in the north. A special cadre drawn from, and responsible to, the Lao Dong (Communist) Party was created to implement the redistribution program. Several People's Courts—groups of local inhabitants drawn together to suggest landowner classifications for their neighbors and to judge the merits of the classifications assigned—were established. These groups, however, often degenerated into vehicles for the satisfaction of personal grudges or selfish claims. Other injustices stemmed from the fact that the land held by people who could fairly be classified as "large owners" was, when divided, insufficient to give the large number of eligible recipients more than token accessions. By the summer of 1956 it was apparent that the new program of agrarian reform was arousing widespread dissatisfaction and open opposition from the peasantry. Corrective measures were applied by the DRV but they came too late to prevent in November 1956, a rebellion in Ho Chi Minh's native province, Nghe An.[18]

Despite the setback caused by the peasant opposition and rebellion, the land reform program was basically completed by October 1956. The "landlord class" was virtually eliminated, and the pattern of small owner-operated farms was expanded to encompass almost the entire agricultural economy.

Subsequently, the regime initiated a series of steps to encourage the peasants to join one of several programs that were ultimately to result in the socialization of agriculture. These steps included manpower exchange teams, cooperatives, and, finally, collective farms. The regime moved cautiously in its socialization program up to the end of 1957, then launched a concerted drive to collectivize agriculture. One year later, 65 percent of the peasants in NVN had been organized into manpower exchange teams and by mid-1960 more than half of NVN's peasant households were enrolled in the agricultural producer cooperatives. The stage had been set for complete collectivization of agriculture, but this would not be accomplished for some time to come.[19]

The DRV made considerable progress in its effort to achieve agricultural self-sufficiency. During this period the DRV succeeded in increasing total rice production, mostly through the reclamation of arable land, to the point where it exceeded the production of any year before Geneva. Rice production enabled the regime, for the first time in the history of the northern region of Vietnam, to export small amounts to India and Indonesia.[20]

This progress was scarcely apparent to the Vietnamese consumer, however. Although the DRV had managed to increase rice production substantially, the annual ration remained only slightly more than the 300 kilograms declared by the regime to be the minimum requirement. Moreover, the variety of the diet was still substandard even by the low standards of pre-World War II Indochina.[21]

In summary, the activities of the DRV in the field of agriculture helped the people of North Vietnam achieve at least a subsistence level diet in the face of adverse conditions. In addition, the DRV's agricultural program succeeded in reconstructing and developing the agricultural economy to the point where it promised to make the north independent of food imports. Finally, the regime laid the basis for the socialization of agriculture. In contrast to both the USSR and Communist China, the DRV seemed to have begun its national planning with full attention to the basic importance of agriculture in its economy. In a further departure from the Soviet agricultural system, which called for the increase in agricultural output per worker through mechanization, DRV planning called for programs of food production that capitalized on the abundance of its manpower and made allowance for the limitations of its industrial capacity. In its national planning the regime demonstrated a pragmatism and flexibility well suited to the difficult situation which it faced.[22]

Reconstruction and Expansion of the Industrial Economy

In order to complete the base on which it hoped to build a viable economy, the regime sought to complement its efforts in agriculture with a program of industrial reconstruction and development. It was hoped that the products of a revived and expanded industrial plant would contribute to the development of economic self-sufficiency and supply North Vietnam with export commodities, which would be traded for products that could not be produced domestically.

The industrial resources of North Vietnam, though substantial when compared with those available in the south, did not qualify the north as an industrialized area. Although there were large numbers of handicraftsmen and some light industry, the few existing large industries were engaged almost exclusively in the extraction of raw materials. North Vietnam's natural endowments presented a brighter picture for the future; it had the only known major coal basin in Southeast Asia and had a potential for the production of cotton, rubber, and other "industrial crops."[23]

Industrial recovery and development in the north, in conformity with the regime's socialist orientation, was planned and controlled by the government. Except for the larger foreign holdings, many of which had been appropriated outright, the regime confined itself to the use of indirect methods to guide industry. It did this by controlling the distribution of raw materials and imported goods and by insuring a market for products at a favorable price through government purchases. The regime was also able to affect the course of industrial development through the granting or withholding of government loans. These controls were exercised by the governmental apparatus pursuant to programs set forth by the Central Planning Commission, which was established late in 1955.[24]

In line with its general policy of subordinating ideology to practicality in order to encourage the swiftest possible economic recovery, the regime made little effort during the reconstruction period to socialize the nation's light industries and handicrafts. Although the regime began reconstructing the large enterprises left by the French, more benefit was expected in the immediate postwar period from the light industries and handicrafts because their recovery could be accomplished quickly and at a small cost, and their reconstruction required little technical skill or capital. Further, the light industries produced essential consumer goods and materials needed in the agricultural recovery program thus reducing the need to import them and freeing more of the country's foreign exchange for the purchase of industrial equipment that could not be produced domestically. Nevertheless, by expanding its productive capacity, the state sector, confined almost entirely to the large industries, increased its share of North Vietnam's total industrial production from 17 percent in 1956 to 36 percent in 1957.[25]

Agriculture and Industry: The Three Year Plan and After

The terror and confusion following the agricultural rebellion in 1956 had upset farming and caused a serious setback in the rehabilitation and industrial reconstruction program begun in 1954. A breathing space had clearly been needed; thus in 1956 and 1957 the DRV had inaugurated modest one year plans. By 1958, however, the DRV apparently believed the time had come to expand its control and the modernization of the nation's economy. In 1958 it launched a well publicized Three Year Plan with ambitious targets for agriculture and industry. The plan called for a substantial increase in agricultural and industrial production, aiming in the first instance to achieve an adequate food supply and greater export surpluses and in the second to lay the foundations for a modern industrialized state. Consonant with Marxist doctrine, the DRV looked ultimately to achieving a high degree of industrialization, but it realistically had to concede in 1958 that the scarcity of technical and managerial skills meant that the country would have to depend on exporting agricultural and mineral raw materials in exchange for machinery and equipment. Thus the primary aim of the Three Year Plan was to increase production of food through the exploitation of North Vietnam's abundant human resources in the slow process toward modern industrialization.[26]

The Three Year Plan had a political as well as an economic aim; state control was to be extended over a wide range of economic activities. In particular, agricultural producers' cooperatives, i.e., collectives, were to be established on a large scale and government control was to be extended in industry by transferring private and mixed enterprises to the "socialist economy." By the end of 1960, the bulk of private industry and commerce had been transformed into joint-stock companies run for the state by their former owners. The state owned nine-tenths of all industry and commerce and four-fifths of all transport. Approximately three-quarters of all petty traders and artisans had been organized in state-controlled cooperatives.[27] In February 1960 Hanoi announced that within the year it hoped to complete "the grouping of peasants and handicraft workers into semi-socialist cooperatives and complete the transformation of private industry and commerce in the form of joint state-private ownership of enterprises."[28]

The DRV continued to emphasize economic rehabilitation during the 1960s. At the opening meeting of the Third National Congress of the Lao Dong Party on 5 September 1960, Le Duan, a member of the Political Bureau, proclaimed the inauguration of the Five Year Plan to begin in 1961. By this new plan the DRV hoped to increase the total value of industrial output 148 percent and agricultural output

96 percent. Once again the emphasis was on agriculture as the basis of industrial growth.[29] A major feature of the Five Year Plan was socialization of agriculture and the rapid obliteration of the private farm. Despite their traditional attachment to private land, the peasant landlords, faced with uneconomical plots, a scarcity of draft animals, and the high delivery quotas of the Five Year Plan, in increasing numbers began enlisting in the Work Exchange Teams, the basic units of the state's agricultural cooperative system. By the end of 1960 the cooperatives included 85 percent of all farming families, and 99 percent of all crops were being produced on these cooperatives. The cooperatives were reorganized in March 1963 and the percentage of all farming families inched up to 87.7. These impressive statistics notwithstanding, the DRV still faced a basic dilemma. With a population increase of 3.5 percent per year, food production had to increase at least 200,000 tons a year to feed the people of North Vietnam. Even the optimistic figures in the Five Year Plan did not provide for such increases.[30]

The DRV Government

In addition to its efforts in the fields of agriculture and industry, the DRV worked in the years after Geneva toward the imposition and consolidation of its political control over the north. To this end, the Communist Party and the governmental structure were reshaped and strengthened. The party tried to streamline its governmental control apparatus and widen its political base, for in spite of its nearly quarter-million membership in 1954, the party was weak in rural areas, suffering from its essentially urban orientation. To avoid the danger of exclusive reliance on one segment of the population, it worked to incorporate into its leadership prominent communist officials from South Vietnam as well as new members from the army and ethnic minorities.[31] With the transfer of the last French-held enclave to the DRV, North Vietnam became more isolated from the west. As the DRV gained wider and tighter control of the country, it acquired more of the distinctive trappings of the communist police state.

In the late spring of 1955, Consul Thomas Corcoran, who maintained the US Consulate in Hanoi, reported that the capital city was submitting readily to communist regimentation. An efficient block leader system had been installed to mobilize the population for parades and demonstrations. Flags, banners, and posters, which depicted the current party line and generated an anti-American fervor, were in evidence everywhere. The DRV made lavish and conspicuous use of sentries and patrols, although there was little danger to the security of the regime. A high degree of police surveillance, farcical people's court trials, Stakhanovite competitions, self-criticism by civil servants, and "brain-washing" of political prisoners marked the conversion of Hanoi from a bastion of French colonialism to the showcase of Vietnamese communism.[32]

JCS and the Prelude to the War in Vietnam 1954–1959

Although the constitution promulgated by Ho Chi Minh in 1946 placed supreme authority in the National Assembly, all important domestic policies actually were framed by the politburo of the party. Moreover, close liaison between party and government was assured by the party's virtual monopoly of key positions at all levels of government. The party leaders centralized governmental authority and reduced the administrative flexibility and local autonomy required by wartime conditions. For example, the wartime administrative "interzones" between the central government and the provinces and municipalities were abolished, and the DRV created three "autonomous regions," ostensibly for the purpose of providing ethnic minorities with some cultural and political autonomy, but in fact for facilitating party and government control of these minorities.

Supreme leadership of the DRV remained in the hands of Ho Chi Minh and a small party coterie. Except for a well publicized trip to Peking and Moscow in 1954, Ho appeared less frequently in the international spotlight, but US intelligence officials believed that because of his great popular appeal as a symbol of Vietnamese nationalism he remained the ultimate authority. With the victory of Dien Bien Phu behind him, the DRV's military commander, Vo Nguyen Giap, appeared to assume greater importance and responsibility in the DRV hierarchy. Even more evident was the rise of Pham Van Dong, appointed Foreign Minister in 1954 and Prime Minister the next year.

Unlike the Communist Party, the Vietnamese People's Army (VPA) was always broadly based, and Vo Nguyen Giap's large, well-trained, and well-equipped force was of major importance in extending communist authority throughout the country. More secure in its national position, the army was able to execute harsh and unpopular policies. Recruited chiefly among the peasantry, and to a lesser extent from the cities and even from the upland minorities, the VPA numbered an estimated 240,000 soldiers in mid-1955, an increase of 60,000 over pre-Geneva figures. United States intelligence officials in 1963 estimated the VPA strength at 380,000 troops, including militia forces of 100,000. The army was organized into fourteen infantry divisions and one artillery division with service and support elements. Large shipments of arms and materiel, imported from Communist China in violation of the Geneva Agreements, resulted in greatly increased firepower and mobility. Intensive training programs had been carried out to improve military effectiveness and insure political loyalty. The US intelligence agencies judged that, in the event of hostilities, the VPA was not only capable of maintaining control over North Vietnam but also of defeating any combination of the military forces of South Vietnam, Cambodia, and Laos. Of particular interest in the period following the Sino-Soviet rift is the fact that Giap, the VPA strong-man, was outspokenly hostile toward the Chinese. In fact, Giap's agents were reported actively engaged in gathering military intelligence inside China in the interest of DRV security.[33]

The Opposition

The regime was hampered in its program of political consolidation by the persistent and mounting opposition of several factions. Organized opposition originated among three groups: the Catholics, certain tribal groups, and the intellectuals. A fourth group, the farmers, were unorganized, but hostile to the land reform programs.

The DRV began seeking Catholic support shortly after its establishment in 1945 and registered some early success owing largely to the nationalistic character of Ho's government. When the Vatican granted diplomatic recognition to the Bao Dai government in 1950, however, relations between the DRV and the Catholic population deteriorated. Shocked by the scale of Catholic emigration following the Geneva settlement, the DRV ordered more liberal treatment of Catholic communities, but petty officials ignored these instructions and provoked further evacuations. The DRV resorted to harassments and finally was forced to halt the Catholic emigration. It launched an intensive propaganda campaign, infiltrated Catholic communities and employed a variety of ruses to attract the laity into state-sponsored activities in order to undermine the authority and prestige of the Catholic hierarchy. At the same time the regime arrested native priests, expelled some French clergy, and used military force to suppress riots in Catholic villages. Although the church managed to retain its national organization despite these pressures, its membership ceased expanding, and its ability to resist further DRV pressure declined. One author has claimed that Catholic migration to the south worked to the advantage of the DRV, as the French had argued it would. The exodus freed land for redistribution and eliminated potential trouble-makers.[34]

Only loosely organized, North Vietnam's tribal communities, living for the most part in strategic border regions, shared a traditional animosity toward the Vietnamese and current hostility toward the political consolidation of their areas under the DRV. The DRV tried to mitigate tribal opposition by establishing the autonomous regions; it had finally to resort to armed force to suppress resistance. Lacking economic resources and adequate organization, the tribesmen were forced to limit their resistance to sporadic guerrilla activity and passive opposition to the regime's attempts to establish its political control. In 1956 the government claimed that since the Vietnam Agreement more than 300 "bandits" had been killed and some 5,700 captured in minority areas.[35]

The nation's intellectuals, although less organized than either the Catholic or tribal minorities, were potentially more dangerous to the regime. In 1956, emulating Mao Tse-tung's "Hundred Flowers" movement, the DRV announced that it would permit different "tendencies," the freedom to discuss and argue political and cultural topics. In response to this dispensation a group of artists and writers in Hanoi began publishing criticism of the DRV and communism in a number of Vietnamese-language publications. Within the space of three months, however, the DRV retracted its policy of press freedom and smashed the movement. In May 1957 the government once more relaxed its attitude and permitted some writers to publish their material freely, but as a result of bitter criticism of governmental policies, the journals were once again closed and the "political thinking and reactionary ideas" of the artists and writers were ruthlessly suppressed. The regime subsequently launched a campaign against revisionism in art and literature; writers and artists by the hundreds were forced into "re-education" courses, some were made to recant, other leading critics were charged with treason and arrested.[36]

The opposition to the regime coalesced in open rebellion in 1956. Though the point at issue was land reform, the occasion allowed the disparate groups to make common cause against the government. The excesses and confusion that accompanied the land reform program had resulted in widespread disillusionment and disaffection among those very groups whose loyalty the regime sought to win. Not only were the small landholders and once powerful landlords in opposition but even the poorest peasants in the tightly organized Vietnamese village society began demonstrating against the government. In some areas local party officials openly supported the dissidents in their complaints. These party members, themselves recently recruited from the rural areas, were repelled by the human suffering resulting from the reforms. The general rural reaction was reflected in the sharp drop in rice tax collection, an index of rice production.[37]

Fearing that rural discontent might lead to barren rice fields, the regime admitted in October 1956 to "grave errors" and embarked on a "mistakes correction" campaign to eliminate the worst of the excesses and restore rural confidence. This spectacular campaign was too late. On 13 November open rebellion broke out in Nghe An province, a center of Vietnamese Catholicism. Land reform was the principal issue, but in part it was also a religious uprising and a revolt of North Vietnamese intellectuals. It was the peasants, however, who paid the high cost of the violence. It was estimated that 50,000 peasants were executed and twice as many arrested. In the end a whole division of regular troops had to be employed to crush the rebellion. Although the DRV succeeded in ending organized resistance, a substantial residue of resentment and potential opposition remained.[38]

DRV Foreign Policy, 1954–1960

According to the Vietnam Agreement, the DRV was to be no more than the regime in de facto control of North Vietnam pending the results of all-Vietnam elections in 1956 that would reunite the northern and southern halves of the nation. But as soon as the DRV became ensconced in Hanoi it began to act as a recognized sovereign nation, and by the end of 1955 the DRV had taken on the unmistakable cast of a permanent communist regime.

In its effort to hasten its economic reconstruction and to achieve political unification, the DRV maintained and encouraged better relations with certain nations of the West. Initially Hanoi looked to France for economic as well as political assistance. France was, in fact, the only great power that was a signatory to the Geneva Agreements and at the same time capable of effective action in South Vietnam, thanks to the military, economic, and political assets still at her disposal there. The DRV hoped that France, disappointed and exasperated by the affronts of the Diem government, might gamble on a unified communist Vietnam with the hope of maintaining its interests. Prime Minister Pham Van Dong emphasized the special relationship between France and the DRV when on 1 January 1955 he declared: "It was with you, the French, that we signed the Geneva agreements, and it is up to you to see that they are respected."[39]

Despite failure of the Sainteny mission early in 1955, the French for a time continued to enjoy amicable relations with the DRV. Once it became clear, however, that France would not grant diplomatic recognition to the DRV or permit the establishment of a DRV diplomatic mission in Paris, relations between the two countries rapidly deteriorated. In 1958 France permitted the DRV to establish a two-man trade delegation in Paris, but like the French mission in Hanoi, this delegation did not enjoy diplomatic privileges. Relations worsened in that year when the DRV held a public spy trial involving a French mission staff member, and, following the suppression of a DRV trade organization operation in France in October 1959, the DRV began harassing the French mission in Hanoi. By 1960 few traces of French influence remained in North Vietnam.[40]

As the principal and strongest supporter of South Vietnam, the United States became the target for DRV vilification and condemnation. After Geneva, the communists blamed the United States for the partition of Vietnam and, from 1956 on, US intervention in the south was constantly denounced as the principle obstacle to reunification. The Diem regime was condemned as the puppet of the US imperialists. This was a line both palatable to the communist bloc and compatible with a north-south rapprochement, offering as it did anti-Americanism as a national adhesive, and at the same time obscuring the ideological issue of communism. Thus the US became, and remained, the primary target of almost all Hanoi's propaganda attacks against the West, and the staging of anti-American demonstrations and exhibits took on the features of a concerted DRV program to discredit US motives and activities in South Vietnam.[41]

It will be recalled that the United States, initially at least, did not adopt an unyielding policy toward North Vietnam. After the Geneva Conference, US policy planners had become divided over the future course of US policy toward Hanoi. Department of Defense officials argued that the United States should consider North Vietnam as already a part of the communist sphere, but other NSC members favored an approach of exploiting available means to prevent North Vietnam from "becoming permanently incorporated in the Soviet bloc." In the end, the latter view prevailed and the NSC adopted an accommodative policy.[42]

JCS and the Prelude to the War in Vietnam 1954–1959

In succeeding years, however, little was actually done to wean North Vietnam from the Soviet bloc. The only policy directly attributable to the NSC decision was the maintenance of the US Consulate in Hanoi. Through this Consulate, the United States hoped to retain some voice and influence in the northern half of the nation. Events soon proved, however, that the DRV was inflexibly hostile to the United States. The DRV harassed the Consulate and its staff continually until the United States had no choice but to close it down in mid-1955.[43]

After the Consulate closed, US policy toward North Vietnam swung gradually around to the hard line suggested by the Department of Defense in 1954. In September 1956, the NSC determined that the DRV should be treated as "not a legal government," that other states should be discouraged from dealing with it, and that the United States should seek to contain and subvert the DRV. This policy remained in force until the end of the Eisenhower administration, reinforced in 1958 by an additional NSC decision to "apply, as necessary to achieve US objectives, restrictions on US exports and shipping and on foreign assets similar to those already in effect for Communist China and North Korea."[44]

Canada and the United Kingdom maintained diplomatic missions in Hanoi after Geneva. Canada's membership on the ICC undoubtedly explained Hanoi's efforts to continue some relationship with that nation. After the cease-fire, some 500 Canadian officials entered North Vietnam. For the most part, however, Canadian contacts with the DRV were limited to those meetings and discussions carried on by the combined ICC with DRV officials.

As a co-Chairman of the Geneva Conference, the United Kingdom, although its mission in Hanoi had no official status, enjoyed a special relationship in Hanoi. Moreover, the presence of this mission and occasional visits by British journalists and parliamentarians seemed to impress some elements of the DRV's hierarchy as something approaching de facto recognition of the regime by London. When the British continued to deny the regime formal recognition, the DRV attitude changed. After mid-1959, DRV propaganda began charging that the British Government had failed to fulfill its responsibilities as a co-Chairman of the 1954 Geneva Conference.[45]

After Geneva, the DRV made a special effort to attract the support of the neutral countries of Asia and Africa for its national aspirations. The DRV worked hard to achieve respectability and to cultivate the friendship of its Asian neighbors. It was largely successful. India, Indonesia, and Pakistan accorded de facto recognition to the DRV, and India and Indonesia established consulates in Hanoi. Indian Premier Nehru and Burmese Premier U Nu made goodwill visits to Hanoi late in 1954, and Pham Van Dong headed a Viet Minh delegation to the Afro-Asian Conference at Bandung in April 1955. However, both India and Indonesia maintained similar representation in the south, and dignitaries visiting the north, such as Indian President Prasad in March 1959, also included South Vietnam in their itineraries. Even in the case of the new African nations the DRV did not succeed in winning acceptance of the Viet Minh regime as the true, and only, Vietnamese Government, although it almost automatically recognized such newly independent states. Yugoslavia was the only country proclaiming itself as "neutral" that extended full recognition to the DRV. Failure to achieve recognition by most of the neutral nations did not discourage the DRV from seeking close relations with these countries. Informal contacts were established through the various Afro-Asian conferences, international youth festivals, and professional meetings. United States intelligence sources agreed that Ho's personal magnetism and Hanoi's continued homage to the principles of neutralism succeeded in enlisting at least some support for the regime among the neutrals.[46]

After Geneva, the Viet Minh leaders moved to cement relations with the communist bloc. In short order, ten communist countries recognized Ho's government and provided accredited diplomatic representation to Hanoi. Relations with the USSR and Communist China became particularly close. Although North Vietnam was apparently attracted to Moscow and Peking for ideological reasons, it was probably drawn even more for practical reasons. After the withdrawal of the French, the DRV economy was soon in dire need of the economic and technical aid that, in the communist bloc, could be provided only by the USSR and Communist China. The first concrete evidence that such aid would be provided came in December 1954, when by the terms of an agreement signed in Peking, the Chinese Communist government undertook to provide equipment to repair road and rail communications and water conservation works throughout North Vietnam and to restore postal and telegraph communications between the two countries. Special attention was paid to the rail network connecting Hanoi with the interior of China, a project of obvious economic and military importance to the Chinese Communists. According to the Hanoi press the first train on the new "intertransport system" left Hanoi bound for Pug Siang, China, on 1 August 1955.[47]

The amount and scope of Communist China's aid to the DRV in 1954–1955 grew to such an extent that by mid-1955 some foreign observers were guessing that the DRV had come under China's domination. The North Vietnamese army had grown heavily dependent upon Chinese equipment and instructors, and Chinese technicians and trade representatives made such an impact on the DRV economy that even the usually optimistic Sainteny remarked to US Consul Corcoran that "it is the Chinese who will replace us here." However, the benefits that the DRV derived from Communist China's aid did not dispel, apparently, the traditional Vietnamese fear and distrust of its northern neighbor. Moreover, a powerful contender for influence in the DRV was now coming on the field.[48]

Early in 1955 the food situation in North Vietnam had become critical. By summer the situation was so grave that the Hanoi government apparently decided to appeal to its Soviet as well as Chinese friends for help. In the summer of 1955 Ho Chi Minh appeared hat in hand in Moscow. The Soviets proved generous; and in the succeeding two years the USSR gave the DRV more than $100 million in economic aid and sent approximately 1,000 specialists to render technical assistance.[49] In addition to this substantial aid, the Soviets provided the DRV with its only source of gasoline, kerosene, and other petroleum products. For the DRV, trade with the USSR—chiefly Vietnamese tropical products for Soviet machinery—provided not only precious commodities but also a market for much of the output of North Vietnamese artisans.[50] By the end of 1955 the Soviet presence in the DRV had become so pronounced that Ambassador Reinhardt suggested that the USSR might be moving to substitute Soviet for Chinese Communist influence in North Vietnam.[51]

Apparently, however, the Vietnamese Communist Party was divided in its loyalties to the USSR and China—a division that increased as the Sino-Soviet rift deepened. Most of the senior Vietnamese communists had been attracted to communism by the power, prestige, and example of the Soviet Union. What is more, the Soviet Union, unlike China, had no history of conflict with Vietnam. On the other hand, it was in Communist China that the majority of them had received their political training and their first experience of communism. Further, the DRV had been born on Chinese soil, and the victory over the French had been due, in substantial measure, to Chinese military aid. That Hanoi found dependence on either of its powerful friends neither desirable nor comfortable was apparent in the fact that after 1955 the DRV made a moderately successful effort to increase North Vietnam's trade with other communist nations (30 percent of total trade in 1959) and noncommunist countries (7 percent in 1959).[52]

During the period 1957–1960, the DRV had considerable success in maintaining comparative freedom of action. Attempting to strike a balance between Moscow and Peking, the DRV press paid approximately equal homage to the USSR and China and sometimes referred to "the bloc of socialist countries and people's democracies headed by the USSR and China."[53] The Sino-Indian border dispute is a case in point. The US Ambassador in Saigon reported in November 1959 that the DRV, which heretofore had remained silent on this question, apparently was now attempting to steer a middle course between the two communist giants. Echoing Khrushchev's 31 October speech, the DRV expressed the hope that the dispute would be settled by friendly negotiations satisfactory to both sides. At the same time Hanoi adopted the Chinese line, that the imperialists, using the "divide and rule" technique, were trying to sow distrust between the Chinese and Indian peoples. The DRV characterized the problem as an "aftermath of colonialism."[54]

In summary, after five years in power, the DRV had succeeded, with the substantial assistance of the USSR and Communist China, in surmounting its most pressing economic ills. It had also established a tight control over the political, social, and cultural life of its populace. In the military sphere, the DRV had enlarged and improved its army into a powerful force capable of defeating any combination of nations in Southeast Asia. And in the process of building a seemingly viable communist state, the DRV had managed to maintain a surprising degree of independence from its two great patrons. With its house in reasonably good order, the DRV now decided, apparently, that the time had come to move on to the achievement, by violence, of its often announced goal, a unified Vietnam.

7

The Republic of Vietnam: 1956, A Year of Progress

By early 1956, Diem had weathered the worst of the political storms that had raged through South Vietnam since Geneva. He had founded a republic, negotiated the withdrawal of French troops, and was in the process of creating the machinery for a democratic government. He had partially resettled the refugees from North Vietnam and had launched various social and economic programs. Reporting on Diem's progress to the National Security Council in March 1956, the Operations Coordinating Board (OCB) observed that for the first time in Vietnam "there is a degree of stability which may permit implementation of reforms and some long range planning in US programs." At the same time the OCB cautioned that Diem's position was still far from secure and his government "not yet effective enough to warrant more than sober optimism." Although hedged with reservations, the report indicated a rising optimism about the future of South Vietnam, in contrast to the "desperate situation" that had existed in Vietnam in 1954 when the last NSC policy statement on Southeast Asia had been issued.[1]

United States intelligence officials believed that Diem had done much to create for himself an effective political power base in South Vietnam. His unwillingness to work with leaders who failed to show complete loyalty narrowed the base of his political support, but Diem had nevertheless confirmed his position as the dominant political leader of South Vietnam. He had built the National Revolutionary Movement into a formidable political machine, the principal source of organized political power in the country. On the other hand, criticism of the domination of the Government of Vietnam (GVN) by Diem's close relatives was mounting throughout South Vietnam and was not confined to communist spokesmen. United States intelligence authorities agreed that nepotism was present in Diem's government but took it mainly as evidence of Diem's continued inability to trust individuals beyond the circle of long-time acquaintances and members of his family.[2]

Elections and a New Constitution

In early March, the South Vietnamese elected, for the first time, a National Assembly. The elections went well for Diem and permitted him to assume unchallenged leadership and control of the government. On the morning of 4 March 1956, beating drums and torchlight parades summoned voters to the polls. Although the communists attempted to disrupt the balloting, over 80 percent of the eligible voters assembled in orderly fashion and cast their ballots. The voters chose 123 deputies from a total of 405 candidates. No openly anti-Diem candidate was elected, although nearly one-third of the government-sponsored candidates were defeated. Of the major parties, the National Revolutionary Movement won sixty-one seats and the Revolutionary Workers Party fifteen.[3]

The new National Assembly settled down at once to draft, under Diem's supervision, a constitution for the Republic of Vietnam which would give the President wide powers, including the power to appoint the first Vice President and to suspend certain civil rights during the life of the first Assembly. After nearly eight months of drafting and redrafting, the National Assembly, in consultation with President Diem, completed the new Vietnamese constitution. Nationwide festivities attended its promulgation on 26 October 1956, the first anniversary of the founding of the RVN.[4]

In its basic outline the constitution resembled that of the United States. It provided for division of governmental authority among executive, legislative, and judicial branches. The President and the members of the newly styled Legislative Assembly were to be elected by universal secret ballot. Citizens were guaranteed most of the basic individual rights contained in the US Bill of Rights. As had been anticipated, however, the constitution lodged most of the governmental power in the executive branch. It provided, moreover, that during the first legislative term the President had the authority to suspend temporarily the right to strike and the exercise of freedom of speech, association, circulation, and the press. Finally, the constitution specifically outlawed communism.

Vietnamese officials explained that a true democracy was an extravagance that South Vietnam, confronted by the communist menace from within and from without, could not presently afford. As law and order were restored, they said, additional democratic freedoms could be progressively introduced. In the meantime, the Vietnamese would trust President Diem to exercise his power with wisdom and justice.[5]

The Republic of Vietnam: 1956, A Year of Progress

The Succession Controversy

Diem's political triumphs had removed all doubt about the future of the French military in Vietnam. The Vietnamese Government had explicitly requested France to complete the withdrawal of French troops at the earliest possible date, and France was complying. By February 1956, the FEC numbered only 15,000 men, with 5,000 scheduled for evacuation in February and 5,000 more in March. The French planned to abolish the High Command in April.

Who would assume France's responsibilities under the Geneva Agreements once the FEC had been withdrawn and the High Command abolished? The French were responsible for protecting and supplying the ICC. They also maintained a liaison mission with the ICC and held co-membership on the French-DRV Joint Armistice Commission (JAC). The ICC Chairman in Saigon believed that if the French cancelled these obligations and the Vietnamese refused to accept them, the commission would probably have to be dissolved sometime during the summer of 1956.[6]

The French wanted written assurance from President Diem that South Vietnam would take over their responsibilities to the ICC and the JAC. Diem, though still refusing to associate his country with the Geneva Agreements, was willing to meet the French halfway. If they would leave a small mission in Vietnam charged with carrying out France's Geneva obligations, he said, the Vietnamese would quietly take over the duty of servicing the ICC.[7]

The United States believed that a plan along the lines of Diem's proposal offered the best hope of solving the problem. In Secretary of State Dulles' opinion, "while we should certainly take no positive step to speed up present process of decay of Geneva Accords, neither should we make the slightest effort to infuse life into them."[8] In short, the United States would not mind if the ICC died but preferred the death to be gradual and quiet.

There was, however, another aspect of the question. The communists were linking the succession problem to Diem's refusal to cooperate with the DRV in holding elections. The USSR, Poland, Communist China, and the DRV bombarded the British with demands that the Geneva Conference be reconvened to examine both of these matters. The British turned down these demands, but, at India's suggestion, proposed that a co-Chairmen's meeting be held when the Soviet leaders visited London in April 1956. The Soviets agreed and when Khrushchev and Bulganin arrived in London representatives of the British and Soviet Foreign Ministers were already at work trying to reach a solution.[9]

Since the summer of 1955 the British position on elections had changed considerably. The British now seemed to be taking a closer look at the distinction between the Geneva Agreements and the Final Declaration of the Geneva Conference. The requirement for elections was contained not in the Vietnam Agreement but in the declaration, and this requirement was really little more than an expression of hope. Probably of more influence on British thinking than the US emphasis at this point had been Diem's political victories. Whatever the reason, the British had grown more optimistic concerning Diem's chances of providing strong leadership for Vietnam and less persistent in urging him to cooperate in holding elections. At the London meeting the British firmly insisted that since consultation between parties had not taken place in 1955, there was no possibility of holding elections in 1956.[10]

The Soviets proved much less aggressive than had been expected. Apparently unwilling to provoke a new crisis over Indochina, they failed to press with their customary vigor the demands of the Chinese Communists and the DRV for a new Geneva Conference to consider the election issue. The negotiations in London lasted almost a month, but the British and Soviet diplomats finally agreed on a course of action. In May the United Kingdom and the Soviet Union sent identical letters to the Governments of North and South Vietnam requesting them to prevent any violation of the military clauses of the armistice agreement and to insure that the political terms of the agreement were carried out. The letters urged the two Vietnamese regimes to agree upon an early deadline for consultations on elections, and to give every assistance to the ICC. The co-Chairmen also appealed to the ICC to continue supervising the armistice and requested France to continue its good offices in support of the ICC, to reach an agreement with the Vietnamese Government to facilitate the tasks of the ICC and the JAC, and to preserve the status quo until these arrangements could be put into effect.[11]

This agreement created the framework for retaining the armistice machinery in Vietnam, but left France and Vietnam to resolve the question of succession. Settlement of this issue became possible in the early summer of 1956 when Diem relaxed his uncompromising stand against publicly associating his country with the Geneva settlement. Replying to the co-Chairmen's notes of May, the President bound South Vietnam to respect the armistice and to provide security for the ICC. With this concession as a point of departure, the French and the Vietnamese found it easier to solve the succession problem. After considerable debate, they reached an agreement in July. In an exchange of notes Vietnam promised to replace the French liaison mission to the ICC; France agreed to maintain its membership on the JAC and to continue bearing the expenses of the ICC.[12]

The formula adopted by the co-Chairmen and complied with by all the interested parties solved few of the basic problems of the armistice. It merely deferred the ordeal of coming to grips with them. In some respects the Department of State believed these problems had been aggravated. For one thing, the accent on elections in the co-chairmen's messages was expected to make the ICC all the more anxious to get the RVN and the DRV together for consultations, and Diem had not changed his mind on this score. For another, although the armistice machinery was still functioning, Diem was unlikely to tolerate indefinitely France's role on the JAC, and even more unlikely to take over this role himself.

On the other hand, the London solution produced important advantages. It carried South Vietnam safely through the crucial month of July 1956, which many diplomats had feared would be a month of crisis. Agreement had also frustrated, for the time being at least, communist efforts to have a nine-power conference convened to discuss Indochina. Finally, although Diem had been forced to abandon his aloof attitude towards the Geneva Agreements, he still enjoyed, by virtue of the ICC's continued presence in Vietnam, a deterrent to aggressive action by the DRV.[13] On balance, Diem had probably gained more than he had lost.

US Aid to RVN

By the fall of 1956 Diem could take justifiable pride in what he had accomplished against heavy odds. Reviewing his accomplishments for General O'Daniel in October 1956, Diem noted that 1955 had been his year of "successful decisions." His country had achieved "political stability, internal security and national independence." His army was loyal, and to a degree, battle-tested. "Vietnam is a democratic Republic now," he stated. The solution of the refugee problem was in sight. Nor had Vietnam "neglected altogether" its economic problems. "We are no longer under French economic control; we control the course of our foreign trade, and the flow of foreign exchange; we have our own National Bank and our own monetary system. Above all, with the help of the United States, we have escaped economic chaos during the formative period of our independence.[14]

Actually, although the economic situation in South Vietnam was no longer chaotic, neither was it encouraging. Normally an agricultural surplus area, South Vietnam had suffered a decline in rice exports since the war, and this factor, coupled with large imports of consumer and capital goods, had resulted in a substantial deficit in the country's balance of payments. Economic problems were further complicated by the withdrawal of French military forces, the termination of France's preferential trade status, and the loosening of French-Vietnamese political ties, which combined to curtail the scale of French industrial and commercial activity in South Vietnam. Diem had declared 1956 a year of economic consolidation, but through the first half of the year he continued to focus attention on security and political issues. Nevertheless, the GVN made some progress in building an organizational structure to replace the institutions of the French colonial period, including an independent national bank, an investment fund, a government-owned commercial bank, and an independent currency.

That South Vietnam had escaped economic chaos or worse was almost entirely due to the large amounts of money and capital goods given to it by the United States. Without US aid, Diem readily admitted, "the seeming air of well being would disappear overnight."[15]

Beginning in 1954 the United States had, for FY 1955, given South Vietnam $325.8 million in economic aid. Although the United States reduced its contribution for economic support in 1956 to $216.3 million, this reduction had been more than offset by the military aid provided during FY 1956. Through its various aid programs, the United States was financing by 1956 about 90 percent of the GVN military budget, 75 percent of South Vietnam's imports, and 65 percent of the combined military-civilian budget.[16]

Most of the economic aid furnished South Vietnam was in the form of defense support. Needed commodities were shipped free of charge to South Vietnam by the United States. These commodities were then sold to the people of Vietnam by the GVN to meet its expenses, most of which were military expenditures. For example, the salaries of the regular military forces were paid from these funds. A total of $488.8 million of defense support aid, administered by the International Cooperation Administration (ICA), was made available to South Vietnam under the FY 1955 and FY 1956 programs.[17]

Other forms of economic aid to South Vietnam included development loans, special assistance funds, contingency funds and surplus agricultural products. The United States also furnished technical assistance in agriculture, industry and mining, transportation and community development. Not only had the United States paid the cost of Operation EXODUS ($56.1 million) but it also bore most of the cost of feeding, housing and resettling nearly 700,000 of these refugees in the two years that followed.[18]

United States military aid to Vietnam was channeled chiefly through the Military Assistance Program (MAP). Administered by the Assistant Secretary of Defense (ISA), MAP aid consisted of the military equipment, supplies, training, and services given to the Vietnamese armed forces as part of the Mutual Security Program. MAP aid to Vietnam for FY 1956, the first year it was programmed, totaled $167 million.[19]

President Diem, although grateful for the aid he had received, was not satisfied that the United States was giving South Vietnam the right kind of aid. This was apparently the inspiration for his letter to General O'Daniel with whom he had enjoyed good relations. Diem probably believed that General O'Daniel would champion his cause in Washington. Thus, along with a lengthy diagnosis of South Vietnam's economic ills, Diem provided a specific prescription for their relief.

He began by giving O'Daniel "a realistic look" at the overall state of the economy. The basis of that economy, Diem noted, was agriculture. But South Vietnam's agriculture was at only 70 percent of the prewar level. Rice exports that in prewar years had reached 1.5 million tons annually were now virtually nonexistent. Livestock had suffered "a catastrophic decline." Industrial production, never significant, was now at the vanishing point. "With the loss of North Vietnam," Diem said, "we have lost our coal, cement, glass works, and our cotton mills. We have become importers of almost everything." And the hard fact was that South Vietnam's exports during 1955 had paid for only 25 percent of its imports. Also part of this discouraging picture were a sharp decline in tax collections, a sharp increase in production costs, rising prices reflecting inflationary pressures, and an artificial rate of exchange.

The Republic of Vietnam: 1956, A Year of Progress

Diem wanted more US economic help and the implication was help on a massive scale—to rebuild highways and rail lines and to build new ones, so that untapped resources in such remote areas as the High Plateau and the Plaine des Joncs could be tapped. He wanted US help to develop "electric power resources, restore the sugar refineries; create a textile and paper industry, bring in more heavy farm equipment to put our abandoned land back into cultivation, etc."

> From now on, therefore, we hope that American aid would assist us in building a balanced agricultural and industrial economy. This is the only way in which we can increase our production and exports, find new sources of employment for our growing population, expand our purchasing power nationally and internationally, develop managerial skills, and give rise to an enterprising middle class.[20]

He intended, Diem told General O'Daniel, to simplify and ease the flow of capital "in full recognition of the profit motive" so that private investment could be persuaded to supplement US aid. He also intended to push ahead with agrarian reform, redistributing land among farmers, but not by seizing it "at the point of a gun" from landlords. He intended to buy it from them when he could find the money. Again the United States could be helpful in furnishing the $20 million that would be needed for the initial payment, about 10 percent of the total value of the land, to the landlords.

South Vietnam had just entered what Diem termed "Year Three of Our Statehood." Almost a century of colonialism had left it nearly devoid of trained native administrative talent. "All the executive and many of the minor posts were in French hands; they neither taught nor encouraged Vietnamese to participate in commerce or industry or practice the liberal professions. The country has hardly any doctors, engineers, technicians and economic specialists of all types and descriptions for private or Government services," Diem stated. Strong efforts were being made to offset the ill effects of this vacuum in native talent by offshore training and inducement of trained Vietnamese to return from France. But again, Diem pointed out, he must have help from the United States, in addition to United States Operations Mission (USOM) specialists, to train his people in the many skills that were so desperately needed in South Vietnam.[21]

The types of aid that Diem sought in his letter to General O'Daniel were generally of a long-term nature from which immediate results could not be expected. Nevertheless, the United States geared its economic aid programs for the next several years to the requirements Diem had outlined.

The Security Threat

It was fortunate for the RVN that these efforts to strengthen the economy and to build up an industrial base could take place in a period of relative peace and security, both in South Vietnam's cities and in the countryside. By the summer of 1956 according to a US intelligence evaluation, the security picture in South Vietnam was substantially brighter than it had been a year before. The sects had been all but destroyed; only an estimated 2,000 remained in small bands scattered about the country. The important sect leaders had been killed, captured, driven out of the country, or induced to rally to the government. Ba Cut, once the most feared and elusive of sect chieftains, had been captured and guillotined.

The communist threat, however, was still real. In the midst of their generally optimistic estimates, in 1956 US intelligence officials injected an ominous note: in the event of large-scale, concerted guerrilla attack, supported by infiltration of men and supplies from the north, relatively large areas of rural Vietnam probably would be lost to government control.[22]

Although the last Viet Minh units had left South Vietnam on 18 May 1955, a year later US and GVN intelligence officials could not estimate accurately the number of active communist agents operating in South Vietnam. The GVN tended to minimize this threat. The VNA Chief of Intelligence maintained that Viet Minh strength in mid-1956 was only 1,360 men in active guerrilla cadres out of a total hostile force numbering 6,000 to 8,000. United States intelligence agencies, however, estimated the communist strength in skeleton battalions and companies at between 8,000 and 10,000 men. Whatever the communists' (now called Viet Cong) numbers, and most sources agreed that they were relatively few in 1956, the communists controlled substantial areas of South Vietnam, particularly the mountain areas along the Cambodian and Laotian borders and the jungle regions of the delta.[23] Since the GVN did not outlaw communism until almost the end of 1956, Viet Cong agents were also able to operate openly in the cities infiltrating the various worker and business movements.[24]

RVN Forces

The French completed the withdrawal of their forces and abolished the High Command in April 1956, leaving only a small military mission to carry out the remaining French responsibilities under the terms of the Geneva Agreements. The completion of the French withdrawal necessitated, more than ever, a strong, well-trained RVNAF.

There was no question of the necessity for maintaining large regular armed forces and extensive police forces, the high cost of which was borne by the United States. The presence of the Viet Cong within the country and the existence of an enemy state across the northern border of South Vietnam posed formidable dangers

The Republic of Vietnam: 1956, A Year of Progress

to the Republic of Vietnam, and in the judgment of US authorities made the support of adequate, trained military and police forces by Diem's government mandatory.

Regular Forces

The mission of the Vietnamese National Army was to maintain internal security. Moreover, as we have seen, it gradually and without NSC sanction was given the added function of temporarily resisting external aggression. As noted earlier, the United States had agreed to support a force goal for all the armed forces of South Vietnam of 150,000 personnel, comprising the Navy and Air Force as well as the VNA, by 1 July 1956. At the beginning of 1956, the VNA alone had almost 156,000 men and officers, including about 16,000 sect troops who had to be integrated into the armed forces by 1 July 1956. The plans developed by MAAG, Vietnam, for organization of the VNA within the approved force goals called for a military strength of 142,000 with a civilian strength of 4,919 (see following chart for detailed organization). The South Vietnamese Navy and Air Force, together accounting for about 7,000, completed the 150,000-man force structure.[25]

By mid-year the VNA had about 145,000 officers and men, organized into four field divisions (8,500 men each), six light infantry divisions (5,225 men each), one airborne group (4,000 men), 13 territorial regiments (1,625 men each), five separate sect regiments, and 15 assorted combat battalions.[26]

Planned Organization, VNA[27]

Activity	Strength Military	Civilian
Armed Forces Headquarters	2,491	449
Field Divisions (4 at 8,500)	34,000	
Light Divisions (6 at 5,225)	31,350	
Airborne RCT	4,000	
Army Troops		
Arms	13,279	
Services	6,409	
Military Regions (3)		
Headquarters Units	4,707	134
Territorial Regiments (13 at 1,625)	21,125	
Other Units	8,999	4,336
Schools and Training Centers	6,000	
Pipeline	9,640	
Total	142,000	4,919

Any part or all of the VNA might be used at the discretion of the President for maintenance of internal security. The territorial regiments had the sole mission of internal security while the divisions had the additional mission of resistance to external aggression. The presence of VNA units throughout the countryside was intended to deter subversion. They were to be employed actively as pacification forces only when the local civilian authorities found themselves unable to cope with such activities.[28]

The VNA had evolved from a loose conglomeration of units, primarily of battalion size, that had fought for the French and that had been dependent upon the French Union military establishment in Indochina. To accomplish the missions now assigned to it, the VNA would require professional skills and competence beyond those currently possessed by its soldiers and officers, regardless of their native ability and past experience under French leadership. The training of the VNA, therefore, was a matter of continuing concern to US military officials. While the Chief, MAAG, had assumed the responsibility for assisting the GVN in training its army in early 1955, he had done so under certain handicaps. His most serious problems were the shortage of US military training personnel and difficulties stemming from the integration of French and US training personnel in TRIM.[29]

With the inactivation of the French High Command in April 1956, TRIM ceased to exist. While this permitted US personnel to operate more freely, it was not immediately accompanied by an increase in US military trainers. The ceiling imposed upon the number of US military personnel in Vietnam did not even allow advisers to be placed with all regiments, although two US advisers in each battalion-sized unit would have been appropriate. United States personnel were detailed to VNA training centers, to units at division level, and to major territorial commands, to supervise the training program. Developed by General O'Daniel in 1955, this program called for further reorganization of the VNA along US lines and the regrouping of units for training. The goal was to bring the VNA to a state of readiness that would render it capable by the end of 1956 of maintaining security within South Vietnam, containing Viet Cong border penetrations, and in the event of invasion, of delaying the invaders for at least 60 days while withdrawing from the 17th parallel to the area of Tourane (Da Nang).[30]

During a visit to Washington in December 1955, General O'Daniel predicted that with six months additional training the VNA would be able to delay any Viet Cong invasion by two to four months. He also stated that by mid-1956 the caliber of the individual VNA soldier would equal that of the Viet Cong.[31]

These predictions stemmed from the expectation that the VNA training program could be carried out smoothly. The program, based on a 25-week cycle, was designed to take the VNA progressively through individual, company battalion, and regimental advanced training. A four-week division exercise would complete the cycle. Unfortunately, the frequent diversion of VNA units from their scheduled training to field operations against subversive elements considerably slowed the rate of training progress. United States officials could do little about this but held some hope that the creation and strengthening of paramilitary forces might relieve the VNA of many of these security missions. Among other deficiencies that hampered the training of the VNA were: (1) lack of uniformity in training and standards because of the varied local interpretations of directives and the absence of supervisors; (2) shortage of qualified Vietnamese personnel as instructors and training directors; (3) shortage of suitable training sites and facilities; (4) lack of experienced officers trained for higher staffs and commands.[32]

This last deficiency, lack of qualified officers, was a very real handicap not only in training but in operations. According to a study prepared by the US Army staff, the VNA required 11,250 officers but had only 7,000. Seventy percent of the company grade officers were qualified for their rank, 30 percent of the field grade officers were qualified, and only 10 percent of the senior officers were qualified. The training of officers for the VNA was therefore an important facet of the overall training program. A combined Staff College and Senior Officers School outside Saigon offered four to five-month courses for about 100 battalion, regimental, and divisional commanders and staff officers. There were also two officer candidate schools. One at Dalat was conducted in the St. Cyr tradition and turned out "excellent" platoon leaders. The other, at Thu Duc, was for reserve officers and turned out "good" platoon leaders.[33]

Perhaps the weakest element of the VNA was its logistical system. Patterned after that of the French Army, it was inadequate to support even peacetime operations. To overcome the deficiencies of the system, including an acute shortage of specialists and technicians, the United States was helping the VNA to develop a logistical system based on US practice. As part of this effort the United States was also providing offshore schooling, special courses in Vietnamese schools, and on-the-job training. Until these efforts were realized, however, the VNA would require the assistance of a large number of US and/or other allied specialists and technical advisers in the supply and maintenance fields.

In terms of equipment the VNA was not too badly off, having inherited a large part of the material and weapons that the United States had sent into Indochina prior to 1955. This in itself presented a problem, however. The VNA had an excess of various types of MDAP equipment. To store and maintain these items placed a considerable burden on the weak logistics system. Despite this burden, President Diem was very reluctant to return any part of the equipment to US control. The Chief, MAAG, noted that the GVN, under the terms of the Pentalateral Agreement, retained title to all MDAP equipment in its possession. "Considerable pressure and tact" would be needed to persuade the GVN to return the excesses. Another serious problem existed with regard to automotive equipment, much of which was in serious disrepair as a result of initially French, and subsequently Vietnamese, substandard maintenance.

General O'Daniel's successor, Lieutenant General Samuel T. Williams, USA, once he was no longer required to cooperate and compromise with French training officers, was able to carry out his training plans more readily. On 29 April 1956 he designated TRIM the Combat Arms and Training Organization (CATO) of the MAAG and gave it sole responsibility for training ground forces.

Temporary Equipment Recovery Mission

An Interagency Costing Team, which returned from Vietnam in January 1956, reported that because of the reduction of French personnel, control of MDAP spares and supplies had been lost. As a result, "the capability of supply of forces in the field in the event hostilities should be resumed in mid-1956 would be virtually non-existent." Furthermore, because of the shortage of US personnel, the French were handling the redistribution of excess MDAP equipment to their own advantage, carefully sorting out the useful items and returning to the United States as excess the unserviceable ones. Secretary Wilson advised Secretary Dulles on 31 January 1956 that the immediate dispatch to Vietnam of a team of 150 to 200 Americans skilled in supply and logistics would save the United States not less that $100 million worth of material.[34] Although the Secretary of Defense did not mention it, such a team would also relieve MAAG's personnel problems by releasing officers for training duties.

The Department of State agreed with the creation of a US Temporary Equipment Recovery Mission with a double purpose of supervising the recovery (identification, inventory, and accounting control) and return of excess MDAP equipment and assisting in the improvement of Vietnamese logistical capabilities. State's agreement was conditional upon the understanding that, while TERM would perform certain training functions inseparable from the task of recovering and maintaining US-origin equipment in Vietnam, such functions should in no case be allowed to become the single or even primary duty of TERM, as distinguished from the MAAG. In addition, the State Department strongly desired that TERM personnel wear civilian clothing whenever possible during their assignment in Vietnam.[35]

There was some initial objection by other countries to the introduction of additional US troops into Vietnam. Although France and the United Kingdom vigorously opposed TERM as a violation of the agreement on Vietnam, they moderated their opposition after India and Canada approved the mission and after the United States made it clear that the project would be carried out despite the foreign objections. The ICC, however, delayed granting its formal approval, and the United States, impatient over the ICC's procrastination, in May 1956 dispatched TERM to Vietnam over the Commission's protest. The first increment of TERM, 48 officers and 38 enlisted men, arrived in late May. The TERM eventually grew to a total strength of 350 and its establishment allowed General Williams progressively to divert more and more of his relatively few officers and men from logistical duties in support of the VNA to CATO.[36]

By the end of 1956, TERM had substantially improved the organization of Vietnamese logistical services and had launched an extensive logistical training program. Perhaps of equal importance, TERM had largely freed MAAG of logistical responsibilities, thus enabling critically needed personnel to be assigned to training activities. Thereafter, the training program gained momentum. In the period 1957–1959, TERM also processed about $650 million worth of MDAP equipment, shipped out excess, removed scrap from collecting points, transferred serviceable material to the RVN forces (more than $300 million worth) and other agencies, and shipped repairable vehicles to Japan for rebuilding (more than 9,000 by mid-1958).[37]

With respect to the VNA, US intelligence authorities in mid-1956 were somewhat less sanguine than General O'Daniel had been in late 1955, stating that the VNA would have to undergo at least six months of uninterrupted training before it reached "minimum operational effectiveness" at division level.[38] Nevertheless, US officials in Saigon believed that the VNA was capable of performing the two missions of maintaining internal security and of delaying any Viet Cong invasion until help arrived.[39]

VNAF and VNN

The French retained exclusive responsibility for training the Vietnamese Navy (VNN) and Air Force (VNAF) and US influence on these services was limited accordingly. As of mid-1956, the VNN and VNAF were still in an embryonic state. The VNAF boasted 3,336 men with an inventory of 143 planes, mostly trainer-liaison and transport types. Although the VNAF had been receiving F-8-F aircraft (piston fighters), it had so far been unable to mount even limited flight operations because of a lack of qualified maintenance personnel. The VNN numbered, including Marine units, 3,616 men with an inventory of three submarine chasers, three coastal minesweepers, 14 amphibious vessels, and 170 smaller amphibious and patrol craft. United States experts considered the VNN in 1956 capable of undertaking river patrol and minor coastal and amphibious operations.[40]

Increase in MAAG Personnel

By the creation of TERM the United States attempted to increase the number of military assistance personnel in Vietnam and at the same time to sidestep the issue of US adherence to the Geneva ceiling. Although the parties to the Geneva Agreements were generally critical of this action, the United States established a new limit of 692 on military assistance personnel in Vietnam, 342 in MAAG and 350 in TERM. In 1957, with the departure of the French Navy and Air Force training missions, MAAG and TERM were reorganized. New Joint Tables of Distribution were approved increasing the combined authorized strength of US military assistance personnel to 736. Of these spaces, 535 were Army, 76 were Navy, 122 were Air Force, and 3 were Marine Corps.[41]

Paramilitary Forces: The Civil Guard

When the war ended in 1954, a number of auxiliary army units with a total strength of nearly 50,000 remained scattered throughout the RVN without specific missions or positive goals. Because these paramilitary units were generally controlled by provincial governors and other regional leaders, and were employed almost as private armies by these men, they represented a potential threat to the central government. At the same time they constituted a potential source of experienced manpower that could be used to advantage in fighting subversion.[42]

On 8 April 1955, Diem had created from these remnant units a Civil Guard (CG). He placed this organization under his Ministry of the Interior. Diem apparently reasoned that by bringing these units under central control in the CG he could eliminate a threat to his government and at the same time create an agency that could relieve the VNA of internal security duties, enforce law and order in the countryside, collect intelligence, and carry out other counter-subversive functions.[43]

Several months earlier, General Collins had approved the formation of a National Police as one of three law enforcement agencies for South Vietnam. He had not, however, agreed to provide any direct US support for such an organization. When Diem formed the Civil Guard, which US officials equated with the National Police, the United States furnished it no weapons or support other than some training assistance and advice.[44]

At President Diem's request, the United States arranged to bring to RVN an advisory and training mission from Michigan State University (MSU). This group, which was under joint contract to USOM and the GVN and which eventually numbered about 25 persons, had begun arriving in RVN in May 1955. The group was charged with providing the GVN with advice and training in government organization and management, specifically including police administration.[45]

The MSU advisers assisted, in coordination with the MAAG and the VNA, in a CG training program, largely in basic military subjects. They insisted, however, that the CG should be a civilian police organization in every respect, located apart from any military encampments and directed and instructed by civilian personnel. They wanted the CG streamlined and armed with weapons and equipment suited to civil police duties. The MSU advisers additionally proposed to the US Mission that the CG be garrisoned permanently in villages rather than being a mobile, transient force. While the CG had a primary mission of maintaining internal security, the

MSU advisers hoped that, in so doing, it could gain for the GVN the confidence and allegiance of the people in the countryside.[46]

The recommendations by US advisers for orienting the CG away from paramilitary organization and operations were not accepted by President Diem. Diem seemed to want a large paramilitary organization deployed widely throughout the provinces and controlled by him through the province chiefs. In November 1955 he transferred the CG from the Ministry of the Interior to his direct control. According to the Deputy Director for Intelligence, Joint Staff, this was only a temporary expedient so that the CG could function as an auxiliary force to the VNA, not as an adjunct of the VNA.

By mid-1956 the CG had a strength of about 51,000, deployed among three military regions of South Vietnam. The majority, 35,000, were stationed in the southern third of the nation, old Cochin-China. In northern South Vietnam, there were about 9,000 CG personnel, and in the central plateau and coastal area about 7,000.[47]

The CG had some fixed post assignments but was basically a patrolling organization. It did not operate in urban areas that had municipal police. Generally, CG units of company size were assigned to each province. From these companies groups of 12 to 40 men patrolled delineated areas of responsibility, operating out of an assigned post. In 1956, however, it had in some instances become necessary to employ companies at full strength in areas being pacified. Once the VNA had established control of an area in which the Viet Cong were engaged in subversion, CG units operating as companies were moved in to assist in further pacification of the area. When pacification was completed, the CG gradually assumed control from the VNA and reverted to normal patrolling in small groups. Chief, MAAG, reported to Washington authorities that in areas in which the CG and the VNA were required to operate simultaneously the commanders coordinated such operations adequately and that there was no duplication between the two. He looked forward to the day when the CG and the other security forces would be trained well enough to handle pacification tasks without VNA assistance. "The VNA can then release its units for much needed combat training," he observed. For the time being, however, pacification requirements exceeded the capabilities of the existing territorial army and CG units.[48]

The MSU advisers and other US personnel involved continued to disagree with Diem over the basic concept of a CG. The United States pressed for a small, centrally controlled civil police force living with the villagers it protected; Diem insisted on a large, decentralized force responsible to him through the province chiefs.[49]

The MSU advisory group gradually accepted the necessity of assigning certain paramilitary responsibilities to the CG, but it continued to stress its civilian character in all recommendations. That Vietnamese police officials and members of the US Country Team agreed with the MSU group did not change President Diem's mind in regard to the CG. In a series of decisions in the summer of 1957, Diem made clear his disagreement. When the US advisers proposed giving the CG powers of arrest and investigation and authorizing it to serve subpoenas, they were supported by Vietnamese police officials but not by the President. Diem also overruled proposals to assign civilian gendarmerie officers, rather than VNA officers on temporary duty, to lead CG units. Further, he resisted a US suggestion that the CG be reduced to a force of 30,000 or less. He remained determined to build a force of at least 50,000 and to use it to augment his military forces.[50]

These differences of opinion were reflected in the important question of equipment. In July 1957, the GVN asked the United States to furnish the CG $60 million worth of heavy equipment. The MAAG and the MSU team, basing their proposals on their concept of the CG as a civilian police organization, proposed a US aid figure of $14 to $18 million for equipment. A compromise was finally worked out in 1958 in which $14 million worth of equipment, including some of the heavy hardware requested by the GVN, would be issued to the CG over a four-year period, with the understanding that the CG was to be reorganized into a civilian operation along the lines proposed by the US advisers.[51]

Little progress, however, was made in changing the features of the CG following this compromise. The $14 million US program for equipping the CG was held in abeyance for almost two years because of the continuing disagreement with the GVN over its status. In January 1959, when the GVN agreed to transfer the CG back to the Ministry of the Interior, the United States agreed to move ahead with its aid program.[52] On 30 June, the MSU group withdrew, leaving the USOM to assume the advisory position.[53]

Two other police agencies maintained by the GVN were the Vietnamese Bureau of Investigation (Surete), a plain-clothes force similar to the FBI, numbering about 5,000 men, and the Gendarmerie. This latter force, which in mid-1956 was being trained by the MSU group, had a current strength of only 572, but 1,000 additional men were being recruited. An eventual strength of 6,000 was contemplated.

Paramilitary Forces: The Self-Defense Corps

The CG was not designed to provide close protection to the individual villages in South Vietnam. In an effort to furnish the villagers some protection against the Viet Cong, Diem had formed, on 27 November 1955, a special organization, the Village Defense Corps. This soon became known as the Self Defense Corps (SDC). He planned to set up individual SDC units in villages, to be activated by the military commander of a specific region and to remain under military control. The SDC would be a static force whose members were native to villages in which they were employed. They would know local conditions thoroughly and would be expected to police and defend the village. These men would perform SDC service as an extra duty, meanwhile keeping their regular jobs. The SDC would not be used as a pacification force since it would be established in villages that had already been cleared of dissidents. A SDC unit would be established in each village of 1,000 or more, the unit consisting of one commander and nine members. The total strength of the SDC was not planned to exceed 60,000 men. The SDC would be controlled by the GVN Secretary of Defense in a chain of command running downward through a Director within the Department of Defense. General O'Daniel and Admiral Stump both supported the concept of the SDC as proposed by the GVN, and recommended that the United States furnish the necessary financial material support.[54]

Because US support was being solicited for the SDC and because the relationship between the CG and the SDC was not clear to Washington, the Secretary of Defense asked CINCPAC and Chief, MAAG, to clarify this relationship and to be precise concerning the organization, functions, and employment of the new organization. On 11 January, General Williams furnished the facts to Washington, pointing out that the CG had quite a different mission from the SDC. The latter was being formed to "provide a fixed organization in each village to protect the people therein from indoctrination and intimidation by the Viet Cong, rebels, bandits and other dissident groups threatening the local security, to give needed assistance to villagers, and to organize anticommunist activities among the population." The VNA would work closely with the SDC, setting it up, training it, and controlling its units. There was no prescribed Table of Organization and Equipment (TO&E) for the SDC, but in general, each unit would have ten men and the total strength would not exceed 60,000. Only rifles, non-US, and some ammunition would be given the SDC by the VNA. No other major weapons or equipment would be supplied. The GVN had no money in its budget, however, to pay salaries of SDC members, averaging about $8.60 per man per month. If the United States were to assume this expense, it would mean a total US expenditure of no more than $6.172 million a year. General Williams stated that, if the United States did not support the SDC, he believed President Diem would nevertheless proceed to build it. He already had some units in being and felt that the SDC was needed to give the villagers the assurance of government protection which was vital to the active popular support of the government in its fight with the Viet Cong.[55]

Following this explanation by Chief, MAAG, and with concurrence by the Country Team, the United States agreed to support a 60,000-man SDC by allocating to the GVN $6.2 million per year for the purpose of paying salaries of the members.[56]

Development of a New Policy Statement

Given the changed and apparently improved situation of South Vietnam by the spring of 1956, the United States undertook the formulation of a new policy statement for the area. Although still recognizing the danger of internal subversion, US Government officials in the course of this policy formulation gave increased emphasis to the threat of external attack against South Vietnam. In devising a

131

new national policy, however, US planners had to consider not only conditions in Vietnam but also the global policies of the US Government. Prominent among US global problems were the thorny issues of the US response to local aggression generally and the US role in limited war. In the latest revision of basic national security policy (NSC 5602/1), the NSC in March 1956 had touched upon these problems in the following language:

> Within the total U.S. military forces there must be included ready forces which, with such help as may realistically be expected from allied forces, are adequate (a) to present a deterrent to any resort to local aggression, and (b) to defeat or hold, in conjunction with indigenous forces, any such local aggression, pending the application of such additional U.S. and allied power as may be required to suppress quickly the local aggression in a manner and on a scale best calculated to avoid the hostilities broadening into general war. Such ready forces must be sufficiently versatile to use both conventional and nuclear weapons. They must be highly mobile and suitably deployed, recognizing that some degree of maldeployment from the viewpoint of general war must be accepted. Such forces must not become so dependent on tactical nuclear capabilities that any decision to intervene against local aggression would probably be tantamount to a decision to use nuclear weapons. However, these forces must also have a flexible and selective nuclear capability, since the United States will not preclude itself from using nuclear weapons even in a local situation.[57]

Almost concurrently with the adoption of NSC 5602/1, the NSC asked the Department of Defense to produce a study in connection with a new statement of policy on Southeast Asia. The Secretary of Defense assigned the Joint Chiefs of Staff responsibility for this study—which was to include estimates of the capability of US forces, with and without nuclear weapons, to deal with local aggression in Vietnam.[58]

Based on the policy outlined in NSC 5602/1, the JCS concept of how to deal with Viet Minh aggression was the subject of an oral presentation made to the NSC by the Chairman, Joint Chiefs of Staff, on 7 June. The Chairman told the NSC that success in halting and repelling a Viet Minh attack depended on prompt and decisive intervention by US mobile forces. Some US support would have to be provided in a matter of hours, and certain essential units would have to be in place within a few days at most. While the VNA fought a delaying action from the 17th parallel to the hill mass around Tourane, the United States would deploy to Vietnam a fast carrier task force; fighter-bomber, interceptor, and transport units totaling two wings and five squadrons, and an Army regimental combat team. The RCT would go ashore at Tourane. As soon as possible, two more RCTs (or Marine regimental landing teams (RLTs)) would be put ashore at Saigon and Cam Ranh Bay.

Most of the fighting would be done by Vietnamese ground forces supported by US air and naval forces. United States ground forces would be provided mainly to help hold vital areas of South Vietnam; and US officers would act as advisers to the VNA. Operations, however, would be conducted under the banner of SEATO. Admiral Radford stressed the importance of vigorously seeking and widely publicizing the support of SEATO nations, even though their contributions would be small. In fact, a combined SEATO command would direct operations designed to check the Viet Minh units at Tourane and ultimately drive them back across the 17th parallel. Depending on circumstances at this juncture, the decision would be made whether or not to occupy North Vietnam.

The US forces would be equipped with nuclear weapons, but according to Admiral Radford, probably would not use them. There were no known military targets in North Vietnam that could not be destroyed by conventional bombing. Only if the Viet Minh concentrated its forces would there be military justification for nuclear warfare. If the Chinese Communists entered the war, however, the situation would be quickly and radically altered. In this event, nuclear weapons would be employed against Chinese air and logistical bases at once.[59]

After NSC discussion of Admiral Radford's presentation, on 7 June the President directed US military authorities to encourage Vietnamese military planning for defense against external aggression along lines consistent with approved US policy and to manifest "in other ways" US interest in assisting Vietnam to defend itself against external attack in accordance with the Manila Pact. The Secretary of Defense assigned this responsibility to the Joint Chiefs of Staff who delegated it to CINCPAC, directing him to prepare a contingency plan for US participation in countering Viet Minh aggression using the military concept contained in the Chairman's presentation. In this directive, the Joint Chiefs emphasized the importance they attached to primary reliance on indigenous ground forces and to the necessity of prompt arrival of US supporting forces.[60]

Following its review of US global policy and of the situation in Southeast Asia in the summer of 1956, the NSC Planning Board published a draft statement of US policy (NSC 5612) toward mainland Southeast Asia. It was intended to supersede NSC 5405 and that portion of NSC 5429/5 covering Indochina and Thailand. The JCS considered the document and informed the Secretary of Defense on 24 August that they found it acceptable from the military point of view subject to several changes. With one exception, the suggested changes were minor. This exception dealt with action in the event of overt communist aggression. The Joint Chiefs advocated advance Congressional authority for the employment of US forces against such aggression rather than waiting until the aggression actually occurred. The NSC did not accept this change, and the draft policy was adopted by the Council on 30 August without substantial revision and approved by the President a week later. The statement, circulated as NSC 5612/1, contained the following guideline for US policy in Vietnam:

> Assist Free Viet Nam to develop a strong, stable and constitutional government to enable Free Viet Nam to assert an increasingly attractive contrast to conditions in the present Communist zone.
> Work toward the weakening of the Communists in North and South Viet Nam in order to bring about the eventual peaceful reunification of a free and

independent Viet Nam under anti-Communist leadership.

Support the position of the Government of Free Viet Nam and all-Viet Nam elections may take place only after it is satisfied that genuinely free elections can be held throughout both zones of Viet Nam.

Assist Free Viet Nam to build up indigenous armed forces, including independent logistical and administrative services, which will be capable of assuring internal security and of providing limited initial resistance to attack by the Viet Minh.[61]

Encourage Vietnamese military planning for defense against external aggression along lines consistent with U.S. planning concepts based upon approved U.S. policy and discretely manifest in other ways U.S. interest in assisting Free Viet Nam, in accordance with the SEATO Treaty, to defend itself against external aggression.[62]

On the same day that the NSC adopted NSC 5612/1, it also revised the paragraph (5-d) of NSC 5429/5 governing US action in the event of aggression in Southeast Asia, the language of which had been somewhat vague. Since NSC 5612/1 contained a more precise statement of US action to meet local aggression in Southeast Asia, the NSC replaced the vague paragraph in NSC 5429/5 with the language of NSC 5612/1. This paragraph provided:

Should overt Communist aggression occur in the Southeast Asia treaty area, invoke the UN Charter or the SEATO treaty, or both, and subject to local request for assistance take necessary military and any other action to assist any state or dependent territory in the SEATO area willing to resist Communist resort to force: Provided, that the taking of military action shall be subject to prior submission and approval by the Congress unless the emergency is deemed by the President to be so great that immediate action is necessary to save a vital interest of the United States.[63]

During the summer of 1956 CINCPAC was keeping pace with the planners in Washington. As directed by the Joint Chiefs of Staff, he submitted on 1 October OPLAN 46-56, a plan for countering overt Viet Cong aggression in Southeast Asia. OPLAN 46-56 was designed to stop communist aggression against South Vietnam as near as possible to the 17th parallel. The salient aspect of the plan was its primary dependence on the Vietnamese forces to defeat the Viet Cong and the "timely application" of US forces. In consonance with Admiral Radford's concept, the plan provided for a US contribution consisting primarily of conventional attacks on selected targets by US air and naval forces and support of VNA forces by US ground forces numbering approximately 12,000 men, including one RCT in Vietnam on D-Day plus 3, one HONEST JOHN Battalion, and 1,200 additional military advisers. One RCT would be held in reserve. Finding the plan in agreement with their guidance, the Joint Chiefs approved it on 19 March 1957.[64]

These statements of policy and military planning were a codification of policies that had been devised and carried out in the two years since approval of NSC 5429/5, the last general statement of US policy toward the Far East, rather than a change in US policy. In August 1954, the outlook in Vietnam had been very bleak. By August 1956, however, the progress made in restoring security and stability to Vietnam and in strengthening the GVN armed forces appeared to vindicate US policy. Moreover, the prospects for the future were hopeful. Even as the NSC adopted the new policy statement on Vietnam, the fledgling National Assembly sitting in Saigon was putting the finishing touches on the first constitution of the Republic of Vietnam. The South Vietnamese were successfully avoiding the elections called for in the Final Declaration of the Geneva Conference; the Vietnamese economy was beginning a period of rapid recovery; and the GVN military forces were "shaping up." At the same time there were signs that the Viet Cong (VC) were losing the support and sympathy of the population. The GVN, it seemed, could face the future with some confidence.

8

South Vietnam, 1957–1959

The years 1957–1959 brought a period of apparent calm to South Vietnam. The government of President Ngo Dinh Diem made further progress in economic development and in strengthening the armed forces. Although Diem's authoritarianism became more and more manifest, no crisis arose during the period to challenge his regime or to stir the United States to undertake a thorough examination of the Vietnamese situation.

The United States government viewed the progress in South Vietnam with enthusiasm. To its policymakers, the stability of 1957 as compared with the chaos of 1954 represented a significant achievement, and the United States was content to continue the policies that had been largely responsible for this progress. Evidence of US satisfaction is found in the fact that the NSC policy on Vietnam, developed in 1956, remained unchanged through 1960.[1]

The Deputy Assistant Secretary of State for Far Eastern Economic Affairs, Howard P. Jones, voiced the optimism that the United States felt toward the situation in Vietnam when he stated on 19 January 1957:

> In Vietnam, even so recently as a year and a half ago, the newly independent government was fighting against tremendous odds for its existence. It was faced with a military and subversive threat from Communist forces north of the 17th parallel; it was confronted by internal strife. Today we find a firmly entrenched nationalistic government under the leadership of President Diem. This government has proved its capacity to survive in the face of Communist external pressure and subversive efforts and at the same time to assume the responsibilities of independence and representative government.[2]

An Operations Coordinating Board progress report on US policy in mainland Southeast Asia, covering the period 5 September 1956 through 13 March 1957, presented a similarly sanguine picture. The report stated that the promulgation of the constitution and the convening of a national assembly emphasized the progress in achieving US objectives in Vietnam. The report added that Vietnam had a "stable free government" and there was "no likelihood that the Republic of Vietnam will pass into or become economically dependent on the communist bloc." Vietnam, the report said, seemed "clearly persuaded that its interests lie in greater cooperation and stronger affiliation with the free world." The OCB also reported progress in the training of the Vietnamese armed forces and in the economic aid programs in Vietnam but warned of several "operating problems or difficulties" facing the United States. South Vietnam continued to face the threat of North Vietnamese aggression and subversion; a budget deficit, a balance of payment gap, and inflation still plagued South Vietnamese economy; and much needed agrarian reform was proceeding extremely slowly.[3]

President Eisenhower in the spring of 1957 joined in the expressions of satisfaction that the United States found with the progress in Vietnam. On May 11 he and President Diem issued a joint statement at the conclusion of a visit by the latter to Washington. In the joint statement, President Eisenhower complimented Diem on the "remarkable achievements" of the RVN since 1954. The joint statement noted that in less than three years a chaotic situation resulting from years of war had been changed into one of "progress and stability" and listed the following achievements of the South Vietnamese Government:

> Nearly one million refugees who had fled from Communist tyranny in North Vietnam had been cared for and resettled in Free Vietnam.
> Internal security had been effectively established.
> A constitution had been promulgated and a national assembly elected.
> Plans for agrarian reform have been launched, and a constructive program developed to meet long-range economic and social problems to promote higher living standards for the Vietnamese people.[4]

This US optimism concerning Vietnam prevailed throughout the years 1957–1959. The OCB progress reports for the remainder of 1957 and 1958 continued to find advances in the development of a representative government. Evidences of this progress were seen in the National Assembly's approval of a national budget, the first ever submitted to a constitutionally elected body in Vietnam, and in President Diem's official visits to the United States, Thailand, Australia, and the Republic of Korea, enhancing both his personal prestige and that of his country.[5]

The Vietnamese armed forces also improved significantly. In August 1957, CINCPAC reported to Washington that the Vietnamese Army had shown "remarkable improvement" during the past year, particularly in logistics and administration, and CINCPAC expected this progress to continue and to extend to the Navy and the Air Force.[6]

Despite the overall tone of optimism, the OCB reports cited several problem areas confronting South Vietnam. Although the government had neutralized communist capabilities for "armed resistance," the threat of "political infiltration and nonviolent subversion" remained. This threat precluded any reduction of forces and presented the United States with the prospect of continued heavy military support costs. The economic situation in Vietnam, while improved, was still far from stable. Vietnam continued to depend on foreign aid, the largest part going to support the military establishment. United States aid counted for approximately 85 percent of imports and two-thirds of the budgetary revenues. The government's agrarian reform program had begun to pick up speed but was still not moving satisfactorily.[7]

In 1958, the OCB reported a new problem facing the United States in Vietnam. President Diem's policy of strict control in the political and economic fields had caused "a certain amount of internal dissatisfaction." Should Diem's exercise of personal authority develop too far, the OCB cautions, there was a danger that "the resultant frustration of government officials might weaken the united support for his regime.... The OCB also noted that Diem's "stern police measures and his emphasis on internal security" had led to increasing criticism of the government.[8]

The following year the OCB reported substantial progress toward meeting US objectives in Vietnam. There was a stable government and the Vietnamese military forces had made a significant improvement under the MAAG training program. The OCB showed increasing concern, however, over the growing authoritarian tendencies of Diem. The Board warned that the Diem government's strong political controls, while seemingly necessary because of the internal security threat, were antagonizing certain elements of the Vietnamese population. Although US action to meet this problem was restricted by the sensitivity of the matter, the OCB suggested that the United States Ambassador might make "discreet suggestions" from time to time for some liberalization of Diem's political control.[9]

During the period 1957–1959, the OCB issued several operations plans for Vietnam outlining detailed courses of action to carry out the provisions of the NSC policy. All of these plans stressed the special importance of Vietnam to the United States because of its "exposed position as an outpost of the free world face-to-face with a powerful and threatening communist regime occupying part of its territory" and because Vietnam was the principal country in the area where a free government and a communist regime completed directly for the same territory and a whole nation. The United States, the plans stated, had made such a substantial investment in Vietnam's independence, and with such success, that the most determined efforts were justified to preserve the integrity and strengthen the position of the country.[10]

All the plans called for continued US support of the Government of Vietnam by diplomatic, military, economic, and psychological means. To accomplish the US objectives, primary reliance was placed on continued economic, technical, and military assistance programs. Military assistance was to be primarily in the form of "adequate support" to the Vietnamese military budget, the provision of US equipment to the Vietnamese armed forces, and the training of Vietnamese military personnel at schools of the US armed forces or at US-staffed schools in Vietnam.[11]

Statistics on US aid to South Vietnam for the years 1957–1959 reveal how these plans were translated into financial support:[12]

US Aid to South Vietnam
(in millions)

	1957	1958	1959
Economic	$281.1	$188.8	$207.1
Military	110.5	53.2	41.9
Total	$391.6	$242.0	$249.0

Throughout the period of US economic aid remained the major category of US assistance to Vietnam. In NSC 5429/2, the earliest statement of US policy toward South Vietnam, the United States had committed itself to help South Vietnam, along with Laos and Cambodia, to maintain "economic conditions conducive to the maintenance and strength of non-Communist regimes," in order that these states might "compare favorably with adjacent Communist areas."[13] From 1954 through 1959, the United States held to this policy, granting $1.2 billion in economic assistance to Vietnam.[14]

Economic Developments and Agrarian Reforms

As the various political and military crises of 1954–1956 subsided, Diem was able to give greater attention to outstanding economic problems. The severity of these problems was such, however, that Diem's programs, even when well advised, were only partially successful. Nevertheless, beneficial results were beginning to appear. A key element in the GVN's program was the Five Year Plan for Economic and Social Development. Initiated at the suggestion of a UN Economic Survey Mission, which visited Vietnam from November 1955 to February 1956, the Five Year Plan was drawn up for the years 1957–1961. Under the plan, 17.5 billion piasters ($500 million at the official exchange rate, approximately $286 million of which would be financed by foreign aid), were to be invested. Primary emphasis and 43 percent of the funds was given to public works and power development in accordance with the GVN's desire to establish a base for future economic growth. At the same time, in recognition of the fact that South Vietnam would continue indefinitely to be, primarily, an agricultural nation, the plan called for the allocation of 22 percent of funds to agricultural development. Twelve percent was allocated to health, education, and housing, and 9 percent to industrial expansion; 14 percent of the funds were unallocated.[15]

Among the objectives of the plan were the complete reconstruction of the existing road and railway systems and the start of construction on 1,000 kilometers of new roads. In addition, new factories would be built for the production of textiles, cement, shoes, tires, glass, and paper. Coal production was expected to keep pace with the increased demands for power that these plans would make. Agricultural development was expected to result in an increase in national income from the renewed cultivation of rice on abandoned lands and increased production of sugar cane, silk, cotton, tobacco, oil seeds, and rubber. There were also livestock, forestry, and fishery programs.[16]

The Five Year Plan was put into effect without fanfare. When it was launched in 1957, the GVN denied it was an approved program, insisting instead that it was being studied. Thereafter the plan's provisions were kept secret. Only in 1961, the terminal year of the plan, did the GVN announce what projects had been undertaken and what funds had been expended under it.[17]

In the years 1957–1959, South Vietnam made modest progress toward achieving the goals of the Five Year Plan. Roads and railroads were reconstructed and textile and coal production was increased. In addition, construction was begun on the following projects: a cement plant at Ha Tien; electro-chemical industries in the Nong Son–An Hoa area; and in the Saigon area a shoe factory, two textile factories, a paper plant, a glass plant, and a Michelin tire plant.[18]

In a country where 80 percent of the people worked the land, agricultural problems were, understandably, of critical importance. It followed, therefore, that in South Vietnam, where 2 percent of the land-owners held 45 percent of the land in 1955, the government's agricultural policies had an immense social and political, as well as economic, bearing. The Indochina War had disrupted the agricultural economy and vitiated the modest gains made by earlier non-communist Vietnamese attempts at agrarian reforms. Reform programs had been initiated in 1947 and 1953, but in both periods the Viet Minh had actually controlled many of the areas where reforms were planned. The landlords had fled these areas, and the Viet Minh had taken advantage of their absence to deed the land to former sharecroppers or squatters. By 1955 the Viet Minh land program had been in effect in some areas of the south for several years. The more cautious reform programs subsequently instituted by the Diem regime, involving regulation of contracts and reimbursement for expropriated lands, seemed to many peasants reactionary or redundant.[19]

The Diem government was neither able nor willing to match the radical simplicity of the Viet Minh grants. Its first agrarian reform was a rent reduction and tenure security program initiated in early 1955. Beginning in 1956 a land transfer program expropriated large estates for resale to tenants. Additionally, the GVN inaugurated land development programs for fallow and virgin lands, an agricultural credit system, and farm cooperatives.[20]

Beginning with the "crash program" and the Collins-Ely Seven-Point Program in 1954, the United States consistently supported agrarian reform in Vietnam.[21] It provided the GVN with technical assistance in agricultural programs and paid the administrative costs of many aspects of the program; it did not, however, provide funds for the purchase of land.[22]

Progress in the agricultural program was at first slow. The landlords were reluctant to cooperate and many of the peasants remained convinced that the land was theirs by order of the Viet Minh. Also, the government program was cumbersome in its bureaucratic detail; its terms were not easy for peasants to meet, and it was often indifferently pushed by government agents.[23]

In 1957, however, the progress of the program was accelerated, owing largely to French agreement to pay one-third of the costs of land expropriated from French landlords. According to an OCB report, by November 1957 the GVN had already set aside about half the total amount needed for the down payments. In the meantime the United States had agreed to pay the administrative costs of the land transfers. Approximately 5 percent of the eligible holdings had been transferred. By the end of 1959, nearly 800,000 tenant farmers had signed tenure agreements with their landlords, another 118,0000 had been designated to share approximately 400,000 hectares (1,100,000 acres) purchased by the government in large estates. In the same period about 600,000 hectares (1,500,000 acres) of land abandoned during the Indochina War had been reclaimed for cultivation.[24]

The wholesome effects of the GVN's agricultural programs began to appear at the end of the decade. From 1955 through 1959 rice production nearly doubled and rubber plantings and production both increased by 20 percent.[25] These gains were largely absorbed, however, by increased domestic consumption. In the period before the sharp escalation of Viet Cong activity brought Diem's agricultural programs to a virtual standstill, neither of these two principal crops became available for export in sufficient quantities to reduce appreciably Vietnam's adverse balance of trade.[26]

From the very inception of the GVN's efforts at economic reforms, the design and implementation of the reforms were subjected to severe criticism; so too was the US economic assistance on which these reforms were based. Criticism of the US aid program in Vietnam generally centered on the charge that the Vietnamese had become overly dependent economically and politically upon the aid program, and that they were becoming "permanent mendicants."[27]

Perhaps the most telling commentary on the GVN's economic progress was made by the Senate Foreign Relations Subcommittee headed by Senator Mike Mansfield in February 1960. After acknowledging the "tremendous achievements" of the Diem regime over the past five years, the Mansfield subcommittee puzzled over the "inescapable fact" that "there had not been any significant reduction in Vietnamese economic dependency on large aid grants from the United States, except those which coincide with Congressional reduction in appropriations for the Mutual Security Act."[28]

Critics of the US aid program also charged that the United States insisted too much on private investment in development projects. Among those criticizing this facet of US aid was Diem himself. The gist of the argument was that many potential investors feared to invest in the existing atmosphere of insecurity; only participation by the state would persuade them to risk their capital. "A more pragmatic American attitude in foreign aid policy would," such critics held, "help to make South Vietnam less dependent on foreign aid."[29]

Nevertheless, few denied that economic progress was being made. In May 1959, NIE 63-59 stated that "South Vietnam has made only limited progress toward basic long-term economic developments in the five years since Independence." But, after explaining how the lack of internal security hampered economic progress, the NIE went on to cite the repaired transportation network, land reform and development program, and the modest industrial development as proof that "South Vietnam is making some economic progress."[30]

The GVN Defense Establishment

In addition to its efforts in the economic sphere, the United States continued to work during the period 1957-1959 toward a strong, effective defense establishment for South Vietnam. This was directly in support of the national policy, expressed in NSC 5612/2, that called for assisting "Free Vietnam" to create armed forces, including independent logistic and administrative services, capable of assuring internal security and of providing "limited initial resistance" to direct attack by North Vietnam.[31]

Direct US military aid furnished South Vietnam from FY 1956 through FY 1959 from appropriated funds totaled $445.7 million. Because the major expenses were incurred in the early years owing to initial requirements for equipment and installations, costs in FY 1959 were much less than in FY 1956, the first year of direct military aid. In FY 1956, $166.8 million in appropriated US funds was given South Vietnam but only $43.8 million was given in FY 1959. During the same period the United States furnished South Vietnam a total of $50.5 million worth of material from excess stocks.[32]

Of the $1.2 billion in US economic aid furnished South Vietnam between 1954 and 1959, a significant amount was expended in defense support. This important category of aid amounted to $255 million in 1957, $174.7 million in 1958, and $177 million in 1959, for a total of $606.7 million.[33]

The RVNAF

The complex structure that had evolved in the Republic of Vietnam Armed Forces by late 1955 remained virtually unchanged. President Diem as Supreme Commander exercised his authority through a Secretary of State for National Defense, a post he occupied. He was served by an Assistant Secretary and by the Director of the Cabinet, through whom orders were transmitted to the Central Organizations (comprising the General Staff, the Inspectorate General for the Armed Forces, and various administrative and fiscal agencies), the Logistical Services, and the Ministerial Services. The Chief of the General Staff had as Deputies the commanders of the Army, Navy, and Air Force.[34]

From the beginning, President Diem had maintained a close interest in the activities of the RVNAF. He participated in all major policy decisions affecting the armed forces, personally approving, for example, all promotions of senior officers.

The ARVN

A General Staff exercised administrative direction over the Army of the Republic of Vietnam (ARVN). Although this group was actually organized and functioned as an army general staff, it supervised the activities of the small naval and air forces of South Vietnam as well. Since the ARVN represented 94 percent of the strength of the RVNAF no one objected strenuously that the General Staff was composed entirely of ARVN officers. The Chief of the General Staff, top military commander of the armed forces, was served by a Chief of Staff who also served as Deputy Chief of Staff for Army. In theory he was the ARVN commander and adviser on army affairs to the Chief of the General Staff. The US influence on the General Staff was quite apparent in its organization although certain features of the French military system had been retained by the Vietnamese.[35]

In the last half of 1957 Diem activated two corps headquarters, giving the Army its first tactical unit headquarters above division level. A third corps headquarters was established in 1959. These organizations were charged with responsibility for assigned operational areas, for planning future operations, for organizing strategic and tactical defense, for training of assigned or attached units, for organizing maneuvers, and for administering organic units. Because of US influence, it was believed that a corps concept very similar to that of the US Army would eventually emerge, with the organization of the corps depending on their particular missions.[36]

On 31 December 1958, President Diem issued a decree creating an ARVN field command. This command was responsible for coordination of the training of all combat units in peacetime and for the direction of combat operations in time of war. This change was made because it was recognized that no individual could function effectively as both the Deputy to the Chief of Staff and as the Commander of the ARVN. This change freed the army staff to concentrate on overall army planning.[37]

The strength of the ARVN, within the overall ceiling of 150,000 for the Vietnamese armed forces that the United States had agreed to support in late 1955, fluctuated to a degree but stood at about 138,000 men and officers late in 1958, slightly below its authorized strength of 140,620. The principal elements of the ARVN at the beginning of 1959 were a central command, two corps headquarters with corps troops, six military region headquarters, 4 field divisions (8,100 men each), 6 light divisions (5,800 men each), 1 airborne group (4,000 men), and various combat and service support units.[38]

Increasingly, throughout this period, internal security duties were turned over to the paramilitary forces, so that the ARVN could, under the guidance of the MAAG, devote more time to training and organizational improvement. Training of the ARVN progressed more readily in the period 1957–1959 than in earlier years. Plans for training drawn up by the General Staff with the advice of the MAAG resembled US Army training plans. The 25-week training cycle was increased to 32 weeks and divided into six phases, starting with basic infantry training and proceeding progressively through division maneuvers during the last two weeks. A longer, 52-week cycle, initiated upon completion of the shorter cycle, continued the training begun in the 32-week course, providing additional general training and advanced unit training. By June 1958 three of the field divisions, two of the light divisions and the airborne group had completed the 32-week cycle and were in the 52-week cycle. The remaining divisions were in the shorter cycle at varying phases.[39]

Strength of Vietnamese Armed Forces

Date	Army	Navy	Air Forces	Totals
1 Jan 54	200,000	1,522	3,434 (57 pilots)	204,956
1 Jan 55	170,000	1,522	3,434	174,956
1 Jan 56	152,000	4,182	3,336 (103 pilots)	159,518
1 Jan 57	138,481	4,818	4,164	147,463
1 Jul 57	133,016	4,721	4,067	141,804
1 Oct 57	129,982	4,800	4,035	138,817
1 Jan 58	131,343	4,870	4,025 (136 pilots)	140,238
1 Apr 58	134,640	4,892	4,082	143,614
1 Jul 58	136,641	5,152	4,271	146,064
1 Oct 58	138,165	5,100	4,590	147,855

President Diem and all of his principal assistants supported a program of developing an ARVN trained by US advisers and modeled along US lines. He had made English language instruction mandatory for all officers to enable US advisers to communicate with them more readily and to facilitate their attendance at US schools and training installations. Basic US Army field and technical manuals had been translated into Vietnamese to widen the dissemination of US tactical principles and training procedures among ARVN personnel.[40]

JCS and the Prelude to the War in Vietnam 1954–1959

Nevertheless, during the period 1957–1959, the lack of qualified officers remained a serious problem. In mid-1958, despite the fact that 2,766 officers were being held beyond their normal date of termination of service, the armed services were short 1,491 officers. Most senior officers were comparatively young, the average age of corps and division commanders in 1958 being only 35. These officers had no experience in handling regimental or larger units in combat, and most had received their training under French tutelage. Consequently, key ARVN officers were being sent by the United States to the US Army Command and General Staff College to acquaint them with US military doctrine.[41]

The principal source of regular officers remained the Military Academy at Dalat, which was changed from a one-year to a four-year school. The Officers Candidate School at Thu Duc provided a six-month course for about 400 students. Graduates were not commissioned immediately but had to serve six months in units before becoming eligible for commission. Graduating classes at Dalat and Thu Duc were too small—the Military Academy, particularly, had difficulty in securing qualified candidates. The Vietnamese Command and General Staff College, whose staff was made up largely of Vietnamese graduates of the US Army Command and General Staff College, offered a five-month staff officer course and ten-month course for field grade offices; but it too had difficulty in obtaining qualified candidates.[42]

The United States also paid for an overseas training program for Vietnamese military students. Between 1 July 1954 and 1 July 1958, 2,037 Vietnamese Army personnel were sent to schools in the United States. Two hundred sixty-one were sent to US-operated military schools outside the United States. Others were sent on general orientation and observer training visits. Ordnance, signal, and engineer technicians were sent to the Philippines for training.[43]

The ARVN was equipped almost entirely with US World War II weapons and vehicles. Most of the infantry weapons and artillery had been used in the Indochina War and by 1959 were, understandably, in poor condition. The GVN had no facilities for production of ordnance material of its own. The ARVN, furthermore, continued to be unable to maintain its ordnance properly. It had too few personnel trained in maintenance. Tools and spare parts were scarce and the ARVN supply distribution and transportation systems were inadequate. The typical Vietnamese soldier had only limited technical knowledge and little appreciation of the need for preventive maintenance. The MAAG, in efforts to remedy these deficiencies, supervised an intensive training program which included the employment of US Mobile Training Teams and contract civilian technicians from the United States and the Philippines, and the training of Vietnamese abroad. Unserviceable vehicles were still shipped to the US Army rebuild facility in Japan.[44]

By early 1957 it had become clear that to build and sustain a truly professional army the GVN must establish a system for conscription. Consequently, on 2 May 1957, Diem instituted a draft. A new law established compulsory 12-month tours of service, with four months of training and eight months with an active unit, for all males 20 and 21 years of age. Conscription began on 1 August 1957 and averaged 480 inductions per week for the reminder of the year; in 1958 inductions reached 720 per week. In March 1958 the GVN set up, under the President, a Permanent Secretariat General of National Defense to plan and supervise mobilization programs. In 1959 the period of service for draftees was extended to 18 months in order to provide more thorough training.[45]

The ARVN divisions, both the field division of 8,100 men and the light division of 5,800 men, were generally considered by US military men to be deficient in firepower, although sufficiently mobile. A test of a larger type division in the summer of 1958 resulted in approval by Army General Headquarters on 1 December 1958 of a new division organization comprising 10,000 men and closely resembling that of a US division. The objective of this revised structure was to achieve organizational standardization and facilitate more economical and efficient employment over the varied terrain of South Vietnam. Additional infantry and engineer troops were added, as well as a 4.2-inch mortar battalion. A program for converting both field and light divisions to the new organization was begun in 1959.[46]

From 1955 to 1958 MAAG and Washington survey teams pressed financial reforms on the GVN and succeeded in bringing about considerable savings in military expenditures. MAAG also advised the GVN on fiscal and budgetary procedures, and the MAAG Comptroller Advisers Group worked closely with Vietnamese specialists in pay and disbursing functions, internal audit, and budgeting. The following table reveals that in a three-year period dollar savings of 84 million were achieved, and that the average cost per man per year in the ARVN declined from $1,320 in 1955 to $1,144 in 1958.[47]

Budget Status 1955–1958
(in millions)

	1955	1956	1957	1958
Vietnam Request	303.0	336.6	233.9	222.4
Approved Budget	286.0	198.4	187.8	171.6
Vietnam Contribution	79.8	20.0	25.0	27.3
US Contribution	125.4	174.3	161.2	144.3
Savings	62.3	4.3	1.4	0.0
Average Paid Strength	169,442	152,077	143,649	150,000
Average Cost Per Man Per Year	$1,320	$1,277	$1,296	$1,144

The VNAF

The air arm of the GVN defense establishment, although administered by the Commander, VNAF, was under actual operational control of President Diem in his post of Secretary of State for National Defense. The mission of the VNAF was to provide air support for the ARVN, including transport, liaison, reconnaissance, evacuation, and air-ground support. From 1955 to 1959, however, it was primarily a training force, and its military capabilities were extremely limited.[48]

Until mid-1957 the VNAF was trained and supported logistically by the French. Upon the withdrawal of French Air force units, the US MAAG assumed both training and logistic responsibility. The VNAF had a total strength in January 1959 of 4,590, of whom 324 were officers. It possessed 148 planes (25 F8F/RF8Fs, 35 C–47s, 10 H–19s, 56 L–19s, 18 AT–6s, 1 Morane-Saulnier 500, 2 C–45s, and 1 Aero Commander) and was organized into a transport group, two liaison squadrons, a composite squadron, a training squadron, and a VIP squadron.[49]

The United States, during 1958 and 1959, gave formal training to VNAF personnel in flying, navigation, electronics, communications, and maintenance at an Air training School in Nha Trang and at base schools at the large fields of Bien Hoa and Tan Son Nhut. Other students were trained in the United States and with USAF units in the Far East. A total of about 375 VNAF personnel were undergoing these various types of training on 30 June 1958. The United States had set an authorized goal of 208 pilots for the VNAF, to be attained by 1963.[50]

The VNN

As in the case of the VNAF, Vietnamese naval forces were trained and supported by the French until mid-1957. As a result, French influence on doctrine and tactics of the VNN was strong. In April 1958, a reorganization of the VNN, based on plans prepared with the assistance of the MAAG, was effected. Under this reorganization the structure of the VNN provided for a Naval Staff of three divisions—Administration, Operations, and Logistics. This staff served the Naval Deputy to the Chief of the General Staff of the Vietnamese Armed Forces. Five commands were established: Naval, Stations and Schools; Naval Supply Center, Saigon; Marine Corps; Sea Forces; and River Forces.[51]

The mission of the VNN was to patrol the coast to interdict junk traffic, to support ground forces, and to mount amphibious landings. United States officials judged the VNN in 1959 to be capable of this mission, including the mounting of a battalion-sized amphibious landing. An important additional function of the VNN was patrolling inland waters. The VNN had proven effective in the Mekong Delta area, using French-developed river warfare techniques against dissident elements.

Training of the VNN in 1959 was progressing at a satisfactory rate, with all training ashore concentrated at the Naval School at Nha Trang. United States Navy advisers served at the school, but the Vietnamese, most of them trained in US schools, performed the actual instruction. Marine Corps training had, until 1959, been generally poor but the arrival of US Marine Corps advisers and the continuing training of Vietnamese marines at US Marine Corps schools promised considerable improvement. The VNN had about 5,100 men and officers, of whom 3,600 were general service and 1,500 were marines. The vessels of the VNN were 7 US submarine chasers, 3 coastal minesweepers, 18 amphibious vessels, and 23 service craft.[52]

Assessment of RVNAF

Throughout the years 1957–1959, US military personnel in South Vietnam were optimistic about the progress made in training and equipping the RVNAF. During this period MAAG quarterly reports, TERM reports, and MAAG country statements all relayed to Washington encouraging assessments of substantial improvements in the readiness and effectiveness of the RVNAF and predicted that these advances would continue. Whereas, in 1955 and 1956, CHMAAG had estimated that the South Vietnamese armed forces could have maintained only limited internal security and would have been unable to retard or delay external aggression without "considerable outside assistance," he noted gradual improvement in 1957, and in mid-1958 he reported that the combat posture of the RVNAF had improved "notably" in the past year. He now considered the RVNAF capable of maintaining internal security as well as containing any minor enemy penetration across the national borders and delaying a full-scale NVN invasion for a week to a week and a half. In addition, he predicted that the RVNAF could hold the Tourane (Nha Trang) base area for another three to four weeks while at the same time maintaining control of key communication centers in the plateau and coastal areas of central Vietnam against enemy guerrilla and infiltrated forces.[53]

While most of this strengthened posture was due to improvements in the ARVN, MAAG Vietnam also cited advances for the VNN and VNAF in the years 1957 through 1959. When MAAG assumed responsibility for the training of the VNN in mid-1957, it was capable only of protecting inland waterways of the southern delta area and could not provide adequate coastal patrol. But by 1959, the VNN could conduct "moderately effective" coastal patrol as well as protecting inland waterways.[54]

The VNAF in the period 1957–1959 was primarily a training force, and in 1959, its combat experience was still extremely limited. The MAAG reports throughout the period maintained that the VNAF was progressing as well as could be expected of an organization of its age and experience.[55]

Another area where US military personnel reported significant advancement was the RVNAF logistical system. In 1957, MAAG found the system incapable of supporting the RVNAF in a wartime operation. This stemmed from the lack of trained personnel in all phases of supply and maintenance and inadequate transportation and supply distribution systems. Throughout the remainder of 1957 and in 1958 and 1959, MAAG reported continuing progress in the development of the RVNAF logistical capabilities. United States advisers and technicians stressed US methods and procedures with particular emphasis in the fields of maintenance, and off-shore and on-the-job training were accelerated.[56]

Officials in Washington were, in varying degrees, encouraged by the improvements of the RVNAF. Operations Coordinating Board progress reports between 1957 and 1959 all noted the enhanced military posture of South Vietnam. In January 1959, the Joint Chiefs of Staff informed the Secretary of Defense that the armed forces of South Vietnam were capable of maintaining internal security and of containing minor penetrations across the national borders.[57] In early September 1959, they forwarded to the Secretary of Defense the following assessment:

> The Army is capable of maintaining internal security and providing initial resistance to a full-scale North Vietnamese Communist invasion across the 17th parallel.
> The Navy has limited capability of conducting a moderately effective coastal patrol and is capable of fulfilling its internal security mission. The Navy has been very effective in river warfare in support of Army operations against dissident elements. Coastal transport would require augmentation in wartime.
> The Marine amphibious capability is limited to the conduct of small-scale landings.
> The capability and combat readiness of the Air Force composite squadron is low. Efforts are being made to improve this capability but are limited by the provisions of the Geneva Accord. The Air Force has no appreciable air defense capability. It does, however, have a fair air transport capability in paratroop delivery, evacuation and air ground support.[58]

Several weeks earlier, the Secretary of Defense had submitted a report to the National Security Council on the status of the Military Assistance Program that was optimistic concerning Vietnam and its armed forces. The United States had, he said, developed South Vietnam into a strategic asset and, unless prepared to "dissipate a valuable resource," it had no choice but to continue support to the Vietnamese armed forces until the situation in Asia permitted a fundamental revision of strategic objectives.[59]

A subcommittee of the Senate Foreign Relations Committee stated in 1960 that:

> As a general objective the military aid program is expected to help develop Vietnamese armed forces adequate for maintaining internal security, for deterring outside aggression, and for offering initial resistance to such aggression if it is not deterred. It is not possible for the subcommittee to say that the military aid program will guarantee achievement of this general goal. But because it operates within a detailed long-range plan it is possible to conclude, at least, that progress is being made toward the creation of the kind of military establishment which those

responsible contend will guarantee the goal. Barring unforeseen developments, moreover, it is also possible to conclude, on the basis of the assurances of the head of the military aid mission in Vietnam, that at least the US Military Aid Advisory group (MAAG) can be phased out of Vietnam in the foreseeable future.[60]

Diem's Attempt at Political Unity

Improvement in the military and economic spheres was only part of the task facing South Vietnam in the late 1950s. While the GVN, with US aid, seemed to be making substantial gains in these areas, at the same time it seemed to be losing the equally vital battle for political unity. In late 1956 a change in the attitude of the Vietnamese toward their government first became discernible. Successively the people's enthusiasm for Diem gave way to tolerance, and tolerance to antipathy.[61] Some of the reasons for this trend in GVN politics lay in Diem's intolerance of political opposition, in his administrative practices, and in his suppression of civil and constitutional rights in the name of internal security.

As early as January 1957, the US Embassy in Saigon reported that Diem, "never tolerant of opposition or criticism," had become "convinced of his own infallibility" and was growing "even less responsive than heretofore to advice which contradicts his basic ideas."[62] The only advisers that Diem seemed to heed were his brothers: Ngo Dinh Nhu, whom the embassy considered "the most important and influential member of the assembly;" Ngo Dinh Thuc, Roman Catholic Archbishop of Hue; and Ngo Dinh Can, who "with no legal authority... treats Central Vietnam as his personal domain."[63] The last member of Diem's inner circle was Mme. Ngo Dinh Nhu, who served along with her husband in the National Assembly.[64]

United States concern over Diem's increasingly authoritarian tendencies grew during 1958 and 1959. Operations Coordinating Board progress reports for these years warned of mounting dissatisfaction in Vietnam over the government's strict political controls and stern police measures. The 1959 OCB Operations Plan for Vietnam suggested that the US Ambassador might, at appropriate times, press for liberalization of Diem's authoritarian controls.[65]

The Joint Chiefs of Staff also recognized that Diem's regime left something to be desired. In September 1959 they called attention to the similar positions of Diem in Vietnam, Chiang in Taiwan, and Rhee in South Korea. The study, prepared in connection with a review of US policy in the Far East, warned that:

> In the case of these three nations, U. S. policy views the heads of government as being synonymous with the government itself. They have come to power as a result of armed revolution, are firmly entrenched, and in practice their systems do not allow a change of chief executives through peaceful constitutional processes. The U. S. thus finds itself without room to maneuver

politically in dealing with these countries, since negotiations are with the chief executives whose actions may or may not be influenced by local or world public opinion.... Since the three men ... are so closely identified with U. S. interests and policies, failure to support them in the international arena, or to allow them to be overthrown violently by the opposition in their counties, would have undesirable repercussions ... throughout the world.[66]

To avoid repetitions of this embarrassing and potentially dangerous situation, the Joint Chiefs of Staff recommended that the United States in the future avoid "personal commitments" of this sort, and seek instead the "development of governmental institutions in the Far East that can survive changing chief executives with little or no disruption."[67]

Although the 1956 constitution had established republican institutions and basic political freedoms, no system of competitive political parties developed in South Vietnam. Diem imposed administrative requirements so restrictive that in practice only puppet opposition parties, such as the government-controlled Socialist Party, were able to function.[68] After 1956 the only political opposition the regime encountered came from the Free Democratic Party of Phan Quang-Dan, which announced in 1958 that it would participate in the 1959 legislative elections. The GVN rejected the party's application for certification; but Dan persisted, ran for the national assembly as an independent candidate, and was elected by the largest majority of any candidate in the Saigon area. The government reacted to Dan's successful election by prosecuting him for violation of the election laws. Dan was convicted and deprived of his assembly seat.[69]

From 1956 to 1959, Diem fashioned the Movement of National Revolution (MNR) into a potent instrument to counter political opposition. The party's program was concerned, almost exclusively, with supporting fully all the policies and actions of Diem. Great pressures were applied to persuade the people to join. In the 1959 elections, for example, party members, often recruited under economic pressure, were compelled to vote for the official candidate or suffer expulsion from the party and loss of economic and civil liberties.[70]

Given the unfamiliarity of the Vietnamese people with free political institutions, the denial of political expression was unfortunate. In the countryside incipient political awareness went unnourished, and in the cities and towns political interest and activity was stifled. Denied any opportunity to develop, the opposition by the end of the decade comprised fragmented and impotent groups of bickering, "coffee-house" politicians.

Repeatedly, during the years 1957–1959, the GVN abridged the constitutional and civil rights of its citizens in the name of internal security. For example, observers reported the existence of "Political Re-education Centers" in South Vietnam, internment camps established apparently for the "political re-education" of communists. The centers, however, bore witness to Diem's violation of civil rights, for citizens could be interned without due process and for an indefinite period.

Although the majority of the inmates of these centers were communist or communist sympathizers, reportedly some were rigid anticommunists whose only crime had been injudicious criticism of the regime.[71]

Central to the case against Diem was the charge that he had restricted the right of free press. When he took office in 1954, Diem had established mild penalties for violation of the press censorship regulations. The trend seemed to be toward greater freedom of the press, but before long Vietnamese newspapers came under close government control, ostensibly because of their sensationalism and irresponsibility. The administration also kept close watch on the foreign press to prevent "abusive attacks on the presidential family or the regime." In addition to censoring the press, GVN officials banned works of fiction that presented the government in an unflattering light.[72]

The years 1958 and 1959 saw the seizure of newspapers for having published news "likely to encourage Communism" in Vietnam, the suspension of others because of moral and financial misconduct on the part of their editors, and the arrest of reporters for alleged communist connections. So-called "popular" demonstrations against newspapers especially critical of the regime also tended to inhibit the development of a spirit of free criticism.[73]

A further example of the GVN's growing political repression was its actions against the Chinese and Montagnard minorities. Nearly ten percent of the population of South Vietnam was non-Vietnamese. The two principal ethnic minorities, the Chinese and the Montagnards, occupied positions of special importance, the one economic, the other geographic.

In 1956, South Vietnam had a population of about 650,000 Chinese, most of whom lived in the Chinese city of Cholon located within Saigon. United States policy toward the overseas Chinese had three aims: to promote anti-communism among them, to encourage them to identify themselves with local governments, and to foster sympathy and support for Nationalist China as a symbol of Chinese resistance to communism.[74] To Diem, however, the Chinese minority represented a group long favored by the French; one with an inordinate influence and, in some respects, a strangle-hold on the Vietnamese economy. Moreover, the separate culture of the Chinese, including separate schools and newspapers, was viewed by Vietnamese nationalists as an affront.[75]

On 21 August 1956, after two years of sporadic harassment, Diem launched a campaign against the Chinese by promulgating an ex post facto decree conferring automatic citizenship on all Chinese born in Vietnam. On 5 September he issued another decree restricting eleven specific occupations—in all of which many Chinese were employed—to Vietnamese citizens. At about the same time, the GVN also ordered that all teaching in the Chinese secondary schools would have to be in the Vietnamese language and with designated texts.[76]

These uncompromising decrees immediately antagonized the Chinese community and aroused its solid opposition. Within a few days the Chinese began withdrawing funds from banks and, in a short time, one-sixth of the currency in circulation had disappeared. Commercial transactions in South Vietnam came to a near standstill. Services normally performed by the Chinese, such as the milling and transport of rice were left undone. The country settled rapidly into a business slump.[77]

Almost immediately after the promulgation of the decree, Nationalist China protested to the GVN on behalf of the Chinese in Vietnam.[78] For its part, the United States counseled moderation to Diem.[79] But for both Diem and the Saigon Chinese the matter had become one of "face." The GVN stubbornly refused to modify its decrees, and the Chinese just as stubbornly refused to obey them.[80] Finally, in July 1957, impressed by now with the damage being done to the economy, the GVN ended a full year of stalemate by easing its strictures on Chinese business activities. Under threat of deportation, some Chinese resumed business under the new regulations. By 1959, the Chinese had reportedly made their accommodation with Diem; the GVN reported that by that time three-fourths of those eligible had accepted Vietnamese citizenship.[81]

The problem of the Chinese minority could not be solved so simply, however. The Chinese congregations—ethnic associations which, under the French, had exercised considerable administrative, police, and revenue control over the Chinese community—continued to be a cohesive force among the Chinese and to oppose the GVN's restrictive policies.[82]

If the Chinese disdained Vietnamese citizenship and culture, the Vietnamese were equally contemptuous of their other sizable ethnic minority, the Montagnard tribesmen. Numbering between 500,000 and 700,000, the Montagnards encompassed, one US observer stated, "every conceivable degree of economic and cultural backwardness."[83] Given to semi-nomadic patch farming, the Montagnards wandered throughout the hilly backlands of Vietnam, nearly half the country. Like the Chinese, they had received special favors from the French, who had used them as a counterweight against the Vietnamese. The GVN was naturally determined to assert its rule over the areas inhabited by the tribesmen, especially because these areas included four-fifths of the nation's land frontier.

The GVN's problem of asserting its control was made difficult by the head start its communist competitors had among the tribesmen. While the GVN for two years concentrated on establishing itself in the more populated lowlands, Viet Cong agents launched a campaign among the tribesmen to win their loyalty. Tribesmen were recruited and sent to North Vietnam for indoctrination and training. The Viet Cong allowed the Montagnards to retain their native dialects and even broadcast propaganda to the Montagnards in their local speech. The communists also pointed with pride to the autonomous regions in the north where the tribesmen's cousins allegedly lived without government interference.[84]

The GVN's program to bind the tribesmen to the central government was twofold: to educate and persuade them to become more loyal and useful citizens; and to resettle in the Montagnard areas small communities of Vietnamese from the lowlands who would serve as examples to the tribesmen and a deterrent to border infiltrators. The first purpose was served by the creation of schools for Montagnards, by demonstration programs in agricultural methods, and by a remarkable insistence that Vietnamese be polite in dealing with the mountain people. Under the latter program, some 40,000 pioneers from the lowlands had been settled in key locales in the highlands by 1959. Despite the GVN's best efforts, friction persisted between the Montagnards, who claimed that the Vietnamese sequestered their best land, and the Vietnamese who were not happy in the primitive highlands. On balance, by 1959 the GVN seemed to have made some progress in allaying the Montagnard's traditional fears, but the government's success in cultivating the tribesmen's loyalty had not yet been tested.[85]

The Insurgency in Vietnam, 1957–1959

Despite the brightened economic situation, the strengthened RVNAF, and the seemingly increased government stability, internal security in South Vietnam did not show a corresponding improvement during the period 1957–1959. At first, it did appear that the insurgency had been brought under control. In fact, however, although the first months of 1957 saw the nadir of the South Vietnamese insurgency, by mid-year the insurgency had begun a gradual upward swing that continued throughout the period.

At the beginning of the period there was good evidence that the Viet Cong were withering away under only sporadic pressure by the GVN. The refusal of the GVN to participate with North Vietnam in national elections in 1956 had signaled the failure of the communist's plan to unify Vietnam through peaceful means, and dealt a severe blow to the strength and morale of the insurgents in the south.[86] Defections became numerous: some VC cadres broke away because of disillusionment with the Hanoi regime; others because they faced another extended campaign—now apparently inevitable—after the long years of fighting. According to ARVN reports, guerrillas captured in operations throughout the south in late 1956 were poorly armed. Their weapons were frequently of local manufacture, knives and daggers often substituting for firearms. United States agencies concurred in the estimate that the VC cadres were probably not receiving regular supplies. Early in 1957 GVN officials estimated that communist military strength had dropped from approximately 10,000 in 1955 to about 1,500.[87]

Captured enemy documents indicated that the VC main preoccupation in the months following the 1956 National Assembly election was survival. In January 1957, a MAAG Intelligence Summary reported that the Viet Cong had been instructed to "lay low, reorganize, propagandize within legal limits, infiltrate government posts including the army, preach peaceful coexistence, and strengthen their cells."[88]

JCS and the Prelude to the War in Vietnam 1954–1959

During the first months of 1957, the ARVN claimed to have killed, wounded or captured large numbers of guerrillas, averaging several hundred a month.[89] For example, for December 1956 and January 1957, the ARVN reported total VC losses of 861, over one-half the currently estimated VC strength in South Vietnam. But despite these losses, the ARVN estimates of VC strength showed no appreciable decrease. MAAG surmised that the ARVN reports of VC losses represented mostly civilian sympathizers, not "hard-core" armed cadres.[90]

In mid-1957 the communists energetically set about rebuilding and revitalizing the VC political and military structure. New political and military cadres were brought in from the north, recruitment was stepped up, and VC units were assigned more men and equipment. During this reorganization the Viet Cong also significantly changed their tactics. More and more, they turned to the use of force and terror as an adjunct to political and economic subversion.[91]

In late June 1957, MAAG reported "a slight but noticeable increase" in VC activity in the southern provinces, with the formation of new units and stepped up propaganda and infiltration. In July, intelligence sources stated that North Vietnam had sent to Cambodia 30 cadres, specialists in political and military organizing, for infiltration into South Vietnam.[92]

In October 1957 President Dem reported that in the past year the communists had killed 412 persons, most of whom had been trained and experienced civilian, military, and police officials loyal to the GVN. From October through December there were approximately 70 VC armed attacks and terrorist acts and more than 50 skirmishes initiated by ARVN troops or security forces. By the end of the year a pattern had emerged. Terrorist action was rather clearly focused on three principal groups: (1) provincial, district, and village officials; (2) rural police and security personnel; (3) community and village leaders. It was discovered, for example, that in the last quarter of 1957, of the 74 acts of terrorism carried out by persons believed to be communist, 67 were perpetrated against Vietnamese falling into the groups enumerated above. Of the remaining seven, four were against ARVN intelligence personnel and three were against members of pro-GVN political groups. In this period, too, US personnel first became targets of VC violence; in October 1957 explosives placed at MAAG installations in Saigon resulted in several casualties. In the same month the US Information Service Center was bombed.[93]

The Viet Cong also undertook a concerted campaign to frighten and coerce the peasants and local officials. Farmers were forced to pay "taxes" either in the form of money or harvested crops, and travelers were often required to pay road, bridge, and river "tolls." The Viet Cong harassed local authorities, burning and robbing their homes and threatening them with assassination if they failed to reveal intelligence information or attempted to inform on VC agents or activities. Reports began to be received in Saigon that in some villages "fear of Communist retaliation has resulted in increasing reluctance on the part of the villagers to act as informants and to otherwise assist security forces."[94]

Terrorism was accompanied by a concerted propaganda campaign with the theme of "normalization" of relations between South and North Vietnam and the "reunification" of the divided nation. At the same time VC propaganda cadres called for the elimination of US "imperialist intervention," evasion of military conscription, and opposition to the GVN land reform program, which they claimed would ultimately make the peasants serfs to the Diem regime.[95]

According to US intelligence officials, the upswing in VC activity that took place in late 1957 was the result of a specific plan of the communist leadership. Meeting in Phnom Penh during October, VC leaders agreed to step up the campaign for reunification, with increased emphasis on terrorism. They hoped that the resulting disorders could be used as evidence of popular desire for reunification, and that, by engendering an atmosphere of insecurity, confidence in the GVN would be eroded.[96]

Viet Cong activity increased, though still on a relatively small scale, during 1958. United States officials did not appear overly concerned. The MAAG biweekly intelligence summaries indicated no cause for alarm, reporting there had been "no great rush" of peasants to rally to the VC cause, and adding that VC successes were confined to more remote areas where the maintenance of internal security was, at best, difficult. ARVN intelligence officers still placed the VC strength in South Vietnam at 1500, although they admitted that the figure might be as high as 2100 if the dissident Binh Xuyen, who had come under communist control, were counted. While warning that there remained "many disquieting indications of subversive strength, a US intelligence survey in July 1958 found that:

> compared with the situation prevailing in late 1954 and early 1955, when South Vietnam was an area torn with bitter conflict between contending forces and when the Saigon government's authority was challenged not only in the countryside but even within Saigon itself, the picture at present is one of relative tranquility.[97]

A MAAG intelligence summary of early spring 1958 stated that the VC overall plan of action for South Vietnam in 1958 called for development of military activities—including the creation of new units, training of additional fifth-column cadres, and increasing terrorism. The Viet Cong divided South Vietnam into two zones: the Guerrilla Zone, where they had both troops and some influence; and the Temporarily Occupied Zone, where local authorities were strong and VC influence weak. In the Guerrilla Zone, the Viet Cong planned expanded activities. These included resisting GVN troops, protecting VC bases, and wooing the people and government troops. In the Temporarily Occupied Zone, the Viet Cong hoped to develop guerrilla bases, aiming at sabotage and winning the people to their cause.[98]

In 1958 assassinations averaged about 15 per month; kidnappings were somewhat higher. Most of the victims were Vietnamese officials, but US personnel began to attract more attention from the Viet Cong. In mid-year, the Viet Cong launched a propaganda campaign designed to promote anti-Americanism in the

ARVN, especially hatred by ARVN soldiers of their US advisers. MAAG sources reported in September 1958 that communist units in South Vietnam had been instructed to: (1) impede the movement of US officers through the countryside by obstructing roads; (2) devise means of terrorizing US military instructors; (3) promote the anti-American movement in south Vietnam. But there was not yet a general call for the slaying or kidnapping of US personnel.[99]

The Viet Cong also made efforts to penetrate the lower echelons of government, the security forces, the labor unions, and political groups. For example, Vietnamese intelligence agents uncovered a communist cell in an SDC unit. The main objectives for the cell were to secure information on troop movements and security operations and to steal arms and ammunition. United States intelligence efforts were directed at government agencies and "semiofficial groups" for the purpose of gathering "intelligence on government policies and programs and on strength, deployment, and specific missions of military and security services, and whenever possible, to subvert or weaken these operations."[100]

Penetration, terror, depredation, and propaganda, though troublesome, did not threaten the continued existence of the Republic of Vietnam. The real threat lay in the growing military strength of the Viet Cong. Operating in small bands of 5 to 50 men, VC units attacked small government forces and installations. Gradually, however, these units grew larger, and their equipment improved. The motley collection of outdated arms typical of the 1955–1956 period was replaced in 1957–1958 by more modern rifles, grenades, and submachine guns. In 1958 the VC units also began to use bazookas, light machine guns, and mortars, as well as transmitting and receiving sets and powered boats.[101]

How much of the improved VC arms and equipment was from stolen or captured stocks and how much came across the borders of South Vietnam was not known. There were good indications that an increasing amount of material was entering the country by land and sea. Overland routes from North Vietnam followed a network of trails through the border areas of Laos and Cambodia, and thence into South Vietnam. Border crossings were made at places where difficult terrain and sparse population made the infiltration of small groups of men almost impossible to detect. In 1958 for the first time intelligence sources began to mention the so-called Ho Chi Minh Trail. This route was already being used "apparently... to smuggle through orders, propaganda material, funds, arms, ammunition, and supplies."[102]

With the hope of slowing the flow of men and materials into South Vietnam, the GVN deployed units to the border regions, stepped up its counter-subversive activities in these areas, and began construction of fortified posts along a portion of the Cambodian border. But given the nature of the terrain and the magnitude of the task, the results were almost predictable. The infiltration of men and material continued; indeed in the late months of 1958, and in 1959, the flow probably increased.[103]

In January 1959 President Diem informed the US Ambassador that the Viet Cong, having failed by other means, were again stepping up terrorism to intimidate the people in the countryside. The tactics being used by the Viet Cong included not only assassinations and kidnappings but increased emphasis on extortions from peasants in the form of "taxes" and "loans." The Viet Cong concentrated also on attacking equipment furnished the GVN by the United States. During the spring of 1959, VC forces damaged by machine gun fire, burning, or explosion 41 tractors, and in a particularly skillful act of sabotage blew up a valuable canal dredge that had been provided to the GVN by USOM.[104]

Unfortunately, the government's handling of the people of the countryside was inept, often alienating the local Vietnamese and making them more amenable to VC influence. South Vietnamese officials at the province and local level frequently dealt with the people using harsh and repressive methods, lessening rather than increasing public confidence in the government. United States Operations Mission officials were receiving increasingly numerous reports of extortion by police officials, arrests without cause, detention without legal proceedings, and other evidences of police malpractice and corruption. "Excesses and corruption on the part of the lower level security and provincial administrative personnel," the US Embassy reported to Washington in August 1959, "reflect adversely on the GVN and may undo much of what might be accomplished by GVN programs designed to assist the people."[105]

South Vietnam's efforts to mount coordinated, supported offensives against the Viet Cong were no more successful in 1959 than they had been in the past. Although plans were developed for such offensives, the GVN failed to provide the required strength, particularly in support forces. The ARVN seemed unable to unsnarl its red tape sufficiently to get logistic support where and when it was needed. Although Diem appointed a central authority to coordinate all internal security activities in the GVN, he neither relieved province chiefs of their authority and responsibility for internal security in their own provinces nor made them subject to the central authority.[106]

United States Embassy officials were critical of Diem's reluctance to reduce the authority of the province chiefs in the field of internal security. They believed that the effectiveness of paramilitary forces was limited by the direct control of the province chiefs of the security agencies in their provinces. It had become more and more difficult to get close cooperation among the ARVN, the CG, the SDC, and the Surete because of provincial autonomy. Without this cooperation the Viet Cong could not, in the view of US Embassy officials, be successfully stamped out.

In the late spring of 1959 US intelligence authorities estimated that the Viet Cong had an active strength of about 2,000 guerrillas, largely in small units scattered along the Cambodian border and the south coast, and in the northern plateau. There were also "several thousand" others, presently inactive, who had access to arms and would participate in guerrilla warfare if directed to do so.[107]

JCS and the Prelude to the War in Vietnam 1954–1959

Statistically, VC activity seems to have risen during 1959. A total of 239 assassinations and 344 kidnappings took place in 1959 as compared with 193 assassinations and 236 kidnappings in 1958.[108] In November 1959, however, the US Embassy reported that the internal security situation was showing some improvement but that it nevertheless remained "a serious problem." It is probable that what appeared to be a reduction in the level of VC activity actually reflected a decision by the Viet Cong to withdraw to their secure bases to reequip, regroup and retrain in preparation for the much higher level of effort that was to come. United States Embassy officials tended to attribute this slackening off to the

> increasing pressure of tougher and more effective GVN counteraction. Viet Cong forces have been reported to be pulling back and regrouping their forces, recruiting new cadres to fill their weakening ranks, and giving greater attention to protecting themselves from GVN penetration and counterintelligence activity.[109]

Proof that this was an overly optimistic analysis of VC motives was to be forthcoming shortly. Even as this moderation in insurgent actions was being noted, the leaders of North Vietnam were preparing to increase the size of their guerrilla apparatus in the south and to step up terrorist activities. This decision to increase pressure on the Diem government may have been taken as early as May 1959, at a meeting of the Lao Dong Party Central Committee. A communiqué issued from this meeting predicted that "the patriotic movement in South Vietnam will become broader and deeper day by day," and pledged that "the entire people will unite to struggle for national reunification. . . . " Pham Van Dong, the North Vietnamese Prime Minister stated in September 1959 "we will be in Saigon tomorrow" and in November told a western official that North Vietnam would "drive the Americans into the sea."[110]

The growing VC activity and the increasing terrorism in South Vietnam aroused little concern in the United States. In fact, Vietnam received scant notice from the American public during the years 1957 through 1959. The US press gave little attention to South Vietnam, and what coverage did find its way into American papers and periodicals presented, for the most part, an encouraging picture of the situation. In this period there were only three permanent resident US correspondents—a free lancer and representatives of UPI and *Time-Life*—in Saigon. From time to time special reporters were sent from the United States, and the larger US newspapers, various magazines, and the wire services had correspondents who covered all of Southeast Asia—operating out of other headquarters, such as Hong Kong—but who only occasionally visited South Vietnam.[111]

In 1957 and 1958 such magazines as *Time, Newsweek, Life, US News and World Report, America,* and *Commonweal* all published reports and articles highly favorable to Ngo Dinh Diem and his government. They presented the South Vietnamese President in such glowing terms as, "the tough miracle man of Vietnam," and, "an authentic patriot," and lauded his "courage" and "tenacity" in meeting the communist threat. These articles all noted the chaos existing in South Vietnam when Diem assumed office in 1954 and reviewed the progress he had achieved since then in creating "an independent national Government." The various articles and reports recognized that Diem still faced significant challenges, but were equally confident that he would overcome them. A recount of Diem's accomplishments of the previous three years, *Time* magazine said in mid-1957, was "a shining vindication of US foreign aid policies."[112]

Encouraging US press reports on South Vietnam continued to appear into 1959. A *New York Times* reporter, Tillman Durdin, went to South Vietnam in April 1959 and filed a series of articles praising the GVN land reform and resettlement programs. Two editorials in the *New York Times* in the spring also lauded Diem and his land reform. *Newsweek* columnist, Ernest K. Lindley, visited South Vietnam in June 1959, after an absence of four years, and wrote enthusiastically of the "striking progress" being made by that "indefatigable, invincible man, President Ngo Dinh Diem." Articles in *Business Week* and the *Wall Street Journal* during the summer of 1959 were similarly optimistic over the progress in South Vietnam.[113]

Amid this symphony of praise for Diem and his government from 1957 to 1959, only an occasional discordant note was heard. David Hotham, a British correspondent, who had spent three years in Vietnam, expressed alarm over the situation there. In two articles in 1957, one in *The Reporter* and the other in *The New Republic*, he charged that reports of success in South Vietnam were "Western propaganda" and "totally untrue." He was convinced that "Western policy in South Vietnam has gone completely off the rails, and unless it is radically changed *now*, will utterly fail in its main objectives." He stated that Diem was not a popular leader and he saw recent terrorist acts as "the red light from which the West should take warning." Bernard Fall, writing in the *Nation* in May 1958, also warned of a developing trend of terrorism in South Vietnam and of a steady deterioration of the economy. He concluded that, despite generous financial and political support by the United States, the Diem government was faced with growing insecurity in the countryside and an economic crisis that threatened to wipe out most of the progress already achieved.[114]

In 1959, a series of articles by Scripps-Howard writer, Albert M. Colegrove, alleged mismanagement of and lack of direction in the US aid program in Vietnam. These charges resulted in hearings before a subcommittee of the Senate Foreign Relations Committee, where Ambassador Elbridge Durbrow, Arthur Gardiner, Director of the US Operations Mission to Vietnam, and the MAAG Chief, Lieutenant General Samuel Williams, all testified that the Colegrove allegations were either false or distorted.[115]

In 1959, US policymakers shared the optimism over Vietnam and its future that was being expressed in the press. Ambassador Durbrow, in testimony before Congress, cited numerous accomplishments wrought by the Diem regime with US assistance. In addition to citing the road construction program and alluding to the nation's economic progress, the Ambassador contrasted the conditions in 1959 with those of five years earlier. "I need hardly tell you," he began, about the devastation and chaos that prevailed in Vietnam when President Diem took over in 1954. The Government controlled little more than the main cities and a few of the roads. Communist and armed sects controlled most of the rest. Today the opposite prevails.

The Communists must hide out in the deep forests, from where they must carry on their sporadic raids.

The Government is becoming more and more effective in curbing these terrorist acts.[116]

As already noted, the Secretary of Defense apparently agreed with Ambassador Durbrow, for a 1959 DOD report to the NSC on military assistance was lavish in its praise of South Vietnam's government:

Vietnam is now a going concern politically, a pivot of U.S. power and influence in Southeast Asia and a deterrent to Communist aggression in Southeast Asia, an effective example of American aid to a friendly regime, a symbol throughout Asia of successful defiance of a brutal Communist threat by an indigenous nationalistic government. Having averted almost certain disaster a few years ago, the U. S. now has a valuable and strategic asset in Southeast Asia.[117]

As it turned out, the progress was more apparent than real. The optimism prevailing in official quarters was based too much on surface appearances. A mere absence of crisis was not necessarily a sign of health; actually, it was a prelude to renewed disturbances of more dangerous dimensions.

Even as US leaders were congratulating the GVN and themselves for a job well done, the Viet Cong were beginning to capitalize on the extensive preparations and careful plans they had made from 1957 to 1959. After more than two years of tearing at the social, economic, and political fabric of South Vietnam, Hanoi had apparently decided that it was ready to overthrow the GVN and reunify North and South Vietnam under communist rule. At Tay Ninh in January 1960, the Viet Cong successfully attacked a regular South Vietnamese regimental command post. The Tay Ninh attack was an earnest of communist intentions and confirmation, in effect, that a new war had begun; but it was a war whose costs and consequences were and would remain unperceived for some time.

Appendix

The Evolution of the Southeast Asia Treaty Organization

The deteriorating French position in Indochina in early 1954 forced upon the United States consideration of a regional security arrangement for Southeast Asia. The basic US aim for this area was to contain communist expansion. At the beginning of 1954, NSC policy to implement this aim called for every effort to prevent France from ending the war in Indochina on terms inconsistent with US objectives. This included attempts to stiffen French resolve in Indochina as well as continued US military assistance for French forces fighting there. But the decision of the Berlin Foreign Ministers at their February meeting to include settlement of the Indochina question in the Geneva discussions, together with the decision by the US government in early April against direct intervention in Indochina, made it highly improbable that France would continue her military efforts.

In commenting for the National Security Council on ways to improve the French position in Indochina, the Joint Chiefs of Staff recommended in January 1954 that the US Government re-examine national strategy toward Indochina, with a view to developing a collective effort in Southeast Asia to counter communism on a regional basis. During February and March the situation in Indochina grew more alarming. The Viet Minh launched their assault on the exposed French position at Dien Bien Phu during the night 13–14 March, capturing two French redoubts within two days, and on 4 April, the French Government put forth a "frantic and belated" request for US intervention.[1]

The US decision to proceed with the formation of a regional coalition in Southeast Asia was made during consideration of this appeal for direct US intervention in Indochina. The National Security Council met on 6 April to consider the French request. The council, however, postponed a decision on intervention and focused, instead, on a proposal for a Southeast Asian coalition. There was some belief that the existence of such an alliance would so strengthen the West's position at the forthcoming Geneva Conference that intervention would become unnecessary. It was also believed that, even should Indochina be lost to the free world, a coalition would increase the political strength of the other noncommunist nations in Southeast Asia. In the end, the council directed US efforts prior to Geneva toward organizing an alliance composed initially of ten nations—the United Kingdom, France,

Vietnam, Cambodia, Laos, Australia, New Zealand, Thailand, the Philippines, and the United States.

Joint Chiefs of Staff support of this position was evident in their views concerning US policy toward the Far East submitted to the Secretary of Defense on 9 April 1954. They advised the Secretary that US policy should be directed toward developing the "purpose and capability" of the non-communist countries of the Far East to act collectively in opposing communism with the "eventual" establishment of a comprehensive regional security arrangement among these noncommunist countries in association with the United States, the United Kingdom, and possibly France.[2]

The United States immediately sounded out its major allies to see if they would be willing to participate in an alliance as envisioned by the National Security Council. Secretary Dulles flew to Europe, conferring first with British Foreign Secretary Eden and then French Foreign Minister Bidault. Secretaries Dulles and Eden agreed that their two countries were "ready to take part, with the other countries principally concerned, in an examination of the possibility of establishing a collective defense, within the framework of the charter of the United Nations, to assure peace, security and freedom of Southeast Asia and the Western Pacific." Secretary Dulles obtained a similar commitment from Foreign Minister Bidault.[3]

The Secretary of State returned to Washington convinced that the loss of Southeast Asia could be prevented "if the free nations having vital interests in the area are united in a determination to preserve peace and freedom in the area." But, scarcely had Mr. Dulles arrived home when Britain hedged on her agreement, claiming that Commonwealth politics dictated the change in policy. As the Colombo Powers, including Commonwealth members India, Pakistan, and Ceylon, were scheduled to meet on 26 April, Mr. Eden explained that it would be "most undesirable" for Britain to give any public indication of membership in a program of collective action until the conclusion of the Colombo Conference. In addition, Mr. Eden felt that the establishment of a working group of the ten nations that did not include India, Pakistan and Ceylon would produce criticism that would be "most unhelpful" at Geneva.[4] The British postponement of any consideration of a Southeast Asian coalition until the conclusion of the Colombo Conference dashed any chance for the establishment of an alliance prior to the Geneva Conference.

Upon his return to Washington after the first phase of the Geneva Conference, Secretary Dulles again raised the possibility of a Southeast Asian alliance. He told a news conference on 25 May that the US position toward collective security in Southeast Asia had long been known, adding that the United States was prepared to participate in such an arrangement under the terms of the Vandenburg Resolution of June 1948—i.e., progressive development of regional collective arrangements for individual and collective self-defense in accordance with the purposes, principles, and provisions of the UN Charter. The United States was not prepared, Secretary Dulles said, to go to the defense of colonialism but was going to go to the defense of liberty, independence, and freedom. "We don't go alone," he concluded, "we go in where the other nations which have an important stake in the area recognize the peril as we do."[5]

In June 1954, Prime Minister Churchill and Foreign Secretary Eden traveled to Washington to meet with President Eisenhower and Secretary Dulles. The visit resulted in a British-US agreement to "press forward with plans for collective defense" in Southeast Asia regardless of the outcome of the Geneva Conference. Immediately after this meeting the two governments established a Joint Study Group on Southeast Asia in Washington. Under Secretary of State Walter Bedell Smith headed the US membership, which included OASD(ISA) representation but none from the JCS.[6]

This Joint Study Group held six meetings during July and worked out draft provisions of a collective defense treaty for Southeast Asia. The conclusion of the Geneva Conference, with the signing of the Agreements on Vietnam, Laos, and Cambodia on 20 July 1954, gave increased impetus to the project.[7]

During the course of the Study Group meetings, there was some disagreement between the two nations over the membership of the proposed alliance, especially over the role of the Colombo Powers—India, Burma, Ceylon, Pakistan, and Indonesia. British representatives believed that the cooperation of these nations was indispensable. The US Government, on the other hand, insisted that, if the treaty were made dependent on the favorable attitude of the Colombo nations, it would be delayed indefinitely. To support its argument, the United States Government cited the denunciations by both India and Indonesia of a proposed treaty. Indian Prime Minister Nehru had, in fact, predicted that such a treaty would reverse the conciliatory trend of the Indochina settlement, adding that the proposed treaty would give protection to countries that did not want it. In the end, Pakistan alone among the Colombo nations agreed to participate in a conference to negotiate a Southeast Asian regional defense treaty.[8]

The JCS reviewed and concurred, on 13 August 1954, in the draft treaty prepared by the US-UK Joint Study Group. They considered it "satisfactory as a point of departure" for negotiations with representatives of the probable initial signatories. They added that the developments at Geneva and in Indochina increased the urgency for a comprehensive US policy with respect to the Far East region as a whole. Until the United States formulated such an overall policy, they said, it would be "severely" handicapped in any negotiation of a collective defense arrangement in Southeast Asia and the Southwest Pacific. Before the provisions of such a treaty could be finally drafted, the Joint Chiefs stated, the United States must make "certain basic decisions" with respect to how far it was willing to go, either in concert with certain noncommunist nations of the Far East or unilaterally, in opposing "further Communist accretions" in this area.[9]

In forwarding the JCS views on the draft treaty to the Department of State, Secretary of Defense Wilson stressed that it should be made clear that no US commitments were implied or intended to equip and maintain indigenous forces or to deploy US forces in such strength as to provide for an effective defense of all of the national territory of each signatory. Military aid to the Southeast Asian pact members should be confined, Secretary Wilson believed, to that necessary to permit those nations to raise and maintain the military forces necessary to ensure internal security, provide a reasonably effective defense against attempted invasions, and instill national confidence.[10]

Three days later, on 20 August 1954, the President approved a new US policy toward the Far East (NSC 5429/2) responsive to the changed situation resulting from the Geneva Conference.[11] The new policy included provision for negotiation of a Southeast Asia security treaty with the United Kingdom, Australia, New Zealand, France, the Philippines, Thailand, and other appropriate free South and Southeast Asian countries desiring to participate. The objectives of such a treaty, as outlined in NSC 5429/2, were to: commit each member to "act promptly to meet the common danger" in the event of an armed attack on the treaty area; provide a possible legal basis for US attack on Communist China should it commit armed aggression endangering US "vital interest"; ensure that, in such an event, other nations would be obligated by the terms of the treaty to support such US action; and avoid limitation of US freedom to use nuclear weapons without involving a US commitment for local defense or for stationing US forces in Southeast Asia.[12]

Representatives of the United Kingdom, France, Australia, New Zealand, and the United States together with those of Pakistan, Thailand, and the Philippines—the only Asian nations willing to join a Southeast Asian regional alliance—assembled in Manila on 6 September to draft a treaty. Although precluded by the Geneva Agreements from participation in military alliances, Cambodia, Laos, and South Vietnam favored having the treaty accord them collective guarantees. South Vietnam even requested permission to send observers to Manila. While the United States supported this request, the United Kingdom, Australia, New Zealand, and Pakistan considered that it would be inconsistent with the "understanding reached at Geneva," and the United States acceded to their view.[13]

A number of issues remained to be resolved at Manila. The United States desired to include Japan, Formosa, and South Korea in the Southeast Asia Pact, if not at the Manila Conference, then at a later date. The other parties to the treaty had made clear their opposition before the conference opened. New Zealand had pointed out that "if a contribution to Southeast Asian defense were to be sought from Japan, the reaction might well be damaging not only from the point of view of the Colombo countries but also from that of the Philippines, even assuming that public opinion in New Zealand and Australia could be induced to swallow it." Japan had no regular military forces, and the United States already had bilateral treaties with Japan and South Korea, New Zealand saw no "overriding military need at this time to have substantial Formosan or Korean forces in SEATO."[14]

The treaty, as finally drafted, did not bar eventual admittance of Japan, Formosa, and South Korea, but any attempts to incorporate them in the treaty area would encounter a number of built-in obstacles. The text of the document delimited a "treaty area" that excluded Korea, Formosa, and Japan, and since unanimous consent of all members was required to expand the treaty area, it appeared unlikely that those governments could be included in the foreseeable future.[15]

A major issue, both at the Manila Conference and in the exchange of views preceding it, was the extent to which the United States would commit military strength to the treaty area. The answer to this question lay in the type of organization that was decided upon. The United States advocated an organization similar to that created by the Australia-New Zealand-United States (ANZUS) security pact. In ANZUS, military representatives of each nation were accredited to the political council to advise on military matters, to make recommendations to their respective Chiefs of Staff, and to transmit to the council recommendations approved by their respective Chiefs of Staff. The other members of the conference wanted an elaborate permanent organization patterned after NATO, with numerous committees of specialists to develop combined regional military plans. This type of structure would give the smaller countries a forum in which they could express their views at any time. It would also bind their own military plans to those of the United States and commit the United States to specific courses of action in the event of aggression; but specific commitments were precisely what the United States sought to avoid.[16]

The NATO concept meant a combined command and staff, with integrated national armies, trained and equipped through generous US assistance, and deployed for the defense of member states. Such a massive organization, besides creating work for itself, would provide the treaty allies with an organ for pressuring the United States to undertake larger obligations than its global responsibilities permitted. By requiring continuous collaboration, it would reduce, without compensating military advantage, US freedom of action in the employment of forces in the Far East. Moreover, it would give other countries of the treaty area power to veto the type and scope of strategic plans evolved.[17] The NATO formula, finally, might conceivably carry the United States into a war Congress had not declared, a possibility that would hardly improve the treaty's chance of ratification by the Senate. The Secretary of State, no doubt, remembered the recent bitter controversy over the Bricker Amendment.[18] Mr. Dulles observed that "it would be extremely unfortunate if Congressional debate were reopened regarding US constitutional questions involving the Executive and Legislative branches, which could well result if the NATO formula were adopted."[19]

The members of the conference were thoroughly familiar with the US viewpoint when the Manila meeting convened. Most of the nations were apparently resigned to accepting an ANZUS type of council that would meet periodically. Australia, nevertheless, made another attempt to moderate the US stand. The Australian delegation introduced an amendment to empower the council to establish "such subsidiary machinery as may be necessary to achieve the military and other objectives of the Treaty." This proposal, if adopted, would have committed the United States to participate in permanent machinery and was therefore unacceptable to the United States. Several days of deliberation by the working group brought about a compromise. The Australians agreed to delete the reference to "subsidiary machinery" and substitute in its place the concept of "consultation." The Joint Chiefs of Staff, by cable, approved this compromise, and the final text stated that "The council shall provide for consultation with regard to military and any other planning as the situation obtaining in the treaty area may from time to time require." This wording was still loose enough to encourage the Australians to persist, and hardly two weeks after the Manila Conference adjourned had they begun pressing the United States to develop procedures for "consultation."[20]

Another issue that proved almost as divisive developed over use, in the US draft of the treaty, of the phrase "Communist aggression" to describe the menace the coalition was designed to combat. All of the conferees recognized the treaty was aimed at communism, but only the US representative wished to say so in the document itself. The British declared that "Communist aggression" was not subject to legal definition and was "needlessly provocative." In addition they feared that it would prejudice the chances of eventually inducing the Colombo Powers to join. Pakistan backed the United Kingdom on this point. But the United States, wanting to avoid treaty forces being drawn into local conflicts, insisted upon inclusion of the phrase. At the conference all seven nations lined up against the United States on the issue. The US delegation, nevertheless, refused to sign a treaty that did not recognize communism as the enemy in Southeast Asia. The remaining delegations finally accepted a compromise advanced by Secretary Dulles. "Communist aggression" was deleted from the text of the treaty, and for it was substituted an "understanding" that US "recognition of the effect of aggression and armed attack" applied "only to communist aggression."[21]

Yet another problem, but one easily resolved, was the provision of collective security guarantees to the former French Associated States. The French delegation, determined to give Peking no pretext for accusing the Manila powers of violating the Geneva Agreements, suggested that specific reference to the Associated States be omitted from the text of the document, proposing instead that the collective protection of the signatories be extended to Cambodia, Laos, and South Vietnam in a separate annex. The other delegations accepted the French plan, and a protocol to this effect was affixed to the final treaty.[22]

All of the members of the conference agreed that economic provisions had to be included in the treaty, mainly as an inducement to the Colombo nations to join at a later date. Of the members who would bear the burden of financing new assistance programs—the United States, the United Kingdom, France, and Australia—none appeared willing to make definite commitments. They agreed merely to "cooperate with one another in the further development of economic measures."[23]

With the various problems successfully solved, the Manila Conference signed the "Southeast Asia Collective Defense Treaty" (SEACDT) on 8 September 1954.

The eight signatory nations declared that an attack upon one would be recognized as dangerous to the peace and safety of the others, and in such an event, each agreed to "act to meet the common danger in accordance with its constitutional processes." The signing states pledged to maintain and develop their capacity "to resist armed attack and to prevent and counter subversive activities directed from without." If the territory, sovereignty, or political independence of any member were threatened "in any other than by armed attack," the parties would consult on the measures to be taken. The "treaty area" was defined as "the general area of Southeast Asia, including also the entire territories of the Asian Parties, and the general area of the Southwest Pacific not including the Pacific area north of 21 degrees 30 minutes north latitude." The SEACDT provided for a council to consider ways of implementing the treaty, and as noted above, an accompanying protocol extended the treaty provisions relating to action in case of armed attack or other threat to Cambodia, Laos, and the southern half of Vietnam. In a separate "Pacific Charter," signed on the same day, the parties proclaimed their intention to resist any attempt "to subvert their freedom or to destroy their sovereignty or territorial integrity" and to cooperate in economic, social, and cultural matters.[24]

The vagueness of the language constituted the real weakness of the treaty. Specific action to be taken in any given situation was not precisely defined, and it was doubtful that aggression would be met with an immediate, decisive and united response. In explaining this deficiency to the Assistant Secretary of Defense (ISA), Vice Admiral A. C. Davis, Deputy Assistant Secretary of Defense (ISA), pointed out that the United States had tried at Manila to attain goals that were not entirely compatible. It had wanted SEACDT to place the communists on notice that future aggression, by whatever means, would evoke collective counteraction. The mechanics of the treaty had, therefore, to be such as to create a feeling of true strength and unity among the participating countries. Yet this end had to be attained without restricting US freedom of action in Asia, without obligating the United States to military aid programs beyond its capabilities, and without impinging on US constitutional limitations in a manner that might jeopardize ratification in the Senate. The document signed on 8 September 1954, thought Admiral Davis, was "in effect a reconciliation of these conflicting objectives," and left Southeast Asia "no better prepared than before to cope with communist aggression."

Nevertheless, Admiral Davis emphasized, the treaty had several important benefits. It provided the nucleus for coordinated defense against communism in Asia. It included features that might someday win over the neutralist nations. At the same time, it expressed economic and political principles that gave the association a broader meaning than that encompassed by its purely military terms. In the final analysis, SEACDT represented more a psychological than a military asset to the regional defense of Southeast Asia.[25]

In the months following the Manila Conference, each signatory nation ratified the Treaty and deposited the instruments of ratification at Manila. On 19 February

1955, the Pact was declared officially in force. To maintain the momentum achieved at the Manila Conference, the signatories had agreed on the desirability of getting on with organizational matters as quickly as possible. Article V of the Treaty had called for the creation of a Council as the supreme organ of the alliance. Subsequently, the members decided that their foreign ministers should meet at Bangkok, Thailand, late in February 1955 to organize this Council and consider basic questions that would determine the future form of the Treaty.

The most important question was that of devising methods to carry out the military provisions of the Pact. For the United States, the answer to this question involved a fundamental tenet of its military policy in the Pacific and Far East—retention of an uncommitted mobile striking force to meet military contingencies that might arise in the area.

A Military Concept for Southeast Asia

The United States, having assumed the leadership in promoting the Southeast Asian alliance, found itself caught between conflicting demands. If the members of the pact, especially the Asian members, were to participate wholeheartedly in collective defense measures, they had to be convinced that the United States was prepared and determined to take military action in the case of an aggression in Southeast Asia. Also, unless the communist rulers of China and North Vietnam were equally convinced of the US ability and willingness to take such action, the primary goal of the Treaty—to deter aggression—probably could not be achieved. At the same time, however, US armed forces were strictly limited by budgetary requirements, and the global responsibilities the United States had already assumed were badly straining available forces. Officials of the United States Government believed, therefore, that it was essential that US forces in the Pacific and Far East not to be tied down to specific geographical commitments in Southeast Asia.

Underlining this conviction, the Joint Chiefs of Staff on 8 October 1954 advised the Secretary of Defense that "the requirement for US freedom of action . . . had been intensified by the terms of the Southeast Asian Collective Defense Treaty. US commitments to Formosa, Japan and Korea, the nations excluded from the treaty, make it imperative that the United States not be restricted by force commitments in the . . . treaty area." And the Secretary of State, explaining the Manila Pact to the President on 2 November, stated that "the responsibilities of the United States are so vast and far-flung that we believe we would serve best not by earmarking forces for particular areas of the Far East but by developing the deterrent of mobile striking power plus strategically placed reserves."[26] This general principle had often been stated by US officials. It was well known in the capitals of the countries allied under the Southeast Asia Pact, and had been widely publicized.

Early in January 1955, with the Bangkok meeting approaching, the Secretary of State asked the Department of Defense to explain how the United States should respond to another war in Southeast Asia. Deputy Secretary of Defense Anderson submitted Secretary Dulles' request to the Joint Chiefs and asked them to recommend a "Concept and Plans for the Implementation, if Necessary, of Article IV, 1, of the Manila Pact." This concept, he said, should provide for a deterrent to overt aggression against Southeast Asian countries that the United States could realistically apply and that the other SEATO powers would find acceptable enough to warrant their support. The deterrent should not only demonstrate unmistakable US intent and the capacity to inflict damage on the aggressor but should also be susceptible to application through US military action with at least token participation by other members of the Pact. Appropriate plans should be developed on the basis that general war would not result from a local conflict unless the aggressor state chose to widen hostilities. Finally, Mr. Anderson asked that the concept be worked out under alternate assumptions that use of atomic weapons would be permitted or that their use "cannot be assured."[27]

The request for such a concept caused serious disagreement in the military establishment, for the Services could not agree among themselves on how best to create an effective deterrent. The conflicting views stemmed from one basic issue: should the United States be prepared to enter any renewed hostilities in Southeast Asia with all elements of its armed forces, including ground troops, or should US participation be limited only to naval and air action?

The services agreed that the conduct of US policy in Southeast Asia had not provided the foundation on which to build a truly effective deterrent. Neither the communists nor the signatories of the Manila Pact had been given any reason to believe that the United States had the means or the intention to block communist expansion into Southeast Asia. As a result, a deterrent could not be created unless the communists were confronted with "demonstrable certainty" that either overt aggression or indigenous rebellion supported by China would trigger instant and effective counteraction by the United States.

The Chief of Staff, US Army, held that "demonstrable certainty" of the capability and intent of the United States to react to either direct or indirect aggression could not be achieved without making specific military commitments to the Treaty area. If either form of communist aggression were to be countered, he reasoned, the enemy had to be defeated on the ground in the area of the attack. This meant US ground troops fighting alongside armies of other Pact members on the mainland of Southeast Asia and supported by US air and naval action against the attacking forces as well as against supply lines in and from China. The Army position, therefore, was that a balanced mobile striking force, composed of land, air, and naval elements, ought to be positioned in the Philippines and earmarked for Southeast Asia. If this force failed to deter aggression, it could be employed in Southeast Asia against aggressor forces.

Opposed to this position, the Navy, Air Force and Marine Corps held that US participation in the event of war in Southeast Asia should be confined to air and naval action. In the initial stage of hostilities, the US contribution at the point of contact would be limited to that necessary to help local forces. The principal US effort, however, would be concentrated on air and naval action against facilities in China used to support the aggressors. If a prolonged local conflict developed, additional US forces, including ground troops, might be deployed to the point of contact. But if general war developed, emergency war plans would be put into execution and the main effort shifted to those areas of the world considered strategically more important.

The question was argued at length among the services, with each side accepting some compromise of their initial positions in an attempt to reach agreement. The Joint Chiefs of Staff twice provided guidance, and in the end an agreed position was endorsed on 11 February 1955.[28]

The concept approved by the Joint Chiefs rejected the Army position that forces should be earmarked for Southeast Asia. The concept for application of US military power under the Manila Pact, said the JCS, should be to deter or to counter aggression by being ready to react promptly with attacks "by the most effective combination of US armed forces against the military power of the aggressor." They explained that these attacks would be launched against targets within the aggressor country, but only against military objectives directly supporting the aggressor action. Atomic weapons would be used on these targets as well as on targets in the immediate area of the attack. If authority for such use were withheld, the concept would still remain valid. But this denial would prevent the most effective employment of US forces, and as a result require larger forces than the United States might feel justified in committing.

In addition to this central thesis, the Joint Chiefs recommended five subsidiary courses of action: (1) continued development of combat-effective indigenous forces, with their structure and training mutually coordinated to develop local leadership and prestige, and with improved capabilities to create a cohesive fighting force through integration of their operations with adjacent indigenous forces and with support by operations of forces of other Manila Pact members; (2) encouragement of other Manila Pact countries to maintain forces in readiness to counter aggression; (3) discussion, in general terms, of unilateral military plans by the military representatives to the council to the extent necessary to insure maximum participation and cooperation by other member nations, but not to the extent that US strategic plans or the availability of US forces for implementing such plans might be revealed; (4) periodic visits by US forces into the area as demonstrations of intent, and for joint and combined training exercises; (5) availability of appropriate mechanism for the employment of US forces in support of friendly indigenous forces in the general area.[29]

Admiral Radford, briefing the Secretary of State on the concept, went into greater detail on what the Joint Chiefs had in mind. If the Chinese attacked Southeast Asia, he said, the US response would be chiefly against the Chinese mainland. Land- and carrier-based air forces would strike air fields, supply depots, and communications lines in South China. To support these operations, Chinese Nationalist troops, assisted by US air and naval units, might invade the mainland in the vicinity of the Formosa Straits, or they might land on Hainan Island or the Straits, or the Liuchow Peninsula. If desirable, another front could be opened in Korea. Thus, the Chinese Communists would find themselves engaged on so many fronts close to home that their effort in Southeast Asia would be seriously compromised. The Admiral believed that the same strategy of air and naval action against the enemy logistical complex would be equally valid if the Viet Minh instead of the Chinese Communists launched an invasion.

When Secretary Dulles mentioned that the decision to use nuclear weapons might be politically difficult to take, Admiral Radford stated unequivocally that the concept was predicated upon the selective use of such weapons. If approval were withheld, the whole question of US involvement would have to be reexamined. In fact, unless nuclear weapons were used, the United States probably could not cope with the situation employing only the available forces.[30]

The International Working Group

The position of the Joint Chiefs of Staff, that the United States could not afford to sacrifice its freedom of action in the Far East by committing forces to SEATO, was unpalatable to other members of the Pact, especially to the Asians. The countries of Southeast Asia were naturally concerned primarily with their own region, and they sought assurance that they would be defended on the ground in Southeast Asia. Counteraction elsewhere might win the war in the long run, but this would be small consolation if Southeast Asia were overrun in the meantime. What they wanted, therefore, were specific US commitments and a combined planning organization to tie US plans securely to those of the other members of the Pact. They persisted in the belief that the United States would, in the end, engage its resources in a SEATO patterned after NATO. In fact, within three weeks after the conclusion of the Manila Conference, Australia requested the views of the United States on military machinery to be set up under the Pact.[31]

This was the central issue when an International Working Group, composed of representatives of the Manila powers, met in Washington during December 1954 and January 1955 to prepare for the SEATO conference to be held in Bangkok in February. Discussions soon assumed a broader framework than the United States had contemplated, for the Asian nations wanted the alliance to establish permanent agencies, especially machinery that would involve the United States in combined military planning for the defense of Southeast Asia.

The Philippine representative was particularly vocal in expressing the Asian viewpoint. He argued insistently that not only must genuine strength be created in the Treaty area but that this strength must be manifest. He proposed repeatedly, the organization of a standing military committee, both to handle military affairs connected with the Pact and to deal with anti-subversive activities.

The US Delegate, Counselor of the Department of State, Douglas MacArthur II, replied that the United States was opposed to creating machinery simply for the sake of having machinery. The ANZUS formula, with military advisors to the members of the council meeting periodically, would suffice. The United States was also opposed to drafting a directive that would in advance dictate to the military advisers any organizational machinery. This should be left to their own deliberations. The Philippine Military Adviser, if he desired, could propose permanent military organization at the first meeting of the military advisers. Mr. MacArthur eventually won the support of the other delegates for this approach, and the problem was deferred. As for anti-subversive activities, the United States felt that these should be the responsibility of each national government, although the members should assist each other unilaterally. Such assistance might, for example, take the form of political action and the exchange of information.[32]

The deep-rooted desire of the Asian members of SEATO for permanent organization also manifested itself in the economic field. Pakistan, strongly backed by Thailand and the Philippines, pointed out that membership in the Treaty, particularly for the Asian members, would impose new strains on the national economies; they proposed that a special section be set up under the council to deal with this matter. The United States, the United Kingdom, and Australia admitted the validity of the argument. They were reluctant, however, to approve anything that might disturb such existing aid programs as the Colombo Plan and the bilateral arrangements between the United States and its Asian allies.[33]

Despite differences of opinion, the representatives to the International Working Group reached agreement on a number of concrete recommendations to the council. They agreed on an agenda for the Bangkok Conference and on organization and procedures of the SEATO Council. Probably more important from the US viewpoint, they adopted the ANZUS system of military advisers, although the Asian members clearly hoped eventually to buttress the advisers with permanent committees. Sooner or later, the United States would have to meet this issue decisively.

The Bangkok Conference: 23–25 February 1955

The Working Group had charted a course for the foreign ministers to follow at Bangkok, and the ministers' deliberations, for the most part, were concerned with the recommendations of the Working Group. At Bangkok, SEATO began to take shape. The supreme organ, as specified by the Treaty, was to be the Council, composed of the foreign ministers of the signatory powers, or their representatives. Because the Council would normally meet only once a year, some means of continuous coordination seemed necessary. Therefore, the conferees decided upon a system of council representatives, whose headquarters would be in Bangkok, and who would be supported by a permanent secretariat. Directly subordinate to the council representatives were three ad hoc subcommittees: one to deal with economic matters; one to deal with information, culture and labor; and a third to deal with counter-subversion. The military advisors to the council members, who were not subordinated to the council representatives, were left to work out their own organization.[34]

Early in the conference, the Department of Defense delegation sensed that the Asian representatives were preparing to bring pressure on the United States for definite commitment of forces and a NATO type of military organization. To check this pressure, the Defense representative advised the Secretary of State both to take the initiative in proposing a meeting of the military advisers during the Bangkok sessions and to make a forceful statement of US intentions concerning the military aspects of the Treaty. Secretary Dulles agreed. During the first closed session, he outlined in detail for the delegates the composition of US armed forces stationed in the Pacific and Far East. Emphasizing the interdependence of Southeast Asia and other regions of the Far East, the Secretary of State declared: "It is much better to have mobile power which is capable of being used whenever circumstances require it... than having the force committed, in segments, to various areas." The Asian delegates apparently found Secretary Dulles' statement so compelling that they did not try to force the issue.[35]

The delegates also accepted the Secretary of State's proposal that the military advisers meet in separate sessions. The military advisers first meeting was held on 24 February and dealt mainly with organizational matters. The delegates agreed that the SEATO military organization would consist of a group of staff planners and a military liaison group, in addition to the advisers. The function of the staff planners would be to meet in advance of the twice-yearly conferences of the advisers to prepare agenda and formulate recommendations on any subject their superiors wished to discuss. The military liaison group was to be established in Bangkok as soon as possible to "provide point of contact between military advisers and between military advisers and the Council." Its members would be military officers, normally service attachés, serving on the staffs of the council representatives.

The Philippine military adviser attempted to inject the question of a "permanent planners group" into the discussions. The other advisers, however, persuaded him that this was a topic more properly suited to discussion by the staff planners. In the assignment of position papers for the first staff planners conference, the Philippines were given responsibility for preparing an "Examination into methods of creating a possible future permanent organizational structure."

To demonstrate that the United States sincerely wanted to implement the Manila Treaty as soon as possible, Admiral Felix Stump, who had been designated the US military adviser, in addition to his duties as CINCPAC, took the initiative in proposing an early meeting of the staff planners and military advisers. The conferees agreed to schedule the first staff planners meeting during April, to be followed in May or June by the first meeting of the military advisers.[36]

Despite the atmosphere of cordiality and unanimity at Bangkok, the Asians still had reservations about the future effectiveness of the Pact. Moreover, nations which were opposed to SEATO were actively recruiting adherents and gaining increased attention in Asia and other continents. At the time of the Bangkok Conference, India's Prime Minister Nehru declared that the Southeast Asia Pact actually increased rather than diminished tension and thereby lessened the security of its members. The principal thesis of the neutralists was that the white man's colonialism, not communism, was the chief enemy. With this thesis they hoped to challenge SEATO and the principle on which it was founded at the Afro-Asian conference, scheduled to be held in Bandung, Indonesia, in April 1955.

The Bandung Conference: 18–24 April 1955

Western diplomats feared that Bandung would produce a collection of platitudes easily interpreted as endorsement of procommunist or neutralist principles, but their fears were only partially realized. The delegates from twenty-nine African and Asian countries represented every shade of political philosophy, but they had in common a fierce independence directed as much against Asian as European domination. The Indian Prime Minister assumed the role of leader of the conference and attempted forcefully, to persuade the delegates to accept his views. When his efforts failed to gain a consensus, Prime Minister Nehru betrayed anger. His failure and his display of temper diminished his prestige and influence.

Shortly before Bandung, Prime Minister Nehru had charged that the Manila Pact and the Bangkok Conference had "upset any possibility of peace—as well as stability—in the Indochinese area." And during the conference, he asserted: "I would consider it to be an intolerable humiliation for any Asian or African country to degrade itself as a camp follower of one side or the other." In effect, Prime Minister Nehru called the Asian members of SEATO "camp followers." General Carlos Romulo, of the Philippines, vigorously defended the Pact. Condemning "starry eyed visionaries dreaming Utopian dreams," General Romulo gave a penetrating analysis of the nature of the communist threat. He then explained in detail the provisions of the Southeast Asia Treaty, emphasizing its nonaggressive character, and attempting point by point to refute Prime Minister Nehru's allegations.[37]

Even more effective from the standpoint of the West was the denunciation of communism by Ceylon's Sir John Kotelawala. Sir John, Prime Minister of an avowedly neutralist country that generally followed Prime Minister Nehru's lead in international politics, denounced the form of imperialism practiced by the communists and called for the Afro-Asians to be equally positive and unanimous in declaring their opposition to all forms of colonialism.[38]

Together with pro-Western speeches by Turkish and Iraqi leaders, General Romulo and Prime Minister Kotelawala made their influence felt in the final communiqué, and the West fared much better than it had hoped. On the other hand, Chou En-lai, Premier of Communist China, by his affability and apparent willingness to compromise, had made a favorable impression on Asians and Africans alike. Bandung created a climate in which neutralism exerted stronger attraction than ever for both the committed and uncommitted states. In so doing, Bandung had its effect on SEATO. The uncommitted states were now less likely to join the Pact, and committed states grew bolder in demanding more substance to SEATO in return for their continued participation.

Setting Up Machinery

While the Asians and Africans were conferring at Bandung, the SEATO staff planners convened at Baguio, in the Philippines, to lay the groundwork for the meeting of military advisers to be held in Bangkok during the summer. The question of permanent organization was still a live issue. The Philippines, in fact, proposed that a permanent military working body, headed by a chairman with a combined staff, be organized immediately. The United States, perceiving that compromise was essential if an open split was to be avoided, backed a plan for creating a small permanent secretariat to serve as a clearing house and communications center for SEATO business. Other, and more vital, questions would, however, be dealt with by ad hoc subcommittees; for example, strategic estimates relating to the defense of Southeast Asia against overt and covert communist aggression, and problems such as logistics, communications, and intelligence common to the nations of the Treaty area.

Admiral Stump believed that the United States, by agreeing to this arrangement, had temporarily headed off any determined insistence on a combined permanent planning group. He asked the Joint Chiefs of Staff to authorize him to give US approval to the secretariat when the advisers met in Bangkok. Although the Chief of Staff, Army, protested that the secretariat portended a larger and more authoritative organization, the Joint Chiefs of Staff interposed no objections to the proposal. They made clear, however, that they would not agree to the evolution of this body into a standing group. The military advisers, meeting at Bangkok in July, approved the establishment of a small secretariat that would function under the authority of the military liaison group.[39]

Despite Admiral Stump's prediction that the secretariat would satisfy the Asians for the time being, it became more and more evident throughout the remainder of 1955 that further compromise was necessary. This was true not only in the military field but in all activities under the Pact. Baguio had demonstrated that the Asians were waiting for the United States to prove its good intentions, and this hopeful waiting was generally reflected in the Southeast Asian press. During a meeting of the council representatives in August, the US member observed "A perceptible anxiety and frustration ... concerning the future development and effectiveness of SEACDT unless substantial progress in Treaty activities can be achieved."[40]

From a "responsible and patriotic Philippine military personality," CIA received the view that the morale of the Asian members was rapidly deteriorating because of the utter lack of accomplishment of SEATO and the allegedly highhanded manner in which the United States was running it. He charged that the Philippines seemed to have a treaty with CINCPAC instead of with the United States. Admiral Stump labeled this report a gross exaggeration but one that nonetheless probably represented the thinking of at least a segment of Philippine military leaders. Even Thailand, one of the United States' staunchest allies in the Far East, was apparently feeling the attraction of neutralism. In November, the US Embassy in Bangkok reported that any sign of reduced US support of SEATO or the Thai defense program would probably encourage the Thai Government to develop an openly neutralist position. And Pakistan, dissatisfied with the ad hoc arrangements for conducting the business of the Treaty, made known its desire for a "large-scale central SEATO organization at least on the civilian side."[41]

The Asian attitude became quite evident at the second staff planners conference, held at Pearl Harbor in November. The Department of Defense observer at the conference was especially impressed with the fact that the Asians were losing interest in the Treaty because the United States would not "provide more definitive military substance" to SEATO. He feared that the United States would have to assent to the concept of a permanent staff organization and possible participation in combined planning. Otherwise, the objectives sought by the United States in promoting the Pact in the first place could not be attained.[42]

The Department of State, too, was beginning to see that the United States would have to make substantial concessions or watch SEATO fall apart. At an ANZUS Council Meeting, held in Washington in September, Secretary of State Dulles had emphasized the necessity of finding means of adding more "substance" to the treaty organization. He repeated this view in conferences with Admiral Radford and other Defense leaders. It was Secretary Dulles' view that the best opportunity for the United States to breathe life into SEATO lay in the field of countersubversion.[43]

By September 1955, it became apparent that the two SEATO organizations designed to cope with subversion in Southeast Asia were inefficient and confused. The separate military and civil committees dealing with subversion had found the military and civil aspects of the problem so interrelated that it only increased the confusion to try to separate them. Almost all of the SEATO members favored a merger of the civilian and military committees. The Philippines, the United Kingdom, and Australia went even further. They advocated the creation of a permanent civil-military standing group to direct SEATO's battle against communist subversion. The United States, in keeping with its uniform policy on SEATO machinery, opposed a standing group.[44]

From the viewpoint of the United States other aspects of the question also had to be weighed. If SEATO became more directly involved in the operational phases of countersubversion, the bilateral arrangements between the United States and its allies would be endangered, and the functions of several other US agencies dealing with countersubversion greatly complicated. Entrusting such functions to SEATO might also jeopardize the division of responsibility for intelligence and espionage among the Departments of Defense, Central Intelligence Agency, and other agencies. Therefore, the United States, while favoring an expanded countersubversive effort and a unified civil-military approach, wished to confine countersubversive activities to exchange of information through a SEATO agency meeting periodically.[45] Yet there obviously existed a need to shore up Asian confidence in SEATO and to increase its activity and efficiency.

On 17 October the Director of Central Intelligence, Mr. Allen Dulles, circulated a proposal to the Secretaries of State and Defense and the Chairman, Joint Chiefs of Staff, for converting the civilian committee to combat communist subversion into a permanent organization, merging it with the military antisubversion committee, and supporting it with a permanent research center. Commenting on the CIA plan, Admiral Stump advised the Chief of Naval Operations that the "formation of some sort of permanent SEATO staff organization may be inevitable." The United States, he added, might have to yield on this point or find itself in no position to refute 'paper tiger' charges."[46]

In keeping with the emerging policy of strengthening SEATO, the Joint Chiefs of Staff, although disagreeing with the specifics of Mr. Allen Dulles' proposal, endorsed the general principle. "The need for more substance to SEATO through permanent staff structure extends to all SEATO activities," they said.

> A permanent executive working group should, therefore, be established under the Council to be responsive to the needs of both the Council Representatives and the Military Advisors. The development now of a permanent staff structure for the coordination of countersubversive activities would probably be the first of a series of proposals for other permanent organization. This could lead to the piecemeal development of permanent SEATO staff structure that would become unwieldy and cumbersome. It is therefore, preferable to develop the permanent structure at the top initially.
>
> ... The Joint Chiefs of Staff recommend that a high level executive working group with a permanent secretariat be established under the Council, outside the SEATO Committee to Combat Communist Subversion (CCCS), to coordinate the work of the technical committees in the fight against Communist subversion.[47]

Concurrently, the United States was also giving serious consideration to relaxing its opposition to a permanent military planning staff. This problem, the Department of State believed, would probably come to a head at the next council meeting, which was to be held at Karachi, West Pakistan, in March 1956. At the request of the Department of State, Admiral Stump's views, both on a permanent military staff and a permanent council, were solicited.

Although he admitted the widespread Asian dissatisfaction with SEATO, Admiral Stump was not convinced that a permanent council and military staff should be created for the time being. In his view, reasons that had prompted the United States to oppose such an organization were still valid, and the ad hoc arrangements were working satisfactorily. Nevertheless, CINCPAC believed that, if political expediency forced a change in the US position, the permanent organization should be developed within a framework acceptable to the United States. He accordingly proposed a plan that provided for evolution of existing ad hoc agencies into permanent agencies. However, this plan was to be executed only if "political pressures made it necessary."[48]

Passing these views on to the Joint Chiefs of Staff, the Chief of Naval Operations endorsed CINCPAC's recommendations and enlarged upon the reasons why the United States should not allow itself to become involved in a permanent staff system. The Asian allies, Admiral Burke explained, were themselves unable to commit forces to SEATO or to provide competent personnel for high-level chairmanships. The Chief of Naval Operations asked the Joint Chiefs of Staff to approve CINCPAC's concept and recommend to the Secretary of Defense that it be adopted as the US position in the event that establishment of a permanent organization became a matter of political necessity.[49]

The Army Chief of Staff disagreed; he believed that Admiral Burke's proposal did not adequately reflect either the current international political and psychological situation or the events that had taken place since the Joint Chiefs of Staff formulated the basic US military position on SEATO in February 1955. He recommended, therefore, that the problem be restudied with a view to revising the basic position. The Joint Chiefs of Staff concurred in General Taylor's proposal.[50]

The Joint Chiefs of Staff again discussed the problem on 21 February 1956. From a strictly military viewpoint, they reasoned, their original concept governing US participation in SEATO remained valid. But, because of increasing pressure exerted by Asian allies for a permanent planning staff, the Joint Chiefs of Staff agreed that their previous decision should be reversed. They stated:

> U.S. commitments elsewhere in the Pacific still require that no U.S. forces be earmarked for SEATO. While this fact prevents agreed combined plans, it does not prevent a small permanent SEATO military staff from participating in combined planning studies where commitments of forces is not involved. If a permanent SEATO military planning staff is inevitable, the U.S. might gain by proposing now the type of organization it desires and, thereby, not only be able

to direct the development of the organization along the lines desired but also by this positive approach, to add "substance" to SEATO.

The Joint Chiefs of Staff added, however, that "Inasmuch as the requirement for a permanent organization stems from political and psychological reasons, the minimum possible military effort should be expended."

The Joint Chiefs of Staff recommended to the Secretary of Defense that, at the Council meeting in Karachi, the United States suggest that the first steps be taken toward setting up a permanent planning staff by modifying existing ad hoc machinery, and that the organizational concept drawn up by Admiral Stump be adopted as the basis for any further expansion. The Secretary of Defense approved these recommendations, and Admiral Stump was authorized to implement them at the Karachi Conference in March.[51]

At Karachi, once it was clear that the United States no longer opposed the principle of a permanent planning organization, the Council promptly adopted it. Following the Council meeting, the SEATO military advisers convened and drew up a proposal for a permanent planning structure. It provided for a small logistical and operational planning staff functioning continuously under the direction of a chief of staff to the military advisers. The advisers themselves, as well as the existing technical subcommittees of the staff planners, would remain on an ad hoc basis. The staff was to be organized and in operation by the time the military advisers met in September 1956.[52]

Acting on Admiral Stump's recommendation, the United States accepted the military advisers' proposals for a permanent planning staff, but agreement on the location of and funding for the staff, as well as securing the necessary office facilities, delayed the actual establishment. Finally, on 1 March 1957, the SEATO Military Planning Office (SMPO) was established in Bangkok. Brigadier General Alfredo M. Santos of the Philippines headed the new SMPO, assisted by a deputy, eight senior national planners representing the member states, over a dozen other national planners, and a military secretariat. Now, after nearly two years of effort, the Asian members had secured the beginning of a permanent organization for SEATO.[53]

With the prospect of more structured planning, the question of US force commitments for SEATO again arose. At conferences in June and September 1956, the military advisers discussed the threat to SEATO under conditions of global war and the need for a strategic concept for this eventuality. At the September meeting, they agreed that each adviser would request his government for political clearance to proceed with such a study. This study would include a review of forces available to SEATO, and on 12 September, the Chief of Naval Operations alerted the Joint Chiefs of Staff that CINCPAC would require "high level policy guidance" on the matter of force commitments.[54]

After a review of the matter, the Joint Chiefs of Staff recommended against any specific force commitments for SEATO, advising the Secretary of Defense on 16 November 1956 that:

The United States should not duplicate the pattern of NATO and its significant standing military forces by earmarking U.S. forces for Southeast Asia. Instead, the United States should maintain mobile striking power readily available for immediate operations and sufficient, in concert with other nations, to defeat overt Communist local aggression in the SEATO area.

The US Government adopted the JCS position, and the Assistant Secretary of Defense (ISA) directed CINCPAC that, although the US policy of making "no specific force commitments" to SEATO remained in effect, he was authorized to reassure the SEATO allies at the next advisers meeting of US support in the event of overt communist aggression. This assurance, the Assistant Secretary added, should be stated "in broad terms of major U.S. forces deployed to the Western Pacific and forces available to CINCPAC for contingency planning with emphasis on the flexibility and mobility of these forces."[55]

The United States not only wished to avoid specific force commitments to SEATO but wanted to avoid a SEATO study of global war altogether. On 9 January 1957, the Joint Chiefs of Staff informed the Secretary of Defense that such a study was impractical "in view of the many imponderables as to Soviet capabilities and courses of action and plans and capabilities of other international defense organizations such as NATO." They recognized, however, that refusal to participate in such studies risked alienation of the Asian SEATO members, and they recommended that the United States avoid the study if it could be done without seriously undermining the confidence of the Asian members. If the Asian members insisted on the study, the Joint Chiefs of Staff would interpose no objection provided that the study was limited to "broad general terms and that agreement could be reached on assumptions regarding the effects of Soviet nuclear weapons and on plans and forces of free world nations and defense organizations outside the treaty area."[56]

The Office of the Secretary of Defense and the Department of State approved the JCS position as a last line of resistance, but hoped to convince the other SEATO members that "planning for a war limited to the treaty area would be adequate for defense in a global war." Such a course of action, they believed, would appear "a diplomatic means of disposing of this study" while still affording "a route for graceful retirement should the Asian members indicate strongly held opposition." The State-OSD approach proved successful. At their next meeting in March 1957, the military advisers decided that "our military studies for limited war will be adaptable for global considerations," since "the residual threat to the mainland of Southeast Asia in a global war would be no greater, and may be less, than in limited war."[57]

In late 1958, the matter of US force commitments for SEATO again arose. At a September 1958 conference, the SEATO military advisers agreed that, for the preparation of outline plans for the introduction of a SEATO force into threatened areas, member nations should agree to base plans on the assumption of an initial requirement for one brigade group or regimental combat team with appropriate naval and air support. They also decided to forward to the SMPO estimates of their forces "which might be available for inclusion in a SEATO force," and to consider the issue further at their next meeting in April 1959.

As a result, on 1 February 1959, CINCPAC requested US positions on SEATO force availabilities and command relations for the forthcoming military advisers conference. With regard to force availabilities, CINCPAC proposed that the United States limit the size of basic forces estimated to be available and include no major supporting forces in the US estimate. Estimates of available US forces for inclusion in a SEATO force, CINCPAC suggested, should not exceed: (1) one Marine BLT or Army BCT; (2) BLT/BCT lift and/or logistic support as required; (3) USAF composite air lift squadron; (4) communications detachment; (5) technical and advisory personnel as required. The Joint Chiefs of Staff endorsed the CINCPAC proposal and it was adopted as the US position, with the provision that "a SEATO force assembled to counter Communist insurgency would be as broadly representative of the member nations as possible and that U.S. participation would be kept to the minimum required by circumstances...."[58]

SEATO's Accomplishments and Failures

In August 1959, SEATO marked its fifth anniversary. In promoting the SEACDT after the Geneva settlement of 1954, the United States had sought a means of checking communist expansion and aggression in Southeast Asia, and during the period 1955–1959, no further territory fell under communist control. It is impossible to determine the role of SEATO in that accomplishment, but in 1959 US officials chose to interpret it as a significant one. Department of State Counselor G. Frederick Reinhardt voiced this view in early 1959:

> SEATO has interrupted the Communists' military march in the Far East. Although the organization, unlike NATO, has no combat forces assigned to it, it had brought confidence to its members and despite the continuing struggle against Communist subversion in Southeast Asia, general tranquility has returned to the area. Quiet conditions have prevailed, and the Southeast Asian nations, relieved of the threat of imminent Communist invasion, have been able to make appreciable progress in programs for social and economic betterment.
>
> With no armed forces of its own and no peacetime military headquarters, SEATO relies upon the mobile striking forces of its members for its defense. Yet SEATO's mere existence has served as an effective deterrent.[59]

In a similar vein, C. Douglas Dillon, Under Secretary of State, proudly pointed out to the SEATO Council in April 1959:

> The true measure of SEATO's worth is the simple fact that since we joined to create its protective shield there has been no Communist aggression against the treaty area. The Nations of Southeast Asia have thus been freed to devote

their primary efforts to the development of their national well-being. When we recall the difficult and unpromising situation in Southeast Asia at the time of SEATO's birth, the significance of this accomplishment becomes apparent.[60]

In 1957, the United States had reluctantly acceded to pressure by the Asian members for a more defined SEATO structure, agreeing to the creation of a permanent planning staff—SMPO. During the next two years, the military advisers and SMPO worked on plans for contingencies such as the defense of Southeast Asia, including East Pakistan, against a Chinese communist-Viet Cong attack; overt communist aggression against the Philippines, military measures to counter communist insurgency, and the establishment of a SEATO force to assist the Royal Government of Laos in combating communist insurgency.[61]

Beginning in 1956, SEATO initiated a series of yearly military training exercises. The first of these, Exercise FIRMLINK held in February 1956, was a ground-air exercise including the forces of all the members except France and Pakistan. During the next several years, the SEATO military exercises fell into three categories: ground-air exercises in Thailand designed to prove and test the capacity of Pact members to aid Thailand in the event of an invasion from the north; combined amphibious operations between the United States and the other members in the Treaty area; and annual naval exercises in the triangle between Singapore, Manila, and Bangkok to standardize procedures and develop cooperation for emergency conditions.[62]

Although SEATO supporters in 1959 could point with pride to the absence of further communist advances during the five years of the treaty's existence, the SEATO-deterrence may, in fact, have influenced the communists to abandon outright aggression for their alternate weapon of subversion, and SEATO's record in the area of antisubversion was not impressive. The United States, the United Kingdom, the Philippines, and Australia helped other states in training police officers and intelligence specialists and members exchanged information about subversive activities. In November 1957, SEATO sponsored a seminar on countering subversion. Philippine President Carlos Garcia opened the meeting in Manila and attendees included officials, educators, publicists, trade union leaders, various other representatives from the eight member states (including Admiral Radford), and three observers from South Vietnam. The main purposes of the seminar were directed toward focusing public opinion on the nature and extent of communist subversion and assisting in the general SEATO effort to expose and counter communist attempts to extend their influence in the Treaty area. But SEATO's principal efforts to counter subversion were restricted to exchanges of information, and the occasion of a SEATO intervention in the aid of a government threatened by communist revolution, initially thought by some observers to be the most likely form of SEATO action in the Treaty area, did not occur.[63]

The Southeast Asia Collective Defense Treaty provided for consultation among the members in case of emergencies, but SEATO consultation in the period 1955 through 1959 was primarily limited to annual Council meetings, which did not include issues of national policy. SEATO consultation was not used in the Formosan offshore crises of 1955 and 1958, the 1957 settlement in Laos, the troubles on the Burmese border, or the Indonesian rebellion of 1958. SEATO ambassadors did meet several times in 1959 on the Laotian situation, culminating in an extraordinary Council meeting in Washington in September 1959. This meeting produced a pledge by the members to abide by their "treaty obligations" and to follow closely "any developments threatening the peace and stability of the treaty area," but no substantive action.[64]

The SEACDT also included provision for mutual self help in economic development, but SEATO activities in this area were modest during the first five years. Australia, alone, instituted a small SEATO-label aid project to strengthen the defense forces of the Asian members with supplies of noncombat material, and there were a handful of small SEATO aid programs concerned with technical training and assistance. SEATO failed to develop an economic aid program largely because the members who would have had to bear the burden of funding such a program, particularly the United States, preferred to channel their aid through bilateral programs.[65]

The economic provisions had been included in SEACDT in 1954 as an inducement to the Colombo nations to join the Treaty, but this did not occur. Neither did the SEATO umbrella of protection against communist aggression entice any additional Asian nations to accede to the Treaty, and in 1959 the SEATO membership remained the same as at the signing of the Manila Treaty in 1954, with Pakistan, the Philippines, and Thailand being the only Asian nations represented.

Although available evidence is not sufficient for a precise evaluation, SEATO may have made an important contribution to the peace and stability of Southeast Asia during the years 1955 through 1959. Its creation internationalized opposition to communist aggression in the region, and SEATO's existence was a factor any potential aggressor nation had to consider. In addition, SEATO accustomed potential allies of a future war in Southeast Asia to working together, fostering cooperation in matters of logistics, communications, intelligence, training, and planning. Even though it still left much to be desired, SEATO had enhanced the prospects of a common front against communist aggression in Southeast Asia, at least, as viewed in the context of the period. Its essential weakness, already perceived by some, would be manifest to the world only at a later time, and under more critical pressures and circumstances.

Abbreviations and Acronyms

ANZUS	Australia, New Zealand, and the United States
ARVN	Army of the Republic of Vietnam
BCT	battalion combat team (Army)
BLT	battalion landing team (Marines)
CATO	Combat Arms and Training Organization
CCCS	Committee to Combat Communist Subversion
CG	Civil Guard
CIA	Central Intelligence Agency
CINCPAC	Commander in Chief, Pacific
DMZ	demilitarized zone
DRV	Democratic Republic of Vietnam
FEC	French Expeditionary Corps
FOA	Foreign Operations Administration
GVN	Government of Vietnam
IAC	Intelligence Advisory Committee
ICA	International Cooperation Administration
ICC	International Control Commission
ISA	International Security Affairs
JAC	Joint Armistice Commission
JSPC	Joint Strategic Plans Committee
MAAG	Military Assistance Advisory Group
MAP	Military Assistance Program
MDAP	Mutual Defense Assistance Program
MNR	Movement of National Revolution
MSU	Michigan state University
NIE	National Intelligence Estimate
NRM	National Revolutionary Movement

NSC	National Security Council
OCB	Operations Coordinating Board
ODM	Office of Defense Mobilization
PMDL	provisional military demarcation line
RCT	Regimental Combat Team (Army)
RLT	regimental landing team (Marines)
RVN	Republic of Vietnam
RVNAF	Republic of Vietnam Armed Forces
RWP	Revolutionary Workers Party
SDC	Self Defense Corps
SEACDT	Southeast Asia Collective Defense Treaty
SEATO	Southeast Asia Treaty Organization
SMPO	SEATO Military Planning Office
TERM	Temporary Equipment Recovery Mission
TO&E	Table of Organization and Equipment
TRIM	Training Relations Instruction Mission
UPI	United Press International
USOM	United States Operations Mission
USSR	Union of Soviet Socialist Republics
VC	Viet Cong
VNA	Vietnamese National Army
VNAF	Vietnamese Air Force
VNN	Vietnamese Navy
VPA	Vietnamese People's Army

Principal Civilian and Military Officers

President and Commander in Chief
Dwight D. Eisenhower   20 Jan 53–20 Jan 61

Secretary of State
John F. Dulles   21 Jan 53–22 Apr 59

Secretary of Defense
Charles E. Wilson   28 Jan 53–08 Oct 57
Neil H. McElroy   09 Oct 57–01 Dec 59
Thomas S. Gates, Jr.   02 Dec 59–20 Jan 61

Deputy Secretary of Defense
Roger M. Keyes   04 Feb 53–01 May 54
Robert B. Anderson   03 May 54–04 Aug 55
Reuben B. Robertson, Jr.   05 Aug 55–25 Apr 57
Donald A. Quarles   01 May 57–08 May 59
Thomas S. Gates, Jr.   08 Jun 59–01 Dec 59

Secretary of the Army
Robert T. Stevens   04 Feb 53–20 Jul 55
Wilber M. Brucker   21 Jul 55–20 Jan 61

Secretary of the Navy
Robert B. Anderson   04 Feb 53–02 May 54
Charles S. Thomas   03 May 54–31 Mar 57
Thomas S. Gates, Jr.   01 Apr 57–07 Jun 59
William B. Franke   08 Jun 59–20 Jan 61

Secretary of the Air Force
Harold E. Talbott   04 Feb 53–13 Aug 55
Donald A. Quarles   15 Aug 55–30 Apr 57
James H. Douglas, Jr.   01 May 57–11 Dec 59

Chairman, Joint Chiefs of Staff
Admiral Arthur W. Radford, USN   15 Aug 53–15 Aug 57
General Nathan F. Twining, USAF   15 Aug 57–30 Sep 60

Chief of Staff, US Army
General Matthew B. Ridgway   15 Aug 53–30 Jun 55
General Maxwell D. Taylor   30 Jun 55–30 Jun 59

Chief of Naval Operations
Admiral Robert B. Carney   17 Aug 53–17 Aug 55
Admiral Arleigh A. Burke   17 Aug 55–01 Aug 61

Chief of Staff, US Air Force
General Nathan F. Twining   30 Jun 53–30 Jun 57
General Thomas D. White   01 Jul 57–30 Jun 61

Commandant, US Marine Corps
General Lemuel C. Shepherd, Jr.   01 Jan 52–31 Dec 55
General Randolph McC. Pate   01 Jan 56–31 Dec 59

Commander in Chief, Far East Command
General John E. Hull, USA   05 Oct 53–01 Apr 55
General Maxell D. Taylor, USA   01 Apr 55–05 Jun 55
General Lyman L. Lemnitzer, USA   05 Jun 55–30 Jun 57
(Disestablished 01 Jul 1957 and functions assumed by USPACOM)

Commander in Chief, Pacific Command
Admiral Felix B. Stump   10 Jul 53–31 Jul 58
Admiral Harry D. Felt   31 Jul 58–30 Jun 64

Chief, US Military Assistance and Advisory Group, Indochina
Major General Thomas J. H. Trapnell, USA   Aug 52–Apr 54
Lieutenant General John W. O'Daniel, USA   Apr 54–Nov 55
Lieutenant General Samuel T. Williams, USA   Nov 55–Aug 60

Notes

Chapter 1. The Geneva Conference and Its Aftermath—1954

1. Terminology for the agreements and final declaration rapidly became confused, both in news media and in official documents and public statements. Geneva Agreements, or Agreement, and Geneva Accords, or Accord, were used indiscriminately to designate all three agreements together; all three plus the final declaration; the agreement on Vietnam only, plus the final declaration; etc. In this volume, Geneva Agreements applies to the three agreements concerning Laos, Cambodia, and Vietnam. When only the agreement concerning Vietnam is addressed, it will be described as the agreement on Vietnam or the Vietnam Agreement. The Final Declaration of the Conference will be identified as the final declaration, distinct from the Geneva Agreements. Exceptions occur in quoted material, where variable usage is often found. For the texts of the Geneva Agreements and the Final Declaration of the Conference see: Council on Foreign Relations, *Documents on American Foreign Relations, 1954* (New York: 1955), pp. 283–314, hereafter *Documents on American Foreign Relations*. See also US Dept of State, *Foreign Relations of the United States, 1952–1954, The Geneva Conference: Korea and Indochina*, vol. 16 (Washington, 1981), pp. 1505–46, hereafter FRUS, 1952–54, Geneva Conference.

2. Protest by the Vietnamese Delegation against the Geneva Conference Agreements, 21 July 1954, *Documents on American Foreign Relations, 1954*, pp. 315–316. See also *FRUS, 1952–54, Geneva Conference*, pp. 1545–46.

3. Declaration by the United States Regarding Final Declaration of the Geneva Conference, 21 July 1954, *Documents on American Foreign Relations, 1954*, pp. 316–317.

4. Joint Franco-Vietnamese Declaration of 28 April 1954, *Documents on American Foreign Relations, 1954*, pp. 269–270.

5. Heads of Agreement on Vietnamese Independence and Vietnamese Association in the French Union, Initialed by France and Vietnam at Paris, 4 June 1954, *Documents on American Foreign Relations, 1954*, pp. 270–272.

6. Richard P. Stebbins (ed.), *The United States in World Affairs*, 1954, (1956), p. 243. *NY Times*, 26 Jun 54, p. 4; 27 Jun 54, pp. IV, 6.

7. *NY Times*, 26 Jun 54, p. 4.

8. *NY Times*, 6 Jul 54, p. 4. Bernard B. Fall, "The Cease-Fire in Indochina—An Appraisal," Far Eastern Survey, Sep 54," pp. 137–138.

9. (U) NIE 63–5–54, "Post-Geneva Outlook in Indochina," 3 Aug 54, Dept of Defense, *United States-Vietnam Relations, 1954–1967 (Pentagon Papers)*, vol. 10 (Washington: GPO, 1971), pp. 692–98, hereafter *Pentagon Papers*.

10. (U) Msg, Paris 481 to State, 4 Aug 54, *Pentagon Papers*, vol. 10, pp. 699–700.

11. Peggy Durdin, "There Is No Truce in Vietnam," *Reporter*, 30 Dec 54, p. 26.

12. Presidential News Conference, 7 Apr 54, transcript in *Public Papers of the Presidents of the United States: Dwight D. Eisenhower, 1954* (1960), pp. 382–383.

13. NSC 5429, 4 Aug 54, CCS 092 Asia (6–25–48) sec 77. For further commentary on NSC 5429, see US Dept of State, *FRUS, 1952–54, East Asia and the Pacific*, vol. xii, pt. 1 (Washington: GPO, 1984), pp. 716–33 and 744–58, hereafter *FRUS, 1952–54, East Asia and the Pacific*, pt. 1.

14. (TS) Memo, JCS to SecDef, "Review of U.S. Policies in the Far East–NSC 5429," 11 Aug 54, same file, sec 79. This memo is reproduced in *Pentagon Papers*, vol. 10, pp. 709–13 and in *FRUS, 1952–54, East Asia and the Pacific*, pt. 1, pp. 719–23.

15. (TS) NSC 5429/1, 12 Aug 54, same file, sec 80. See also NSC meeting minutes, 12 Aug 54 in *FRUS, 1952–54, East Asia and the Pacific*, pt. 1, pp. 719–23.

16. (TS) NSC 5429/2, 20 Aug-54, same file, sec 81. This document is reproduced in *Pentagon Papers*, vol. 10, pp. 731–41 and in *FRUS, East Asia and the Pacific*, pt. 1, pp. 769–76.

17. For a full account of the Manila Conference and the resulting SEACDT, see Appendix.

18. (TS) NSC 5429/3, 19 Nov 54, CCS 092 Asia (6–25–48) sec 88. This document is also reproduced in *FRUS, 1952–54, East Asia and the Pacific*, pt. 1, pp. 972–82.

19. (TS) Memo, JCS to SecDef, "Current U.S. Policy toward the Far East (NSC 5429/3)," 26 Nov 54 (derived from JCS 1992/420), same file. This JCS memo is reproduced in *FRUS, 1952–54, East Asia and the Pacific*, pt. 1, pp. 992–94.

20. (TS) NSC 5429/4, 10 Dec 54, same file, sec 89. NSC 5429/4 is reproduced in part in *FRUS, 1952–54, East Asia and the Pacific*, pt. 1, pp. 1035–38.

21. (TS) Memo, JCS to SecDef, "Current United States Policy in the Far East (NSC 5429/4)," 17 Dec 54, same file. The JCS memo is reproduced in *FRUS, 1952–54, East Asia and the Pacific*, pt. 1, pp. 1050–51.

22. (TS) NSC 5429/5, 22 Dec 54, same file, sec 90. NCS 5429/5 is reproduced in *FRUS, 1952–54, East Asia and the Pacific*, pt. 1, pp. 1062–72.

23. This study was not completed and approved by the National Security Council until March 1957 (NSC 5701/1, 8 Mar 57).

24. (TS) NSC Action No. 1295, 5 Jan 55. (TS) Memo, ActgSecDef to CJCS et al., "Current U.S. Policy Toward the Far East—NSC 5429/5," 30 Dec 54, CCS 092 Asia (6–25–48) sec 90. (TS) Memo, ExecSecy, NSC to NSC, "Current U.S. Policy Toward the Far East," 6 Jan 55, CCS 092 Asia (6–25–48) (2) sec 1.

Chapter 2. Three Troubled Months—August–October 1954

1. (S) Msgs, Saigon 460 to State, 6 Aug 54, DA IN 77122; 580, 14 Aug 54; 751, 26 Aug 54; 758, 26 Aug 54, DA IN 81273. (C) Msgs, Saigon 515 to State, 10 Aug 54; 601, 16 Aug 54, DA IN 78405; 733, 25 Aug 54, DA IN 80878. The following messages are reproduced in US Dept of State, *Foreign Relations of the United States, 1952–54, Indochina*, vol. xiii, pt. 2 (Washington, GPO, 1982), hereafter cited as *FRUS, 1952–54, Indochina*, pt. 2; Saigon msg 460, p. 1923; Saigon msg 580, pp. 1945–48; Saigon msg 758, pp. 1985–87.

2. (TS) Msgs, Saigon 1036 to State, 16 Sep 54; 1204, 24 Sep 54. Saigon message 1036 is reprinted in *FRUS, 1952–54, Indochina*, pt. 2, pp. 2030–31. See also Spector, *The Early Years*, p. 236.

3. (S) Msgs, Saigon 370 to State, 29 Jul 54; 759, 27 Aug 54. (S) Msgs, Paris 598 to State, 12 Aug 54; 781, 23 Aug 54; 873, 30 Aug 54. (C) Msg, Paris 849 to State, 28 Aug 54. (S) Msg, State 934 to Saigon, 8 Sep 54. (S) Msgs, Saigon 1059 to State; 1061; 1076; 17 Sep 54. (TS) Msg: State 997 to Paris, 17 Sep 54. (TS) Msg, Paris 1171 to State, 18 Sep 54. (TS) Msg, Saigon 1122 to State, 20 Sep 54. The following documents are reprinted in *FRUS, 1952–54, Indochina*, pt. 2: Saigon msg 370, pp. 1890–91; Saigon msg 759, pp. 1988–90; Paris msg 598, pp. 1935–36; Paris msg 873, pp. 1997–99; Saigon msg 1061, p. 2033; State msg 997, pp. 2034–35.

4. (S) Msgs, Saigon 933 to State, 9 Sep 54; 953, 954, 10 Sep 54. (TS) Msgs, Saigon 971 to State, 11 Sep 54; 1076, 17 Sep 54. (U) Msg, Saigon 1107 to State, 19 Sep 54, DA IN 645055. The following messages are reprinted in *FRUS, 1952–54, Indochina*, pt. 2: Saigon msg 933, pp. 2014–15; Saigon msg 953, pp. 2015–16; Saigon msg 971, pp. 2018–19.

5. The US Military Assistance Advisory Group (MAAG) Indochina, was established in the summer of 1950 to provide assistance to the forces of France and the Associated States in Indochina. Lieutenant General John W. O'Daniel was appointed Chief, MAAG Indochina, in April 1954. Between 1950 and mid-1954, the US provided approximately $2.753 billion in military assistance to the French and native troops, almost completely re-equipping them with modern weapons and vehicles.

6. (TS) Msgs, Saigon 1036 to State; 1043, 16 Sep 54; 1119, 19 Sep 54. (S) Msg, Saigon 1250 to State, 27 Sep 54, DA IN 87877; 1278, 30 Sep 54, DA IN 88724 (1 Oct 54). (TS) Msg, CHMAAG Indochina MG 3228 A to CJCS, 22 Sep 54, DA IN 86638. The following messages are

reproduced in *FRUS, 1952–54, Indochina*, pt. 2: Saigon msg 1036, pp. 2030–31; Saigon msg 1119, pp. 2038–39; Saigon msg 1250, pp. 2075–78; Saigon msg 1278, pp. 2103–05. Ronald Spector observes that there was a difference between General O'Daniel and Ambassador Heath in how best to deal with General Hinh during this period. O'Daniel maintained that Hinh was basically honest and would cooperate with Diem while Heath believed that the American general was naive on this subject. Spector, *The Early Years*, pp. 233–35.

7. (S) Msg, Saigon 794 to State, 29 Aug 54.

8. In return for cooperation, often purely nominal, France had for some time given the Cao Dai, the Hoa Hao, and the Binh Xuyen subsidies of money and equipment.

9. (S) Msgs, Saigon 1150 to State; 1154, 21 Sep 54; 1162, 22 Sep 54; 1185, 23 Sep 54. (S) Msg, Saigon 1231 to State, 25 Sep 54, DA IN 87675. (U) Msg, Saigon 1226 to State, 25 Sep 54, DA IN 647750. The following messages are reproduced in *FRUS, 1952–54, Indochina*, pt. 2: Saigon msg 1150, pp. 2041–44; Saigon msg 1154, pp. 2044–45; Saigon msg 1185, pp. 2048–52.

10. (OUO) Msg, Saigon 1286 to State, 1 Oct 54, DA IN 88899. (S) Msgs, Saigon 1313 to State, 2 Oct 54; 1321, 4 Oct 54.

11. About 177,000 men of the FEC were stationed in Indochina at the close of the Geneva Conference.

12. (TS) Dept of State, Briefing Session Summary, 27 Sep 54, ELaC Memo 15, 4 Oct 54, CCS 092 Asia (6–25–48) BP pt 14.

13. (S) Dept of State, ELaC D–1/1, "Establishment and Maintenance of a Stable Anti-Communist Government of Vietnam," 23 Sep 54; ELaC D–1/3, "Other Major Political Questions, Draft Minute of Understanding," 27 Sep 54; (TS) ELaC VM–1, "Minutes of Opening Political Session...," 30 Sep 54; (S) ELaC Memo 16 "Minute of Understanding," 4 Oct 54; CCS 092 Asia (6–25–48) BP pt 14. (TS) Msgs, State 1298 to Saigon, 30 Sep 54; 1327, 1 Oct 54. State msg 1327 is reproduced in *FRUS, 1952–54, Indochina*, pt. 2, pp. 2110–11.

14. (S) Msg, State 737 to Paris, 28 Aug 54.

15. (S) Dept of State, ELaC D–3/1, "US Financial Assistance to French Union Forces in Indochina...," 24 Sep 54, CCS 092 Asia (6–25–48) BP pt 14.

16. (TS) Dept of State, ELaC VM–1, "Minutes of Opening Political Session...," 30 Sep 54; ELaC VM–3, "Minutes of Economic Session of Franco-American Bilateral Talks...," 2 Oct 54; same file.

17. (S) Msg, State 610 to Paris, 18 Aug 54, same file, sec 81. (S) Dept of State, ELaC D–1/2, "US Relations with Cambodia, Laos and Vietnam," 23 Sep 54, same file, BP pt 14. (S) Dept of State "A US Policy for Post-Armistice Indo-china," 12 Aug 54. The following documents are reproduced in *FRUS, 1952–54, Indochina*, pt. 2: State msg 610, pp. 1957–59 and Dept of State, "... Policy for Post-Armistice Indochina," pp. 1937–38.

18. (S) Msg, Paris 715 to State, 20 Aug 54. (S) Msg, State 737 to Paris, 28 Aug 54. (C) Dept of State, ELaC Memo 14, "French Position Papers re Military Aid and Economic Assistance to the Associated States," 28 Sep 54, CCS 092 Asia (6–25–48) BP pt 14. Paris msg 715 is reproduced in *FRUS, 1952–54, Indochina*, pt. 2, pp. 1964–67.

19. (TS) Dept of State, ELaC MC–2, "Memorandum of Conversation, Smith-La Chambre Meeting, September 29, 1954," 6 Oct 54, same file.

20. (TS) Dept of State, ELaC Memo 20, "Report to the Secretary of State on Franco-American Bilateral Talks October 8, 1954," 22 Oct 54, same file.

21. (TS) Msg, State 1194 to Paris for Heath, 1 Oct 54. (S) Msgs, Paris 1413 from Heath to State, 4 Oct 54; Saigon 1361 to State, 7 Oct 54. The following messages are reproduced in *FRUS, 1952–54, Indochina*, pt. 2: State msg 1194, pp. 2109–10; Paris msg 1413, pp. 2115–17; Saigon msg 1361, p. 2118.

22. (S) Msgs, Saigon 1330 to State, 5 Oct 54; 1382, 8 Oct 54; 1397, 10 Oct 54; 1434, 13 Oct 54; 1487, 18 Oct 54; 1493, 19 Oct 54. The following messages are reproduced in *FRUS, 1952–54, Indochina*, pt. 2: Saigon msg 1397, pp. 2128–29; Saigon msg 1434, pp. 2135–38.

23. (S) Msg, Saigon 1513 to State, 21 Oct 54, DA IN 93686 (22 Oct 54). (TS) Msg, Paris 1807 to State, 28 Oct 54.

24. (S) Msg, Saigon 1513 to State, 21 Oct 54, DA IN 93686 (22 Oct 54). (C) Msg, Saigon 1571 to State, 25 Oct 54. (S) Msg, Saigon 2007 to State, 29 Nov 54.

25. (C) Msg, USARMA Saigon MC 817-54 to CSUSA, 14 Oct 54, DA IN 98990 (15 Oct 54), CCS 092 Asia (6-25-485) sec 84. (S) Msg, USARMA Saigon MC 825-54 to DA, 23 Oct 54, DA IN 94015, same file, sec 86. (S) Msg, Saigon 1513 to State, 21 Oct 54, DA IN 93686 (22 Oct 54).

26. "Report of Senator Mike Mansfield on a Study Mission to Vietnam, Cambodia, Laos," 15 Oct 54, 83d Cong., 2d sess., S. Com on Foreign Relations, pp. 11, 14.

27. (C) Msg, Saigon 1478 to State, 17 Oct 54, DA IN 92546. (S) Msg, Saigon 1501 to State, 20 Oct 54. (C) Msg, Paris 1608 to State, 16 Oct 54. The following messages are reproduced in *FRUS, 1952–54, Indochina*, pt. 2: Saigon msg 1501, pp. 2145–46; Paris msg 1608, pp. 2141–42.

28. (TS) Msgs, State TODUL 14 to Paris; State 1678 to Saigon and Paris; 22 Oct 54. The President's letter had been drafted in August and a copy made available to the French, but delivery had been held up pending clarification of the Vietnamese political situation. (TS) Msg, Joint State-Defense (State 1679) to Paris and Saigon, 22 Oct 54. The following messages are reproduced in *FRUS, 1952–54, Indochina*, pt. 2: State msg 1678 to Paris and Saigon, pp. 2159–60 and Joint State-Defense msg 1679, pp. 2161–62.

29. (TS) Msgs, Paris 1718 to State, 24 Oct 54; 1736, 25 Oct 54. Paris msg 1718 is reproduced in *FRUS, 1952–54, Indochina*, pt. 2, pp. 2168–69.

30. (TS) Msgs, State 1565 to Paris, 29 Oct 54; Paris 1835 to State; 1836, 30 Oct 54. The following messages are reproduced in *FRUS, 1952–54, Indochina*, pt. 2: State msg 1565, pp. 2193–94; Paris msg 1835, pp. 2196–97.

31. See chap. 3.

32. (S) Msg, Saigon 1609 to State, 27 Oct 54. Saigon msg 1609 is reproduced in *FRUS, 1952–54, Indochina*, pt. 2, pp. 2188–2190.

33. Ibid.

34. (S) Dept of State, ELaC Memo 16, "Minute of Understanding," 4 Oct 54, CCS 092 Asia (6-25-48) BP pt 14.

35. (S) Msg, Paris 2080 to State, 15 Nov 54. Paris msg 2080 is reproduced in *FRUS, 1952–54, Indochina*, pt. 2, pp. 2246–50.

36. Ibid. (S) Msg, Saigon 1611 to State, 27 Oct 54. Saigon message 1611 is reproduced in *FRUS, 1952–54, Indochina*, pt. 2, pp. 2190–91.

37. See *The Joint Chiefs of Staff and the First Indochina War, 1947–1954* (Washington, D.C.: Office of Joint History, 2004), p. 11.

38. (TS) Msg, Paris 646 to State, 15 Aug 54. (S) Msg, Saigon 494 to State, 8 Aug 54. Paris message 646 is in *FRUS, 1952–54, Indochina*, pt. 2, pp. 1948–49.

39. (C) Msg, Saigon 795 to State, 29 Aug 54. (S) Msgs, Saigon 507 to State, 10 Aug 54; 721, 24 Aug 54. (TS) Msg, Paris 646 to State, 15 Aug 54. On 20 October, Amb. Dillon reported a conversation with Jacques Raphael-Leygues, French Union Counselor and reputedly a member of the Mendes-France "brain-trust" on Indochinese affairs. Sainteny, said Raphael-Leygues, had convinced the government that South Vietnam was doomed and that the "only possible means of salvaging anything was to play Viet Minh game and woo the Viet Minh away from Communist ties in hope of creating a Titoist Vietnam which would cooperate with France and might even adhere to French Union." When the rift appeared between France and the United States over the government to be supported in Saigon, the French deferred to the United States in order to obtain financial support of the FEC and to fix responsibility for eventual loss of South Vietnam on the United States. General Ely, said Raphael-Leygues, was not fully "au courant" with these facts and was "playing straight game of honestly cooperating with United States." (C) Msg, Paris 1665 to State, 29 Oct 54. The following messages are reproduced in *FRUS, 1952–54, Indochina*, pt. 2: Saigon msg

795, pp. 1994–95; Saigon msg 507, pp. 1931–32; Saigon msg 721, pp. 1980–84; Paris msg 646, pp. 1948–49.

40. *NY Times*, 11 Dec 54, 3:7; 12 Dec 54, 42:1. (C) Msgs, State 2413 to Saigon, 13 Dec 54; Paris 2542 to State, 14 Dec 54.

41. (S) NIE 63-7-54, 23 Nov 54, pp. 4, 7–8. NIE 63-7-54 is reproduced in *FRUS, 1952–54, Indochina*, pt. 2, pp. 2286–2301.

42. (S) Msgs, Paris 1883 to State, 3 Nov 54; State 1737 to Paris, 10 Nov 54; Paris 2018 to State, 11 Nov 54. State msg 1737 is reproduced in *FRUS, 1952–54, Indochina*, pt. 2, p. 2238.

43. (S) Paris 366 to State, 27 Jul 54; 715, 20 Aug 54. The following messages are reproduced in *FRUS, 1952–54, Indochina*, pt. 2: Paris msg 366, pp. 1879–81; Paris msg 715, pp. 1964–66.

44. (S) Msgs, Paris 366 to State, 27 Jul 54; 438, 30 Jul 54. Paris msg 438 is reproduced in *FRUS, 1952–54, Indochina*, pt. 2, pp. 1896–98.

45. Ibid.

46. (C) Msg, Paris 849 to State, 28 Aug 54. *NY Times*, 17 Sep 54, p. 3; 28 Sep 54, p. 1.

47. *NY Times*, 27 Aug 54, p. 5; 3 Sep 54, p. 5; 30 Dec 54, p. 1. (S) Msgs, State 740 to Paris, 30 Aug 54; Saigon 580 to State, 14 Aug 54. Saigon msg 580 is reproduced in *FRUS, 1952–54, Indochina*, pt. 2, pp. 1945–48.

48. (U) Msgs, Paris 1545 to State, 12 Oct 54, DA IN 654436; 1668, 21 Oct 54. (C) Msg, Paris 2360 to State, 4 Dec 54. *NY Times*, 20 Oct 64, p. 12; 30 Dec 54, p. 1.

49. *NY Times*, 10 Oct 54, p. 1; 21 Oct 54, p. 11.

50. *NY Times*, 29 Oct 54, 5:3. (TS) Memo, OCB, Working Group on Indochina to Chm, OCB, "Special Status Report on Indochina . . . ," 14 Dec 54.

51. (LOU) Msg, Saigon 2114 to State, 6 Dec 54, DA IN 103403.

52. (S) Intelligence Advisory Committee, IAC-D-93/2, "Vietminh Violations of the Geneva Agreements Through 31 December 1954." (Hereafter cited as IAC, *Vietminh Violations*.) (S) Msg, CHMAAG Indochina MG 3267A, 1 Oct 54, CCS 092 Asia (6–25–48) sec 84.

53. (S) IAC, *Vietminh Violations*. (S) Msg, Saigon 383 to State, 30 Jul 54, DA IN 75514.

54. (S) Msg, Saigon 2070 to State, 3 Dec 54, DA IN 103027. (S) IAC, *Vietminh Violations*.

55. Ibid.

Chapter 3. The Collins Mission

1. (TS) Ltr, Pres to GEN Collins, 3 Nov 54, CCS 092 Asia (6–25–48) sec 88.

2. (TS) Msg, Saigon 1686 to State, 3 Nov 54. Saigon msg 1686 is reproduced in *FRUS, 1952–54, Indochina*, pt. 2, pp. 2203–04.

3. (TS) Memo, Collins to SecState, "Report on Vietnam to the National Security Council," 20 Jan 55, CCS 092 Asia (6–25–48) (2) sec 3. (Hereafter cited as Collins Report to NSC.) The Collins Report is reprinted in US Dept of State, *Foreign Relations of the United States, 1955–1957, Vietnam*, vol. I (Washington: GPO, 1985), pp. 54–57, hereafter *FRUS, 1955–57, Vietnam*.

4. Ibid. (S) Msg, Saigon 2004 to State, 29 Nov 54, DA IN 101696–S, CCS 092 Asia (6–25–48) sec 88. Saigon msg 2004 is reproduced in *FRUS, 1952–54, Indochina*, pt. 2, pp. 2315–2319.

5. As a concession to LTG Navarre's rank consciousness, LTG O'Daniel had taken a one-grade reduction in rank upon assignment to MAAG in the spring of 1954. With GEN Navarre's replacement by GEN Paul Ely, O'Daniel's three-star rank was restored in August 1954.

6. (TS) Msg, CHMAAG Indochina MG 2062Z to DA, 27 Jul 54, DA IN 74737, CCS 092 Asia (6–25–48) sec 76. (TS) Msgs, Saigon 301 to State, 24 Jul 54; 366, 29 Jul 54. The following messages are reproduced in *FRUS, 1952–54, Indochina*, pt. 2: CHMAAG Indochina, 27 Jul 54, pp. 1883–85; Saigon msg 366, pp. 1889–90.

7. (S) Memo, JCS to SecDef, "US Assumption of Training Responsibilities in Indochina," 4 Aug 54 (derived from JCS 1992/367), CCS 092 Asia (6–25–48) sec 77. (S) Ltr, SecDef to SecState,

12 Aug 54, same file, sec 80. The JCS memo to SecDef, 4 Aug 54 is reproduced in the *Pentagon Papers*, vol. 10, pp. 701–02, while the SecDef letter to SecState 12 Aug 54 is reproduced in *FRUS, 1952–54, Indochina*, pt. 2, pp. 1938–39. See also Spector, *The Early Years*, pp. 223–224.

8. (S) Ltr, SecState to SecDef, 18 Aug 54, App to Encl to JCS 1992/388, 3 Sep 54, same file, sec 82. This letter is reproduced in *FRUS, 1952–54, Indochina*, pt. 2, pp. 1945–56.

9. (TS) NSC 5429/1, 12 Aug 54, same file, sec 80.

10. (S) Msg, State 610 to Paris, 18 Aug 54. (TS) Memo, JCS to SecDef, "US Assumption of Training Responsibilities in Indochina," 22 Sep 54 (derived from JCS 1992/393), CCS 092 Asia (6–25–48) sec 83. The following documents have been reproduced in *FRUS, 1952–54, Indochina*, pt. 2: Paris msg 610, pp. 1957–59; JCS memo to Sec Def, 22 Sep 54, pp. 2088–89.

11. (S) State Dept. ELaC D2–4, "Development and Training of Indigenous Forces in Indochina," 24 Sep 54, CCS 092 Asia (6–25–48) BP pt 14.

12. (TS) Memo, JCS to SecDef, "Retention and Development of Forces in Indochina," 22 Sep 54 (derived from JCS 1992/394), same file, sec 83.

13. (TS) Ltr, SecState to SecDef, 11 Oct 54, App to Encl to JCS 1992/402, 15 Oct 54, same file, sec 84. This letter is reproduced in *FRUS, 1952–54, Indochina*, pt. 2, pp. 2132–35.

14. (TS) Memo, JCS to SecDef, "Development and Training of Indigenous Forces in Indochina," 19 Oct 54 (derived from JCS 1992/404), same file, sec 85. This memo is reproduced in the *Pentagon Papers*, vol. 10, pp. 771–74.

15. The Operations Coordination Board was a major subsidiary organization of the National Security Council. It functioned as the coordinating and integrating arm of the NSC for all aspects of implementation of national security policy.

16. (TS) CM–117–54 to D/JS, 21 Oct 54, Encl to JCS 1992/406, 21 Oct 54; (TS) JCS 1992/407, 22 Oct 54; (TS) Msg, State 1678 to Saigon and Paris, 22 Oct 54; (TS) Msg, Jt State-Defense (State 1679) to Saigon and Paris, 22 Oct 54; CCS 092 Asia (6–25–48) sec 85. (TS) NSC Rcd of Action, 218th Mtg, 22 Oct 54. The following documents are reproduced in *FRUS, 1952–54, Indochina*, pt. 2: Joint State/Defense msg 1679, pp. 2161–62; NSC memo of record, 218th Meeting, extracts, pp. 2153–60.

17. (S) Msg, Saigon 1609 to State, 27 Oct 54. Saigon msg 1609 is reproduced in *FRUS, 1952–54, Indochina*, pt. 2, pp. 2188–90.

18. (S) NIE 63–7–54, 23 Nov 54. This NIE is reproduced in *FRUS, 1952–54, Indochina*, pt. 2, pp. 2286–2301.

19. (S) Msg, Saigon 2104 to State, 29 Nov 54, DA IN 101696–S, CCS 092 Asia (6–25–48) sec 88. Saigon msg 2104 is reproduced in *FRUS, 1952–54, Indochina*, pt. 2, pp. 2315–19.

20. (S) Msgs, Paris 1927 to State, 5 Nov 54; 2036, 12 Nov 54; 2211, 25 Nov 54; 2240, 28 Nov 54. (S) Msg, Saigon 1807 to State, 12 Nov 54. (C) Msgs, Paris 2272 to State, 30 Nov 54; 2290, 1 Dec 54. (U) Msg, Paris 2193 to State, 23 Nov 54. The following messages are reproduced in *FRUS, 1952–54, Indochina*, pt. 2: Paris msg 1927, pp. 2210–13; Saigon msg 1807, pp. 2238–41; Paris msg 2290, pp. 2327–28. See also Spector, *The Early Years*, p. 237.

21. (S) Msg, CHMAAG Indochina (Collins) 1795 to OSD, 11 Nov 54, DA IN 98060. (S) Msg, DEF 970965 to CHMAAG Indochina, 13 Nov 54.

22. (TS) Msg, Saigon 1830 to State, 15 Nov 54, DA IN 99015, CCS 092 Asia (6–25–48) sec 87. Saigon msg 1830 is reproduced in *FRUS, 1952–54, Indochina*, pt. 2, pp. 2250–56. See also Spector, *The Early Years*, pp. 237–238.

23. (TS) Memo, JCS to SecDef, "Indochina," 17 Nov 54 (derived from JCS 1992/4I2), same file. (TS) Ltr, ASD(ISA) to SecState, 26 Nov 54, Encl to JCS 1992/421, 30 Oct 54, same file, sec 88.

24. (S) Msg, Saigon 1761 to State, 8 Nov 54. (TS) Msg, Saigon 1830 to State, 15 Nov 54, DA IN 99015, CCS 092 Asia (6–25–48) sec 87. Saigon msg 1761 is reproduced in *FRUS, 1952–54, Indochina*, pt. 2, pp. 2224–25.

25. (C) Msg, FAO Washington USFOTO 263 to Paris and Saigon, 24 Nov 54, same file, sec 88.

26. (TS) Msg, Paris 2433 to State, 8 Dec 54. (S) DA, ACofS, G–2 Intelligence Estimate of the "Defensive Capabilities of Southeast Asia Pact Nations," 1 Mar 55, CCS 092 Asia (6–25–48) (2) BP pt 1.

27. (TS) Msg, Saigon 2168 to State, 9 Dec 54, CCS 092 Asia (6–25–48) sec 89. (S) Msg, Saigon 2025 to State, 30 Nov 54.

28. (S) Msg, Saigon 1854 to State, 16 Nov 54.

29. Ibid. (TS) Msg, Saigon 1830 to State, 15 Nov 54, DA IN 99015, CCS 092 Asia (6–25–48) sec 87. (C) Msg, Saigon 1920 to State, 21 Nov 54. Saigon msg 1830 is reproduced in *FRUS, 1952–54, Indochina*, pt. 2, pp. 225–56.

30. (TS) Msg, State 2046 to Saigon, 19 Nov 54. (S) Msgs State 2070 to Saigon, 22 Nov 54; 2126, 26 Nov 54. The following messages are reproduced in *FRUS, 1952–54, Indochina*, pt. 2: State 2046, pp. 2271; State 2070, pp. 2277–79; State 2126, pp. 2307–08.

31. (TS) Msg, Saigon 2250 to State, 13 Dec 54. (S) Msg, Saigon 2024 to State, 30 Nov 54. (C) Msg, Saigon 2261 to State 14 Dec 54, DA IN 105051, CCS 092 Asia (6–25–48) sec 89. The following messages are reproduced in *FRUS, 1952–54, Indochina*, pt. 2: Saigon 2250, pp. 2362–66; Saigon 2024, pp. 2319–21; Saigon 2261, pp. 2366–68.

32. (TS) Msg, Paris 2601 to State, 19 Dec 54. Paris msg 2601 is reproduced in *FRUS, 1952–54, Indochina*, pt. 2, pp. 2400–06.

33. (TS) Msg, Saigon 2455 to State and Manila, 25 Dec 54. Saigon msg 2455 is reproduced in *FRUS, 1952–54, Indochina*, pt. 2, pp. 2423–25.

34. (TS) Msgs, Paris 2270 to State, 31 Dec 54; 2870, 7 Jan 55. (TS) Msg, State 2766 to Saigon, 7 Jan 55. Paris msg 2270 is reproduced in *FRUS, 1952–54, Indochina*, pt. 2, pp. 2440–44. Both Paris msg 2870 and State msg 2766 are reproduced in *FRUS, 1955–57, Vietnam*, pp. 22–24.

35. (S) Msg, Paris 2797 to State, 3 Jan 55. (TS) Msgs, Saigon 2660 to State, 9 Jan 55; 2663, 10 Jan 55, DA IN 109948; CCS 092 Asia (6–25–48) (2) sec 1. The following messages are reproduced in *FRUS, 1955–57, Vietnam*: Saigon msg 2660, pp. 29–30; Saigon msg 2663, pp. 30–32.

36. (S) Msgs, Saigon 2453 to State for DOD, 24 Dec 54, DA IN 10729. (TS) Msg, Saigon 2676 to State, 10 Jan 55. (S) Msg, Saigon 2876 to State, 22 Jan 55, DA IN 113240. Saigon msg 2453 is reproduced in *FRUS, 1952–54, Indochina*, pt. 2, pp. 2415–17.

37. (TS) Msg, Paris 3064 to State, 20 Jan 55. (TS) Msg, State 2629 to Paris, 24 Jan 55. Msg 2629 contains a copy of the letter from Secretary Dulles to Premier Mendes-France and is reproduced in *FRUS, 1955–57, Vietnam*, pp. 59–60.

38. (TS) Msg, Paris 3195 to State, 28 Jan 55. (TS) Msg, State 2726 to Paris, 1 Feb 55. (C) Msg, Saigon 3343 to State, 11 Feb 55, DA IN 117991, CCS 092 Asia (6–25–48) (2) sec 4. These messages are reproduced in *FRUS, 1955–57, Vietnam*: Paris 3195, pp. 70–71; State 2726, pp. 71–72; Saigon 3343, pp. 84–86.

39. (S) Msg, Saigon 2075 to State, 4 Dec 54. Saigon msg 2075 is reproduced in *FRUS, 1952–54, Indochina*, pt. 2, pp. 2340–41.

40. (TS) Msg, Saigon 2303 to State, 17 Dec 54, DA IN 105690.

41. (S) Msg, Saigon 2811 to State, 17 Jan 55; 3340, 11 Feb 55. (TS) Collins Report to NSC.

42. (S) Msg, Saigon 2004 to State, 29 Nov 54, DA IN 101696–S, CCS 092 Asia (6–25–40) sec 88. (S) Msg, Saigon 2110 to State, 6 Dee 54. Saigon msg 2004 is reproduced in *FRUS, 1952–54, Indochina*, pt. 2, pp. 2315–19.

43. (TS) Msg, State 1565 to Paris, 29 Oct 54. (S) Msg, Paris 1896 to State, 4 Nov 54.

44. (S) Msgs, Saigon 1919 to State, 21 Nov 54; 1935, 23 Nov 54. (S) Msg, State 2070 to Saigon, 22 Nov 54. State msg 2070 is reproduced in *FRUS, 1952–54, Indochina*, pt. 2, pp. 2277–79.

45. (S) Msg, Saigon 1967 to State, 24 Nov 64, DA IN 100745. Saigon msg 1967 is reproduced in *FRUS, 1952–54, Indochina*, pt. 2, pp. 2301–02.

46. (TS) Msgs, Saigon 2250 to State, 13 Dec 54; 2285, 15 Dec 54; 2303, 17 Dec 54, DA IN 105690. The following messages are reproduced in *FRUS, 1952–54, Indochina*, pt. 2: Saigon 2250, pp. 2362–66; Saigon 2303, pp. 2379–82.

47. (S) Msg, Saigon 2334 to State, 17 Dec 54. Saigon msg 2334 is reproduced in *FRUS, 1952–54, Indochina*, pt. 2, pp. 2396–97.

48. (S) Msgs, Saigon 1906 to State, 20 Nov 54; 2285, 15 Dec 54; 2234, 17 Dec 54. The following messages are reproduced in *FRUS, 1952–54, Indochina*, pt. 2: Saigon 1906, p. 2272; Saigon 2285, pp. 2375–78; Saigon 2234, pp. 2396–98.

49. (S) Msg, Saigon 1906 to State, 20 Nov 54. For reproduction of Saigon 1906 see footnote 48.

50. (S) Msgs, Saigon 2022 to State, 30 Nov 54; 2259, 14 Dec 54; 2583, 5 Jan 55. (C) Msg, Saigon 3451 to State, 17 Feb 55.

51. (S) Msg, Saigon 2259 to State, 14 Dec 54.

52. (S) Msg, Saigon 2583 to State, 5 Jan 55. (C) Msg, Saigon 3451 to State, 17 Feb 55.

53. (S) Msgs, Saigon 2022 to State, 30 Nov 54; 2259, 14 Dec 54; 2583, 4 Jan 55.

54. (C) Msg, Saigon 3451 to State, 17 Feb 55.

55. Ibid.

56. (S) Msgs, State 2555 to Saigon, 20 Nov 54; 2112, 24 Nov 54. The following messages are reproduced in *FRUS, 1952–54, Indochina*, pt. 2: State 2055, pp. 2274–75; State 2112, pp. 2303–06.

57. (U) Msg, Paris 2601 to State, 19 Dec 54. Paris msg 2601 is reproduced in *FRUS, 1952–54, Indochina*, pt. 2, pp. 2400–05.

58. (S) Msg, Paris 2987 to State, 14 Jan 55.

59. (S) Msg, Saigon 2894 to State, 22 Jan 55.

60. (TS) Msg, Saigon 2250 to State, 13 Dec 54. Saigon msg 2250 is reproduced in *FRUS, 1952–54, Indochina*, pt. 2, 2362–66.

61. (TS) Msg, Saigon 2303 to State, 17 Dec 54. Saigon msg 2303 is reproduced in *FRUS, 1952–54, Indochina*, pt. 2, pp. 2379–2382. Note that the message is dated 16 December 54 in the FRUS volume rather than 17 December.

62. (U) Memo, Heath to Robertson, "Comments on Saigon Telegram 2303," 17 Dec 54, Pentagon Papers, vol. 10, pp. 824–825. The Heath memo is also reproduced in *FRUS, 1952–54, Indochina*, pt. 2, pp. 2350–52.

63. (U) Memo of Conversation, Senator Mike Mansfield, Asst SecState Walter S. Robertson, et al., "Vietnam and Southeast Asia," 7 Dec54, the *Pentagon Papers*, pp. 806–808. This memo is also reproduced in *FRUS, 1952–54, Indochina*, pt. 2, pp. 2350–52.

64. (U) Msg, Paris 2601 to State, 19 Dec 54. Paris msg 2601 is reproduced in *FRUS, 1952–54, Indochina*, pt. 2, pp. 2400–05.

65. (S) Msg, State 2872 to Saigon, 13 Jan 55. (TS) Msg, Paris 3034 to State, 18 Jan 55. The following messages are reproduced in *FRUS, 1955–57, Vietnam*: Msg 2872, pp. 32–33; Msg 3034, pp. 45–47. In the latter message to the State Department from Paris on 13 January 1955, Secretary Dulles cabled that the French had apparently misinterpreted his views. He explained that the US had not made any commitment to "change Diem or associate Bao Dai with any such change except in event his failure to make progress makes an alternative desirable." Dulles noted that his most recent information from Saigon was that "Diem is gaining popular support. . . . ", p. 33.

66. (U) Msg, State 2585 to Saigon, 24 Dec 54, Pentagon Papers, vol. 10, pp. 853–855. This message is also reproduced in *FRUS, 1952–54, Indochina*, pt. 2, pp. 2419–20.

67. (TS) Memo, SecDef to JCS, "Reconsideration of US Military Programs in Southeast Asia," 5 Jan 55, Encl to JCS 1992/431, same date, CCS 092 Asia (6–25–48) (2) sec 1.

68. (TS) Memo, to SecDef, "Reconsideration of US Military Program, Southeast Asia," 21 Jan 55 (derived from JCS 1992/438), same file, sec 2. JCS 1992/438), same file, sec 2. Editorial

Note, *FRUS, 1955–57, Vietnam*, pp. 57–58, refers both to the Secretary of Defense and JCS memos. Both memos are reprinted in *Pentagon Papers*, vol. 10, pp. 860–63.

69. (TS) Collins Report to NSC.

70. (S) Msg, Saigon 2562 to State, 4 Jan 55. (C) Msgs, Saigon 2568 to State, 4 Jan 55; 2703, 11 Jan 55. (FOUO) Msg, Saigon 3039 to State, 30 Jan 55.

71. (TS) Collins Report to NSC. General Collins' oral remarks to the National Security Council are contained in Memorandum of Discussion at the 234th Meeting of the National Security Council, Washington, January 27, 1955, reproduced in *FRUS, 1955–57, Vietnam*, pp. 62–70.

72. (TS) Memo, SecDef to JCS, et al., "Report on Vietnam for the National Security Council," 3 Feb 55, Encl to JCS 1992/447, 7 Feb 55, CCS 094 via (6–25–48) (2) sec 4.

73. (S) Msg, Saigon 3253 to State, 7 Feb 55. Saigon msg 3253 is reproduced in *FRUS, 1955–57, Vietnam*, pp. 78–79.

74. (C) Msg, Saigon 2895 to State, 22 Jan 55. (S) Msg, Saigon 3102 to State, 1 Feb 55. (C) Msg, Paris 3092 to State, 21 Jan 55. (S) Msg, Paris 3316 to State, 7 Feb 55.

Chapter 4. The Crisis of April and May 1955

1. (TS) Msg, Saigon 2581 to State, 5 Jan 55. Message 2581 is reproduced in *FRUS, 1955–57, Vietnam*, pp. 17–19. For additional information about the sects and the April–May crisis see Spector, *The Early Years*, pp. 243–251.

2. For further treatment of TRIM, see Chapter 5.

3. (TS) Msg, Saigon 2581 to State, 5 Jan 55. (S) Msgs, Saigon 3797 to State, 10 Mar 55; 4373, 6 Apr 55. Both messages 2581 and 3797 are reproduced in *FRUS, 1955–57, Vietnam*, pp. 17–19, and 116–119.

4. (OUO) Msg, Saigon 2807 to State, 17 Jan 55. (S) Msgs, Saigon 3381 to State, 14 Feb 55; 3470, 18 Feb 55.

5. (S) Msgs, Saigon 3156 to State, 3 Feb 55; 3296, 9 Feb 55; 3470, 18 Feb 55. Message 3156 is reproduced in *FRUS, 1955–57, Vietnam*, pp. 75–76.

6. (S) Msg, Saigon 4078 to State, 23 Mar 55.

7. (S) Msg, Paris 3654 to State 1 Mar 55. This message is reproduced in *FRUS, 1955–57, Vietnam*, pp. 97–99.

8. (S) Msg, Saigon 3462 to State, 18 Feb 55.

9. (C) Msgs, Saigon 3754 to State, 8 Mar 55; 3861, 13 Mar 55.

10. (S) Msgs, Saigon 3797 to State; 3812, 10 Mar 55. (S) Msg, USARMA Saigon MC 938–55 to DA for G–2, 15 Mar 55, DA IN 125334, CCS 092 Asia (6–25–48) (2) sec 6. Messages 3797 and 3812 are reproduced in *FRUS, 1955–57, Vietnam*, pp. 116–122.

11. (C) Msg, State to Paris, 21 Feb 55. (S) Msgs, Paris 3654 to State, 1 Mar 55; 3896, 15 Mar 55. Message 3654 is reproduced in *FRUS, 1955–57, Vietnam*, pp. 97–99.

12. (OUO) Msg, Saigon 4038 to State, 22 Mar 55. (S) Msg, Saigon 4050 to State, 23 Mar 55.

13. (S) Msg, Saigon 4050 to State, 23 Mar 55.

14. (S) Msg, Saigon 4050 to State, 23 Mar 55; Saigon 4084 to State, 24 Mar 55.

15. (S) Msgs, Saigon 4051 to State, 23 Mar 55; 4096, 24 Mar 55. Paradoxically, Wintrebert was the only important French official in Saigon who wholeheartedly believed in the policy of supporting Diem. General Collins, in explaining Wintrebert's conduct said: "I believe Wintrebert, who is really a fine young man friendly to Diem, became a bit panicky after talking to Diem evening 21st."

16. (S) Msgs, State 3384 to Paris, 25 Mar 55; Saigon 4096 to State, 24 Mar 55; Paris 4070 to State, 23 Mar 55; 4108, 24 Mar 55; 4151, 26 Mar 55. Message 3384 is reproduced in *FRUS, 1955–57, Vietnam*, pp. 146–147.

Notes to Pages 64–70

17. (S) Msgs, Paris 4107 to State, 24 Mar 55; Saigon 4123 to State, 24 Mar 55; State 3384 to Paris, 25 Mar 55; State 4197 to Saigon, 28 Mar 55. Message 4197 is reproduced in *FRUS, 1955–57, Vietnam*, pp. 150–51.

18. (S) Msg, Saigon 4070 to State, 23 Mar 55. (LOU) Msg, Saigon 4157 to State, 28 Mar 55.

19. (S) Msg, USARMA Saigon MC 945–55 to DA for G–2, 27 Mar 55, DA IN 128188, CCS 092 Asia (6–25–48) (2) sec 6. *NY Times*, 27 Mar 55, p. 33.

20. (S) Msg, Saigon 4192 to State, 29 Mar 55. *Washington Post*, 29 Mar 55, p. 4. Message 4192 is reproduced in *FRUS, 1955–57, Vietnam*, pp. 158–59.

21. (S) Msg, Saigon 4213 to DA, 30 Mar 55, DA IN 128901. *NY Times*, 30 Mar 55, p. 1. General Ely initially denied the government reports that General Jacquot had interfered with Vietnamese troop movements. He declared that the VNA had been issued without question all the gasoline and ammunition it had requested. However, a few days later, Ely remarked that the French had never restricted gasoline or ammunition "except for a few hours" during the fighting of 29–30 March. (S) Msg, Saigon 4292 to State, 2 Apr 55. (TS) Msg, Saigon 4349 to State, 6 Apr 55. Messages 4213 and 4292 are reproduced in *FRUS, 1955–57, Vietnam*, pp. 163 and 180–84.

22. (S) Msg, Saigon 4230 to State, 30 Mar 55. Message 4230 is reproduced in *FRUS, 1955–57, Vietnam*, pp. 164–67.

23. Ibid. (S) Msg, Saigon 4264 to State, 31 Mar 55; 4292, 2 Apr 55. These messages are reproduced in *FRUS, 1955–57, Vietnam*, pp. 164–67, 171–74, 180–84.

24. (S) Msgs, Saigon 4220 to State, 4230, 30 Mar 55; 4241, 31 Mar 55; 4292, 2 Apr 55. Messages 4230 and 4292 are reproduced in *FRUS, 1955–57, Vietnam*, pp. 164–67 and 180–84.

25. (TS) Msgs, Saigon 4263 to State, 31 Mar 55; 4348, 5 Apr 55. Both messages are reproduced in *FRUS, 1955–57, Vietnam*, pp. 171–74 and 205–08.

26. (TS) Msg, Saigon 4382 to State, 7 Apr 55. Message 4382 is reproduced in *FRUS, 1955–57, Vietnam*, pp. 215–221.

27. (TS) Msg, Saigon 4263 to State, 31 Mar 55. Message 4263 is reproduced in *FRUS, 1955–57, Vietnam*, pp. 168–71.

28. (TS) Msg, Saigon 4399 to State, 7 Apr 55. Message 4399 is reproduced in *FRUS, 1955–57, Vietnam*, pp. 218–21.

29. (TS) Msgs, State 4438 to Saigon, 9 Apr 55; 4466, 11 Apr 55; 4575, 16 Apr 55. Messages 4438 and 4575 are reproduced in *FRUS, 1955–57, Vietnam*, pp. 229–31 and 250–52. In a Memorandum of a Conversation between the Director of the Office of Philippine and Southeast Asian Affairs and Senator Mansfield, dated 8 Apr 55, and not cited in the footnote, the Senator is quoted as saying: "Ngo Dinh Diem and Ho Chi Minh are the only two national leaders in Vietnam....Dropping Diem now would probably lead to chaos and disintegration." Senator Mansfield believed that even with supporting Diem that the chances of "saving Free Vietnam" were small. "But the importance of Southeast Asia is so great that we must take even that chance." This Memorandum is reproduced in *FRUS, 1955–57, Vietnam*, pp. 221–22.

30. (S) Msgs, Paris 4200 to State, 28 Mar 55; 4281, 4285, 2 Apr 55. (TS) Msgs Paris 4328 to State, 5 Apr 55; 4395, 9 Apr 55; State 3510 to Paris, 4 Apr 55. Message 3510 is reproduced in *FRUS, 1955–57, Vietnam*, pp. 194–95.

31. (TS) Msg, State 3622 to Paris, 12 Apr 55. (TS) Msg, Paris 4498 to State, 16 Apr 55. Message 3622 is reproduced in *FRUS, 1955–57, Vietnam*, pp. 244–45.

32. (TS) Msg, Paris 4503 to State, 17 Apr 55. Message 4503 is reproduced in *FRUS, 1955–57, Vietnam*, pp. 251–54.

33. (U) Msgs, Saigon 4661 to State, 19 Apr 55; 4663, 20 Apr 55; *Pentagon Papers*, vol. 10, pp. 912–913, 918–922. Messages 4661 and 4663 are reproduced in *FRUS, 1955–57, Vietnam*, pp. 260–65 and 268–70.

34. (U) Memo, Dep ASD(ISA) to ASD(ISA), 25 Apr 55, *Pentagon Papers*, vol. 10, pp. 937–940.

35. (TS) Msg, Paris 4576 to State, 21 Apr 55. (S) Msg, Paris 4659 to State, 26 Apr 55.

Notes to Pages 70–80

36. (TS) Msgs, State 4757 to Saigon, 27 Apr 55; State 3828 to Paris, 27 Apr 55; 3849, 28 Apr 55. A memorandum for the record, dated Washington, 27 Apr 1955, contains a "Summary of Remarks of General Lawton Collins" in which the general is quoted as stating that "there was no question of Diem's honesty, anti-communism and anti-colonialism, but he is so completely uncompromising...and monastic that he cannot deal with realities like the Binh Xuyen and the Cao Dai....", *FRUS, 1955–57, Vietnam*, pp. 292–93.

37. (U) Msg, Saigon 4844 to State, 27 Apr 55. (OUO) Msg, Saigon 4845 to State, 27 Apr 55.

38. (S) Msg, Saigon 4860 to State, 28 Apr 55. (U) Msgs, Saigon 4881 to State, 28 Apr 55; 4943, 30 Apr 55. *NY Times*, 29 Apr 55, p. 1.

39. (S) Msgs, Saigon 4926 to State, 29 Apr 55; 4951, 30 Apr 55. (C) Msg, Saigon 4928 to State, 29 Apr 55. (TS) Msg, Paris 4746 to State, 30 Apr 55. Message 4926 is reproduced in *FRUS, 1955–57, Vietnam*, pp. 316–19.

40. (S) Msg, Saigon 4956 to State, 30 Apr 55. This message is reproduced in *FRUS, 1955–57, Vietnam*, pp. 328–331.

41. (S) Msg, Saigon 4944 to State, 30 Apr 55. (OUO) Msg, Saigon 4957 to State, 30 Apr 55.

42. *NY Times*, 1 May 55, p. 1. (OUO) Msg, Saigon 4961 to State, 1 May 55.

43. *NY Times*, 2 May 55, p. 1.

44. Msgs, Saigon 4882 to State, 28 Apr 55; 4926, 29 Apr 55; 4953, 30 Apr 55. (C) Msg, Saigon 4908 to State, 29 Apr 55. These messages are reproduced in *FRUS, 1955–57, Vietnam*, pp. 303–05, 316–19, 327–28 and 315–16.

45. (S) Msgs, Saigon 4953 to State, 30 Apr 55; 4988, 1 May 55. Both messages are reproduced in *FRUS, 1955–57, Vietnam*, pp. 327–28 and 340–44.

46. (C) Msg, Saigon 4039 to State, 4 May 55.

47. (S) Msgs, Saigon 5005 to State, 5006, 2 May 55; 5047, 5049, 5053, 5054, 4 May 55. (S) Msgs, State 4867 to Saigon, 3 May 55; Paris 4814 to State, 4 May 55. Messages 4867 and 5047 are reproduced in *FRUS, 1955–57, Vietnam*, pp. 353–55 and 357–59.

48. (C) Msg, Saigon 5103 to State, 6 May 55. *NY Times*, 6 May 55, p. 1.

49. (TS) Msg, State 4831 to Saigon, 1 May 55. This message is reproduced in *FRUS, 1955–57, Vietnam*, pp. 344–45.

50. (TS) Msg, Paris SECTO 8 to State, 8 May 55. This message is reproduced in *FRUS, 1955–57, Vietnam*, pp. 372–78.

51. (TS) JCS 1992/460, 9 May 55, CCS 092 Asia (6–25–48) (2) sec 8. This JCS document is reproduced in *Pentagon Papers*, vol. 10, pp. 971–74 and is quoted extensively in "Telegram from the Acting Secretary of State to the Secretary of State, at Paris," 9 May 55 and reproduced in *FRUS, 1955–57, Vietnam*, pp. 380–82.

52. (TS) Msg, Saigon 5154 to State, 9 May 55.

53. (TS) Msg, Paris SECTO 36 to State, 11 May 55. This message is reproduced in *FRUS, 1955–57, Vietnam*, pp. 393–99.

54. (S) Msg, Paris SECTO 42 to State, 12 May 55. This message is reproduced in *FRUS, 1955–57, Vietnam*, pp. 401–05.

55. (U) Msg, Saigon 5187 to State, 10 May 55. (C) Msgs, Saigon 5188 to State, 10 May 55; 5258, 14 May 55. (S) Msg, Saigon 5209 to State, 11 May 55.

56. (U) SNIE 63.1–2/1–55, 2 May 55, *Pentagon Papers*, vol. 10, pp. 955–957. This document is reproduced in *FRUS, 1955–57, Vietnam*, pp. 346–50.

Chapter 5. The Outlook Brightens in South Vietnam

1. The question of elections was dealt with by the Geneva conferees in paragraph seven of the Final Declaration: "The Conference declares that as far as Vietnam is concerned, the settlement of the political problems... should permit the Vietnamese people to enjoy the basic freedoms, guaranteed by the democratic institutions to be established after holding

general free elections by secret ballot... the general elections shall be held in July 1956, ... Consultations shall be held on this matter between competent representative authorities of the two areas beginning on July 20, 1955."

2. (S) Msgs, State 35 to Saigon, 5 Jul 55; 53, 6 Jul 55; 80, 9 Jul 55; 155, 14 Jul 55; 179, 16 Jul 55. (S) Msg, Paris 69 to State, 6 Jul 55. (S) NIE 63.1-3-55, 11 Oct 55. Message 69, 6 Jul 55, is reproduced in *FRUS, 1955-57, Vietnam*, pp. 478-79. SecState Special Assistant for Intelligence memo to SecState, 27 Jul 55 refers to NIE 63-1-55, 19 Jul 55. The author of the memo observes that while the North Vietnamese "would not agree to complex and elaborate safeguards..." they probably would accept "some form of neutral (but not UN) supervision." *FRUS, 1955-57, Vietnam*, pp. 498-99. The text of NIE 63-1-55 is reprinted in *Pentagon Papers*, vol. 10, pp. 993-96.

3. (TS) NSC 5519, 17 May 55, CCS 092 Asia (6-25-48) (2) sec 8. NSC 5519 is reproduced in *FRUS, 1955-57, Vietnam*, pp. 410-12.

4. (TS) Memo, JCS to SecDef, "U.S. Policy on All-Vietnam Elections (NSC 5519)," 25 May 55 (derived from JCS 1992/463), same file. See also Deputy Asst SecState for Far Eastern Affairs memo to SecState, dtd 8 Jun 55, pp. 436-38. Note on bottom of p. 438 quotes the suggested JCS revision to NSC 5519.

5. (TS) Paragraph 5d set forth the action the US would take as follows: In the event of Communist overt armed attack in the area covered by the Manila Pact prior to the entering into effect of the Pact, take actions necessary to meet the situation, including a request for authority from Congress to use US armed forces, if appropriate and feasible. When the Pact is in effect, be prepared to oppose any Communist attack in the Treaty area with US armed forces if necessary and feasible, consulting the Congress in advance if the emergency permits.

6. (TS) Memo ExecSecy NSC to NSC, "U.S. Policy on All-Vietnam Elections," 13 Jun 55, same file, sec 9.

7. (S) Msg, State 5267 to Saigon, 27 May 55. (TS) Msg, State 4362 to Saigon, 6 Apr 55. (S) Msg, Saigon 5711 to State, 7 Jun 55. Messages 5267 and 4362 are reproduced in *FRUS, 1955-57, Vietnam*, pp. 422-23 and pp. 210-11. Ronald Spector observed that the United States "never adopted a firm policy on the question of elections. In general, Washington leaders saw them as something to be delayed rather than eliminated." Spector, *The Early Years*, p. 304.

8. (S) Msgs, Saigon 5731 to State, 8 Jun 55, State 5347 to Saigon, 3 Jun 55; 35, 5 Jul 55.

9. *NY Times*, 17 Jul 55, p. 7.

10. Ibid., 22 Jun 55, pp. 1-2.

11. Ibid., 21 Jul 55, p. 6.

12. (S) Msg, Paris SECTO 12 to State, 15 Jul 55.

13. (LOU) Msg, Saigon 298 to State, 20 Jul 55. (S) Msg, Saigon 341 to State, 21 Jul 55. (OUO) Msg, Saigon 352 to State, 22 Jul 55. (C) Msg, State 215 to Saigon, 20 Jul 55. *Washington Post*, 21 Jul 55, p. 1; 22 Jul 55, p. 4.

14. (S) Msg, State 220 to Saigon, 20 Jul 55. *Washington Post*, 22 Jul 55, p. 7. Message 220 is reproduced in *FRUS, 1955-57, Vietnam*, pp. 490-91.

15. (C) Msg, State 344 to Saigon, 30 Jul 55. *Washington Post*, 22 Jul 55, p. 7.

16. *Washington Post*, 22 Jul 55, p. 7.

17. (S) Msgs, Saigon 5677 to State, 6 Jun 55; State 5438 to Saigon, 11 Jun 55.

18. (S) Msgs, Saigon 5705 to State, 7 Jun 55; 5731, 8 Jun 55.

19. (C) Msgs, Paris 5513 and 5514 to State, 16 Jun 55; 5701, 21 Jun 55; 5776, 29 Jun 55. (S) Msg, Saigon 5969 to State, 24 Jun 55; Paris 27 to State, 2 Jul 55; 183, 12 Jul 55.

20. (C) Msg, Saigon 381 to State, 23 Jul 55. (S) Msgs, Paris 1460 to State, 29 Sep 55; 1757, 14 Oct 55.

21. (S) Msg, Paris 2889 to State, 17 Dec 55. (C) Msg, Paris SECTO 17 to State, 17 Dec 55. Message SECTO 17 is reproduced in *FRUS, 1955-57, Vietnam*, pp. 600-02.

22. (C) Msg, Paris 2886 to State, 17 Dec 55. *NY Times*, 1 Nov 55, p. 8. (S) Msg, Saigon 2671 to State, 5 Jan 56.

23. (TS) Msg, Saigon 5609 to State, 2 Jun 55. (TS–NOFORN) Memo, DDI to CJCS, "Relationship between France and the Diem Government in South Vietnam," 1 Jun 55. Message 5609 is reproduced in *FRUS, 1955–57, Vietnam*, pp. 431–32.

24. (S) NIE 63.1–3–55, 11 Oct 55, pp. 4–5. *NY Times*, 6 Nov 55, p. 33.

25. (TS–NOFORN) Memo, DDI to CJCS, "Relationship Between France and Diem Government in South Vietnam," 1 Jun 55. (LOU) Msg, Saigon 1354 to State, 21 Sep 55. (S) Msg, Saigon 2117 to State, 17 Nov 55. (C) Msg, Saigon 2192 to State, 22 Nov 55. The remnants of the Hoa Hao armies broke into roving guerrilla bands that were decimated and further fragmented by a second offensive begun in November. (S) Msg, Saigon 3498 to State, 28 Feb 56. Spector remarks that the campaign against the sects delayed the training of the Vietnamese Army. Spector, *The Early Years*, pp. 252–53.

26. (S) Msg, Saigon 2420 to State, 8 Dec 55.

27. (S) Colonel Lansdale outlined much of his pacification philosophy and a description of civic action activity in Vietnam at a meeting of the National Security Operations Coordinating Board's Special Working Group on Vietnam. See Memorandum of Discussion, 7 Nov 55, reprinted in *FRUS, 1955–57, Vietnam*, pp. 572–76. For a description of Lansdale's activities in Vietnam see his memoir, *In the Midst of Wars* (New York: Harper and Row, 1970), and Spector, *The Early Years*, pp. 240–43.

28. (S) JCS 1992/468, 15 Jul 55, CCS 092 Asia (6–25–48) (2) sec 9.

29. (S) Msg, JCS 988351 to CINCPAC, 12 Sep 55 (derived from JCS 1992/477), same file, sec 11. (S) Memo, JCS to SecDef, "Training of the Vietnamese Army," 1 Nov 55 (derived from JCS 1992/490), same file, sec 14. (C) N/H of JCS 1992/490, 2 Dec 55, same file.

30. (S) Msg, Saigon 1468 to State, 28 Sep 55.

31. (S) Msgs, Saigon 1483 to State, 29 Sep 55; 2378, 6 Dec 55. Message 1483 is reproduced in *FRUS, 1957–59, Vietnam*, pp. 547–48.

32. *NY Times*, 19 Oct 55, p. 1.

33. Ibid., 24 Oct 55, p. 1.

34. (S) Msg, Saigon 1846 to State, 25 Oct 55. Message 1846 is reproduced in *FRUS, 1955–57, Vietnam*, pp. 565–66.

35. (U) Msg, Saigon 1857 to State, 27 Oct 55. (S) Msg, Saigon 1867 to State, 27 Oct 55. (U) Msg, Saigon 2297 to State, 20 Nov 55. (OUO) Msg, Saigon 1911 to State, 30 Oct 55.

36. Dai Viet (National Party of Greater Vietnam) was a nationalist party dating to World War II.

37. (C) Msg, Saigon 3244 to State, 10 Feb 56. (S) NIE 63–56, 17 Jul 56. (C) Dept of State, PST 5/50, "Karachi Conference, Background Paper on Viet-Nam," 16 Feb 56, CCS 092 Asia (6–25–48) (2) sec 20. NIE 63–56 is reproduced in part in *FRUS, 1955–57, Vietnam*, pp. 720–21. The entire text is published in *Pentagon Papers*, vol. 10, pp. 1068–81.

38. (S) Msg, Saigon 2378 to State, 6 Dec 55. (C) Dept of State, PST 5/50, "Karachi Conference, Background Paper on Viet-Nam," 16 Feb 56, CCS 092 Asia (6–25–48) (2) sec 20.

39. TRIM Briefing, in (TS) Report of Visit of LTG Bruce C. Clarke, Commanding General, US Army, Pacific to Western Pacific and Southeast Asia, 6–29 Sep 55 (hereafter cited as Clarke Report), vol. III, CCS 092 Asia (6–25–48) (2) BP pt 5. For further details on TRIM, see Spector, *The Early Years*, pp. 240–42 and 251–52.

40. Ibid.

41. (S) Msg, CHMAAG Vietnam MG 1191 F to CNO, 17 Nov 55, DA IN 181427, CCS 092 Asia (6–25–48) (2) sec 15. (S) Msgs, State 2520 to Saigon, 24 Jan 56; Saigon 4070 to State, 7 Apr 56.

42. (S) Briefing by CHMAAG Indochina, in (TS) Clarke Report. (S) Msg, Saigon 186 to State, 14 Jul 55, CCS 092 Asia (6–25–48) (2) sec 9. (TS) Msg, CHMAAG Indochina to CINCPAC, 9 Aug 55, same file, sec 10. These messages are reproduced in *FRUS, 1955–57, Vietnam*, Saigon msg 186, pp. 484–85; CHMAAG msg to CINCPac, pp. 506–10.

43. (TS) Msg, CHMAAG Indochina to CINCPAC, 9 Aug 55, same file.

44. (TS) Msg, CINCPAC to OSD, 10 Aug 55, same file. (TS) Memo, JCS to SecDef, "Revised Force Bases for Vietnam, 19 Aug 55" (derived from JCS 1992/472), same file. (S) Msg, Saigon 186 to State, 14 Jul 55, same file, sec 9. The JCS memo to SecDef is reproduced in *FRUS, 1955–57, Vietnam*, p. 522.

45. (S) JCS 2099/466, 14 Mar 55, CCS 092 (8–22–46) (2) BP pt 7. (S) JCS 2099/603, 7 Apr 56, same file, BP pt 9. (TS) Memo, JCS to SecDef, "Objectives for the Department of Defense International Security Plan," 1 Mar 55 (derived from JCS 2101/189), CCS 381 US (1–31–50) sec 52. (TS) JCS 2099/540, 17 Nov 55, CCS 092 (8–22–46) (2) sec 20.

46. (S) Msg, Saigon 186 to State, 14 Jul 55, CCS 092 Asia (6–25–48) (2) sec 9. (TS) Msg, CINCPAC to DA for OSD, 30 Jul 55, same file, sec 10. (TS) NSC 5612/1, 5 Sep 56, same file, sec 26. Saigon message 186 is reproduced *FRUS, 1955–57, Vietnam*, pp. 484–85.

47. (S) Msg, CHMAAG Indochina MG 125 A to CNO, 10 Feb 55, DA IN 117629, same file, sec 4.

48. (S) Msg, CINCPAC to CNO, 28 Feb 56.

49. (S) Msg, CINCPAC to CNO, 2 Nov 55, CCS 092 Asia (6–25–48) (2) sec 15.

50. (S) Memo, JCS to SecDef, "Raising U.S. Military Personnel Ceiling of MAAG Vietnam" (derived from JCS 1992/500), 9 Dec 55, same file, sec 16. The entire memo is reprinted in *FRUS, 1955–57, Vietnam*, pp. 598–99.

51. (S) Ltr, SecDef to SecState, 13 Dec 55, N/H of JCS 1992/500, 14 Feb 56, same file. This letter is quoted in *FRUS, 1955–57, Vietnam*, note number 3, p. 615.

52. (S) Rpt, Intelligence Advisory Committee, "Vietminh Violations of the Geneva Agreements through 31 December 1954," 21 Jan 55; (S) Memo, DDI JS to CJCS, "Emerging Pattern-South Vietnam," 22 Nov 55. (S) Memo, DDI JS to CJCS, "Comments by LTG O'Daniel on 12 Dec 55," 19 Dec 55. See also Memo from the Deputy Asst SecState for Far Eastern Affairs, 1 Mar 55, *FRUS, 1955–57, Vietnam*, pp. 95–96 for another listing of Viet Minh truce violations. See also Spector, *The Early Years*, pp. 310–11.

Chapter 6. Developments in North Vietnam

1. (S) Msg, Saigon 458 to State, 5 Aug 54, DA IN 76895.

2. (U) "Exodus Report on a Voluntary Mass Flight to Freedom, Viet-Nam, 1954," Dept of State Bulletin, 5 Feb 55, pp. 223–24. Hereafter cited as Exodus Report. For further discussion of the evacuation of refugees from the north, see Spector, *The Early Years*, pp. 225–27.

3. (TS) Memo, W. J. Lederer to CINCPAC, "Report on Trip to Indochina," 30 Aug 54.

4. Exodus Report, pp. 226–28. (S) Msgs, Saigon 613 to State, 17 Aug 54; 723, 25 Aug 54, DA IN 80795.

5. (S) OCB Status Report, "Indochina Economic and Financial Programs," 3 Nov 54, CCS 092 Asia (6–25–48) sec 86. (S) Msg, USARMA Saigon MG-815-54 to DA, 12 Oct 54, DA IN 91346, same file. (C) Memo, COMAMPHIBSQDN ONE to ADM Radford, "Statistical Summary Indochina Evacuation," 20 Dec 54.

6. (S) OCB Report, "Detailed Development of Major Actions Relating to 'U.S. Objectives and Courses of Action with Respect to Southeast Asia' (NSC 5405) and Portions of NSC 5429/5 from March 16 through November 16, 1955," 29 Nov 55; (S) OCB Report, "Progress Report on 'U.S. Objectives and Courses of Action with Respect to Southeast Asia' (NSC 5405) and Portions of NSC 5429/5," 29 Nov 55; CCS 092 Asia (6–25–48) (2) sec 16.

7. (S) Msg, Saigon 3726 to State, 5 May 55. (C) Msgs, Saigon 5146 to State, 9 May 55; 5239, 13 May 55. (LOU) Msg, Saigon 5679 to State, 6 Jun 55. (S) Msg, Hanoi 1345 to State, 22 May 55. *NY Times*, 21 May 55, p. 5; 23 May 55, p. 4; 1 Jun 55, p. 8; 26 Jun 55, p. 6. (U) Dept of State, Publication No. 7308, "A Threat to the Peace," Pt 1, Dec 61, p. 6.

8. (S) Msg, CHMAAG Indochina MG 0022 B to OSD, 10 Jan 55, DA IN 110057, CCS 092 Asia (6–25–48) (2) sec 1. (S) Msg, Saigon 2759 to State, 15 Jan 55.

9. (S) Memo, Dep ASD (ISA) to CJCS, "MDAP Equipment in Indochina," 30 Jun 55.

10. (S) Msgs, Saigon 2759 to State, 15 Jan 55; 2874, 21 Jan 55; 4159, 28 Mar 55. (C) Msg, Saigon 3355 to State, 12 Feb 55. (S) Msg, Paris 3565 to State, 23 Feb 55. Message 4159 is reproduced in *FRUS, 1955–57, Vietnam*, pp. 151–54. *FRUS, 1955–57, Vietnam*, also reproduces the following documents that relate to the evacuation of the MDAP material from the north: Memo of Conversation, Dept of State, 18 Jan 1955, pp. 48–52; Collins to the Dept of State, 10 Feb 55, pp. 81–82; Collins to Dept of State, 10 Mar 55, pp. 116–19.

11. (S) Msgs, Paris 2883 to State, 7 Jan 55; 3091, 21 Jan 55. (C) Msg, Paris 3306 to State, 7 Feb 55. (S) Msg, Saigon 2985 to State, 27 Jan 55.

12. (S) Msg, Paris 3394 to State, 11 Feb 55. (S) Msg, Paris 3452 to State, 16 Feb 55. Message 3452 is reproduced in *FRUS, 1955–57, Vietnam*, pp. 89–90. According to the US Consul in Hanoi, the French were "definitely thinking in terms of Titoism for [North] Vietnam," Consul in Hanoi to State Dept, 7 Mar 55, *FRUS, 1955–57, Vietnam*, p. 110.

13. (C) Msgs, State 2846 to Paris, 11 Feb 55; Saigon 3355 to State, 12 Feb 55. (S) Msgs, Paris 3582 to State, 17 Feb 55; 4263, 1 Apr 55; 4409, 12 Apr 55.

14. William Kaye, "A Bowl of Rice Divided: The Economy of North Vietnam," P. J. Honey (ed.), *North Vietnam Today: Profile of a Communist Satellite* (1962), p. 106. James Price Gittinger, "Communist Land Policy in North Vietnam," *Far Eastern Survey*, August 1959, p. 113. Donald Lancaster, *The Emancipation of French Indo-China* (1961), pp. 368, 372–373. For a discussion of DRV policy of independence, see Harold C. Hinton, *China's Relations with Burma and Vietnam* (1958), p. 17. For its program of economic independence, see M. M. Avsenev, *The Democratic Republic of Vietnam, Economy and Foreign Trade* (Joint Publications Research Service) (Leningrad: 1960), p. 168.

15. (U) NIEs 63.1-55, 19 Jul 55; 10–55, 12 Apr 55. (S) Msgs, Saigon 3637 to State, 4 Mar 55; 2159, 20 Nov 55; Hanoi 4 to State, 1 Jul 55. Reproduction of NIE 63–1-5 is cited in footnote 2, Chapter 5.

16. Theodore Shabad, "Economic Developments in North Vietnam," *Pacific Affairs*, March 1958, pp. 45, 51.

17. Gittinger, "Communist Land Policy in North Vietnam," p. 113. Avsenev, *The Democratic Republic of Vietnam, Economy and Foreign Trade*, pp 27, 109. Bernard Fall, *The Viet Minh Regime, Government and Administration in the Democratic Republic* (1956), p. 117.

18. For a full discussion of the land reform program, see Gittinger, "Communist Land Policy in North Vietnam," pp. 117–120.

19. For material on the stages of collectivization, see (C) NIS 43C, sec 61, pp. 13–15; and sec 60, p. 4.

20. Shabad, "Economic Developments in North Vietnam," pp. 47–48. Kaye, "A Bowl of Rice Divided: The Economy of North Vietnam," p. 116.

21. Shabad, "Economic Developments in North Vietnam," pp. 46–47.

22. (C) NIS 43C, sec 55, p. 9. (S) NIE, 63–59, 26 May 59, pp. 8–9.

23. P. H. M. Jones, "The Industry of North Vietnam," *Far Eastern Economic Review*, 22 Sep 60. (C) NIS 43C, sec 60, p. 10. Shabad, "Economic Developments in North Vietnam," pp. 42ff. Avsenev, *The Democratic Republic of Vietnam, Economy and Foreign Trade*, pp. 55–57, 83ff.

24. Avsenev, *The Democratic Republic of Vietnam, Economy and Foreign Trade*, pp. 75–82. (C) NIS 43C, sec 60, p. 17.

25. Avsenev, *The Democratic Republic of Vietnam, Economy and Foreign Trade*, pp. 71, 76–77, 168.

26. (S) NIS 43C, sec 55, p. 8. Kaye, "A Bowl of Rice Divided," p. 108.

27. Kaye, "A Bowl of Rice Divided," p. 109.

28. *NY Times*, 10 Feb 60, p. 6; Kaye, "A Bowl of Rice Divided," pp. 108–109.

29. *NY Times*, 6 Sep 60, p. 18.

30. Bernard B. Fall, *The Two Viet-Nams* (1963), pp. 154, 164–166.

31. (S) NIE 63–55, sec 55.

32. (S) Msg, Hanoi 1364 to State, 23 May 55. See also Msg, Hanoi 1312, 17 May 55, reproduced in *FRUS, 1955–57, Vietnam*, pp. 413–14.

33. (S) NIE 63–55. (S) *US Army Handbook for Vietnam*, Sep 62, p. 103.

34. (S) NIS 43C, sec 55, p. 55–5. Fall, *The Two Viet-Nams*, p. 154.

35. (S) NIS 43C, sec 55, p. 55–5.

36. (S) NIS 43C, sec 55, p. 55–6. Honey, *North Vietnam Today*, pp. 82–87.

37. Gittinger, "Communist Land Policy in North Vietnam," pp. 118–119.

38. Bernard B. Fall, "Crisis in North Viet-Nam," *Far Eastern Survey*, January 1957, pp. 12–15. Gittinger, "Communist Land Policy in North Vietnam," p. 179. Frank Trager (ed.), *Marxism in Southeast Asia: A Study of Four Countries* (1959), p. 162. See also Msg, Saigon 1718 to State, 23 Nov 56, relating to the Diem government's protest of North Vietnamese action in putting down the uprising in Nghe An Province, reproduced in *FRUS, 1955–57, Vietnam*, pp. 751–52. A note at the bottom of page 751 describes the start of a series of reports about events in North Vietnam.

39. P. Devillers, "The Struggle for Unification of Vietnam," *The China Quarterly*, January–March 1962, p. 8.

40. (S) NIS 43C, sec 55, p. 55–17. Lancaster, *The Emancipation of French Indo-China*, p. 364.

41. (S) NIS 43C, sec 55, p. 55–17. Devillers, "The Struggle for Unification of Vietnam," p. 11.

42. (TS) Memo for the NSC Planning Board, "Review of US Policy in the Far East," 3 Aug 54, CCS 381 Far East (11–28–50) sec 22.

43. *NY Times*, 29 Oct 54, p. 5. (S) Msg, Hanoi 1364 to State, 23 May 55. (C) Memo, DepDir Intel to CJCS, 25 Nov 55.

44. (TS) NSC 5612/1, 5 Sep 56, Encl to JCS 1992/565, 11 Sep 56, CCS 092 Asia (6–25–48) (2) sec 26. (TS) NSC 5809 2 Apr 58, same file, sec 38. (S) NSC 6012, 25 Jul 60, JMF 9150/9105 (11 Jul 60). NSC 5612/1 and NSC 5809 are reprinted in *Pentagon Papers*, vol. 10, pp. 1082–95 and 1113–33. Portions of NSC 5809 are reprinted in an editorial note, US Dept of State, *Foreign Relations of the United States, 1958–1960, Vietnam* (Washington: GPO, 1986), vol. I, pp. 34–5; hereafter *FRUS, 1958–60, Vietnam*.

45. (S) NIS 43C, sec 55, pp. 55–16 to 55–17. (S) Msg, Saigon 2597 to State, 28 Jun 58.

46. The DRV constantly reiterated the Five Principles of Coexistence, those international standards of peaceful coexistence subscribed to by the Prime Ministers of China and India in 1954. (S) NIS 43C, sec 55.

47. (S) Msg, Hanoi 1364 to State, 23 May 55. (S) NIE 63.1–55, 19 Jul 55. Lancaster, *The Emancipation of French Indo-China*, pp. 368–369. Shabad, "Economic Development in North Vietnam," p. 49.

48. (S) Msg, Hanoi 1312 to State, 17 May 55. Russell H. Fifield, *Diplomacy of Southeast Asia, 1945–58* (1958), p. 118. Nguyen Ngoc Bich, "Vietnam, an Independent View," *The China Quarterly*, January–March 1962, pp. 105–111. Message 1312 is reproduced in *FRUS, 1955–57, Vietnam*, pp. 413–14.

49. Avsenev, *The Democratic Republic of Vietnam, Economy and Foreign Trade*. Hinton, *China's Relations with Burma and Vietnam*, p. 21.

50. (OUO) Msg, Saigon 2010 to State, 8 Nov 55. Shabad, "Economic Development in North Vietnam," p. 53.

51. (OUO) Msg, Saigon 2010 to State, 8 Nov 55.

52. Honey, *North Vietnam Today*, p. 14. (S) NIS 43C, sec 60, p. 60–15.

53. Hinton, *China's Relations with Burma and Vietnam*, p. 17.

54. (C) Msg, Saigon 1809 to State, 28 Nov 59.

Chapter 7. The Republic of Vietnam: 1956, A Year of Progress

1. (S) OCB, "Progress Report, 'U.S. Objectives and Courses of Action with Respect to Southeast Asia' (NSC 5405 and Portions of NSC 5429/5)," 14 Mar 56, CCS 092 Asia (6–25–48) (2) sec 21.

2. (S–NOFORN) Dept of State, IR No. 7256, 23 May 56, pp. 44–46.

3. (S) NIE 63–56, 17 Jul 56. *NY Times*, 4 Mar 56, p. 1. This NIE is reproduced in part in *FRUS, 1955–57, Vietnam*, pp. 720–21. The full text is reprinted in *Pentagon Papers*, vol. 10, pp. 1068–81.

4. (S) NIE 63–56, 17 Jul 56.

5. *NY Times*, 25 Oct 56, p. 33.

6. (S) Msg, Saigon 2190 to State, 2 Nov 55.

7. (S) Msgs, Saigon 2086 to State, 14 Nov 55; 2206, 23 Nov 55. (C) Msg, Paris 3783 to State, 21 Feb 56.

8. (S) Msg, State 1901 to Saigon, 2 Dec 55. This document is reprinted in *FRUS, 1955–57, Vietnam*, pp. 594–95.

9. (S) Msgs, State 2563 to Saigon, 27 Jan 56; 2914, 27 Feb 56. (C) Msg, State 2789 to Saigon, 15 Feb 56.

10. (S) Msgs, Saigon 2137 to State, 18 Nov 55; 2777, 10 Jan 56; State 3432 to Saigon, 12 Apr 56. *NY Times*, 10 Apr 56, p. 2.

11. (S) Msgs, Paris SECTO 32 to State, 6 May 56; State 3749 to Saigon, 11 May 56. (S) NIE 63–56, 17 Jul 56. Msg SECTO 32 is reproduced in *FRUS, 1955–57, Vietnam*, pp. 678–79. For NIE 63–56 see footnote 3 of this chapter.

12. (S) NIE 63–56, 17 Jul 56. (C) Msg, Saigon 287 to State, 24 Jul 56.

13. (S) Msg, State 3749 to Saigon, 11 May 56.

14. (C) "Diem's Paper Re Their Needs (Economic) from General O'Daniel," n.d. [Sep 56] (hereafter cited as Diem's Paper). Diem's Paper is shown as an attachment to a message from the Deputy Director, Plans, CIA to Asst SecState, 27 Sep 56. Both the memorandum and attachment are reproduced in *FRUS, 1955–57, Vietnam*, pp. 742–45.

15. (C) Diem's Paper.

16. (U) AID, "U.S. Foreign Assistance and Assistance From International Organizations, July 1, 1945–June 30, 1962," [Revised], p. 69. (S) NIE 63–56, 17 Jul 56, p. 8.

17. (U) State-Defense-ICA, "A Summary Presentation, MSP, FY 1960," Mar 59, AID, S&R Div. Rpt by Subcom on State Department Organization and Public Affairs to S. Com on Foreign Relations, 30–31 Jul 59, 86th Cong, 1st sess, pp. 203–204 (hereafter cited as "Situation in Vietnam"). See also the discussion in Spector, *The Early Years*, pp. 306–08.

18. "Situation in Vietnam," p. 42. (S–NOFORN) Dept of State IR 7256, 23 May 56, pp. 57–58.

19. (S–NOFORN) ASD(ISA), Mutual Security Program: Fiscal Year 1958 Estimates; World-Wide Summary Statements, No 105; East and Pacific, No. 105; Non-Regional Programs, No. 105.

20. (C) Diem's Paper, pp. 6–7.

21. The United States Operations Mission was the field level office of the Foreign Operations Administration, which was established on 1 August 1953 and was responsible for continuous supervision, general direction, and coordination of all foreign assistance operations, under the policy direction of the Secretaries of State, Defense, and Treasury.

22. (S) NIE 63–56, 17 Jul 56, pp. 9–10. For this NIE see footnote 3 of this chapter.

23. Viet Cong (VC) is a derogatory contraction of the Vietnamese term "Vietnamese communist" that came into general use in 1956–1957 in referring to the communist guerrillas and terrorists operating in South Vietnam. (U) SORO, *US Army Handbook for Vietnam*, p. 324. (S) Rpt, Dept of State, RFE 59, "Situation and Short-Term Prospects in South Vietnam," 3 Dec 63.

24. (S) NIE 63–56, 17 Jul 56. (S) Dept of State, Intelligence Brief 2070, 13 Feb 57. (S) NIE 63–57, pp. 10–11. (S) Dept of State IR 7197, 6 Apr 56, p. 6. P. J. Honey, "Democracy in the

Republic of Vietnam," in S. Rose (ed.), *Politics in Southern Asia* (1963), p. 204. Dept. of State Intelligence Brief, No. 1876, 7 Feb 56 contains much the same information cited here and is reprinted in *FRUS, 1955–57, Vietnam*, pp. 637–39 as is NIE 63-2-57, 14 May 57, pp. 818–19. The latter document is also reproduced in the *Pentagon Papers*, vol. 10, pp. 1101–02.

25. (S) Memo, COL F. F. Evans (OASD/ISA/FER) to Dir FER/ISA, 16 Jun 59, ISA File 200 Vietnam (16 Jun 59), RG 330, case 63A–1672, FRC. The Evans memo is reproduced in *FRUS, 1958–60, Vietnam*, pp. 209–12.

26. (S) NIE 63–56, 17 Jul 56, p. 9. Memo, Joint Staff, 13 Apr 56, Subj: Defense Information Relating to the US AID Program for Vietnam, reproduced in *FRUS, 1955–57, Vietnam*, pp. 672–73. For further discussion, see Spector, *The Early Years*, pp. 262–68.

27. (S) Country Statement on MDAP, Non–NATO Countries, 15 Jan 56, CCS 092 (8–22–46) (2) sec 24, and BP pt 8. (Hereafter cited as US Country Statement, 1955.)

28. (S) Msg, CHMAAG, Vietnam 1469A to OSD, 11 Jan 56.

29. (S–NOFORN) NIS 43D, "South Vietnam," chap. 8.

30. (S) US Country Statement, 1955.

31. (S) Memo, DDI, JS to ASD(SO) "Emerging Pattern-South Vietnam," 21 Dec 55, CCS 092 Asia (6–25–48) (2) sec 17.

32. (S) US Country Statement, 1955.

33. (TS) CSAM 32–56 to JCS, 16 Feb 56, CCS 092 Asia (6–25–48) (2) sec 20. See also Spector, *The Early Years*, pp. 282–86.

34. (S) Ltr, SecDef to SecState, 31 Jan 56; N/H of JCS 1992/500, 20 Feb 56, same file. The status of the recovery program as of March 1956, according to the Department of State, was as follows: The total cost of equipment sent to Indochina during the war was $1.2 billion, of which $941 million was military hardware. Of this $941 million, $154 million had been turned over to Cambodia and Laos, $198 million was still in the possession of the FEC, and $81 million had been declared excess and shipped out of Vietnam. Of the estimated $508 million remaining, the bulk was in the nominal custody of the Vietnamese, but in fact lay in unprotected supply dumps without proper maintenance. (C) Msg, State 3225 to Paris, 3 Mar 56. The SecDef letter is reproduced in *FRUS, 1955–57, Vietnam*, pp. 626–27.

35. (U) Ltr, DepUSecState to SecDef, 1 May 56, *Pentagon Papers*, vol. 10, pp. 1057–58. (C) Jt. State/Def Msg (State 3430) to Saigon, 12 Apr 56. Message 3430 is reproduced in *FRUS, 1955–57, Vietnam*, pp. 669–71. For additional information see Spector, *The Early Years*, pp. 257–62.

36. Msgs, State 2950 to Saigon, 29 Feb 56; 2981, 2 Mar 56. (S) Msgs, State 3292 to Saigon, 30 Mar 56; 3722, 7 Apr 56. (C) Msg, Saigon 309 to State, 25 Jul 56. (S) "MAAG Vietnam Quarterly Activities Report No. 1 for period ending 31 May 1956," 10 Jun 56, CCS 092 Asia (6–25–48) (2) BP pt 10. Memo from Deputy Asst SecState for Far Eastern Affairs to SecState, 23 Mar 56, Subj: Despatch of "Temporary Equipment Recovery Mission to Vietnam," states that the US Embassy in New Delhi reported that the Indian government "would not consider our proposed operation inconsistent with the Geneva Agreement if its purpose was to reduce the volume of armament in South Vietnam." This memo is reproduced in *FRUS, 1955–57, Vietnam*, pp. 666–68.

37. (S) US Country Statement, 1956. (S) OCB, "Progress Report on U.S. Policy in Mainland Southeast Asia (NSC 5612/1)," 14 Mar 57, CCS 092 Asia (6–25–48) (2) sec 31. (S) MAAG-Vietnam Narrative Statement, Nov 58—with changes through September 59, pp. 43–43.1.

38. (S) NIE 63–56, 17 Jul 56, p. 6.

39. (S) US Country Statement, 1956.

40. (S) NIE 63–56, 17 Jul 56, pp. 9–10.

41. (TS) Study, "US National Policy Toward Vietnam, 1945–1962," OCMH, DA, p. 52. (TS) Study, "The U.S. Army Role in The Conflict in Vietnam," OCMH, DA, chap. 3, p. 39. The size of the MAAG remained a matter of sensitivity as illustrated by an exchange of letters between the State and Defense Departments relative to limits on the number of

US personnel in Vietnam in the spring of 1957. See Asst SecDef (ISA) letter to Asst SecState for Far Eastern Affairs, 15 Apr 57, *FRUS, 1955–57, Vietnam*, pp. 780–82, and Asst SecState for Far Eastern Affairs letter to Asst SecDef (ISA), 6 May 57, *FRUS, 1955–57, Vietnam*, pp. 793–94.

42. (TS) Manuscript, "U.S. Policy Toward Vietnam Since 1945," 23 Jul 62, p. 43, OCMH, DA. For further discussion of Vietnamese paramilitary forces including the Civil Guard and the Self Defense Corps, see Spector, *The Early Years*, pp. 320–25.

43. (S) NIS 43D, chap. 8, "Armed Forces," p. 29. John D. Montgomery, *The Politics of Foreign Aid* (1962), pp. 64–70.

44. (S) Memo, DDI, JS to CJCS, "Vietnamese Civil Guard and Police, Origin and Current Status," 3 Jul 56.

45. (TS) Memo, OCB Secretariat Staff to Board Assistants, "Detailed Development of Major Actions Relating to Southeast Asia (NSC 5405 and portions of NSC 5429/5) from March 16 through September 16, 1955," 2 Dec 55, CCS 092 Asia (6-25-48) (2) sec 16. (S) NIS 43D, sec 55, "National Policies," p. 11. Montgomery, *The Politics of Foreign Aid*, p. 64. For further discussion of the Michigan State mission see Spector, *The Early Years*, pp. 321–23 and *FRUS, 1955–57, Vietnam*, notes at bottom of pp. 65–66.

46. Montgomery, *The Politics of Foreign Aid*, pp. 66–68.

47. (S) Memo, DDI, JS to CJCS, "Vietnamese Civil Guard and Police, Origin and Current Status," 3 Jul 56.

48. (S) Msg, CHMAAG, Vietnam 1469A to OSD, 11 Jan 56.

49. Montgomery, *The Politics of Foreign Aid*, pp. 68–70. Montgomery's account of the Civil Guard case is based on the files of the MSU team. For an illustration of the differences between the MSU group and President Diem, see: "Memo of a Conversation Between the President of the Republic of Vietnam and the Chief of the Military Assistance Advisory Group in Vietnam," 13 Oct 57, reproduced in *FRUS, 1955–57, Vietnam*, pp. 851–53.

50. Montgomery, *The Politics of Foreign Aid*, pp. 68–70.

51. (S) Msg, Saigon 400 to State, 29 May 59.

52. Ibid.

53. Montgomery, *The Politics of Foreign Aid*, p. 69.

54. (S) Memo, DDI, JS to CJCS, "Vietnamese Civil Guard and Police, Origin and Current Status," 3 Jul 56. (S) Msg, CINCPAC to CNO, 13 Dec 55.

55. (S) Msg, DEF 994892 to CINCPAC, (n.d.) Jan 56. (S) Msg, CHMAAG Vietnam 1469A to OSD, 11 Jan 56.

56. (S) OCB, "Progress Report, 'US Objectives and Courses of Action with Respect to Southeast Asia' (NSC 5405 and Portions of NSC 5429/5)," 11 Jul 56, p. 3. CCS 092 Asia (6-25-48) (2) sec 24.

57. (TS) NSC 5602/1, 15 May 56, CCS 381 U.S. (1-31-50) sec 61. NSC 5602/1 was superseded on 2 Apr 58 by NSC 5809. The section on Vietnam in the new paper, however, remained the same. (TS) JCS Hist Div, "Vietnam, 1 January 1956–31 March 1963: A Brief Chronology of Significant Events," 24 Apr 63.

58. (TS) Memo, SecDef to JCS, "Basic National Security Policy—NSC 5602/1," 21 Mar 56, CCS 381 U.S. (1-31-50) sec 62. For the relationship of this study to NSC 5519, NSC 5429/5, and NSC 5612/1, see (TS) Encl to Memo, ExecSecy, NSC to NSC, "Current U.S. Policy Toward the Far East (Review of para 5-d of NSC 5429/5)," CCS 092 Asia (6-25-48) (2) sec 23.

59. (TS) JCS 2101/233, 9 Jun 56, CCS 381 U.S. (1-31-50) sec 63. See also Paper Presented by the Chairman of the Joint Chiefs of Staff at the 287th Meeting of the National Security Council, 7 Jun 56, reproduced in *FRUS, 1955–57, Vietnam*, pp. 703–09 and Spector, *The Early Years*, p. 271.

60. (TS) Memo, SecDef to JCS, "Capability to Deal with Local Aggression in Vietnam," 16 Jul 56, CCS 092 Asia (6-25-48) (2) sec 24. (TS) SM-582-56 to CINCPAC, 11 Jul 56, same file.

See also Memorandum of Discussion at the 287th Meeting of the National Security Council, 7 Jun 56, reproduced in *FRUS, 1955–57, Vietnam*, pp. 695–703 and Chairman, JCS letter to CINCPAC, 14 Jun 57, reproduced in *FRUS, 1955–57, Vietnam*, pp. 712–13. In his letter, Radford refers to a CINCPAC draft OPLAN 49–56 that calls for an amphibious operation against Vinh in North Vietnam. CINCPAC telegram to Chief of Naval Operations, 1 Jun 56, reproduced in *FRUS, 1955–57, Vietnam*, pp. 689–91, provides the general concept of the plan. For contingency planning, see Spector, *The Early Years*, p. 272.

61. In response to a Presidential query, the JCS on 21 December 1956 defined the term "limited initial resistance" as: "Resistance to Communist aggression by defending or delaying in such manner as to preserve and maintain the integrity of the government and its armed forces for the period of time required to invoke the U.N. Charter and/or SEACDT or the period of time required for the U.S. Government to determine that considerations of national security required unilateral U.S. assistance and to commit U.S. or collective security forces to support or reinforce indigenous forces in defense of the country attacked." (TS) Memo, JCS to SecDef, "U.S. Policy in Mainland Southeast Asia (U)," 21 Dec 56 (derived from JCS 1992/583), CCS 092 Asia (6–25–48) (2) sec 29.

62. (TS) Memo, JCS to SecDef, "U.S. Policy in Mainland Southeast Asia (NSC 5612); Change to Current U.S. Policy Toward the Far East (NSC 5429/5)," 24 Aug 56 (derived from JCS 1992/562), CCS 092 Asia (6–25–48) (2) sec 25. (TS) Note by ExecSecy, NSC to NSC, "U.S. Policy in Mainland Southeast Asia," 5 Sep 56; (TS) NSC 5612/1, same subj, 5 Sep 56, same file, sec 26. A partial text of NSC 5612/1, "US Policy on Mainland Southeast Asia," is reprinted in Pentagon Papers, vol. 10, pp. 1082–95.

63. (TS) Memo, ExecSecy, NSC to NSC, "Current U.S. Policy in the Far East," 5 Sep 56, same file, sec 26. See revised paragraph 5–d of (TS) NSC 5429/5, 22 Dec 54, CCS 092 Asia (6–25–48) sec 90; and paragraph 19 of (TS) NSC 5612/1, 5 Sep 56, CCS 092 Asia (6–25–48) (2) sec 26.

64. (TS) CINCPAC OPLAN 46–56, 1 Oct 56, CCS 381 (4–16–49) BP pt 4. (TS) SM–221–57 to CINCPAC, l9 Mar 57 (derived from JCS 2054/164, 19 Mar 57), same file, sec 10. See also Spector, *The Early Years*, p. 272.

Chapter 8. South Vietnam, 1957–1959

1. (TS) NSC 5612/1, 5 Sep 56, CCS 092 Asia (6–25–48) (2) sec 26. NSC 5612/1 was revised and reissued in April 1958 as NSC 5809. The revision dealt with the sections on Laos, Malaya, Singapore, and Thailand, but NSC 5809 made no changes with regard to Vietnam. (TS) NSC 5809, 2 Apr 58, same file, sec 38. See footnote 62, chap. 7 relative to reproduction of NSC 5612/1.

2. Address, Howard P. Jones, DepAsstSecState for Far Eastern Economic Affairs before the Boise Valley World Affairs Association, Boise, Idaho, 19 Jan 57, reproduced in Dept of State *Bulletin*, 18 Feb 57, pp. 263–268.

3. (S) OCB Progress Report on US Policy in Mainland Southeast Asia (NSC 5612/1), 14 Mar 57, CCS 092 Asia (6–25–48) (2) sec 31.

4. Joint Statement, President Eisenhower and President Ngo Dinh Diem, 11 May 57, reproduced in Dept of State *Bulletin*, 27 May 57, pp. 851–52. See Spector, *The Early Years*, pp. 304–05 for a discussion of some of the criticisms of the Diem regime at this time. In an extensive report to the Department of State, the US Ambassador to South Vietnam, Elbridge Durbrow, in December 1957 expressed his concern about recent trends: "Certain problems now discernible have given us a warning which, if disregarded, might lead to a deteriorating situation in Viet Nam within a few years." See Durbrow Despatch to Dept of State, 5 Dec 57, with enclosure, reproduced in *FRUS, 1955–57, Vietnam*, pp. 869–84, hereafter Durbrow Despatch, 5 Dec 57, *FRUS, 1955–57, Vietnam*.

5. (S) OCB Progress Report on Southeast Asia (NSC 5612/1), 6 Nov 57, CCS 092 Asia (6–25–48) (2) sec 35. (S) OCB Progress Report on Southeast Asia (NSC 5612/1), 28 May 58, same file, sec 39.

6. (S) Msg CINCPAC to CNO, 18 Aug 57, same file, sec 34.

7. (S) OCB Progress Report on Southeast Asia (NSC 5612/1), 6 Nov 57, same file, sec 35. (S) OCB Progress Report on Southeast Asia (NSC 5612/1), 28 May 58, same file, sec 39.

8. (S) OCB Progress Report on Southeast Asia (NSC 5612/1), 28 May 58, same file.

9. (S) OCB Report on Southeast Asia (NSC 5809), 12 Aug 59, JMF 9150/9105 (12 Aug 59). (S) OCB Operations Plan for Vietnam, 9 Jan 59, JMF 9155.3/9105 (9 Jan 59).

10. (TS) OCB Outline Plans of Operations with Respect to Vietnam, 12 Apr 57, CCS 092 Asia (6–25–48) (2) BP 7; 4 Jun 58, same file, BP 9; and 9 Jan 59, JMF 9155.3/9105 (9 Jan 59). The OCB Operations Plan for Vietnam, 4 Jun 58, is reproduced in *FRUS, 1958–60*, pp. 40–54.

11. Ibid.

12. (U) AID, "US Foreign Assistance and Assistance from International Organizations, July 1, 1945 – June 30, 1962 (Revised)," p. 69.

13. (TS) NSC 5429/2, 20 Aug 54, CCS 092 Asia (6–25–48) sec 81.

14. (U) AID, "U. S. Overseas Loans and Grants... July 1, 1945 – June 30, 1966," p. 57.

15. Franklin D. Rosebery, "Experiment in Planning Economic and Social Development, 1956–1957," in Richard W. Lindholm (ed.), *Vietnam: The First Five Years* (1959), pp. 193–95. UN Economic Survey to the Republic of Vietnam, *Toward the Economic Development of the Republic of Vietnam* (1959), p. 5.

16. Francis J. Corley, "Economic Stabilization in Viet Nam," *Review of Social Economy*, Summer 1958, pp. 154–57. Rosebery, "Experiment in Planning Economic and Social Development, 1956–1957," pp. 294–96. Bernard B. Fall, *Two Vietnams* (1963), p. 299.

17. Bernard B. Fall, "South Vietnam's Internal Problems," *Pacific Affairs*, September 1958, p. 249. Fall, *Two Vietnams*, p. 298.

18. Fall, *Two Vietnams*, pp. 299–300.

19. Wolf Ladejinsky, "Agrarian Reform in the Republic of Vietnam," chap. 9 in Wesley R. Fishel, *Problems of Freedom: South Vietnam Since Independence* (1961), pp. 155–162. J. Price Gittinger, "Progress in South Vietnam's Agrarian Reform (I)," and "... (II)," *Far Eastern Survey*, January and February 1960, pp. 1–5; 17–21. As land reform adviser in the US Operations Mission in Vietnam, Wolf Ladejinsky reported to the US Ambassador in June 1955 on "the sad state of the agrarian reform; the poor progress of settling refugees on land, and the problems presented by local administration." See Memo from the Land Reform Adviser...to the Ambassador..., 7 Jun 55, *FRUS, 1955–57, Vietnam*, pp. 456–58.

20. Ladejinsky and Gittinger describe agricultural developments in detail. Ladejinsky was Diem's personal adviser for agrarian reform; Gittinger was a USOM Saigon agricultural adviser from 1955 to 1959. Montgomery, *The Politics of Foreign Aid*, pp. 122–28.

21. See chap. 3.

22. Gittinger, "Progress on South Vietnam's Agrarian Reform (II)," pp. 17, 21 and 22.

23. (S) Msg, Saigon 80 to State, 7 Jul 56. Desp, Saigon 200 to State, 15 Jan 57. Fall, "South Vietnam's Internal Problems," p. 250.

24. (S) OCB Progress Report on Southeast Asia (NSC 5612/1), 6 Nov 57, CCS 092 Asia (6–25–48) (2) BP 8. Gittinger, "Progress in South Vietnam's Agrarian Reform (I)," pp. 1, 4. Ronald Spector, however, noted that in the Mekong Delta in 1960, "only 23 percent of the farmers ... owned any land at all, and about 56 percent of those lived on two acre farms, one acre of which was rented. Spector, *The Early Years*, pp. 309–10.

25. Milton C. Taylor, "South Vietnam: Lavish Aid, Limited Progress," *Pacific Affairs*, Fall 1961, p. 250.

26. "United States Aid Program in Vietnam," Report by Subcom on State Department Organization and Public Affairs to S. Com on Foreign Relations, 26 Feb 69, 86th Cong., 2d sess (hereafter cited as "US Aid Program in Vietnam," S. Com on Foreign Relations, 26 Feb 60). Taylor, "South Vietnam: Lavish Aid, Limited Progress," pp. 242–56.

27. Taylor, "South Vietnam: Lavish Aid, Limited Progress," p. 256. (S) Interdepartmental Committee on Certain US Aid Programs, "Vietnam," 25 Jul 56, circulated with NSC 5610, 3 Aug 56, CCS 092 (8–22–46) (2) BP pt 10.

28. "US Aid Program in Vietnam," S. Com on Foreign Relations, 26 Feb 60, p. 10.

29. UN Economic Survey to the Republic of Vietnam, p. 246. Brian Crozier, "The Diem Regime in Southern Vietnam," *Far Eastern Survey*, April 1955, pp. 49–56. Russel H. Fifield, *The Diplomacy of Southeast Asia* (1958), p. 316.

30. (S) NIE 63–59, 26 May 59.

31. (TS) NSC 5612/2, 5 sep 56, CCS 092 Asia (6–25–48) (2) sec 26. Also see partial text of document in *Pentagon Papers*, vol. 10, pp. 1082–95.

32. (C) ICA, OS&R Report, "US External Assistance, Obligations and Other Commitments, July 1, 1945 through June 30, 1959," 16 Mar 60.

33. Ibid. "US Aid Program in Vietnam," S. Com on Foreign Relations, 20 Feb 66, p. vi.

34. (S–NOFORN) NIS 43D, "South Vietnam," chap. 8, "Armed Forces," Jan 59 (hereafter cited as NIS 43D).

35. (S–NOFORN) NIS 43D, p. 7.

36. Ibid., p. 10.

37. Ibid., p. 8.

38. (S–NOFORN) NIS 43D, see Chart A – Strength of Vietnamese Armed forces. (C) MAAG Vietnam Narrative Statements, 25 Nov 58, MAAG Vietnam General Administrative Files, 1958 (Washington National Records Center). For a discussion of the restructuring and composition of the Vietnamese Army see Spector, *The Early Years*, pp. 295–302.

39. (S–NOFORN) NIS 43D, pp. 17–18.

40. Ibid., p. 14.

41. Ibid.

42. Ibid., pp. 4–6, 19.

43. Ibid., p. 19. See also Spector, *The Early Years*, pp. 282–86.

44. NIS 43D, pp. 23–25.

45. (C) Quarterly Activities Report of MAAG Vietnam, 1 Jun 57–31 Aug 57, MAAG Vietnam Gen Admin Files, 1957. (C) MAAG Vietnam Country Statement, 31 Dec 57, same file. (C) Quarterly Activities Report on MAAG Vietnam, 1 Mar 58–31 May 58, same file, 1958. (S) Msg, Saigon 1471 to State, 24 Jan 59.

46. (S–NOFORN) NIS 43D. (C) Hq MAAG Vietnam, Eighth Quarterly Special TERM Report, 19 Jun 58, MAAG Vietnam, 1 Mar 58–31 May 58, MAAG Vietnam Gen Admin Files, 1958. See also Spector, *The Early Years*, pp. 296–99.

47. (C) Quarterly Activities Report of MAAG Vietnam, 1 Mar 58–31 May 58, MAAG Vietnam Gen Admin Files, 1958.

48. (S–NOFORN) NIS 43D, pp. 36–7.

49. Ibid., p. 37.

50. Ibid., p. 38.

51. Ibid., pp. 31–34.

52. Ibid., p. 32.

53. (C) MAAG Vietnam Country Statement, 15 Jan 56, CCS 092 (8–22–46) (2) BP pt 8. Ibid., 21 Jan 57, 15 Jul 57, and 22 Jan 58, MAAG Vietnam Gen Admin Files, 1957 and 1958. (C) Hq MAAG Vietnam, Narrative Study, 24 Aug 58, MAAG Vietnam Gen Admin File, 1958.

54. (C) MAAG Vietnam Country Statement, 15 Jul 57, MAAG Vietnam Gen Admin Files, 1957. (S) JCSM–368–59 to SecDef, 4 Sep 59 (derived from JCS 2101/367), JMF 4060 (14 Aug 59).

55. (U) Hq MAAG Vietnam, Quarterly Activities Report, 7 Mar 57, MAAG Vietnam Gen Admin file, 1957. (C) Hq MAAG Vietnam, Narrative Study, 25 Nov 58, same file, 1958. (S) JCSM-368-59 to SecDef, 4 Sep 59 (derived from JCS 2101/367), JMF 4060 (14 Aug 59).

56. (C) MAAG Vietnam Country Statement, 15 Jul 57, MAAG Vietnam Gen Admin File, 1957. Hq MAAG, TERM Reports, 19 Nov 58, and 13 Jan 61, same file, 1958. See also Spector, *The Early Years*, pp. 299–300.

57. (TS) JCSM-8-59 to SecDef, 13 Jan 59 (derived from JCS 1992/684), CCS 092 Asia (6-25-48) (2) sec 42.

58. (S) JCSM-368-59 to SecDef, 4 Sep 59 (derived from JCS 2101/367) to JMF 4060 (14 Aug 59).

59. (S) DOD Report to NSC, "Status of the Military Assistance Program," 14 Aug 59, same file.

60. "US Aid Program in Vietnam," S. Com on Foreign Relations, 26 Feb 60, pp. 8–9.

61. (S) NIE 14.3/53–61, "Prospects for North and South Vietnam," 15 Aug 61, p. 7. Honey, "Democracy and the Republic of Vietnam," p. 215.

62. (C) Desp, Saigon 200 to State, 15 Jan 57.

63. Anonymous, "A New Look at Vietnam," *Far Eastern Economic Review*, 11 Jan 62, p. 49. See also Spector, *The Early Years*, p. 279.

64. Wesley R. Fishel, "Problems of Democratic Growth in Vietnam," chap. 2 of Fishel (ed.), *Problems of Democratic Growth in Vietnam Since Independence*, p. 28.

65. (S) OCB Progress Report on Southeast Asia (NSC 5612/1), 28 May 58, CCS 092 Asia (6-25-48) (2) sec 39. (S) OCB Progress Report on Southeast Asia (NSC 5809), 12 Aug 59, JMF 9150/9105 (12 Aug 59). (S) OCB Operations Plan for Vietnam, 9 Jan 59, JMF 9155.3/9105 (9 Jan 59). For further expressions of US dissatisfaction with the Diem regime, see Durbrow Despatch, 5 Dec 57, *FRUS, 1955–57, Vietnam*, pp. 869–84.

66. (TS) SM-902-59 to SpecAsst to JCS (NSC Affairs), 11 Sep 59 (derived from JCS 1992/730), JMF 9150/9105 (19 Jun 59).

67. Ibid.

68. Robert G. Scigliano, "Political Parties in South Vietnam Under the Republic," *Pacific Affairs*, December 1960, pp. 341, 345–46.

69. Ibid., p. 340.

70. Honey, "Democracy and the Republic of Vietnam," pp. 207–08.

71. Ibid., p. 210.

72. Anonymous, "A New Look at Vietnam," p. 48.

73. (C) Desp, Saigon 377 to State, 24 Apr 58. Fishel, *Problems of Freedom: South Vietnam Since Independence*, p. 23.

74. (TS) NSC 5612/1, 5 Sep 56, CCS 092 Asia (6-25-48) (2) sec 26.

75. (S) OCB, "The Overseas Chinese and US Policy" (draft), 6 Sep 56, same file, BP pt 7. Joseph Buttinger, "The Ethnic Minorities in Vietnam," chap. 6 in Fishel, *Problems of Freedom: South Vietnam Since Independence*, pp. 110–18.

76. (C) Desp, Saigon 200 to State, 15 Jan 57. (U) Msg, CHMAAG Vietnam 5148 to CINCPAC, 5 Jan 57.

77. Ibid., Lindholm, *Vietnam: The First Five Years*, p. 113. Buttinger, "The Ethnic Minorities in Vietnam," p. 110.

78. (C) Msgs, Saigon to State, 823, 8 Sep 56; 1171, 6 Oct 56; 1322, 20 Oct 56. Bernard B. Fall, "South Vietnam's Chinese Problem," *Far Eastern Survey*, May 1958, pp. 67–68.

79. (S) Msg, Saigon 1001 to State, 22 Sep 56. (C) Desp, Saigon 200 to State, 15 Jan 57.

80. (C) Desp, Saigon 200 to State, 15 Jan 57.

81. Buttinger, "The Ethnic Minorities in Vietnam," p. 119.

82. (S) Msg, Saigon 3479 to State, 18 Jan 60.

83. Buttinger, "The Ethnic Minorities in Vietnam," p. 105.

84. Lindholm, *Vietnam: The First Five Years*, pp. 135–39.

85. Buttinger, "The Ethnic Minorities in Vietnam," pp. 106–07. William Henderson, "The Republic of Vietnam Land Redevelopment Program," chap. 7 in Fishel, *Problems of Freedom: South Vietnam Since Independence*, p. 130. (S) Desp, Saigon 295 to State, 12 Mar 59. See also Spector, *The Early Years*, p. 308.

86. (S) NIE 63.2/2–57, "The Prospects for North Vietnam," 14 May 57, p. 6. Philippe Devillers, "The Struggle for the Unification of Vietnam," *The China Quarterly*, January–March, 1962, p. 15.

87. (U) Dept of State Pub No 7308, *A Threat to the Peace, North Vietnam's Efforts to Conquer South Vietnam*, pp. 43–44. (S) Desp, Saigon 243 to State, "Summary of Internal Security Situation in Vietnam: November 1957, #7," 7 Jan 58. (S) SEATO "Rpt of the 12th Mtg of SEATO Security Experts," pp. 66–68. (C) MAAG Vietnam Intelligence Summary (hereafter cited as MAAGV ISUM) No. 1–57, 2 Jan 57, MAAG Vietnam Gen Admin File, 1957. (S) NIS 43D, Jul 58, p. 57-7. William J. Duiker quotes a Vietnamese historian of the Democratic Republic of Vietnam as writing that this period "was the darkest hour for the revolutionary cause." See Duiker, *Ho Chi Minh* (New York: Hyperion, 2000), p. 510; hereafter, Duiker, *Ho Chi Minh*.

88. (C) MAAGV ISUMs 1–57, 2 Jan 57; 3–57, 1 Feb 57; 4–57, 15 Feb 57; 7–57, 1 Apr 57; 8–57, 15 Apr 57; 9–57, 1 May 57; MAAG Vietnam Gen Admin File, 1957.

89. For ARVN reports of VC losses, see MAAG Vietnam Biweekly Intelligence Summaries in the MAAG Vietnam Gen Admin Files.

90. (C) MAAGV ISUM 5–57, 1 Mar 57, MAAG Vietnam Gen Admin File, 1957.

91. (U) Dept of State Pub No. 7308, pp. 3–4. (S) NIE 14.3/53–61, 15 Aug 61, p. 3.

92. (C) MAAGV ISUMS 13–57, 1 Jul 57; 16–57, 16 Aug 57; MAAG Vietnam Gen Admin file, 1957.

93. (S) NIS 43D, Jul 58, pp. 57–3, 57–11, 57–12. *NY Times*, 8 Oct 57, p. 5.

94. (S) NIS 43D, p. 57–12.

95. Ibid.

96. (S–NOFORN) Desp, Saigon 277 to State, "Summary of Internal Security Situation in Vietnam: December 1957, #8," 3 Feb 58. Ambassador Durbrow in December 1957 reported that since late summer, the Diem regime was more concerned with security matters because of an increase in terrorist attacks. See Durbrow Despatch, 5 Dec 57, *FRUS, 1955–57, Vietnam*, p. 870. Ronald Spector notes that in 1957 much of this terrorist activity was accomplished by Communist forces in the south without direct support from the north. Spector, *The Early Years*, p. 312.

97. (C) MAAGV ISUM 3–58, 1 Feb 58, MAAG Vietnam Gen Admin File, 1958. (S) NIS 43D, pp. 57–1—57–3.

98. (C) MAAGV ISUM 5–58, MAAG Vietnam Gen Admin File, 1958.

99. (S–NOFORN) Desps, Saigon 295 to State, "Summary of Internal Security Situation in Vietnam: September and October, No. 14," 12 Mar 59; 337, "Summary... February and March 1958, No. 10," 24 Apr 58; 401, "Summary... November and December 1958, No. 15," 29 May 59. MAAGV ISUMs 5–58, 1 Mar 58; 11–58, 1 Jun 58; 14–58, 16 Jul 58; 16–58; MAAG Vietnam Gen Admin File, 1958.

100. (S) NIS 43D, p. 57–10.

101. Ibid., p. 57–12.

102. Ibid., p. 57–9.

103. Ibid., p. 57–12.

104. (S–NOFORN) Desps, Saigon 42 to State, 30 Jul 59; 71, 21 Aug 59.

105. Ibid.

106. Ibid.

107. (S) NIE 63–59, "Prospect on North and South Vietnam," 26 May 59, p. 4. NIE 63–59 is reproduced in *FRUS, 1958–60, Vietnam*, pp. 201–03. The document is also published in the *Pentagon Papers*, vol. 10, pp. 1190–95.

108. (S) SNIE 63.1–60, "Short Term Trends in South Vietnam," 23 Aug 60, p. 3.

109. (C) Msg, Saigon 133 to State, 4 Nov 59.

110. (C) Dept of State Report 8276, "North Vietnam Increases Pressure on South Vietnam," 7 Jun 60. William J. Duiker noted that the 15th Plenum of the Central Committee of the Vietnamese Worker's Party in January 1957 approved a "strategy of revolutionary war to bring about the reunification of the two zones of the country... but the relative degree of political and military struggle to be applied was left unresolved." Duiker, *Ho Chi Minh*, p. 512. See also Spector, *The Early Years*, pp. 330–31.

111. Hearings, *Situation in Vietnam*, Subcom on State Department Organization and Public Affairs of S. Foreign Relations Com, 86th Cong, 1st sess, pp. 26–27.

112. "The Tough Miracle Man of Vietnam," Life, 13 May 57, pp. 156–76. "The Courage of Ngo Dinh Diem," *Commonweal*, 19 Apr 57, p. 53. "Diem's Achievement," *America*, 1 Feb 58, p. 501. Ernest K. Lindley, "A Friend Named Diem," *Newsweek*, 20 May 57, p. 40. "Indo-China: Another Place Where Reds Are Losing," US News and World Report, 1 Mar 57, pp. 83–84. "Foreign Aid Repaid," Time, 20 May 57, p. 25.

113. *NY Times*, 2, 4, 6, 11, and 12 Apr 59, 19 May 59. *Wall Street Journal*, 16 Jun 59. Ernest K. Lindley, "An Ally Worth Having," *Newsweek*, 29 Jun 59, p. 31. "Vietnam's Gains Spur Red Terror," *Business Week*, 18 Jul 59, pp. 56–58.

114. David Hotham, "South Vietnam – Shaky Bastion," *The New Republic*, 25 November 1957, pp. 13–16. Hotham, "Vietnam: Trouble in North, South, and the Future," *The Reporter*, 21 February 1957, pp. 36–38. Bernard B. Fall, "Will South Vietnam Be Next?," *Nation*, 31 May 1958, pp. 489–93.

115. Hearings, *Situation in Vietnam*, Subcom on State Department Organization and Public Affairs of S. Foreign Relations Com, 86th Cong, 1st sess.

116. Ibid.

117. (S) DOD, "Report of Defense Dept to NSC: Status of the MAP as of 30 June 1959," 14 Aug 59, JMF 4060 (14 Aug 59).

Appendix. The Evolution of the Southeast Asia Treaty Organization

1. Unless otherwise stated all information in the introductory section of this appendix is from Office of Joint History, *The Joint Chiefs of Staff and The First Indochina War, 1947–1954*, (Washington, D. C.: GPO, 2004).

2. (TS) Memo, JCS to SecDef, "United States Strategy for Developing a Position of Military Strength in the Far East (NSC Action No. 1029–B)," 9 Apr 54 (derived from JCS 1776/452), CCS 383.21 Korea (3–19–45) sec 150. JCS memo to SecDef, 9 Apr 54, attached to SecDef to NSC, 10 Apr 54 are both reproduced in *FRUS, 1952–54, East Asia and the Pacific*, pp. 412–20.

3. Joint Statements, SecState Dulles and Foreign Secretary Eden, 13 Apr 54; SecState Dulles and Foreign Minister Bidault, 14 Apr 54; reproduced in Dept of State *Bulletin*, 26 Apr 54, pp. 622–23.

4. Statement, SecState Dulles, 15 Apr 54, reproduced in Dept of State *Bulletin*, 26 Apr 54, p. 623. (TS) Msgs, Paris DULTE 3 to Actg SecState, 22 Apr 54; Geneva DULTE 7 to Actg SecState, 26 Apr 54; State TEDUL 37 to Geneva, 6 Mar 54. Geneva DULTE 7 msg is reproduced in *FRUS, 1952–54, Geneva Conference*, pp. 370–71.

5. News Conference, SecState, 25 May 54, reproduced Dept of State *Bulletin*, 7 Jun 54, pp. 862–63.

Notes to Pages 165–168

6. Joint Statement President Eisenhower and Prime Minister Churchill, 28 Jun 54, reproduced in Dept of State *Bulletin*, 12 Jul 54, p. 49.

7. (TS) Report to the Jt US-UK Study Group on Southeast Asia, 17 Jul 54, Att to JCS 1992/360, 22 Jul 54, CCS 091 Asia (6–25–48) sec 75. This document is reproduced in *FRUS, 1952–54, Geneva Conference*, pp. 370–71.

8. Ibid. (S) Dept of State, SEAP Special 2, "Summary of Meeting in Secretary's Office," 5 Aug 54; SEAP D–3 "UK Invitations to the Colombo Powers and Replies...," 6 Aug 54; CCS 092 Asia (6–25–48) sec 77A. NY Times, 17 Aug 54, p. 3; 26 Aug 54, p. 1. SEAP Special 2, 5 Aug 54 is reproduced in *FRUS, 1952–54, East Asia and the Pacific*, 705–08.

9. (TS) Memo, JCS to SecDef, "Report of Joint US-UK Study Group of Southeast Asia," 13 Aug 54 (derived from JCS 1992/375), CCS 092 Asia (6–25–48) sec 80.

10. (U) Ltr, SecDef to SecState, 17 Aug 54, Encl to JCS 1992/382, same file, sec 81. The letter is reproduced in *FRUS, 1952–54, East Asia and the Pacific*, pp. 737–39.

11. For detailed coverage of NSC 5429/2 see chap. 1.

12. (TS) NSC 5429/2, 20 Aug 54, CCS 092 Asia (6–25–48) sec 81. NSC 5429/2 is reproduced in *FRUS, 1952–54, East Asia and the Pacific*, pp. 769–76.

13. Stebbins, *The United States in World Affairs, 1954*, pp. 257–58. (S) Msgs, State 750 to Saigon, 25 Aug 54; 795, 27 Aug 54; 799, 27 Aug 54. (S) Msg, Manila SECTO 2 to State, 2 Sep 54, DA IN 82471, CCS 092 Asia (6–25–48) sec 82.

14. (S) Dept of State, SEAP D–4, "New Zealand Memoranda on 'SEATO'," 6 Aug 54, same file, sec 77A.

15. (S) Memo, VADM A. C. Davis, DepASD (ISA) to SecDef, "Report on the Manila Conference," 14 Sep 54, same file, sec 82. (Hereafter cited as Report on the Manila Conference.)

16. (S) Report on the Manila Conference. (TS) Ltr, SecDef to SecState, 17 Aug 54, Encl to JCS 1992/383, 19 Aug 54, CCS 092 Asia (6–25–48) sec 81. On 17 Aug 54, Secretary of Defense Wilson addressed two letters to Secretary Dulles. In the first and formal letter to Dulles, he transmitted the views of the JCS. In the second and informal note, Wilson wrote," I have the minimum amount of optimism about what really can be accomplished at this stage." See *FRUS, 1952–54, East Asia and the Pacific*, pp. 737–40. The quote is on p. 739.

17. (S) Memo, VADM Davis to JCS, "Southeast Asian Collective Defense Organization," Encl to JCS 1992/361, 23 July 54, same file, sec 76. (S) Ltr, R. B. Anderson, ActgSecDef to Robert Murphy, DepUSecState, 19 Aug 54, Encl to JCS 1992/385, 21 Aug 54, same file, sec 81.

18. A constitutional amendment proposed by Senator John Bricker of Ohio in the spring of 1953 to limit the Executive Branch's treaty making powers. The proposed amendment would have given Congress the "power to regulate all Executive and other agreements" and required appropriate legislation before a treaty became "effective as internal law." In subsequent congressional debate, a number of revisions were suggested, but the Senate rejected the amendment and the various revisions in early 1954.

19. (S) State Dept, SEAP D–28a, "UK Redraft of Article IV," 27 Aug 54, CCS 092 Asia (6–25–48) sec 81.

20. (S) Report on the Manila Conference. (S) Msgs, Manila SEATO 1 to OSD, 2 Sep 54, DA IN 82324; Manila SECTO 5 to State, 3 Sep 54, DA IN 82324; Manila SECTO 5 to State, 3 Sep 54, DA IN 82592; DEF 967212 to Manila, 3 Sep 54. Encl to JCS 1992/389, 3 Sep 54; CCS 092 Asia (6–25–48) sec 82. Manila Msg Sect 5 is reproduced in *FRUS 1952–54, East Asia and the Pacific*, pp. 793–94.

21. (S) Report on the Manila Conference. (S) Dept of State, SEAP D–13/1, "UK Cabinet Views Re Article IV Southeast Asia Treaty," 28 Aug 54, same file, sec 82.

22. (S) Report on the Manila Conference.

23. (C) Dept of State, SEAP D–6, "UK Views on Economic Measures for Southeast Asia," 23 Aug 54; (S) SEAP D–6/1, "Australian Memoire on SEATO," 23 Aug 54; (S) SEAP D–11, "French Proposals Re the Preamble and Article III," 26 Aug 54; CCS 092 Asia (6–25–48) sec

81. (S) Report on the Manila Conference. (S) Dept of State, SEAP D-9, "U.S. Position on Economic Cooperation," 26 Aug 54, State Dept files. State SEAP D-9 is reproduced in *FRUS, 1952–54, East Asia and the Pacific,* pp. 793–94.

24. Text of SEACDT and Pacific Charter reproduced in Dept of State *Bulletin,* 20 Sep 54, pp. 393–96.

25. (S) Report on the Manila Conference.

26. (TS) Memo, JCS to SecDef, "Military Consultation under the Southeast Asia Collective Defense Treaty," 8 Oct 54 (derived from JCS 1992/400), CCS 092 Asia (6–25–48) sec 84. (TS) Encl B to JCS 1992/446, 3 Feb 55, CCS 092 Asia (6–25–48) (2) sec 4.

27. (TS) Memo, DepSecDef to JCS, 6 Jan 55, Encl to JCS 1992/433, 7 Jan 55, same file, sec 1.

28. (TS) JCS 1992/422, 25 Jan 55; (TS) Memo, CMC to JCS, "Concept and Plans for the Implementation, if Necessary, of Article IV, 1, of the Manila Pact," 27 Jan 55; same file, sec 3. (TS) JSPC 958/234/D, 8 Feb 55; same file, sec 4.

29. (TS) Memo, JCS to SecDef, "Concept and Plans for the Implementation, if Necessary, of Article IV, 1, of the Manila Pact," 11 Feb 55 (derived from JCS 1992/448), same file. The JCS memo is reproduced in the Pentagon Papers vol. 10, pp. 885–87. See also Memo for Record, Joint State Defense Meeting, 14 Feb 1955, US Dept of State, *Foreign Relations of the United States, 1955–57, East Asian Security, Cambodia, Laos* (Washington: GPO, 1990), vol xxi, pp. 34–36, hereafter *FRUS, 1955–57, East Asian Security.*

30. (TS) Memo for Record by RADM G. W. Anderson, "Concept and Plans for the Implementation, if Necessary, of Article IV, 1, of the Manila Pact," 15 Feb 55.

31. (S) Memo, DepSecDef to JCS, 4 Oct 54, Encl to JCS 1992/399, 5 Oct 54, CCS 092 Asia (6–25–48) sec 84.

32. (C) Dept of State, Minutes of Mtg, "Manila Pact Working Group," 28 Dec 54; Dept of State, Memo of Conversation, "Military Arrangements Under the Manila Pact," 6 Jan 55; CCS 092 Asia (6–25–48) (2) sec 1. (S) Dept of State, Minutes of Mtg, "Manila Pact Working Group," 6 Jan 55; Dept of State, MP(IWG)D–2/1, 6 Jan 55; MP(IWG)D–2b, 18 Jan 55; Dept of State, Minutes of MTG, "Manila Pact Representatives," 13 Jan 55; Dept of State, MP(IWG)D–4/3, 26 Jan 55, same file, BP pt 1.

33. (S) Dept of State, MP(IWG)D–5, 21 Jan 55; (S) Dept of State, Minutes of Mtg, "Manila Pact Representatives," 21 Jan 55; (C) 2 Feb 55; 4 Feb 55; same file.

34. Dept of State *Bulletin,* 7 Mar 55, pp. 371–74. The US Ambassador to Thailand was subsequently designated Council Representative in addition to his other duties.

35. (S) Msg, Bangkok SECTO 15 to State, 24 Feb 55, CCS 092 Asia (6–25–48) (2) sec 5. (S) Memo, VADM Davis to SecA, et al., "Department of Defense Contribution to and Participation in the Bangkok Conference," 29 Mar 55, same file, sec 6.

36. (S) Memo, VADM Davis to SecA, et al., "Department of Defense Contribution to and Participation in the Bangkok Conference," 29 Mar 55, same file. (S) Msg, Bangkok SECTO 29 to State, 24 Feb 55, DA IN 121333, same file, sec 5.

37. *NY Times,* 23 Apr 55, p, 2. *Washington Post,* 1 Apr 55. (U) "General Carlos P. Romulo's Speech, Encl 5 to (S) Memo, ExecO, OCB to OCB, "Bandung Conference of April 1955," 12 May 55, CCS 092 Asia (6–25–48) (2) BP pt 1.

38. (S) "Speech on Colonialism by Sir John Kotelawala, Prime Minister of Ceylon," Encl 6 to Memo, ExecO, OCB to OCB, "Bandung Conference of April 1955," 12 May 55, same file.

39. (TS) Rpt, Military Staff Planners Conference, Southeast Asia Collective Defense Treaty, Baguio, P. I., April–May 1955, same file. Hereafter cited as Baguio Staff Planners Report. (TS) Record of Procedures and Decisions Reached at the Military Advisers Meeting at Bangkok on 6–8 July 1955, same file, BP pt 3. Hereafter cited as Bangkok Military Advisers Report. (S) Msg, CINCPAC to CNO, 150001Z May 55, same file, sec 8. (TS) Memo, CSA to JCS, "Military Staff Planners Conference, SEACDT, April–May 1955," 1 Jun 55, same file, sec 9. (TS) JCS 1992/464, 24 May 55, same file.

40. (S) Msg, CINCPAC to CNO, 150001Z May 55, same file, sec 8. (S) Desp, Bangkok 116 to State, 31 Aug 55.

41. (S) Ltr, ActgDCI to CJCS, 12 Sep 55. (TS) Msg, CINCPAC to CJCS, 17 Sep 55, Encl to Ltr, Cabell to Radford, 20 Sep 55. (S) Msg, Bangkok 1284 to State 4 Nov 55. (C) Msg, Bangkok 2957 to State, 19 Jan 56, DA IN 195109.

42. (TS) Memo, Dir, OFMA to ASD(ISA), "Report on the SEATO Military Staff Planners' Conference, Pearl Harbor, T. H., 1–15 Nov 1955," 1 Dec 55, CCS 092 Asia (6–25–48) (2) sec 15.

43. (S) Dept of State, TAN–MC–1, 30 Sep 55, CCS 381 (2–18–51) sec 4. (S) JIC 579/75/D, 10 Nov 55, CCS 092 Asia (6–25–48) (2) sec 15.

44. (TS) Baguio Staff Planners Report. (TS) Bangkok Military Advisers Report. (TS) Rpt, Southeast Asia Collective Defense Treaty, Military Staff Planners Conference, Military Anti-Subversion Committee, Manila, P. I., Sep 55, 092 Asia (6–25–48) (2) BP pt 3. (TS) Msgs, CINCPAC to CNO, 090057Z Sep 55; CINCPAC to JCS, 122012Z Sep 55; same file, sec 12. (TS) Memo, GEN G. B. Erskine, USMC, DirOSpOpns to DepSecDef "Meeting of the Southeast Asia Collective Defense Treaty (SEACDT) Counter-Subversion Committee," 3 Oct 55. (TS) Philippine Position Paper, MPSPG(E) (55) Baguio, "Military Participation in Combatting Communist Subversion," in Baguio Staff Planners Report. (TS) Msg, CINCPAC to CNO 090057Z Sep 55, CCS 092 Asia (6–25–48) (2) sec 12. (S) Msg, JCS 988444 to CINCPAC, 13 Sep 55, same file. (C) Msg, Bangkok 1413 to State, 18 Nov 55, same file, sec 15.

45. (TS) Msg, JCS 988087 to CINCPAC, 7 Sep 55 (derived from JCS 1992/478), same file, sec 11. (TS) Memo, Erskine to DepSecDef, "Meeting of the Southeast Asia Collective Defense Treaty (SEACDT) Counter-Subversion Committee," 3 Oct 55.

46. (TS) Ltr, DCI to CJCS, 17 Oct 55, Encl to JCS 1992/493, 25 Oct 55, CCS 092 Asia (6–25–48) (2) sec 14. (TS) Memos, Erskine to CJCS, 13 and 17 Oct 55, Encls A and B to JCS 1992/494, 25 Oct 55, same file. (S) Msg, CINCPAC to CNO, 230211Z Nov 55, same file, sec 15.

47. (TS) Memo, JCS to SecDef, "Recommendations for Broadening the Scope of the SEATO Committee on Countersubversion," 20 Dec 55 (derived from JCS 1992/507), same file, sec 17.

48. (S) Msg, CINCPAC to CNO, 052218Z Jan 56, Encl B to JCS 1992/519, 25 Jan 56, same file, sec 19.

49. (S) JCS 1992/519, 25 Jan 56, same file.

50. (S) JCS 1992/525, 9 Feb 56, same file, sec 20.

51. (TS) Memo, JCS to SecDef, "Southeast Asia Collective Defense Treaty (SEATO) Staff Organization, 21 Feb 56 (derived from JCS 1992/528); (TS) N/H of JCS 1992/528, 29 Feb 56; CCS 092 Asia (6–25–48) (2) sec 20.

52. Communique on the Meeting of the SEATO Council, Karachi, 8 Mar 59, reproduced in Dept of State *Bulletin*, 19 Mar 56, pp 447–449. (TS) Msg, CINCPAC to ASD(ISA), 21 Mar 56, CCS 091 Asia (6–25–48) (2) sec 21.

53. (TS) Memo, JCS to SecDef, "Southeast Asia Collective Defense Treaty (SEATO) Staff Organization," 4 Apr 56 (derived from JCS 1992/534), same file, sec 22. (TS) Memo, ASD(ISA) to CJCS, same subj, same file, sec 23. Report by SecyGen of SEATO, "Development of SEATO in Its Third Year" Mar 58, reproduced in Dept of State Bulletin, 13 Mar 58, pp. 509–516. George Modelski (ed.), *SEATO, Six Studies* (1962), pp. 24–25.

54. (TS) Msgs, CINCPAC to CNO, 061005Z Sep 56 and 152006Z Sep 56, CCS 092 Asia (6–25–48) (2) sec 26. (TS) JCS 1992/567, 17 Sep 56, same file, BP pt 6.

55. (U) Memo, JCS to SecDef, "U.S. Force Commitments to the SEATO," 16 Nov 56 (derived from JCS 1992/576), same file, sec 27A. (TS) Memo, ASD(ISA) to CJCS, same subj, 29 Nov 56; N/H of JCS 1992/576, 6 Dec 56; (TS) Msg, DEF 914526 to CINCPAC, 5 Dec 56; same file, sec 28.

56. (TS) Memo, JCS to SecDef, "Proposed SEATO Planning Study Regarding a Strategic Concept for Defense of Treaty Areas under Conditions of Global War," 9 Jan 57 (derived from JCS 1992/586), same file, sec 29.

57. (TS) Ltr, ASD(ISA) to Asst SecState, FEA, 4 Feb 57, Encl to JCS 1992/590, 6 Feb 57, same file, sec 30. JHO, *The Joint Chiefs of Staff and National Policy, 1957–1960*, p. 220.

58. (S) Msg, CINCPAC to JCS 010202Z Feb 59; (S) JCS 1992/702, 13 Mar 59; (S) JCSM–103–59 to SecDef, 23 Mar 59 (derived from 1992/702); (S) Memo, ASD(ISA) to CJCS, 7 Apr 59, N/H of JCS 1992/702, 9 Apr 59; (S) Msg, JCS 957702 to CINCPAC, 8 Apr 59; JMF 9060 (20 Mar 59).

59. "What SEATO Means to the United States," an address by G. Frederick Reinhardt, Counselor Dept of State, before Int'l Relations Club, U of SC, 5 Mar 59, reproduced in Dept of State *Bulletin*, 23 Mar 59, pp. 395–398.

60. Address, USecState C. Douglas Dillon, before 5th SEATO Council, Wellington, New Zealand, 8 Apr 59, reproduced in ibid., 27 Apr 59, pp. 602–604.

61. SEATO Report, "Development of SEATO in Its Third Year," Mar 58, reproduced in Dept of State *Bulletin*, 24 Mar 58, pp. 509–516. JHO, *The Joint Chiefs of Staff and National Policy, 1957–1960*, p. 219.

62. Modelski, SEATO, Six Studies, pp. 40–41. (U) SEATO Pub. 3653P–12, SEATO Military Exercises, pp. 3–16. (U) SEATO Pub. 3653P–22, *SEATO Record of Progress, 1950–59*, p. 8.

63. Final Communique of SEATO Seminar on Countering Communist Subversion, 29 Nov 57, reproduced in Dept of State *Bulletin*, 23 Dec 57, p. 993. Modelski, *SEATO, Six Studies*, p. 41.

64. Modelski, *SEATO, Six Studies*, pp. 28–29. SEATO Press Release, Washington, 28 Sep 59, reproduced in Dept of State *Bulletin*, 19 Oct 59, p. 565.

65. Modelski, *SEATO, Six Studies*, pp. 41–42. Richard P. Stebbins, *The United States in World Affairs, 1958*, (1959), pp. 284–285.

Index

Africa: 112–13
Agriculture
   collectivization of: 102–05
   in North Vietnam: 102–05
   in South Vietnam: 140–43
Annam: 25
Anticommunist doctrine, Asian: 87
Army of the Republic of Vietnam: 144–47, 149,
      155, 159. *See also* Vietnamese National Army.
Assistant Secretary of Defense International
      Security Affairs: 18, 120
Associated States
   relationships with France: 3–4, 28, 31–32, 38
   US aid for: 22, 23–24
Australia: 8–9, 13

Ba Cut: 61, 62, 63, 85, 86, 122
Bac, Tran Van: 4
Bandung Conference: 99–100, 112
Bangkok Conference: 57
Bao Dai
   Catholic support for: 109
   French support for: 22–23
   and proposed national assembly: 51, 52
   relationship with Binh Xuyen: 20, 56, 61, 71
   relationship with Diem: 4, 6, 20, 21, 22, 53, 57,
      61, 63–64, 69–70, 71, 73–74, 76–77, 88–89
   relationship with General Hinh: 21, 22, 41, 85
   relationship with the French: 5, 53, 63–64, 69,
      76, 85–86, 89
   support from sects: 20, 56, 62–63
   and US policy in Vietnam: 41, 70
   US policy toward: 22–23, 24, 53–54, 62–63,
      74–75
Basic National Security Policy: 39–40, 131–32
Binh Xuyen: 6, 19, 36, 56, 157
   control of the National Police: 61, 65–66, 68,
      69, 71
   control of the Surete in Saigon: 24–25, 50, 59,
      61, 64–66, 68, 69, 71
   desire to control the Ministry of the Interior:
      25, 50
   and the French: 71–74, 85
   military forces: 71–74, 85–86
   refusal to participate in a coalition government:
      21–22, 64–66
   relationship with the Diem government: 21–22,
      41, 57–58, 64–66, 69, 71–74, 76, 85, 86
   support for Bao Dai: 20
   and the "United Front of Nationalist Forces":
      62–64
Bulganin, Nikolay: 82, 83, 117
Burke, Admiral Arleigh: 93
By, General Nguyen Van: 41

Cambodia: 2, 3, 9, 13, 19, 31, 32, 33, 34, 38, 54, 56,
      86, 140, 156, 158
Can, Ngo Dinh: 89, 151
Canada: 2, 3, 34, 99, 112, 126
Cao Dai: 6, 19, 36
   clashes with Hoa Hao: 25
   forces in Cochin-China: 25
   military forces: 24–25, 59, 60, 61, 62, 64, 66,
      85–86
   relationship with the Diem government: 21–22,
      49, 50, 57–58, 59, 62, 66, 72, 85
   role in the provinces: 60, 85–86
   and the "United Front of Nationalist Forces":
      62–64
Catholics: 99, 109–10
Central Intelligence Agency: 14, 16
Chairman, Joint Chiefs of Staff: 132
Chan, Le Ngoc: 21
Charbonnages du Tonkin: 101–02
Chau, Nguyen Huu: 83–84
Chief, MAAG: 125, 129, 131
   personnel: 92–94, 124, 126
   reports: 149–50
   responsibility for training the Vietnamese
      National Army: 44, 90, 124
Chief of Naval Operations: 10, 11, 93
Chief of Staff of the Air Force: 10, 11
Chief of Staff of the Army: 11, 12
China, Peoples Republic of
   and all-Vietnam elections: 117, 118
   economic assistance for North Vietnam: 113–14
   and the Geneva Conference of 1954: 1–2
   proposed potential retaliatory actions against:
      17–18, 133
   and rice for North Vietnam: 102
   role in the Far East: 8, 9–10
   support for the Vietnamese People's Army:
      108, 113
   trade embargo against: 15–16, 17, 18
   US policy to disrupt relations of with the USSR:
      11, 12, 14, 15

Index

US policy toward: 8, 9–12, 14, 15–18, 82
  violations of the Geneva Agreement: 108
China, Republic of: 14, 15
Chinese population in Vietnam: 153–54
Cholon, Vietnam: 64–66, 71, 73, 153
Chou En-lai; 83
Chuong, Tran Van: 4
Civil Guard: 128–30, 159
Civilian internees: 2
Cochin-China: 25, 129
Colegrove, Albert M.: 161
Collins, General J. Lawton, USA: 19, 35, 77
  and all-Vietnam elections: 80
  and analysis of the role of the sects: 60, 62, 63, 64
  and Bao Dai: 53–55
  and the French Expeditionary Corps: 43, 54, 75–76
  and land reform: 47–48
  mission in Vietnam: 35
  objectives in Vietnam: 36–37, 56
  promotion of a national assembly for South Vietnam: 51–52, 73
  relationship with General Ely: 35–37, 40, 43–44, 45–46, 47, 49
  reports: 56, 67–68
  and strengthening the Diem government: 49–50, 51–52
  and US assistance to the Vietnamese National Army: 41–42, 44–45, 46–47, 54, 56, 75–76, 128
  and US support for Diem: 53–55, 56–57, 63–64, 65–68, 69–70
Collins-Ely Minute of Understanding: 45–47, 90
Combat Arms and Training Organization: 126
Commandant of the Marine Corps: 10, 11
Commander in Chief, Pacific: 87, 92, 93, 98, 131, 133, 134, 138
Communist Party (North Vietnam): 103, 106–08, 114
Communists
  ability of Diem to prevail against: 77, 131, 152–53
  outlawed in South Vietnam: 116
  and the Revolutionary Committee of the Congress: 73
  subversive pressures in the villages: 86–87, 155–57
  US policy objectives regarding: 8–10, 13–18, 133–34, 153
Congress of Elected Representatives: 73–74
Corcoran, Thomas G.: 33, 107, 113

Dan, Phan Quang: 152
Daridan, Jean: 20–21, 22, 25, 63, 64
Defense, US Department of
  and strength of the Vietnamese National Army: 42
  and US policy in the Far East: 8, 10, 14, 15–16
  and US policy in Southeast Asia: 132, 133
  and US policy toward North Vietnam: 111, 112
Defense, US Secretary of: 93–94, 150, 162

Deputy Director for Intelligence, Joint Staff: 86, 94, 129
Diem, Ngo Dinh: 115, 119
  and all-Vietnam elections: 79–80, 81–82, 117
  American press treatment of: 160–61
  antipathy toward France: 20, 30
  Bao Dai opposition to: 20, 21
  and the Binh Xuyen: 41, 57–58, 61, 64–66, 69, 71–74, 76, 85, 86
  British support for: 117–18
  and the Chinese minority population: 153–54
  and the Civil Guard: 128, 129–30
  and consultations with the Viet Minh: 80, 81, 82
  and development of the constitution: 116, 135
  and economic issues: 119, 120–21, 140–43
  efforts to create discord between the sects: 61
  French lack of enthusiasm for: 20–21, 22–23, 26, 27, 30, 52–55, 68–69, 79
  and the Geneva Final Declaration: 4–5, 79–80, 82, 117, 118, 119
  and land reform: 48, 56, 141–42
  and personal control of the government: 49–50, 51, 66–67, 70, 77, 88, 115–16, 129–30, 137, 139, 151–52
  personality: 4, 25, 26, 57, 65, 66–68, 72, 75, 88, 151
  and proposed national assembly: 51–52, 56, 88, 116
  public support for: 5, 19, 20, 57, 87–88, 89, 90, 151, 161
  and refugees: 99
  relationship with Bao Dai: 4, 6, 20, 21, 22, 24, 63–64, 69, 71–74, 76–77, 88–89
  relationship with Binh Xuyen: 64–66, 69, 71–74, 76
  relationship with General Hinh: 19–20, 21–22, 24, 25, 27–28, 41
  relationship with province chiefs: 159
  relationship with the French: 6–7, 52–53, 71–77, 83–85, 117, 118
  relationship with the sects: 59–64, 76, 85–86
  relationship with the Vietnamese National Army: 6–7, 19–20, 21, 24–25, 41, 83–86, 88, 124, 125
  and the Revolutionary Committee of the Congress: 73–74
  and role of the sects in government: 20, 21–22, 49–50, 57–58, 59, 66
  and the sects' military forces: 60
  and the Self Defense Corps: 130, 131
  suppression of civil and constitutional rights: 151, 152–54, 159
  as Supreme Commander of the military forces: 143–44, 148, 159
  US support for: 19–23, 24, 26–28, 35, 52–55, 63–64, 65–67, 68–70, 74–76, 87–88, 89–90, 161–62
  and the Viet Minh: 75
  and Vietnamese membership in the French Union: 84

Index

Dillon, C. Douglas: 23–24, 27, 28, 30, 31, 55
Do, Tran Van: 4, 66, 67, 68, 70
Dong, Pham Van: 82, 108, 111, 112, 160
Duan, Le: 106–07
Dulles, John Foster: 117
   messages to France: 30
   reports from Collins: 67–68
   and US aid for Vietnam: 22, 23, 24, 27, 48–49, 99–100, 126
   and US support for Diem: 54–55, 68–69, 70, 74–75, 76
   and US support for the Vietnamese National Army: 39, 46, 47, 55
   and US training for the Vietnamese National Army: 38–39, 40, 45
Durbrow, Elbridge: 161–62
Durdin, Tillman: 161

Eden, Anthony: 81, 83, 99–100
Eisenhower, Dwight D.
   and Bao Dai: 62–63
   "falling domino" principle: 7
   and France: 26–27, 28
   and General Collins: 35
   and military intervention in Vietnam: 1, 19, 133
   and NSC 5429/1: 11–12
   and NSC 5429/4: 17
   and NSC 5429/5: 18
   and support for Diem: 26–27, 138
   and US policy toward the Far East: 11–12, 17, 18
Ely, General Paul: 32, 77
   advice to Diem: 25, 50
   efforts to promote a coalition government: 20, 21, 22
   efforts to restrain Diem: 65–66
   and land reform: 47–48
   and plans for the defense of South Vietnam: 43–44
   promotion of a national assembly for South Vietnam: 51, 52
   and refugees: 99–100
   relationship with General Collins: 35–37, 40, 43–44, 45–46, 47, 49
   relationship with Heath: 27
   and role of the French military in Vietnam: 65
   and the Sainteny Mission: 29–30
   and sect military units: 60, 64
   and security of French citizens in Vietnam: 72–73
   support for Diem: 23, 24, 54–55, 63, 64, 66–67, 68, 72–73
   and US equipment in North Vietnam: 100–101
   and US support for the French Expeditionary Corps: 43
   and US training for the Vietnamese National Army: 40, 44, 45–46, 47

Fall, Bernard: 161
Faure, Premier Edgar: 74–75, 76, 83, 101
Food shortages: 102, 107, 113–14
Foreign Operations Administration: 14, 100–101
France
   and arming of the sects: 59, 60
   and autonomy of the Vietnamese National Army: 39, 41, 44–45, 46, 47
   and the Binh Xuyen: 65–66, 69, 71–72
   cooperation with Americans on refugee issues: 98–99
   coordination of policy with the United States: 68–70, 74–77
   diplomatic relations with Vietnam: 84
   and direct US aid to Indochinese states: 23–24
   and direct US aid to Vietnam: 27, 48–49
   economic interests in North Vietnam: 29–30, 84, 101–02, 111
   economic relationship with South Vietnam: 7, 119, 121
   economic relationships with the Associated States: 32, 48, 84–85
   efforts to create discord between the sects: 25
   and elections in Vietnam: 29–30, 80, 82, 83
   and ethnic minorities in Vietnam: 153, 154
   evacuation of refugees from North Vietnam: 98–99
   and the Geneva Agreement of 1954: 1–2, 45–46, 79–80, 82, 111, 117, 118
   and independence for the Associated States: 31, 38
   and independence for Vietnam: 3–4, 31–32, 36, 38
   and MDAP equipment: 100–101, 126–27
   and North Vietnam: 28–30, 32–34, 84, 97–98, 101–02, 111
   obligations under the Geneva Agreement: 117, 118, 122
   plans for deposing Diem: 69–70, 71–74, 85–86
   policy toward Indochina: 28–30, 31–32
   policy toward the Viet Minh: 28–29, 36
   public opinion in: 31, 80
   and refugees from North Vietnam: 98
   relationship with Bao Dai: 63–64, 69–70, 71–72, 86
   relationship with Diem: 6–7, 20–21, 22, 23, 26, 27, 30, 52–55, 65–66, 68–70, 71–77, 79, 83–86
   reliance on US financial support: 23
   and the Royal Khmer Army: 38
   and the Southeast Asia security treaty: 8–9, 13
   support for General Hinh: 20, 22
   support for Tam: 20–21, 27
   support for the sects: 85–86
   and training for the Vietnamese Air Force: 127
   and training for the Vietnamese National Army: 39, 44–46, 90–91
   and training for the Vietnamese Navy: 127
   transfer of governmental functions to South Vietnam: 32
   US policy regarding French relations with her former Indochinese colonies: 9
   US pressure on to support Diem: 26–27

Index

and US responsibility for the security of South Vietnam: 43–44, 45
and US support for the French Expeditionary Corps: 4, 22, 23, 28, 42–43
and the Vietnamese National Army: 38–39, 71–72
withdrawal of the French Expeditionary Corps from Vietnam: 75–76, 83–85, 90–91, 92, 117, 122

French Expeditionary Corps
MDAP equipment for: 100–101
morale: 45
role in South Vietnam: 32, 38–39, 42–43, 64, 75–76, 83–85, 124
strength in Vietnam: 42–44, 117
US financial support for: 22, 23, 28, 42–43
withdrawal from Vietnam: 75–76, 83–85, 90–91, 92, 117, 122, 124

French Union
forces in Vietnam: 2, 100–101
membership of the Associated States: 32
military operations in South Vietnam: 25–26
Vietnamese membership in: 3–4, 31, 84, 85

Gambiez, General Jean: 66
Gardiner, Arthur: 161
Geneva Agreements: 117–18
Chinese violations of: 108
Diem's refusal to sign: 4–5, 29, 79–80, 82, 117, 118, 119
and elections in Vietnam: 2–3, 6, 9, 29, 79–83
enforcement of. *See* International Control Commission.
and foreign forces in Vietnam: 37–38, 45–46, 92–95, 126, 127–28
French obligations under: 117, 122
North Vietnamese violations of: 33–34
possible violations of by the United States: 45–46
and refugees: 98
restrictions on foreign aid to South Vietnam: 6

Geneva Conference
Final Declaration of the Conference: 2–3, 4–5, 79–80, 110, 112, 117–18. *See also* Geneva Agreements.
Final Declaration on Indochina: 2–3, 117–18
US positions at: 1, 111

Giao, Phan Van: 57
Giap, General Vo Nguyen: 6–7, 33, 108
Guerrilla warfare: 5–6, 94, 155–56, 159

Haiduong, Vietnam: 97, 98
Haiphong, Vietnam: 32–33, 34, 97–98, 99, 100, 101–02
Hanoi, Vietnam: 32–33, 97, 98
Heath, Donald H.
efforts to promote a coalition government: 20–21, 22
efforts to stabilize the Diem government: 27–28

reports on the situation in Vietnam: 25, 98
support for Diem: 23, 24, 25, 26–27, 53, 54
and US support for the French Expeditionary Corps: 43
and US training for the Vietnamese National Army: 38, 40

Hinh, General Nguyen Van: 7, 69, 76
cooperation with the sects: 20
plans for a coup d'etat: 19–20, 21, 41
relationship with Bao Dai: 21, 22, 24, 41, 57, 71, 85
relationship with Diem: 19–20, 21, 24, 25, 27–28, 36, 41
relationship with the French: 20, 25
US pressure on: 25, 27

Ho Chi Minh: 29, 30, 83, 99–100, 101, 102, 108, 109, 113–14
Ho Chi Minh Trail: 158
Hoa-Hao: 6, 19, 36, 53
clashes with Cao Dai: 25
forces in Cochin-China: 25
French support for: 85
and land reform: 48
military forces: 24–25, 59, 60–61, 64, 85–86
relationship with the Diem government: 21–22, 49, 50, 57–58, 59, 66, 72, 76, 85–86
role in the provinces: 60–61, 85–86
and the "United Front of Nationalist Forces": 62–64

Hoi, Buu: 20, 30, 53, 57, 69
Hon Gay coal mines, Vietnam: 100–101
Hoppenot, Henri: 84
Hotham, David: 161
Huu, Tran Van: 20, 49, 53, 57, 69

India: 2, 3, 34, 82, 112, 114, 117, 126
Indonesia: 112
Interagency Costing Team: 126
International Control Commission: 2–3, 34, 46, 81, 82–83, 93, 99–100, 112, 117, 118, 119, 126
International Cooperation Administration: 120

Jacquot, General Pierre: 65, 77
Japan: 127
Joint Armistice Commission: 2, 117, 118
Joint Chiefs of Staff
assessment of Republic of Vietnam Armed Forces: 150
and commitment of US forces to battle in Vietnam: 81
and need for a comprehensive US policy toward the Far East: 8, 10–11, 14, 17
and NSC 5429: 8, 10–11
and NSC 5429/3: 14
and reviews of US policy toward Vietnam: 55–58, 151–52
and role of the Vietnamese National Army: 39–40, 75

and size of the Vietnamese National Army: 39, 42, 92
and trade embargo on Communist China: 17
and training for the Vietnamese National Army: 38, 39–40, 44, 87
and US or French withdrawal from Vietnam: 75
and US policy on all-Vietnam elections: 80–81
and US policy regarding Viet Minh aggression: 132, 133, 134–35
and US policy regarding violations of the Geneva Agreement: 16
and US policy toward Communist China: 10–11, 12, 14, 15–16, 17
and US policy toward Diem: 75
and US policy toward North Vietnam: 10
and US policy toward Southeast Asia: 132
and US support for the French Expeditionary Corps: 43
and US troops in Vietnam: 81, 93–94
and Viet Minh threat to South Vietnam: 42
Joint Strategic Plans Committee: 42
Jones, Howard P.: 137

Khmer Resistance Forces: 33
Khrushchev, Nikita: 117
Kidder, Randolph: 57, 72–73
Korean War: 1–2

La Chambre, Guy: 30, 31, 100
  and elections in Vietnam: 29
  reports on conditions in Vietnam: 25
  and the Washington Conference: 22–23, 24, 27, 53, 57
Land reform: 7, 27–28, 37, 48, 55, 56, 99, 102, 103–05, 109, 110, 121, 138, 139, 141–43, 157, 161
Laniel, Joseph: 3–4, 31
Lansdale, Col. Edward G., USAF: 87
Lao Dong Party: 103, 106–07, 160
Laos: 19, 56
  and the Geneva Conference of 1954: 2, 3
  relationship with France: 31
  relationship with South Vietnam: 32
  and the Southeast Asia security treaty: 13
  US policy toward: 9, 54, 140
  Viet Cong operations in: 158
  Viet Minh operations in: 33, 34
Le, Col. Nguyen Ngoc: 71
Lindley, Ernest K.: 161
Loc, Buu: 3, 4, 20, 22–23, 57
Luyen, Ngo Dinh: 4, 49–50

MacArthur, Douglas, II: 24
Macmillan, Harold: 74–75
Manila Conference: 13
Manila Pact: 13, 39, 43–44, 56, 57, 62, 75, 81, 133
Mansfield, Mike: 26, 54, 68, 142
Mansfield Report: 26

Mekong River: 32, 148
Mendes-France, Pierre: 20–21, 27, 28, 29–30, 102
  policy toward South Vietnam: 31, 32, 83–84
  and support for the Diem government: 53, 54–55
  and US aid to Vietnam: 48–49
  and US training for the Vietnamese National Army: 45–46, 47
Michigan State University: 128–30
Military Assistance Program: 120, 150–51
Minh, Col. Ho Thong: 21, 46–47, 49–50, 56, 64–65, 66, 67
Molotov, V. M.: 83, 99–100
Montagnards: 153, 154–55
Movement of National Revolution: 152
Mutual Defense Assistance Program
  equipment for the Vietnamese National Army: 39, 92–93, 125
  evacuation of equipment from North Vietnam: 100–101
  French control of: 100–101, 126
  objectives: 92
  US recovery of equipment provided by: 126–27
Mutual Security Act: 23, 68, 142
Mutual Security Program: 120

National Intelligence Estimates: 5–6, 77, 122, 143
National Police: 65, 66, 68, 69, 71, 128
National Revolutionary Congress of the Vietnamese People: 72
National Revolutionary Movement: 89, 115–16
National Security Council
  Collins reports to: 56–57
  consideration of NSC 5429/3: 17–18
  and efforts to stabilize the Diem regime: 26, 27–28, 115, 137–38
  and plan to stabilize Vietnam: 40
  and policy regarding use of US forces in Southeast Asia: 12, 131–35
  reports from the Secretary of Defense: 150
  and role of the Vietnamese Armed Forces: 92, 123
  and trade embargo against Communist China: 15–16, 17, 18
  and US aid to Indochinese countries: 23
  and US policy toward North Vietnam: 111–12
  and US training for the Vietnamese National Army: 39, 40
  and US troops in Vietnam: 93–94
National Security Council Planning Board
  and NSC 5429: 8–10, 11–12
  and NSC 5429/3: 13–18
  and NSC 5612: 133
  and US policy on all-Vietnam elections: 80–81
National Security Council policy statements
  NSC 162/2: 39–40
  NSC 5405: 133
  NSC 5429: 8–10
  NSC 5429/1: 11–12, 39
  NSC 5429/2: 11, 12, 15, 39, 140

225

Index

NSC 5429/3: 13–18
NSC 5429/4: 17
NSC 5429/5: 17, 18, 81, 133, 134–35
NSC 5519: 80–81
NSC 5602/1: 132
NSC 5612: 133
NSC 5612/1: 133–34
NSC 5612/2: 143
Nationalist China: 153, 154
Nehru, Jawaharlal: 82, 83, 112
New Zealand: 8–9, 13
Nghe An Province: 104, 110
Ngo, General Nguyen: 72
Nguyen, General Lam Than: 53, 62, 63
Nhu, Ngo Dinh: 4, 49–50, 89, 151
Nuclear weapons: 132, 133

O'Daniel, Lt. Gen. John W.: 94, 119, 120, 121, 125, 131
  efforts to promote a coalition government: 21, 50
  and MAAG personnel problems: 92–94
  and MDAP equipment: 100
  and refugees: 98
  and US support for Diem: 27–28
and US training program for the Vietnamese National Army: 37–38, 40, 41, 44, 45, 46, 47, 90, 91–92, 124, 127
Office of Defense Mobilization: 8, 10, 14, 15–16
"Operation Exodus": 98, 99, 120
Operations Coordination Board: 40, 115, 137–39, 142, 150, 151
OPLAN 46-56: 134

Pacification: 86–87, 129
Pakistan: 13, 112
Pathet Lao: 33
Philippine Islands
  and the Southeast Asia security treaty: 8–9, 13
  and training for the Vietnamese National Army: 87, 146
Phuong, General Nguyen Thanh: 50, 62, 63, 64, 72, 85
Poland: 2, 3, 34, 117
Press censorship: 153
Prisoners of war: 2
Propaganda, communist: 157–58
Provisional Constitutional Act: 89
Provisional National Conference: 5
Public opinion
  French: 31, 80
  US: 69–70, 74–75, 160
  Vietnamese: 69, 76, 80

Quat, Phan Huy: 49–50, 53, 54, 67, 68, 69, 70

Radford, Admiral Arthur W.: 40, 45, 87, 94, 132–33, 134
Refugees
  care of: 7, 36, 37, 98–99, 120
  evacuation of: 98, 99, 120
  North Vietnamese efforts to impede: 33, 98, 99–100, 109
  resettlement of: 9, 48, 99, 138, 161
  US payment of the costs of caring for: 120
Reinhardt, G. Frederick: 77, 81, 88, 89–90, 92, 114
Republic of Vietnam Armed Forces: 143–47, 149–51. *See also*: Vietnamese Air Force; Vietnamese National Army; Vietnamese Navy.
Reunification of Vietnam
  elections regarding: 2–3, 6, 9, 29, 79–81, 135, 155
  US policy regarding: 10, 80, 111, 133–34
Revolutionary Committee of the Congress: 72, 73–74, 85, 89
Revolutionary Workers Party: 89, 116
Rice production: 7, 25, 50, 102, 104, 106, 110, 119, 120, 141, 142
Robertson, Walter: 24, 54
Royal Khmer Army: 38
Rubber production: 7

Sabin, Rear Adm. Lorenzo S.: 98
Saigon, Vietnam
  fights for control of: 64–66, 71–74, 82–83, 98–99
  loyalty of the Surete to Diem: 24–25
  port of transferred to Vietnam: 32
  and refugees: 98–99
  role of Bien Xuyen in: 6, 24–25, 61, 64–66, 71–74
  Viet Minh role in: 5
Sainteny, Jean: 29–30, 84, 101–02, 111, 113
Salan, General Raoul: 22
Sang, Lai Van: 65–66, 71
Self Defense Corps: 130–31, 158, 159
Sino-Soviet relations, US policy to disrupt: 11, 12
Smith, Walter Bedell: 22–23, 24, 27, 48–49, 53, 100
Soai, General Tran Van: 50, 61, 62, 63, 85, 86
Southeast Asia, US policy toward: 8–9, 13, 15, 18, 55–58, 131–35
Southeast Asia Collective Defense Treaty: 13, 14
Southeast Asia Treaty Organization: 81, 92
  role in defense of South Vietnam: 132–33, 134
  and training for the Vietnamese National Army: 87
  US efforts to create: 8–9, 13, 57
Special United States Representative in Vietnam: 35
Stassen, Harold: 23
State, US Department of
  and elections in Vietnam: 29, 81, 89–90, 118
  and enforcement of the Geneva Agreement: 117
  estimates of refugees from North Vietnam: 100
  and MDAP equipment: 126
  plan to stabilize Vietnam: 40
  protests to France: 21

and strength of the Vietnamese National Army: 42
support for US training for the Vietnamese National Army: 38–39
and US adherence to the Geneva Agreement: 93
and US policy in the Far East: 14
and US policy toward Communist China: 16, 17
and US support for Diem: 53–54, 64
and US support for the French Expeditionary Corps: 43
and US support for the Vietnamese National Army: 93
State, US Secretary of: 18, 93. *See also* Dulles, John Foster.
Stump, Admiral Felix B.: 87, 92, 93, 131

Tac, Pham Cong: 50, 62, 85
Tam, Nguyen Van: 7, 20–21, 27, 50, 53, 57, 69
Task Force 90: 98, 99
Taylor, General Maxwell D.: 87
Terrorism by the Viet Cong: 155–58, 159, 160
Thailand: 56
  and the Southeast Asia security treaty: 13
  US policy toward: 54
The, Trinh Minh: 61, 62, 63, 64, 72, 74
Thuc, Ngo Dinh: 151
Tonkin, Vietnam: 29, 30, 33, 34, 97–102
Tourane, Vietnam: 132, 133, 149
Training
  for the Civil Guard: 128–29
  by the French: 39, 44–46, 90–91, 127
  for the Self Defense Corps: 131
  by the United States: 37–38, 44, 45–46, 47, 56, 87, 90–91, 124, 126–27, 138, 139, 145
  for the Vietnamese Air Force: 127
  for the Vietnamese National Army: 37–38, 39, 44, 45–46, 47, 56, 75–76, 86–87, 90–91, 124–26, 127, 138, 139, 144, 145, 146–47
  for the Vietnamese Navy: 127
Training Relations Instruction Mission: 60, 90–91, 92, 124, 125–26
Ty, General Le Van: 41, 66, 71, 72

U Nu, Premier: 112
Union of Soviet Socialist Republics
  and all-Vietnam elections: 117, 118
  and the Geneva Conference of 1954: 1–2, 82, 83
  relationship with North Vietnam: 113–14
  US policy to disrupt relations of with Communist China: 11, 12, 14, 15
"United Front of Nationalist Forces": 62–64, 66, 71, 76
United Kingdom: 1–2, 8–9, 13, 74–75, 80, 82, 83, 112, 117–18, 126
United Nations Economic Survey Mission: 140
United States
  and communist threat to Southeast Asia: 8–10, 13–18, 133–34, 153
  and creation of a Southeast Asia security treaty: 8–9, 13
  evaluation of the importance of Vietnam: 7–8
  and the Geneva Agreement of 1954: 1–2, 3, 117
  objectives in Vietnam: 68, 133–34, 137–38, 139, 153
  policy regarding all-Vietnam elections: 9, 29, 80–81, 117, 134
  policy regarding Chinese people in Vietnam: 153, 154
  policy regarding independence for former French colonies in Indochina: 9
  policy regarding reunification of Vietnam: 10, 80, 111, 133–34
  policy toward China: 8, 9–12, 14, 15–18, 82
  policy toward North Vietnam: 9, 111–12
  policy toward Southeast Asia: 8–9, 13, 15, 18, 55–58, 131–35
  and potential use of nuclear weapons: 132, 133
  pressure on France to support Diem: 26–27
  and resettlement of refugees from North Vietnam: 9
  support for paramilitary forces in South Vietnam: 128–31
  support for the Diem government: 19–23, 24, 26–28, 35, 52–55, 63–64, 65–67, 87–88, 89–90, 133–34, 137–38, 139–40, 161–62
  technical assistance to South Vietnam: 120, 141, 146
  training for government officials in South Vietnam: 128–29
  training for the Vietnamese Air Force: 148
  training for the Vietnamese Navy: 148–49
  troops sent to Vietnam: 126–28, 138–39
United States aid
  for the Associated States: 22
  economic aid to South Vietnam: 119–21, 139–40, 141, 142–43, 161
  for the French Expeditionary Corps: 22, 23, 28, 42–43
  French reliance on: 1, 22, 23, 28
  given directly to Indochinese states: 23–24
  given directly to Vietnam: 26–27, 48–49, 122–23, 143
  threats to diminish if Diem was deposed: 21–22
US Army Command and General Staff College: 146
US Congress
  and aid for the French Expeditionary Corps: 23
  and US aid for Indochinese countries: 23
  and US support for Diem: 54, 68, 69–70, 74
US Embassy, Saigon, reports on internal security situation in Vietnam: 159, 160
US Information Service Center, Saigon: 156
US Marine Corps: 149
US Military Aid Advisory Group, Indochina: 37–38, 45–46, 92–94
US Military Aid Advisory Group, Saigon: 39, 40

227

Index

US Military Aid Advisory Group, Vietnam: 92–94, 123, 147, 151, 156
   and the Civil Guard: 128–29, 130
   Comptroller Advisers Group: 147
   evaluation of the progress of the RVNAF: 149
   Intelligence Summary reports: 155–56, 157–58
   logistical support for the Vietnamese National Army: 126–27
   personnel: 37–38, 45–46, 92–94, 124, 126, 127–28, 156
   and training for Vietnamese military forces: 39, 40, 125–26, 127, 139, 145, 146, 148, 149
US Military Attaché, Saigon, reports from: 25, 99
US Mobile Training Teams: 146
US Navy
   advisors to the Vietnamese Navy: 149
   and evacuation of refugees from North Vietnam: 99
United States Operations Mission: 128–29, 130, 159, 161
US Senate Foreign Relations Committee: 150–51, 161
US Temporary Equipment Recovery Mission: 126–27, 149

Vien, Bay: 41, 61, 62, 63, 64–65, 66, 71, 73, 76, 85
Vien, General Le Van: 22, 24, 25, 27–28, 36, 50
Viet Cong: 155–62. *See also* Viet Minh.
   efforts to erode confidence in the Diem government: 155–57
   equipment: 155, 158
   and guerrilla warfare: 155–56, 157, 159, 160
   and the Montagnards: 154–55
   strength: 155–56, 157, 159
   terrorism practiced by: 155–58, 159, 160, 161
   US personnel as targets of: 156, 157–58
Viet Minh (People's Army of Vietnam). *See also* Viet Cong.
   army divisions: 6–7
   control of North Vietnam: 32–34, 97
   efforts to prevent emigration from North Vietnam: 33, 98, 99–100
   French policy toward: 27–28, 36, 101–02
   and the Geneva Conference of 1954: 2, 5, 94–95
   guerrilla activities of: 5–6, 94
   infiltration into local groups: 155–62
   infiltration into sect leadership: 86–87
   influence in South Vietnam: 5–6, 86, 94–95, 155
   and land reform in North Vietnam: 103
   and land reform in South Vietnam: 141–42
   operations in Annam: 25
   protests to the International Control Commission: 46
   refusal by Diem to consult with: 80, 81, 82
   relationship with Communist bloc countries: 113–14
   respect for: 103
   and the Revolutionary Committee of the Congress: 73
   role in Saigon: 5
   role in villages: 5, 6, 86–87, 94, 155–58

   strength in the provinces: 36, 122
   truce violations in South Vietnam: 33, 34, 94–95
   US evaluation of: 5–6, 155–56
   US policy regarding aggression by: 132, 133–35
Vietnam, Democratic Republic of
   agricultural economy: 102–05, 106–07
   and all-Vietnam elections: 117, 118, 155
   and Catholics: 99, 109–10
   Central Planning Commission: 105
   collectivization of agriculture: 102–05, 106–07
   expansion of military forces: 33
   Five Year Plan: 106–07
   foreign policy: 109–14
   French economic interests in: 29–30, 84, 101–02, 111
   and the Geneva Conference of 1954: 2, 97
   government of: 107–08
   industrial economy: 105–07
   and intellectuals: 109–10
   National Planning Board: 103–04
   propaganda against the United States: 111, 112, 156, 157
   rebellion in: 110
   refugees from: 33, 97–100, 109
   and reunification: 155, 157, 160, 162
   Three Year Plan: 106–07
   and tribal communities: 109
   US policy toward: 9, 11
   Viet Minh control of: 32–34
   withdrawal of French forces from: 97–98
Vietnam, Republic of
   and all-Vietnam elections: 79–80, 135, 155
   anticommunism activities: 77, 131, 152–53
   communist threat to: 122–23, 138–39, 155–62
   competency of local officials: 25
   and conscription: 146–47
   constitution for: 116, 135
   development of a constitution for: 72, 76, 88, 89, 138, 152
   economic issues: 7, 27–28, 37, 47–49, 119–21, 135, 138–39, 140–43, 147, 153–54, 161
   efforts by Ely to promote a coalition government for: 20
   efforts by Heath to promote a coalition government for: 20
   elections for a national assembly: 72, 76, 88, 89, 116
   financial reforms: 48, 147
   Five Year Plan for Economic and Social Development: 140–41
   French role in the economy of: 7, 119, 121
   French transfer of some functions to: 32
   French Union forces in: 2, 100–101. *See also* French Expeditionary Corps.
   General Collins' objectives regarding: 36–37, 49–50, 56
   governmental structure: 4–5
   hostility toward the International Control Commission: 82–83
   independence from France: 3–4, 31–32, 36, 38
   infrastructure: 7, 140–41, 143

Index

lack of competitive political parties in: 151–52
lack of trained professionals: 121
Ministry of Agriculture: 48
Ministry of Defense: 49–50, 90, 131
Ministry of National Defense: 4
Ministry of the Interior: 4, 25, 27, 49, 50, 128, 129, 130
national assembly: 50–52, 87–90, 116, 135, 138
National Police: 65–66
operations against the Viet Cong: 159
organization of the government of: 4–5
paramilitary forces: 128–31, 145, 159
Permanent Secretariat General of National Defense: 147
police agencies: 128–30, 159
Political Re-education Centers: 152–53
prospect of civil war: 19, 62–68, 72–73
referendum on role of Bao Dai: 88, 89
refusal to sign the Final Declaration on Indochina: 2–3, 4–5, 29, 79–80, 117–19
relationship with Cambodia: 32
relationship with Laos: 32
restrictions on foreign aid to: 6
role of politico-religious sects in: 6, 49
and the Southeast Asia security treaty: 13
treatment of ethnic minorities: 153–55
US economic aid to: 119–21, 138–39, 140
US efforts to build democratic institutions in: 36–37, 49–50
US technical assistance to: 120, 139, 150
Viet Cong infiltration from the North: 156, 158–59
and Viet Minh violations of the Geneva Agreement: 33, 34
Vietnamese Air Force: 42, 91, 123, 127, 144, 148, 149, 150
Vietnamese Command and General Staff College: 146
Vietnamese National Army. *See also* Army of the Republic of Vietnam.
  administration of: 41, 86–87, 90, 144
  air support for: 148
  autonomy of: 39, 41, 44–45, 46, 47
  Chief of Intelligence: 122
  and the Civil Guard: 128, 129–30
  conscription for: 146–47
  demobilization of: 91–92
  dependence on French leadership: 25–26, 32, 38–39, 40–41, 44, 75–76, 83–84, 117
  and Diem: 6–7, 19–21, 24–25, 41, 83–86, 88, 124, 125
  effectiveness of: 25–26, 40, 149
  equipment for: 39, 125, 127, 139, 143, 146
  fighting against the Binh Xuyen: 65–66, 71
  formation of: 6–7
  and the French: 6–7, 38–39, 41, 44–46, 65–66, 71–72, 75–76, 83–85, 90–91, 124, 144
  General Staff: 41, 86–87, 90, 144, 145
  integration of sect units into: 60, 61, 66, 85, 123
  logistical support for: 25–26, 40–41, 75–76, 84, 125, 126–27, 138, 143, 146, 149–50, 159
  loyalty of leaders to Diem: 19–20, 21, 22, 24–25, 41, 85, 88
  mission: 39, 41–42, 44, 92, 123, 124, 128, 132
  morale: 7, 42
  officer training: 87, 90–91, 125, 145, 146
  officers: 7, 40–41, 88, 125, 145–46
  operations against the sects: 71–74, 85–86, 91
  organization of: 7, 39–40, 41, 42, 44, 47, 86–87, 91–92, 123, 124, 144–45, 147
  and the pacification program: 86–87, 91, 124, 129
  and plans for a coup d'etat: 21, 25
  role in internal security: 39, 42, 43, 145, 149, 150, 156, 157
  role in response to invasion: 39, 42, 91, 92, 132–33, 134–35, 149, 150
  role of the sects in: 57–58, 60
  and the Self-Defense Corps: 131
  strength: 38, 39–40, 41–42, 46–47, 60, 91–92, 123, 144–45
  territorial regiments: 124
  training for: 37–38, 44, 45–46, 47, 56, 75–76, 86–87, 90–91, 124–26, 127, 144, 145, 146–47
  US efforts to improve the loyalty of: 27, 36, 40
  US financial support for: 42, 47, 60, 91–92, 119–20, 122–23, 139–40, 143, 147, 150–51
  US training for: 37–38, 44, 45–46, 47, 56, 87, 90–91, 124, 126–27, 138, 139, 145
Vietnamese Navy: 42, 91, 123, 127, 144, 148–49, 150
Vietnamese People's Army: 108, 113–14
Village Defense Corps: 130
Villages
  alienation of local Vietnamese in: 159
  protection for: 128–31
  Viet Cong role in: 155–62
Viet Minh role in: 5–6, 86–87
Vinh, Nguyen Trung: 3–4
Vy, General Nguyen Van: 21, 66, 71, 72, 77

Washington Conference (1954): 22–24, 26, 27, 28, 30, 48, 57
Williams, Lt. Gen. Samuel T., USA: 125–26, 131, 161
Wilson, Charles E.
  and MDAP equipment: 126
  review of US policy toward Vietnam: 55
  and US troops in Vietnam: 93–94
Wintrebert, Michel: 63, 65

Xuan, General Nguyen Van: 20, 22, 24, 25, 26, 27–28, 36, 57

Yugoslavia: 113

www.ingramcontent.com/pod-product-compliance
Lightning Source LLC
Chambersburg PA
CBHW082115230426
43671CB00015B/2711